The Russian Image of Goethe

VOLUME TWO

The Russian Image of

GOETHE

Goethe in Russian Literature of the
Second Half of the Nineteenth Century

ANDRÉ von GRONICKA

University of Pennsylvania Press
PHILADELPHIA

This work was published with the support of the Haney Foundation.

Library of Congress Cataloging in Publication Data

Von Gronicka, André, 1912–
    The Russian image of Goethe.

    Includes bibliographies and indexes.
    Contents: v. 1. Goethe in Russian literature of the
first half of the nineteenth century—v. 2. Goethe in
Russian literature of the second half of the nineteenth
century.
    1. Goethe, Johann Wolfgang von, 1749–1832—Appreciation
—Soviet Union.   2. Goethe, Johann Wolfgang von, 1749–
1832—Influence.   3. Goethe, Johann Wolfgang von, 1749–
1832—Translations, Russian.   4. Russian literature—19th
century—History and criticism.   I. Title.
PT2173.R8V66   1985   831'.6   84-28060
ISBN 0-8122-7985-9 (v. 1)
ISBN 0-8122-7986-7 (v. 2)

Printed in the United States of America

To
my beloved wife
and
life's companion, Hilde

CONTENTS

Preface

This second volume of *The Russian Image of Goethe* covers the second half of the nineteenth century and the first two decades of the twentieth. It is a seamless continuation of the first volume, chronologically and methodologically. I try to avoid the rigorisms and excesses of the numerous movements and schools of literary criticism that preceded the inception of my study or chased each other during my work on it: Positivism and *Geistesgeschichte* and *Marxist Literatursoziologie*, neo-Criticism and *Neue Sachlichkeit*, and, more recently, *Rezeptionsgeschichte* and Deconstruction, among others. I did profit from all of these, selecting what I found to be most helpful in my investigation. The resulting approach may well be called "eclectic," a characterization I am prepared to accept.

The readers I address are those for whom I wrote the first volume: Slavists and comparativists who are versed in Russian but are not specialists in German literature and Goethe research. On the other hand, I also speak to those among the comparativists, Germanists, and nonspecialized readers who are interested in Goethe's reception in Russia but lack a knowledge of the Russian language. It is for them that I quote the Russian sources liberally, and translate the quotations verbatim rather than paraphrasing them. (All translations are my own unless otherwise indicated.) I draw on a wealth of statements by Russian authors, major and minor, on Goethe and his works, which I found scattered throughout their diaries, letters, essays and reviews, and I analyze and evaluate, from the perspective of the writers' time and of our own, their creative response to the *personae*, scenes, themes, and "familiar quotations" (geflügelte Worte) in Goethe's total *oeuvre* as far as it was known to them.

As in the first volume so again in this second, I introduce biographical, social, and historical materials, that may not be strictly relevant to my central theme, but that help the non-specialist place the Goethe image of the Russian writers into the context of their lives and times. My foremost aim throughout the study is to give my readers the most comprehensive and authentic impression of the Russian writers' reaction to Goethe, the man and the artist.

Intentionally I do not reach out beyond Russia to other Slavic lands, but concentrate on the presentation of the *Russian* reception of Goethe, confident that such a focused presentation will, at the same time, offer the reader a survey in some depth of the development of Russian literature in the time span under discussion. As the well known scholar, Victor Zhirmunski observes: "The history of the creative reception and theoretical interpretation of Goethe's work in Russian literature illuminates with varying degrees of intensity the entire history of that literature." [1] Another authority in the field, Michael Gorlin, even suggests that the study of Russia's reception of Goethe "mirrors [that country's] entire *cultural* development—at least in its main facets." [2]

Finally, a word about the transliteration system: I continue use of the "Library of Congress System II," which I adopted in the first volume, as the least confusing to the nonprofessional reader. I deviate from this system only in the transliteration of words ending in "-iĭ." Thus, "russkiĭ" becomes "russki" and proper names such as Dostoevskiĭ and Zhirmunskiĭ become Dostoevski and Zhirmunski in my transliteration.

Philadelphia, 1985

Acknowledgments

It is my pleasure to gratefully acknowledge the encouragement received from friends and colleagues, in this country and abroad, and the expert advice and unstinting assistance of the directors and staffs of the Ost-Europa Institut, the Staatsbibliothek in Munich, the Bibliothèque Nationale in Paris, the Slavic Division of the New York Public Library, and the Interlibrary Loan Departments at the University of Texas (Austin) and the University of Pennsylvania. I am greatly indebted to Professors Victor Terras and Heinz Moenkemeyer, who gave liberally of their time and expertise to a critical reading of parts of the manuscript.

I also wish to express my sincere appreciation for the assistance given me by the Guggenheim Foundation with a second Fellowship, by the American Council of Learned Societies, by the National Endowment for the Humanities, and by the University of Pennsylvania through its program of liberal research leaves. Portions of this volume which have appeared in article form are now published with the kind permission of the editorial boards of the *Germanic Review* and *The Germano-Slavica. A Canadian Journal* and of the editors of the *Festschriften* in honor of Professors Adolf Klarmann and Heinz Moenkemeyer. I am grateful for their cooperation.

CHAPTER ONE

I. S. Turgenev: A Study in Ambivalence

Among the Russian admirers and critics of Goethe, Ivan Turgenev (1818–1883) was unquestionably one of the most accomplished in the German language and the most knowledgeable in German philosophy and belles lettres. The well-known Slavist Victor Terras states categorically: "He [Turgenev] was philosophically and otherwise the most universally literate of all Russian writers." [1] His interest in Goethe was the most sustained, his insight into the poet's personality and works was remarkable.

To be sure, Turgenev's view of Goethe was, to a considerable degree, derivative. I recognize in it the attitudes characteristic of Nikolai Stankevich and his "Circle," of the Russian Romanticists, and in striking contrast to these, the critical opinions of the "Westerners," of Vissarion Grigorievich Belinski and Aleksandr Ivanovich Herzen.* And yet, with these various echoes and outright borrowings, Turgenev's image of Goethe is strikingly original. His attitude toward the German poet is basically one of sustained admiration, yet he is capable of sharp criticism, like that in his account of his visit to Weimar. On entering Goethe's house, he was at once disappointed, indeed outright offended, by its decor. He minces no words in his criticism: "I have always suspected that Goethe had the worst taste in sculpture, painting, and architecture; the author of *Faust*, of *Hermann und Dorothea*, of those countless, inimitable poetic creations appears as a kind of untalented, pedantic, heavy-handed schoolman whenever it is a matter of the visual arts." [2] Despite such critical observations, Turgenev always prided himself on being a "sworn Goetheist," a "zakliatyi Gëteanets." [3]

Turgenev's early publications clearly show Goethe's influence. "Parasha," a narrative poem with which the young author made his literary debut in 1844; the essay on Goethe's *Faust* (1845); *Hamlet of the Shchigry District* (1849); his novellas *Iakov Pasynkov* (1855), *Faust* (1856), and *Asia* (1856); and his novel *Rudin* (1856) are all influenced by the German poet, particularly by his *Faust*. In his influential work *The Spirit of Russia*, T. Masaryk points out Turgenev's debt to Goethe "in a literary, artistic and philosophic sense"

---

*I have discussed these in Volume I.

1

and adds, "His *Faust* became a sort of starting point for Turgenev's own artistic endeavors,"[4] an opinion fully borne out by my investigation.

Turgenev's letters are replete with references to and quotations from a broad range of Goethe's works. The German poet takes first place by a wide margin among the long list of classical and modern writers whom Turgenev refers to and cites. Schiller is a distant second.

As so many other Russian Goethe-enthusiasts and even some of his critics, Turgenev liked to enlist Goethe in support of his views and theories of the most varied kind and quality. Thus, in an early letter (1839) to his friend Timothy N. Granovski he draws on Goethe's ballad "Der Gott und die Bajadere" in order to buttress with the master's authority the notion—possibly borrowed from Hegel's *Aesthetics*—that "in the Indian race the vegetative nature still predominates."[5] In another letter, Turgenev waxes rapturous over the vitality and passion alive in the *Roman Elegies*: "I cannot stop reading Goethe. This reading sustains me in these listless days. What treasures I continue to discover in him! Just think of it—up to this moment I had not read his *Roman Elegies*. What life, what passion, what vitality breathe in these verses. Goethe in Rome, in the embrace of a Roman woman!" He is particularly impressed with Elegies III, V, VII, XII,[6] and XV. "These elegies have suffused my blood as with a stream of fire—how I yearn for love!" He despairs of ever experiencing this "heavenly gift," which—he is convinced—would change his very nature: "If I were to fall in love, oh how kind, how pure, how sincere, how rich I would become!"[7]

I have quoted this letter at some length as one example among many that show how deeply and personally affected young Turgenev was by the words of the poet. Turgenev extols Goethe as his guide and teacher, and not only as his but as the great "teacher of us all."[8] He councils his lifelong love Pauline Viardot, the great diva of the day, to read Goethe's drama *Iphigenie auf Tauris* as a guide and inspiration in interpreting her role in Gluck's opera of the same name: "La tragédie de Goethe est certainement belle et grandiose, et la figure qu'il a tracée est d'une simplicité antique, chaste et calme . . . peut-être trop calme. . . . Je crois que ce rôle vous ira à marveille, d'autant plus que vous n'avez pas besoin de faire une effort pour vous élever à tout ce qu'il y a de noble, de grande et de vrai dans la création de Goethe—tout cela se trouvant naturellement en vous."[9] What subtle flattery there is in that final phrase!

A letter that speaks eloquently of Turgenev's admiration for the philosophical thoughts of his great teacher is his lengthy epistle, in flawless German, to Bettina von Arnim. Clearly, Turgenev's admiration is sparked not so much by Bettina the charming hostess in whose salon he was no stranger, but by Bettina the devoted apostle of Goethe, the eloquent transmitter of Goethe's pantheistic world view which so enraptured young Turgenev.[10]

Like many another Goethe admirer, Turgenev had his favorite Goethe quotations, which are ubiquitous in his essays and letters. One of these is the famous lines of the *Lustige Person* in the "Vorspiel auf dem Theater": "Greift nur hinein ins volle Menschenleben! / Ein jeder lebt's, nicht vielen ist's bekannt, / Und wo ihr's packt, da ist's interessant." [11] In these lines Turgenev found a pithy expression of his artistic credo, of his untiring effort to reach out into the fullness of human life and to render its essence with ultimate faithfulness.

In "On the Occasion of *Fathers and Children* [his novel *Ottsy i Deti*]," that revealing self-defense of his method of composition—and not only in that masterpiece—Turgenev addresses the young generation, in particular the budding artists and writers among them, urging them to follow the advice of Goethe: "And so my words go out to you, my brethren: 'Greift nur hinein ins volle Menschenleben. . . .'" And Turgenev goes on to define the "reaching into life's depth," this "grasping" and "capturing" of the essence of nature, of characters and their milieu. He sees in this ability to comprehend and give artistic form to reality the very mark of talent. "But," he goes on, "talent alone is not enough. The artist, to be worth his salt, must also possess honesty, an unbending, unyielding honesty with regard to his own sensations." And finally, the artist "needs freedom, an unlimited freedom of perception, and he needs education, he needs knowledge." [12] This excerpt may serve as a striking instance of Turgenev's habitual use of quotations from Goethe as springboards from which to launch and subsequently to expand on the message nearest his heart, to lend weight and authority to that message.

To cite one more example, in a letter to Herzen, Turgenev quotes from Goethe's drama *Torquato Tasso*: "Der Mensch (der europäische Mensch) ist nicht geboren frei zu sein." [13] And he insists, "No, brother, no matter how you twist and turn, the old fellow [starik: Goethe] is right . . . —and why is he right?" Turgenev has his answer ready: "In nature we meet at every step with examples of societies of slaves with subdivisions into classes (bees, e.g.), and of all the European nations it is precisely the Russians who, compared with all the others, feel the least need of freedom." [14] Having delivered this thrust, Turgenev takes off from Goethe's words to expound a favorite theme of his, "gradualness," an idea central to his world view, [15] the evolutionary rather than revolutionary development of the cultural and sociopolitical life of nations, a theory that was also close to Goethe's heart. Only the gradual process of education, Turgenev insists to his more radical friend, can cure Russian society from its reactionary tendencies: "Take science, take civilization, and carry out the cure by means of these homeopathic remedies little by little" [16] is his urgent advice to Herzen and his friends on the left of the political spectrum.

In view of these and many more striking instances [17] of the inspirational influence of Goethe's words on Turgenev, I cannot agree with Zhirmunski when he argues, "The majority of Turgenev's Goethe quotations play in his writings a purely literary role as habitual formulae characteristic of the conversational style—with its literary embellishments and allusions—of the aristocratic intelligentsia," and then goes on to contrast Turgenev's Goethe quotations with those by Stankevich, Mikhail Bakunin, and Herzen, which, according to him, had a "basic significance in the establishment and development of their world view."[18] I would argue that Turgenev's Goethe references and quotes have the same "basic significance" in shaping his philosophy of life and art, and I would agree with Katharina Schütz that "das häufige Erwähnen Goethes . . . ein untrügliches Zeichen dafür ist, dass Turgenew in ihm seinen geistigen Führer erkannt hat. . . . Ohne Zweifel erblickt der russische Dichter in Goethe die Erfüllung dessen, was er selbst anstrebt."[19] Turgenev supports my opinion. Throughout his life he was intent on keeping his growing reputation as a Goethe adept, if not a Goethe scholar, untarnished and demanded of himself and of others exactness in quoting the admired poet and teacher. He had given Otto Lewald, a lawyer-acquaintance, an autograph in which he "had quoted three verses of Goethe and had made two mistakes!" This, he admits in a letter to his friend and translator Ludwig Pietsch, "ist mir unangenehm, man könnte glauben ich wäre nicht Goethefest." And he begs his friend "fussfällig" to go to Lewald, to give him the enclosed corrected autograph and to take back the faulty one. Then he adds with that rough humor bordering on vulgarity, of which he was quite capable, "Nehmen Sie das andere—und wischen Sie sich damit den Podex, hätt' ich gesagt, wenn nur das Papier nicht so hart wäre."[20] There are other instances[21] of his spirited defense of his "Goethefestigkeit," which has been attested to by many of his contemporaries.[22]

It cannot be my task to offer a full listing of the Goethe references and quotations in Turgenev's correspondence, especially since such a listing has been compiled by Schütz as well as by Elias Rosenkranz.[23] After a brief biographical introduction, I will deal in detail with Turgenev's view of Goethe as reflected in his essayistic and belletristic writings.

Biographical Background

From his youth to his dying day, Turgenev felt a deep attachment to Germany and an abiding respect, even admiration, for its exceptional achievements in philosophy and literature. Germany became his second fatherland. He traveled widely within its borders, knew Silesia, the "schwäbische Schweiz," the Taunus, the Black Forest, and the Rhine, which together with the picturesque valley of the Aar and the romantic town of Sinzig, he described so lyrically in his novella *Asia*. He frequently visited Munich, Heidelberg, Karlsruhe, and Germany's famous spas. As a student he spent about two years * in Berlin, and as a celebrated author he had a sumptuous villa built in Baden-Baden, made it his steady residence until the Franco-Prussian War (1870–1871), and longed for that "beloved, peaceful idyl" whenever he had to leave it.

As a boy of four, Ivan traveled with his family to Switzerland by way of Königsberg, Berlin, Dresden, Karlsbad, and Augsburg. In Bern the boy's life nearly came to a tragically premature end when he almost fell into the famous bear pit and was snatched from certain death at the last moment by the firm hand of his father.[24] And it was again his father's firm hand that set the boy to writing a diary at least twice a week, alternating the writing of it between Russian, French, and German, training that served Turgenev well throughout his life.[25]

Before Turgenev reached his teens, he was fortunate to have a German tutor who was able to win his confidence and to instill in him a love of the German language that remained with him for the rest of his life. He preferred it to French, and it was German that he habitually used when expressing his most intimate feelings.[26]

At the age of nine, Turgenev was placed in a Moscow boarding school run by a German. There he remained for two years (1827–1829), further perfected his German, and was introduced to the works of Schiller by a fair-souled instructor who could not read a line of the poet without shedding tears of rapture.[27] At this time Goethe does not seem to have been among his readings.[28] "The decade 1833 to 1843 were years of intense study at the Universities of Moscow, St. Petersburg, and Berlin; of travels in Italy and Switzerland; and of friendships with Nikolai Stankevich and Mikhail Bakunin. They were his *Lehrjahre*," [29] which confirmed him in his "Westernism." As Turgenev writes in his autobiographical sketch, "I threw myself headfirst into the German sea [during his stay in Berlin], . . . and when I finally surfaced from its waves I reappeared as a 'Westerner' and have always remained one." [30] Turgenev does not exaggerate. Among the "Westerners" he was the most consistent and outspoken, not even excluding Herzen, who had his flirtations with Slavophilism and whose glorification of the Russian peasant commune Turgenev criticized.[31] Turgenev proudly proclaimed himself a "rooted, incorrigible Westerner." [32] For him there existed no curtain between East and West. He "never recognized that insuperable line which some cautious and even some overly eager but poorly informed compatriots insist on drawing between us and that Europe to which, after all, Russia is so closely tied with ties of race, lan-

---

*Two semesters in 1838 and again a large part of the year 1841.

guage, and faith." He knows Russia to be "one of the main members of the Indo-Germanic cultural and linguistic family." And he poses a question:

Admitting the combined influence of Greece and Rome on the Germano-Romanic world, how can one possibly deny the influence of this filially related kindred world on us? Can it be that we are so little *sui generis*, so feeble, as to be afraid of any and every foreign influence and wave it off, childishly, lest it corrupt us? I, for one, do not assume this to be true. . . . I judge by my own experience; my devotion to the cultural foundations laid by the West has in no way hindered me from developing a lively feeling for and protecting jealously the purity of the Russian tongue.[33]

This eager openness toward the culture of the West was decisive in kindling Turgenev's interest in and growing admiration of Goethe.

At the University of Berlin, where he enrolled in the spring of 1838, Turgenev studied "Roman antiquity with Zumpt,[34] Greek literature with Böckh,"[35] history with Leopold von Ranke, and, most intensively, Hegel's philosophy with Professor Werder, who enlivened and enhanced his lectures with copious quotations from Goethe, especially from the Second Part of *Faust*.[36]

The university was not the only attraction Berlin had to offer the culture-hungry Russian. He frequently attended performances at the opera and the theater and came away with an unforgettable impression of the thespian talent of Klara Stich and of Karl Seydelmann in the role of Mephisto.

The salon of Rahel Varnhagen was open to Turgenev, and he was a welcome guest in the hospitable home of the Frolows, where, as he puts it, "I came to hold my tongue, to gape and listen."[37] And there was indeed much to listen to and to observe. Alexander von Humboldt, at the height of his fame, was an honored guest, and Varnhagen von Ense, an early champion of Aleksander Pushkin, and Bettina von Arnim were frequently present.[38]

In those Berlin years young Turgenev found his way into Goethe's world. Aside from the theater, with its famous *Faust* performances, and the salons of Rahel and the Frolows, hothouses of a fervent Goethe cult, there was the famous Stankevich "Circle," to which Turgenev was introduced in 1838. Here Goethe was celebrated as the "admired sage," an "all-embracing giant of poetry."[39] Turgenev, impressionable and enthusiastic, was caught up in this uncritical worship. He read the poet voraciously and even tried his hand at translating, but relatively little came of these efforts: "Klärchens Lied" (the "Soldatenliedchen") from Goethe's *Egmont*, the twelfth Roman Elegy, and, as the most successful rendering, the "Last Scene from Goethe's *Faust*," the dungeon scene.[40]

Turgenev's uncritical devotion to Goethe proved short-lived. It was the devotion of Turgenev the Idealist, the Romantic. As Schütz observes,

"Turgeniews Begegnung mit Goethe steht zunächst durchaus unter romantischem Vorzeichen." [41] But soon the rationalist temper of the socially conscious "objective realist asserted itself." [42] A. Yarmolinski succinctly characterizes this important reorientation: "Though to a lesser degree than the other members of Stankevich's coterie, Turgenev also was beginning to turn his attention away from ethical self-culture to the duties of man as a citizen of the uncouth, inert, abused, pregnant Russia in which he lived. Belinski helped him on his way." [43]

Turgenev's first meeting with Belinski took place in the fall of 1842 in St. Petersburg upon Turgenev's return from Berlin. This first acquaintance developed into a lasting friendship the following summer in the idyllic surroundings of the "Forest Institute" (Lesnoi Institut) near St. Petersburg. "Here we truly found each other," Turgenev reminisces in his autobiographical sketch:

We saw each other almost every day and took frequent walks in the pine groves surrounding the institute. We would settle on the dry, soft moss strewn with fine pine needles, and it was here that we had those endless conversations touching on the most varied subjects but centering on philosophy and literature. I had recently returned from Berlin, where I had studied the philosophy of Hegel. Belinski questioned me, listened, took issue, developed his ideas. . . . [44]

And these ideas had a strongly anti-Hegelian bent. In 1840, Belinski, who had been as ardent a Hegelian and admirer of Goethe as any member of the Stankevich "Circle," had one of his violent reorientations. It came to him with the suddenness and force of a revelation that his Hegelian "reconciliation with reality" had been "a tragic error." From this sudden revelation, from this violent "unreconciliation with reality," there flowed an impassioned reaction to his former positions all along the line—aesthetic, social, and political.

Goethe was now condemned for his egoism and social and political indifference, for his reprehensible *Fürstendienertum*; the poet Goethe was dismissed as out of step with modern times, as "dead in the present," as "a king deposed." Belinski's sharpest attacks on Goethe were concentrated in the years 1841 through 1843, the very period in which his meeting with Turgenev took place and their acquaintance ripened into friendship.

But even before their meeting, Turgenev had contact with Belinski's revolutionary ideas, expressed in a sharply critical article on Vladimir Benediktov, [45] a fashionable poet of the day. Turgenev vividly recaptures his reaction to Belinski's attack on his favorite poet in his "Recollections of Belinski": [46]

One morning a student-friend of mine dropped in and in great indignation reported that in the Café Beranger was an issue of the periodical *The Telescope* with an article by Belinski in which this "kritikan," this pseudo-critic, had dared to raise his hand against our idol Benediktov. Immediately I went off to Beranger, read the entire article, and naturally, just like my companion, flared up with indignation. But—strangely enough—both during my reading and afterward, to my great consternation and even anger, something within me involuntarily agreed with that "kritikan," found his argument convincing, irresistible. I was ashamed of this most unexpected reaction and tried to suppress that inner voice. Among my comrades I sounded off with even sharper criticism against Belinski and his article, . . . but in the depths of my soul something kept whispering to me that *he was right*. . . . A little time passed, and I no longer read Benediktov.[47]

The "inner voice" that "kept whispering" to Turgenev was the voice of the "objective realist." That voice made him receptive to Belinski's anti-Romantic, anti-Idealistic, "social" aesthetics. It prepared him to respond to Belinski's critical view of Goethe, enabled him to make Belinski's strictures of the man and the artist, at least in part, his own. Belinski's attacks on Goethe were to echo clearly in Turgenev's first major pronouncement on Goethe's personality and work in his review of M. Vronchenko's translation of Goethe's *Faust*.[48] Nowhere in his entire opus, essayistic or belletristic, was Turgenev to be again as close to the critical position of Belinski and Herzen as in his *Faust* essay.[49]

This is not to say that Turgenev altogether abandoned his idealistic aesthetics nurtured on Schelling and Hegel. Yarmolinsky puts it well when he argues, "[The] subsequent changes in his [Turgenev's] mental attitude could not erase, though they obscured, the idealistic notions that had taken hold of him during his formative years [especially during his two terms at the University of Berlin]: a reliance on consciousness, a profound appreciation of such generous if general values as Art, Freedom, Humanity."[50] *Au fond*, Turgenev remained kin to the Romantics[51] and never joined such radical materialists as Nikolai Chernyshevski and Dimitri Pisarev, even though he came to admit the timeliness, effectiveness, and even the need of their message in the Russia of serfdom and black reaction.[52] But on the other hand, he also never made common cause, either in art or in politics, with the "Pure Poets," with Afanasi Fet, for example, and never accepted their gospel of "l'art pour l'art."[53]

Such middle ground as Turgenev occupied is a notoriously exposed, dangerous, and ungrateful position. His stance between the ever more sharply clashing ideological camps drew on him many a vicious attack and caused him much anguish, but it also secured for him the freedom that he cherished above all else, the freedom from all constrictive ideological ties. Basically, he hated all "systems" and rigid theories, especially in aesthetics.[54]

This attitude lends his critical as well as his belletristic writings a quality of ambivalence, even of outright contradictoriness, which makes it difficult at times to lay hold of his message. There is in his critical argument a certain lack of logical consistency that sometimes leads him into outright self-contradictions. Yet he would put up with all this, arguing that life itself is never simplistic, but complex and full of inconsistencies. He would never simplify his task as a responsible thinker and artist by putting on ideological blinkers, or tie his artist hands with rigid systems or unyielding prejudices. Repeatedly Turgenev proclaimed the freedom and autonomy of the artist as the sine qua non of all true art: "Believe me," he urges, "a genuine talent never serves extraneous ends but finds satisfaction in himself. Only those who cannot excel take up some assigned theme or carry out a program." [55]

The *Faust* Essay

Turgenev's interpretation of Goethe's *Faust* [56] is, at the same time, his single most comprehensive and penetrating statement of his view of Goethe, of the poet's attitudes in life and art. Turgenev sets the stage for his discussion of Goethe's drama most effectively by characterizing the spiritual orientation of the Russian intelligentsia in the mid-1840s. The years of the Romantic adulation of Goethe, he tells us, are gone forever: "Now the common sense of the Russian public demands solid proof—not of Goethe's greatness as a poet (that our public knows better than we do) but rather proof that his *Faust* is really such a gigantic creation." Turgenev promises to satisfy his modern readers by giving them not high-blown paeans but a down-to-earth critical examination of the work.

Beginning his exposition with a survey, informed even if derivative, of the German literary scene in the mid-eighteenth century, that is, at the time of Goethe's birth, Turgenev praises Martin Wieland, Friedrich Klopstock, and in particular Gotthold Lessing for their contributions to German culture and specifically to belles lettres and critical literature, but he concludes that "none of these was destined to express in a positive, comprehensive manner the essential characteristics of his nation and his time." That supreme achievement was to be Goethe's. Turgenev finds the source of this achievement in Goethe's uniquely "German" personality. Goethe's penchant for self-perfection, "Bildungssucht," Goethe's suspicion of politics, his asocial, even antisocial, bent, his emphasis on the private, the purely "human" aspects of life—all these salient traits of Goethe's character our critic recognizes as being typically German. For Turgenev "there is no other people who can be, to such an extreme degree, purely and solely 'human.'" In his view "the German is an individual first and foremost and a citizen last and least."

Turgenev was to experience a gradual change of mind on this point as he observed during his long life the antisocial, individualistic German change into a well-disciplined, loyal citizen of his burgeoning fatherland who set aside philosophy and the humanities in pursuit of glory on the battlefield of wealth and power in the heady *Gründerzeit* (1871–1873). Turgenev actually came to fear the arrogant victor in the Franco-Prussian War, which he recognized as the seedbed of more horrible wars to come.[57] But those days were still three decades in the impenetrable future for the young author of the *Faust* critique.

The claim that it was Goethe who had first expressed with his personality and work the spirit of his nation was not new. The Romanticists, as well as Belinski and Herzen, had sounded that theme. With Turgenev, however, it becomes a central aspect of his image of the German poet. Especially in his *Faust* essay he returns to it time and again: "It was Goethe who was destined to fully encompass and express with his personality the essential characteristics of his people. . . . His greatness consisted in his unique ability to reflect in a creative manner all the strivings, all the hopes and desires, of his people. As the great German poet he conceived his *Faust*."

In view of these reiterations of Goethe's preeminence as the national poet, it is startling to find Turgenev in his essay on Friedrich Schiller's *Wilhelm Tell* (1804) bestowing the laurel on that poet rather than on Goethe. He tells us that it is "Schiller, even more than Goethe, who deserves that highest satisfaction a poet can enjoy, that of having expressed the innermost essence of his people." And he goes on: "As a human being and a citizen, Schiller stands above Goethe, even though he ranks below him as an artist and, generally, as a personality."[58] However inconsistent this statement may seem, it does introduce another salient feature of Turgenev's Goethe image: the critical view of Goethe the "human being and citizen," which we find especially pronounced in the *Faust* essay.

Turgenev shares with a majority of his compatriots their predilection for the *young* Goethe, for the author of the early poems, of *Werther* and of *Faust*, Part One. The Italian journey he sees as the great divide separating the passionate, vital Goethe of his "Sturm und Drang" (Storm and Stress) period from the "all too calm"[59] classical Goethe: "After the fateful journey there appeared the multitude of remarkable, profoundly reasoned, and perfectly rounded works to which, nonetheless, *we* [Turgenev] *prefer the spontaneously passionate and disorderly inspirations* of his youth."[60] In the young Goethe, Turgenev recognizes "the foremost representative of his generation, of the generation of Sturm und Drang. Goethe alone fulfilled the high promise of these *Kraftgenies* by dint of the wholeness, soundness, balance, and vitality of his nature," while others, "the Lenzes and Klingers, and the whole lot of them, failed." Characteristically, Turgenev equates Sturm und Drang with Romanticism.[61] The author of the Part One of *Faust* is a Romantic, he insists, and as such "he is a poet first and foremost, a poet and nothing else." It is in this all-determining character trait that Turgenev finds "all of his [Goethe's] greatness but also all of his weakness."

Here we touch the very core of Turgenev's ambivalent valuation of Goethe, his bifocal view of him. Together with the Russian Romanticists, under the influence of his friend Nikolai Stankevich, impelled by his own artistic nature, Turgenev extols Goethe's all-embracing genius and recognizes, more clearly perhaps than the Romanticists, the full complexity of this poet:

With the ability to abandon himself passionately, madly, Goethe combined the gift of constant self-analysis, of an instinctive observation of his own passions characteristic of the poet. With an infinitely varied and receptive imagination he combined common sense, an artist's unfailing tact, and a striving toward totality. He himself *was* that totality, he was—as the saying goes—all of a piece; with him life and poetry were not divided into two separate worlds. His life *was* his poetry and his poetry *was* his life.

And then Turgenev comes to his central theme: "The first and the last word, the Alpha and Omega, of his [Goethe's] whole life, was, as is the case with all poets, his own *ego*, but in that *ego* you find the whole world. . . . Everything earthly is reflected in his soul, simply, effortlessly, faithfully." In these words of Turgenev one all but hears Evgeni Baratynski's famous paean to the "all-encompassing" Goethe:

> Sein Atem war eins mit dem atmenden All,
> Er verstand das Gemurmel der Quellen,
> Des Laubes Geflüster, des Schauers Schall,
> Und hörte die Knospen schwellen.[62]

And Turgenev continues: "This all-embracing greatness of Goethe's personality exerts on us such a powerful influence that a little poem, the "Song of Klärchen," in which nothing more is said than the trite fact that there is no happiness in life without love strikes us as a veritable revelation that could not possibly have occurred to us or, for that matter, to anyone else." Thus far, Turgenev's image of Goethe retraces the Romantic view of the German genius. But the positive aspects of that image can suddenly appear in a sharply critical light, Goethe's ego, here extolled as world-encompassing, can shrink to a solipsistic, alienated, hopelessly egocentric self.[63]

Some critics—Erich Hock, for instance—see in this ambivalence a mark of Turgenev's immaturity, the inability of the young author of the *Faust* essay to understand the complex nature and role of the poet.[64] I see it as a natural outgrowth of Turgenev's dilemma, which remains basically unresolved throughout his life. Examined from the point of view of aesthetics, this dilemma proves to be characteristic of the writer standing midway between Romanticism and Realism.[65] From the sociopolitical standpoint, Turgenev's dilemma presents itself as the dire predicament of the cosmopolitan liberal in times of a greatly intensifying polarization between the conservative camp and the progressive camp, between reaction and revolution.[66] Turgenev the Romantic grants the poet ultimate freedom and celebrates his self-assertive ego as the source of all truly creative achievements. As the socially conscious Realist, he frowns on that self-centered ego and castigates it as antisocial, solipsistic, and alienated and demands of the poet self-effacement in social service.[67]

Belinski, in his anti-Hegelian period, had "deposed" his onetime idol Goethe the "king." Turgenev does not go so far, yet he does follow his guide and mentor in denying Goethe true modernity. Goethe, he argues, was the representative of an age of transition. He was still too much caught up in the past to enter fully the new age of "sociality" (social 'nost').* Turgenev explains:

In his [Goethe's] time, in that transitional as yet undefined time, the poet could afford to be merely an individual. The old social structure had not yet collapsed in Germany; nonetheless, one began to feel stifled in that society. The new age was merely dawning; there was not as yet a sufficiently firm supporting ground for a person who would no longer be satisfied with a life of dreams and fancies. Every German went his own way and either refused to acknowledge any duties or else submitted selfishly or thoughtlessly to the existing order.

According to Turgenev, the Germans—and that included Goethe, of course— had not yet developed a sense of social responsibility; they had remained indifferent to the suffering of the masses, blind to the potential greatness of the simple people. Goethe, together with his fellow intellectuals, had not yet achieved even a modicum of social consciousness. Turgenev exclaims: "Just look what a sad role the people play in his *Faust*! Those are people . . . such as we find in the paintings of Teniers and Ostade. . . . In Goethe's work, people pass before our eyes not as the ancient chorus in the classical tragedy but as the choristers in the latest opera."[68]

Unquestionably, ideology is here clouding Turgenev's vision and tricking his ear. He seems insensitive to the vitality and vigor in the merriment of a free peasantry under the traditional village linden tree which Goethe has caught so inimitably in his scene.[69] He does not recognize the self-assured dignity in the bearing of the old peasant as he offers Faust the brimming cup—a

---

*Translation of French *société* and Belinski's favorite term.

very different bearing from that of a Russian serf and hardly that of a "chorister in the latest opera." There is a fine irony in the fact that Turgenev's ideologically blinkered view of this colorful peasant-scene bears striking resemblance to Wagner the archphilistine's reaction to it in Goethe's drama. Both criticize it, Wagner from the conservative point of view, Turgenev from the liberal democratic viewpoint.

The same prejudicial view is manifested in Turgenev's comments on the student scene.[70] He would have us hear "an aristocratic, supercilious irony" in Goethe's voice "as he makes fun of that poor young fellow who so humbly approaches Faust for his advice." Again Turgenev misses the point. It is, after all, not the poet but the sarcastic Mephisto who speaks here, and not at all with "aristocratic, supercilious," ironic intonations but with sardonic irony aimed not so much at the student as at the petrified institutions, the dusty academic system, and the questionable mores of society.

To cap his misinterpretation of this scene, Turgenev makes of the humble student—surely against every intention of Goethe—a "representative of the entire young generation, which is incapable of rising to the heights of genius." Then, thrusting home his attack against the "aristocratic Goethe," he has him pose the captious question: "What right has that stupid crowd to disturb the sublime peace, the lonely joys, and the sufferings of genius?" Clearly, Turgenev strives to emulate, or rather to outdo, Belinski and Herzen in their attacks on Goethe, the antisocial, haughty Olympian, coldly superior to the hoi polloi.

Continuing in this vein, Turgenev then traces Goethe's growing alienation from his social environment, his mounting indifference to the epochal events of his time, the decline of his poetic powers into the lifeless allegory of his late works:

The poet's flair for receptivity and artistic reproduction, which had always been so powerfully developed in Goethe's soul, finally became dearer to him than the actual content of life. Not life itself preoccupied and enthralled him, but *life as an object of poetry*. Goethe imagined that he stood at the summit of spiritual contemplation, while actually he was looking down on all terrestrial life from the heights of his cold, aging ego. He was proud of the fact that all the mighty social upheavals taking place around him could not even for a moment perturb his equanimity, the calm silence of his soul. Like a mighty cliff he would not let the waves move him—and as a result he fell behind his times, even though his observing mind strove to evaluate and understand all the extraordinary, contemporary events. But after all, with the mind alone one cannot truly understand anything living. . . . All human existence turned into an allegory for him.

And yet with these critical strictures Turgenev was quite capable of combining a positive view of Goethe as the "protector of all that is human, of all that is rooted in earth, vital, as the sworn enemy of all that is pseudo-idealistic and supranatural." He praises Goethe the "courageous champion, who as the first one came forward in defense of the rights of man." But then he adds, significantly, "not of [the rights] of humanity as a whole but of the rights of the individual, passionate, discrete human being." Goethe was "the first to show us that in such a being there is hidden an indomitable strength, that such a being can live without any external support, that his is the right and the opportunity for happiness, and that he need not be ashamed of that happiness, despite all the unresolved doubts that haunt him, despite the feebleness of his religious faith and of his personal convictions."

Such then is Turgenev's ambivalent view of Goethe as the aloof, cold, egocentric poet devoted exclusively to his art, and at the same time as the protector and champion of modern man, who discovers for us the individual's self-sufficient independence, his inalienable right to a happy life even in the modern world without religious faith and strong convictions. But note that even in his *praise* there is an important reservation, a negative note: he acclaims Goethe as the champion of the "discrete human being," not of society as a whole, not of the masses. Once again there is here more than a hint of Goethe's lack of a sense of sociality, a lack of a commitment to a comprehensive reform of the human lot.

We find this same ambivalence, even contradictoriness, in Turgenev's interpretation of Goethe's *Faust*: "*Faust* is a purely human, or—to be more precise—a purely egoistical [read: egocentric], work." * It is for Turgenev the most complete expression of the epoch "in which society had reached its own negation, when every citizen had become an individual, when the battle between the old and the modern times had finally been joined and people had come to deny all absolute authority except human reason and nature. The French actualized this autonomy of human reason in [political] action, the Germans in theory, in philosophy, and in poetry." And Turgenev reiterates his basic view of the Germans as predominantly individualistic, and "private" in their outlook on and bearing in life: "Generally speaking, the German is not so much a citizen as he is an individual. With him purely human problems take precedence over social."

Turgenev now leads the discussion back to his central theme: Goethe, precisely because he is a typical German, a national poet, was singularly endowed "to evoke *Faust* from the depths of his all-embracing and, at the same time, deeply egocentric nature [!]"—he could create that "purely human or

---

* "Egoism" was used at the time of Turgenev's essay (1845) still as a philosophical term roughly equivalent to our present-day term "egocentricity."

more precisely purely egocentric work" with an "egoist *pur sang*" for its hero. Turgenev characterizes Goethe's Faust as a "theorizing egoist, a self-adulating, learned, daydreaming egoist. He does not strive to conquer science, to comprehend analytically his own self." His ego is the center of Faust's universe. "For Faust society does not exist. He is completely, blindly wrapped up in himself; he expects salvation solely through his own self." In this self-centeredness Turgenev recognizes Faust's as well as his creator's tragic aberration, their fatal flaw. According to Turgenev, "the cornerstone of man is not his self as an indivisible entity, but rather mankind-as-a-whole, society with its eternal, immutable laws."

Turgenev finds Goethe's dramatic masterpiece saturated from beginning to end with the "one-sidedness of Faust's egocentric nature." From this point of view *Faust* becomes for him "the most extreme expression of Romanticism, Romanticism being the apotheosis of the self." For Turgenev there is in Goethe's entire drama only one scene that stands out as an important exception, "the mighty appearance of the Earth Spirit,[71] in whose thunderous words" Turgenev hears "the voice of Goethe the pantheist, of that Goethe who sought and found refuge in the all-embracing quiescent 'substance' of Spinoza whenever his own limited self began to bore him." On the other hand, the self-centered egoism of Faust is displayed, according to the Russian critic, nowhere more crassly than in Faust's relationship with Gretchen. Turgenev leaves us guessing about how far he would have us recognize in Faust's behavior Goethe's own attitude toward his many loves.

Of Gretchen, Turgenev has surprisingly little to say. He treats her with condescending irony: "She is as lovely as a flower, as transparent as a glass of water, as easy to grasp as two-times-two is four; she is a kindly German girl quite devoid of passion, she exudes the bashful charm of innocence and youth and is, to tell the truth, quite—stupid." One cannot be sure with what voice Turgenev is speaking here—with the voice of the eccentric aesthete who considers this stupid innocent beneath serious consideration, or with the voice of the progressive cosmopolite who makes short shrift of the "kindly German girl" of bourgeois extraction, or with the voice of Belinski, that full-fledged feminist, who would have considered Gretchen merely a backward and "stupid" victim of male oppression. Clearly, Gretchen is not Turgenev's type, no sister to his heroines. One might find some distant resemblance to Lisa of *The Nobleman's Nest*, but with that all comparison would end. And yet such is the complex ambivalence of Turgenev's reactions to Goethe's protagonists, that he is by no means totally insensitive to Gretchen's true nature. He finds her comparable to Shakespeare's Ophelia, and in his discussion of the dungeon scene, so masterfully translated by him, he even raises Gretchen "a thousand times higher than the clever Faust."

Up to this point it may appear that Turgenev's view of Faust is altogether negative, but this is by no means the case. In Goethe's hero, Turgenev recognizes "not only the sick child of the none-too-healthy Middle Ages" but also, far more perceptively, the representative man at the threshold of the modern era: "In him a new beginning has found its forceful expression, the beginning of the newest epoch," of the autonomy of human reason, the epoch of criticism, of "reflection." Faust's penchant to "contemplate and reflect on his own feelings" marks him as a thoroughly modern man: "The presence of the element of negation and 'reflection' is the distinguishing characteristic of the contemporary generation; 'reflection'—that is our strength and our weakness, our ruin and our salvation."

The other representative of this "new beginning" is Mephisto. At times, in Turgenev's interpretation, he appears superior to Faust as the more "faithful expression" of the "critical spirit of the eighteenth century, of the epoch of Voltaire." Turgenev asks, "Is not Mephisto frequently a boldly articulated Faust? And are not his speeches the most faithful expression of the innermost impulses and convictions of Goethe himself?" Turgenev's answer to this question is not as clear-cut as its assertive tone would suggest. In other parts of the essay, Turgenev emphasizes not the preeminence of Mephisto but rather the *identity* of Faust with Mephisto: "Faust is that self-same Mephisto or, to put it more precisely, Mephisto is the abstract, personified[72] element of the total personality of Faust; he is 'personified negation.'" And negation, in Turgenev's interpretation, is also a central element of Faust's nature: one cannot but feel the inner, insoluble ties that bind Faust to Mephisto; one cannot but acknowledge these two figures to be the manifestation of one and the same personality, of the personality of their creator. It is precisely in Goethe's ability to embrace *both* elements—eternal striving *and* absolute negation, Faust as well as Mephisto—that Turgenev finds the true measure of Goethe's greatness. Goethe rises above the "limited genius," Byron precisely because "*he* was able to bear in his soul a Mephisto without being destroyed, yes, even without suffering," a strength that Turgenev finds lacking in Byron's "problematically torn nature." In Goethe's "classically calm soul all contradictions are a priori resolved."

Turgenev's characterization of Mephisto as "acerbic, malevolent, and derisive," as a "destructive force," must not lead us to conclude that he saw in Mephisto exclusively negative traits. Far from it. In his very role of "absolute negation," Mephisto represents for Turgenev "a positive and a creative impulse ushering in a new epoch." Of course, being the harbinger of the modern age, he had to appear as *radical* negation, for only as such an absolute force could he hope to overcome the stubborn resistance of the entrenched past. He is in Hegelian terms—and we know Turgenev's immersion in Hegel's philosophy—the "antithesis" to the "thesis" of the established order of the feudal Middle Ages. He is the "acid solvent of the calcified past." In short, for Turgenev, he is a liberating, creative force helping to usher in the "synthesis" of the modern age.

And yet Turgenev denies Mephisto true greatness. "Mephisto is far from being the 'majestic Satan.' He is but a 'puny devil from among the lowest subalterns.'" Why this surprisingly low ranking of Mephisto? Turgenev's answer is that Mephisto, like Faust, like Goethe himself, is still caught up in the age of individualism. He is the devil not of those strong, socially conscious "new people of action" whom Belinski and Herzen and, with them, Turgenev are calling for, but of the self-centered, eternally theorizing, and temporizing members of the Russian intelligentsia. He is the devil of those "timid souls exclusively preoccupied with their own doubts and quandaries, he is the devil of lonely, alienated, endlessly agonizing people deeply troubled by some miniscule contradiction in their private life, of people who would pass by a worker's family dying of hunger with complete philosophic indifference." In sum, Mephisto, like Faust and Goethe himself, is lacking the essential quality of greatness: social consciousness and compassion.

Ironically, Turgenev cannot deny Mephisto a degree of greatness for a purely negative reason. He cannot deny it to him because of his "powerful influence over that vast multitude of youths who, by his grace [as a hellish Pied Piper] or, to put allegory aside, by the grace of their own timid and egoistical introspection never were able to escape the narrow circle of their own dear ego." Clearly, Turgenev has lost touch with Goethe's text.[73] Here again, as so often in his letters, Goethe's words have become for Turgenev a convenient springboard from which to launch one of his favorite ideas, this time his criticism of the "superfluous man." Mephisto can be dropped as a dispensable allegory, and what comes into bold focus is Turgenev's characterization of the decadent generation of solipsistic Russian youths tragically caught up in their problematical, limited "dear ego." Self-indulgent, obsessive "reflection" is here presented from its darkest side as the "lost" generation's "greatest weakness."

Throughout the study, Turgenev's attention centers on the figures of Faust and Mephisto. The other personae are given short shrift. We recall Turgenev's surprisingly brief remarks on Gretchen, his cursory mention of Wagner as the "Urphilister" and of the Student as the butt of Mephisto's irony and the "representative of the young generation." All the other protagonists of *Faust*, Parts One and Two are merely alluded to (Martha, for instance, or Oberon and Titania) or passed over in total silence.

In his essay "Hamlet and Don Quixote" (1860),[74] Turgenev carries forward his analysis of Mephisto by comparing him with Hamlet. In both he recognizes the "beginning of negation," with the decisive difference that Shakespeare's Hamlet remains "enclosed in the circle of human nature" while Goethe, with his penchant for abstraction and allegory, "separates his Mephisto from all that is purely human." Goethe's Mephisto is a supranatural figure, especially in the Second Part of *Faust*, and as such draws sharp criticism from "objective realist" Turgenev. Shakespeare's Hamlet, on the other hand, never transcends human reality. Hamlet's "negation" is not "absolute," as is Mephisto's. "He may doubt the existence of the good, but he does not doubt the existence of evil, and he joins in uncompromising battle with it." Good and evil, truth and falsehood, beauty and ugliness—they do not fuse and mingle for Hamlet into one haphazard, mute, and dull nothingness, as they do, according to our critic, in the cynical indifferentism of the absolute nihilist Mephisto. "Hamlet does not laugh the demonically indifferent laughter of Mephisto; his bitter smile expresses that melancholy sadness that speaks of his sufferings and reconciles us with him. . . . Hamlet's skepticism is not indifferentism, and from this fact derive his importance, his worth, and his dignity." Clearly, Turgenev's sympathies lie wholly with Hamlet, the suffering human being, Shakespeare's realistic creation, "enclosed in the circle of human nature." Mephisto as a demonic figure stands too close to allegory, too obviously transcends human reality (especially in Part Two) so as not to chill the sympathies of Turgenev, that sworn enemy of all that is allegorical and abstract.

Though there is no explicit mention of Faust in "Hamlet and Don Quixote," I agree with Schütz that Hamlet is basically the Faust figure once again, but this time seen through the eyes of a more mature Turgenev: "Faust ist von neuem vor Turgeniew erstanden, aber nicht mehr in der Gestalt des alten Faust der Vergangenheit, sondern als lebendige Verkörperung von einem der beiden Grundgesetze der menschlichen Natur." Hamlet-Faust and Don Quixote become in this essay the two antithetical forces of "immobility and motion, of conservatism and progress," of the centripetal and the centrifugal impulses. Hamlet-Faust is no longer dismissed as the egocentric "superfluous man" but rather accepted as the valid, in fact, necessary representative of the one manifestation of nature, of the "Nordic" spiritual, introverted, contemplative, brooding, while Don Quixote is seen as the representative of the antithetical "Mediterranean," sensuous, extrovert, activist pole of nature in its totality. And again I would agree with Schütz when she points out the resemblance of these contrasting yet complementary manifestations in Turgenev's interpretation to Goethe's concept of "Systole und Diastole," of the "Ein und Ausatmen der Welt, in der wir leben, weben und sind." [75]

On the other hand, Turgenev's identification of Faust with Hamlet indicates how far the Russian critic has moved from Goethe's original in his view of the Faust figure. The element of *striving*, central in Goethe's conception, has for Turgenev lost in importance to such a degree that it no longer can serve as a salient trait clearly differentiating Goethe's Faust from Shakespeare's Hamlet. In Turgenev's view of Faust and Hamlet, the traits of *reflection* and *negation* that are characteristic of both figures are seen as being so dominant that they enable Turgenev to establish the complete identification Faust = Hamlet.

But let us return once more to the *locus classicus* of Turgenev's effort to grasp the full complexity of Goethe's personality and of his dramatic master-piece, to his seminal essay on *Faust*. Throughout the essay, Turgenev focuses, very characteristically for this champion of spontaneity and realism, on Part One of the tragedy. For him "the entire first part of *Faust* . . . is imbued with unconscious verity; it possesses organic unity. . . . Truly, thinking of *Faust* you feel that everything in it is absolutely necessary, that there is nothing su-perfluous here." Yet to be precise, it is not the entire Part One that meets with Turgenev's approval. The "Intermezzo of the Golden Wedding of Oberon and Titania" is denigrated as the product of "Goethe's passion for allegory," and such phantasmagoric scenes as the "Hexenküche" and the "Walpurgisnacht" receive no mention whatever.

The Second Part of the tragedy is summarily dismissed:

The final judgment on that second part has been pronounced. All these symbols, these types, these contrived groupings, these mystifying speeches, Faust's journey into the world of classical antiquity, the cleverly woven interactions of these allegorical person-ages and events, the pitiful, paltry denouement of the tragedy that roused so much discussion—that entire second part finds a sympathetic reception only among the dod-dering oldsters (young or old in years) of the present generation.[76]

That "pitiful denouement that roused so much discussion" preoccupies Turgenev as well. As the "objective realist," he cannot accept Faust's apoth-eosis as a believable resolution of the tragedy. He rejects it as "an allegori-cal, cold, strained invention" of the old Goethe. At the same time, he is convinced that a truly satisfactory resolution could not possibly have been achieved by anyone at the "present stage of our spiritual development." It cer-tainly was not achieved by Goethe, but then, Turgenev argues, Goethe had no need of a believable resolution. And he draws the startling conclusion that "Goethe's consciousness of his own inner strength sufficed him." It is reflected in "Faust's majestic indifference," and this majestic indifference is "the real and final resolution of all the unsolved and unsolvable questions and doubts." We recall, "In Goethe's classically calm soul all contradictions are a priori resolved."[77]

Turgenev scoffs at the notion that "the Romanticists, barely risen from the innermost depths of the old order, should have been endowed with a knowledge we [citizens of the modern age] do not yet possess," and he reiterates his unshakeable conviction that "any resolution that does not take place *within* human reality is unnatural." At the same time, he has to admit that "of another kind of resolution we can only dream."

This conviction does not leave him despondent. "Let Faust be a fragment!" he exclaims. As an unfinished fragment it is the faithful mirror of an unfinished, fragmentary epoch. It is "the precise expression of an age for which the sufferings and joys of Faust were the highest possible sufferings and joys and for which Mephisto's irony was the most merciless of ironies!" In its unfinished state lies the true greatness of Goethe's masterpiece as an imperishable milestone on mankind's way from the Middle Ages to the very threshold of the modern epoch of "sociality."

Turgenev felt himself to be a representative citizen of such an age of transition. He often spoke of himself as of a "writer between two epochs." [78] He too, like Goethe in his tragedy, was not prepared to give final "realistic" answers. May not this be the highly personal reason why he accepted the "unnatural" denouement, the "unfinished" state of Goethe's tragedy? And may not this be also a reason why Turgenev dismissed the social message of the Second Part of *Faust* with a captious question, "Which honest reader would believe that Faust was really enjoying the 'moment of highest bliss' because his utilitarian plans are crowned with success?" Of course, there is another reason why Turgenev passes over, in virtual silence, the famous scene of Act V,[79] in which Faust demonstrates his sense of "sociality," his desire to strive with a free people on free soil for the improvement of their common lot. Emphasis on this scene would have clashed too crassly, even for the ambivalent Turgenev, with his view of Faust—and of Goethe—as the unregenerated egocentrics bent solely on their personal salvation. Turgenev's slighting of the famous scene has drawn and continues to draw sharp rebukes from Soviet critics.[80]

In the final remarks of the essay, Turgenev provides us with the clearest insight into the very source of his ambivalent view of Goethe and his tragedy. He concludes: "In the life of every one of us there is an epoch when *Faust* appears to us the most remarkable creation of the human mind, when it satisfies all our demands. But there follows another period in our lives, when we no longer accept *Faust* as a majestic and splendid creation, when we move forward toward other goals, following other leaders of lesser talent perhaps, but endowed with the greatest strength of character." And Turgenev repeats his central argument: "As a poet, Goethe does not have his equal, but now we are not in need of mere [!] poets. . . . We have come to resemble (alas, not completely as yet) those people who at the sight of a beautiful painting of a beggar cannot take pleasure in its "artistic execution" but rather are disturbed and saddened by the thought of the existence of beggars in our time." We can hear Belinski prompting from the wings, but of course it is not Belinski alone. We can trace the central message of this passage back to the "Young Germans," to Wolfgang Menzel and Ludwig Börne, and forward in time to such radical materialists as Chernyshevski and Pisarev. It expresses most poignantly Turgenev's dilemma. As a fellow artist by temperament and endowment, he cannot but deeply admire Goethe's genius, but as a follower of Belinski, imbued by him with the spirit of "sociality" which, moreover, came so naturally to Turgenev, having been awakened in him by early sordid experiences at Spasskoe (his mother's feudal estate), Turgenev cannot but censure Goethe's stance as a "mere poet," as the asocial, even antisocial, human being.

The concluding remarks of the essay reveal still another tension in the makeup of its author, Turgenev's twofold allegiance to his native Russia *and* to his cultural homeland Europe. He calls on his Russian compatriots to read *Faust* with utmost attention. He is convinced that Goethe's work is of greater value to its Russian readers than to Germans, who have been doting on this "Buch des Lebens" far too long, but that to dote on one's past, no matter how beautiful, is sure to prove counterproductive. The Germans should finally leave Faust's study, where to this day they are sitting side-by-side with Wagner, that archphilistine, and are daydreaming in a cave like Frederick Barbarossa of popular legend. "High time," Turgenev exclaims, "that the Germans stop dealing with transcendental problems and put their *Faust* aside."

On its Russian audience, on the other hand, the drama is sure to produce a most salutary effect: "This work will awaken in us many a thought. . . . And perhaps, reading *Faust* [this mirror of an age in transition], we will finally understand that the decomposition of the elements constituting a society need not always signal its death." Of course, the Russian reader must not expect to find in Goethe's work a faithful reflection of his own image, of his temperament, his way of feeling and thinking, his way of life:

We Russians are not aiming [as does the German Faust] to master life by means of ultimate, all-encompassing knowledge. Faust's striving toward transcendent goals is alien to us.[81] All our doubts and all our convictions arise and develop not as they do with the Germans; our women do not resemble Gretchen, our devil is not Mephisto. . . . To our common sense, much in *Faust* will seem strange and capriciously contrived (the Golden Wedding of Oberon and Titania, for example . . .).

And yet "despite its German exterior [!]," Goethe's *Faust* is "a work more readily understood by us than by any other people." The reason for this is that the Russian, not being caught up in blind admiration of the work, can keep a critical distance, and at the same time, as a member of the European cultural community, not lacking sensibility or the necessary background and intellectual equipment, he is able to grasp its message more soberly and soundly: "We will not thoughtlessly genuflect before *Faust*, because we are Russians, but we will understand and admire Goethe's mighty creation, because we are Europeans."

Here we recognize the characteristic stance of Turgenev—and not of him alone but of all the foremost "Westerners." They are deeply conscious of their twofold indebtedness to their native Russia as well as to their intellectual homeland, Europe. Though knowledgeable, empathetic participants in European culture, they keep a critical distance, are proud of their "otherness," and would not "thoughtlessly genuflect" before the achievements of the West.

In stressing the "otherness" of the Russian people, Turgenev stands in a time-honored tradition.[82] Of course, there is no question that the Renaissance and the Reformation had bypassed Russia and that the Age of Enlightenment had dawned relatively late and feebly for the Russian intelligentsia. This is reason enough for Russians not to have developed, indigenously, the admiration of classical antiquity, the Faustian striving, the penchant for self-cultivation, the cult of personality—all traits typical of Western man and of the Germans in particular. Yet there is overwhelming evidence, to which the present study hopes to add its share, of the Russians' ability to understand, to appreciate, and to participate intensely in the West's cultural and sociopolitical movements once they are brought into contact with them.[83] We recall the *Liubomudry*, those "lovers of wisdom," who all but outdid the Germans in their cultivation of the Romantic spirit. Nikolai Stankevich was an inspiring leader of his "Circle," of a whole generation of young Russians, into the esoteric world of German philosophy, but he also fervently and eloquently championed the cult of Goethe and even shared the Germans' *Italiensehnsucht* and *Bildungsdrang*. At the other pole of the cultural and sociopolitical spectrum stand the Belinskis and the Herzens, with their eager embrace of the critical spirit of the "Young Germans," of the radical preachments of the "Young Hegelians," and of Saint-Simon and Fourier in France. And there is Turgenev himself, that foremost example of the Russian's desire and outstanding ability to participate with a sharply observant eye and an open though critical mind in the cultural and artistic currents swirling around him in Berlin, Paris, and London.

Turgenev's dictum that as a *Russian* he would not bend a knee before Goethe's *Faust* but that as a *European* he would understand and admire the work, though a memorable *bon mot*, proves all too simple and pat in his case. One must not forget that Turgenev had been an expatriate for much of his adult life and had been thoroughly Europeanized. Thus, his admiring as well as critical attitudes toward Goethe are characteristic of him both as a Russian and as a European. Clearly, his view of Goethe as an egocentric, antisocial poet was motivated quite as much by his long, intensive exposure to European thought as by his Russian heritage. He had thoroughly absorbed the critical attitude toward the German poet initiated by the "Young Germans" and by Menzel and Börne and transplanted to Russia by Belinski.[84] On the other hand, it was a Russian, Nikolai Stankevich, whose influence, as we remember,[85] fortified Turgenev's abiding admiration of Goethe as the "greatest poet of more recent times," as the "sage teacher of us all."

In the context of my study there is no need to enter into a detailed discussion of Turgenev's analysis and evaluation of Vronchenko's translation and his "Survey of Both Parts of *Faust*."[86] They are of interest only as proof of Turgenev's extraordinary control of the German language and of his mastery of the finest nuances of the idiom far exceeding Vronchenko's.[87] Moreover, Turgenev's incisive critique of the translation also offered him the opportunity to characterize Goethe's unique style and to define its origin. For Turgenev this style has no equal in German literature. Not even Schiller could match it in its "energetically passionate simplicity." With this definition Turgenev characterized, specifically, the masterpieces of Goethe's Sturm und Drang period. But even in such "classical" works as *Tasso* and *Iphigenie*—"with their artistic, at times even artificially contrived embellishments," not to Turgenev's taste—he detects "far fewer archaisms than in the latest works of Schiller." The source of this unique style he finds in Goethe's "innate realism." Goethe's talent "developed in immediate contact with his everyday life, and his entire being was imbued with the liveliest sense of reality." Furthermore, Turgenev singles out the extraordinary "plasticity" of Goethe's style, which he traces to the poet's unequaled ability to achieve complete harmony between form and content. This harmony, in turn, he recognizes to be the result of Goethe's world view expressed in the famous lines of his poem "Epirrhema": "Müsset im Naturbetrachten / Immer eins wie alles achten; / Nichts ist drinnen, nichts ist draussen: / Denn was innen, das ist aussen."[88] Finally, Turgenev emphasizes the "organic" nature of Goethe's works. They are not, he argues, products of abstract ratiocination, they are not "invented." The best of them grew out of an experience that engaged the total personality of the poet, "his mind as well as his heart. . . . They grew as the fruit grows on its tree."[89] To be sure, Turgenev is speaking here of Fëdor Tiutchev's poems, but by implication he recognizes these very qualities in the form and content of Goethe's creations as well. He even compares, explicitly, Tiutchev's best lyrics to "those *Gelegenheitsgedichte* which Goethe called for"[90] and created. We recall Turgenev's characterization of the insoluble vital bond between Goethe's life and works: "His life *was* his poetry and his poetry *was* his life."

Critics, in their evaluation of Turgenev's *Faust* essay, present a wide range of opinions. Prague Slavist A. Bem stands at the negative pole of the spectrum, Schütz at the positive pole.[91] Bem finds nothing but commonplaces, "landläufige Urteile," in Turgenev's interpretation of Goethe's work: "Seine [Turgenev's] Auslegung des *Faust* bringt meines Erachtens nichts grundlegend Neues. Was seinen ablehnenden Standpunkt gegen den II. Teil des *Faust* betrifft, so ist auch hier Turgeniew nicht nur nicht ursprünglich, sondern sinkt auf die Stufe der landläufigen Urteile über dieses grandios angelegte Werk Goethes hinab."[92]

I cannot follow Bem in his denial to Turgenev of all originality. To be sure, Turgenev did have "close contacts with the contemporary German [critical] literature,"[93] but this does not mean, as Bem implies, that he accepted unquestioningly the German critics' interpretations and evaluations. While not agreeing with some of Turgenev's interpretations, I do recognize in much of his analysis a degree of originality, as, for instance, in his characterization of Mephisto as the "puny devil" of a generation of "superfluous," decadent youths, or in his view of the Second Part of *Faust* as a fragment, and his very personal reason for approving that open-ended denouement of the play. There can be no doubt that the essay on *Faust*, even if it does not represent "eine bedeutsame Etappe in der Geschichte der Auslegung des Goetheschen Drama auf russischem Boden," must be seen as the *locus classicus* of Turgenev's searching encounter with Goethe and his masterpiece. From it radiate lines of influence to his other essays[94] as well as to his early novellas and novels. Thus, it is not difficult to recognize in the protagonists of these early works, in the Hamlet of the Shchigry District, for example, or in Rudin, the "hero" of Turgenev's first novel by that name, certain salient personality traits that make them kith and kin to Turgenev's image of Faust as drawn in his essay. They are in essential aspects of their characters the selfsame problematical Romantics, "eternally theorizing, . . . daydreaming egoists," who have been influenced by their immersion in German Idealist philosophy and Romantic poetry, who ponder and proclaim transcendental ideals but are incapable of a single socially beneficent act and "pass by a worker's family dying of hunger with complete philosophical indifference," who are, in sum, representatives of the "superfluous people" so prevalent among the Russian intelligentsia of those days.

The Belletristic Works

With the narrative poem "Parasha,"[95] Turgenev made his literary debut. The influence of Goethe's *Faust* on the poem has been recognized by A. Bem, Katharina Schütz, and Erich Hock. All three critics see it as a minor Russian counterpart to the German drama. As Bem puts it, in "Parasha" "wird Russland, das Land der Stille und der freudlosen Ruhe dem deutschen Lande, dem Lande des Strebens . . . gegenübergestellt." [96] I read the poem as Turgenev's statement in "images" of central themes in his essay on *Faust*, namely, that "Faust's striving toward transcendent goals is alien to the Russians," that "Russian women do not resemble Gretchen," and that the "Russian devil is not Mephisto." Coming from the essay, one cannot but recognize that in "Parasha" Turgenev set out to demonstrate these insights. His "Parasha" is indeed no sister of the German Gretchen, nor is her lover, Victor, a German Faust. When Bem characterizes Victor as a seducer and equates him in that role with Goethe's hero,[97] he quite misses Turgenev's intention in creating this character, namely, to draw the figure of his Victor as differently as possible from Faust's. His Victor is a typical member of the Russian landed gentry of the mid-nineteenth century. He is a very proper suitor, careful not to press his affections in an unseemly manner on Parasha. Both parents welcome Victor as the future son-in-law. The mother watches with tears of joy the burgeoning affections between the young people in hopes he would declare himself; she has her wish fulfilled—with dire consequences. The narrator thinks he hears "the laugh of Satan!" [98] Turgenev leaves his readers with no doubt as to the true nature of his hero. He tells us explicitly: "My Victor was no Don Juan." [99] He could have said with equal justice, "My Victor was no Faust."

As to Parasha, far from being kin to Gretchen she is a modern-day Tatiana,[100] transplanted from the habitus of Pushkin to the milieu of mid-nineteenth-century Russia and transformed in keeping with the *Zeitgeist*. Again, I have to disagree with Bem, who sees in Parasha's loveless marriage Turgenev's "parody of Gretchen's tragedy." [101] Rather, I recognize in the Russian author's sensitive, searching, gently ironic portrayal of Parasha his intent to define realistically a Russian woman's status and sad fate in her marriage to a typical member of the landed gentry. Delineating her, Turgenev is intent on setting off his heroine as sharply as possible against Gretchen, that "kindly German girl." Why else would Turgenev have stressed so insistently the Russianness of his Parasha? He calls her the lovely child of Russian steppes, the daughter of Mother Russia: "I look at you—you breathe the magic loveliness of Russian steppes; you are the daughter of our Russ' [poetic term for Russia]." [102]

The figure that links the Russian poem explicitly to Goethe's *Faust* is Mephisto. The German devil is at length compared with and contrasted to his Russian counterpart, as if in pointed proof of the essay's statement "Our devil is *not* Mephisto." Here is how Turgenev elaborates the difference:

> Doch unser Dämon ist kein deutscher Teufel
> Der ist ein Grübler und ein Sonderling,

> Unheimlich—närrisch; unser ist dagegen
> Ein rundlicher, einfältiger Biedermann;
> Er weiss sich unter Menschen zu bewegen
> Und macht den feinen Herrn so gut er kann.[103]

Turgenev's Russian devil, as he first appears, is devoid of all supranatural traits, a totally realistic figure, "fat and rather simple" (tolst i prostovat).[104] Yet next to him, or perhaps as this inconspicuous devil's magical transformation, Turgenev introduces into his poem the "majestic Satan," whom he had missed in Goethe's *Faust*. This "laughing Satan" is not the puny devil of the "superfluous people," a role Turgenev had assigned to Goethe's Mephisto. This Satan is a terror-inspiring presence whose fierce, sardonic gaze fixes on Parasha and her lover and, reaching out beyond them, encompasses the width and breadth of the vast Russian realm with paralyzing power. He is a truly mythical figure, the grandiose, terrifying personification of those evil forces that Turgenev knew were holding Russia in their tyrannical grip:

> Und Grau'n
> Ergreift mich, denn nicht mehr nach meiner Schönen
> Und ihrem Freund blickt Satan: gross und weit
> Scheint sich ganz Russland vor ihm auszudehnen . . .
> Wie um der Wolken Saum zur Abendzeit
> Des Wetterleuchtens rote Flammen blitzen,
> Zuckt's grell durch seiner dunklen Wimpern Ritzen
> Und um die schmalen Lippen windet sich
> Ein boshaft Lächeln, langsam schauerlich.[105]

Pushkin's *Onegin*[106] has been pointed to as the primary source of Turgenev's inspiration for "Parasha," by its content and especially by its form, its rhythms, rhymes, and meters.[107] My analysis indicates the measure of influence Goethe's drama had on Turgenev's first literary effort.

The insistent presence of Goethe and his world in young Turgenev's thoughts is quaintly demonstrated in the very first of his famous *Notes of a Huntsman* (*Zapiski Okhotnika*), in the tale of the two Russian peasants, "Khor' and Kalinych" (1847).[108] Into this most indigenously Russian of his narratives Turgenev introduced the names of Goethe and Schiller by way of a startling comparison. The Russian peasant Khor', a down-to-earth, worldly-wise, successful type he compares to Goethe, and Kalinych, his inseparable friend and complete antipode, this dreamer and visionary of the tender heart, he compares to the fair-souled, idealistic Schiller of the "Ode to Joy": "Seid umschlungen Millionen!"

It is indicative of young Turgenev's preoccupation with the German world that Goethe and Schiller, their contrasting personalities, and their lasting friendship would enter the poet's mind while portraying two Russian peasants in their Russian setting. It should be added at once that when his friends and advisers pointed out to the beginner the tasteless blunder of the incongruous comparison, which ruffled the sensibilities of his aristocratic Russian readers as an unheard-of insolence,[109] Turgenev was quick to remove the German names from all subsequent editions of the tale.[110]

The next group of works[111] has a common theme: the effect of the immersion in the currents of German Idealism and Romanticism on members of the Russian intelligentsia. Already in "Parasha" Turgenev had touched on it: Victor, the "hero" of the tale, had been abroad; "his agile mind had brought from there a heavy freight of unproductive [besplodnykh] phrases and many doubts, results of cunning, timid observations." "All his life he had nourished his mind with strangers' thoughts."[112] This characterization of Victor is but thinly veiled autobiography. Young Turgenev, returning from Berlin, had times when he too doubted the value of the fruits of education he was bringing home to Russia and had his fears of having "nourished his mind with strangers' thoughts." This theme, merely touched on in "Parasha," is fully developed in the novella *Hamlet of the Shchigry District*,[113] which presents its author's most acerbic view of German Idealism, that includes for Turgenev Goethe's entire *Weltanschauung*.*[114]

To blunt the cutting edge of his critique, Turgenev places it into the mouth of a Russian "Hamlet,"[115] an unbalanced individual who, under the influence of Romanticism, that "apotheosis of the ego," with its cult of genius, had developed an *idée fixe*: he yearned to be an "original," a person completely *sui generis*. "To have your own odor [!], yes your own odor—that's it!" This is the Shchigry Hamlet's loftiest dream, his ultimate goal. Tragically for him, he is soon forced to realize that far from developing into a unique personality he had hopelessly retrogressed, had been stunted by his education at home and abroad into a most ordinary nobody. At Moscow University he had been drawn into one of those "Circles," a "Kruzhok"[116] that flourished in the hothouse atmosphere of the Romantic culture with its Goethe cult in the 1830s and 1840s. Here he tells us he "had lost all chance at self-directed development, had been trained in empty loquacity, . . . had been infected with the

---

*We may recall that Turgenev had attended Professor Werder's Berlin Hegel lectures, which were interlaced with copious quotes from Goethe, especially from the Second Part of *Faust*. This was but one of the many ways in which German Idealism and Goethe's *Weltanschauung* became inextricably interwoven in Turgenev's mind.

literary mange, and finally had found himself stripped of every vestige of native strength and freshness of soul."

From Moscow the Shchigry Hamlet had gone abroad to sit at the feet of the coryphaei in the hallowed lecture halls of Berlin University. Here he had "studied assiduously his Hegel" and had come to "know his Goethe by heart." But he asks, "What benefit could I derive from Hegel's *Encyclopedia*[117]—and not from it alone but from all German philosophy? . . . Why did I not stay at home and study life surrounding me right here? I would have come to know Russia's present needs, its future, and, moreover, as to the so-called mission in life, I would have seen mine clearly." Instead, he had "yearned for the Good, the True, and the Beautiful" and had lost all contact with reality. "Reflection [that curse of the Russian intelligentsia] ate into my very being and destroyed every vestige of my natural, unaffected self."

Such is the somber picture Turgenev paints in this satirical novelette of the disastrous effect of study abroad, of exposure to fair-souled Idealism and starry-eyed Romanticism and explicitly to Goethe's world: the Shchigry Hamlet had come to "know his Goethe by heart," and that achievement had contributed to his undoing.

Apollon Aleksandrovich Grigor'ev, one of the most dedicated admirers of Goethe among the Slavophiles,[118] took Turgenev to task for having traced the Shchigry Hamlet's "sickness" to the influence of German Idealism and of Goethe. With biting irony he writes:

Only in one respect is Hamlet mistaken. His sickness has not been caused by his study of German philosophy and Goethe. No matter that he intones, "I have studied Hegel, dear Sir, and know my Goethe by heart!" Not Goethe and not Hegel can be blamed for the poor fool's feeling duty-bound to "read German books at the very place of their origin" and to marry the daughter of a German professor. No, the fact is that this pitiable Hamlet of the Shchigry District had—*in the first place*—always been a sick visionary and—*in the second place*—had been ruined by a superficial encyclopedism or, to be more precise, by the disjointedness and fragmentariness of his knowledge.[119]

Grigor'ev's attack is justifiable, yet as a perceptive reader of Turgenev he must have known that Turgenev, in his deep-seated ambivalence, was quite capable of the diametrically opposite view of German Idealism and Romanticism and, with it, of Goethe, in their influence on members of the Russian intelligentsia.

In the novella *Iakov Pasynkov* (1855),[120] Turgenev presents such a diametrically opposite view. He paints a radiant portrait of the "last Romantic," who had been nurtured on German philosophy, on the poetry of Schiller, and who had developed into an ideal human being to whom Turgenev—thinly disguised as the authorial narrator—looks back in longing, love, and admiration in an attitude diametrically opposed to the critical view he had presented not only in the *Shchigry Hamlet* but also in his essay on *Faust*.

For a proper understanding of this difference in attitude, it is important to keep chronology in mind. The *Faust* essay had been written in 1845, the *Shchigry Hamlet* in 1849, that is, at a time when the anti-Hegelian and anti-Romantic influence of Belinski on Turgenev was at its height. In 1855, when the *Pasynkov* novella was written, that influence was on the wane. Now Turgenev was facing the radical materialists Nikolai Chernyshevski and Nikolai Dobroliubov, whom he had dubbed "snake and rattlesnake." Theirs was a provocative challenge to his aesthetics rooted in Romanticism. *Pasynkov* was Turgenev's answer to that challenge, a deeply felt defense of Romanticism, with Schiller chosen here as its chief representative.*

Some contemporary critics, Vasili Botkin and Aleksandr Druzhinin foremost among them, were greatly impressed with Turgenev's courage in writing this paean to Romanticism at a time of the ascendancy of radical materialism.[122] Panaev congratulated Turgenev on this spirited defense: "Only one, who was himself a poet, who had himself experienced all those Romantic transports and raptures, strivings and convictions, could come to its [Romanticism's] defense so fervently and with such success."[123] As such a born poet, Turgenev raised his monument to Pasynkov, that "last Romantic," and concluded his tribute to him with these words of heartfelt farewell: "Rest in peace impractical man, fair-souled idealist! And may God give to all those practical people,[124] to whom you have always been a stranger and who even now may be laughing at your shade, may God give to all these a chance to experience even one-hundredth of those pure delights, with which, despite a cruel fate and cruel people, your poor and humble [smirennyi †] life was beautified."

In *Hamlet of the Shchigry District*, Turgenev had subjected German Idealism and Romanticism, and with them the world of Goethe, to sharp criticism; in *Iakov Pasynkov* he had extolled them. In *Rudin* (1855),[125] his first sociological novel,[126] he strives to maintain a balanced view of his idealistic past, of that *unbewältigte Vergangenheit* with which he was trying, in the course of a full decade (1845–1855), to come to terms.[127]

Once again the hero of the novel, Rudin, is a "last Romantic," a "last Mohican." He is introduced to us, not without a noticeable touch of irony, as

---

*Pasynkov reads to the narrator of the novella—a thinly disguised Turgenev—Schiller's "poem 'Resignation'[121] . . . and so many others," and both are "swept off somewhere into some radiant, mysteriously beautiful world."

†Though *smirennyi* is usually translated "humble," it implies much more. It characterizes a person who has come to terms with himself and who now lives content and in peace with the world. It is an apt antonym to the German *strebend*.

the inspired seer of Romantic imagination who "is possessed of the well-nigh highest secret, the secret of musical eloquence." But Turgenev is quick to cast a shadow on his Romantic hero by introducing Rudin's implacable enemy, the realist Pigasov. Listening to one of Rudin's inspired monologues, Pigasov grumbles under his breath, "Nothing but words, nothing but empty words."

Turgenev highlights this tragic shortcoming of Rudin in a powerful scene. Having awakened admiration, affection, and love in Natalia Alekseevna, having declared his love for her in enthralling words, Rudin ignominiously collapses when put to the test of eloping with his beloved against the wishes of her mother. And Natalia responds with devastating disdain: "Is that how you translate into action your lectures on freedom, on self-sacrifice! But obviously there is a long way from your words to action. You have proved yourself a coward!" Turgenev is here passing the harshest possible judgment on the grave shortcomings of his fainthearted Romantic Idealist.

And yet, at the same time, Turgenev stresses that this gifted Romantic had actually lifted Natalia with his eloquent, empathetic readings from Romantic works far above her everyday existence:

What sweet moments did Natalia experience when . . . Rudin read to her from Goethe's *Faust* or Hoffmann or the "Letters" of Bettina or Novalis. . . . Rudin, totally immersed in German poetry, in the German Romantic and philosophical worlds, drew her after him into those sacred lands. . . . From the pages of the book Rudin held in his hands [Goethe's *Faust*] there poured, like melodious streams, marvelous images, new luminous thoughts into her soul and heart, deeply stirred by the noble joy of lofty emotions, and quietly there was ignited in her the sacred spark of rapture.*

It is Rudin's friend, Lezhnev, who expressed most clearly Turgenev's ambivalent attitude toward Rudin and his world of German Idealism. In their university days, as members of a Romantic "Circle," Rudin and Lezhnev had been close to one another. Lezhnev recalls those "golden days," when the young men would meet in animated discussions: "The eyes of each and every one were bright with rapture, cheeks aflame and hearts a-pounding as we talked of God, of truth, about the future of mankind, of poetry. Sure, some-

---

*Soviet critic M. O. Gabel' has singled out Rudin's love of Germany, his immersion in German philosophy, poetry, and music, and his resultant estrangement from Russian traditions and culture as the basic cause of Rudin's tragic fate, as the fatal flaw of the "superfluous man [lishnyi chelovek] of the 1830s and 1840s." According to this critic, "there was no ambivalence in the author's [Turgenev's] evaluation of the hero. His view of him . . . remained [a critical one] to the end [of the novel]; he never softened his criticism, did not rehabilitate Rudin." (M. O. Gabel', "Tvorcheskaia Istoria Romana *Rudin*," *Literaturnoe Nasledstvo* 55, 25/26.) Both the textual history of the novel and its final version emphatically disprove Gabel's claim.

times we talked nonsense, enthused over bagatelles, but what of that. . . . We parted, deeply moved, joyous, honest. . . . Yes! Those were good times, and I don't want to think that they passed away without a trace!" This was surely a picture of the "Kruzhok" very different from the one Turgenev had drawn in *Hamlet of the Shchigry District*!

Lezhnev's friendship with Rudin was not to last; Rudin's flawed character soon disrupted it. But even as Lezhnev speaks of his subverted friendship, he is ambivalent in his attitude toward Rudin. He readily admits that Rudin is "an exceptionally clever person," then adds emphatically, "But basically he is empty." Rudin's apparent cleverness is altogether derivative, "his thoughts were not born in his own mind: he borrowed all of them from others." Having echoed a theme familiar to us from "Parasha" and the *Shchigry Hamlet*, Lezhnev executes a turnabout and defends Rudin: "Granted that he did not speak his own ideas—so what of that. When Rudin spoke, all that had been disjointed bits of knowledge and fragmented thoughts suddenly assembled, grew coherent, luminous, rose before us like an imposing edifice."

But once again Lezhnev turns from defense to renewed attack. He accuses Rudin of not being honest with himself, of merely acting the role of the passionate man, all the while being as "cold as ice." Such is the ambivalence of Lezhnev-Turgenev toward the Romantic Idealism of Rudin, nurtured by Schiller, Goethe, and the Romantic poets.

In the course of the novel the preponderantly critical stance of the author toward Rudin changes decidedly in Rudin's favor. In Lezhnev's parting words the full measure of Turgenev's sympathy for and self-identification with the "last Romantic" becomes explicit:

Our paths through life did part, and yet look how close we are to one another. You realize, we speak with but a single tongue, we understand each other at the merest hint, we have grown up together on the selfsame emotions. Look, brother, how few of us remain; we two of us, we are the last Mohicans! It was all well and good to part ways, even to attack each other in those long-past years when there was much of life ahead of us. But now that our ranks grow thin, when the new generations are passing us by, moving toward goals that are not ours, in these times we must hold together. And so, brother, let's clink glasses and let's sing as of old: *Gaudeamus igitur!* *

---

*In an "Epilogue" (added in the fall of 1855) Turgenev has Rudin "humble himself, adjust to circumstances, reach out only for near goals to be of some use, no matter how modestly." Thus Rudin approaches Turgenev's ideal of the "humble" person, dedicated to self-effacement in socially useful activity, an attitude that is the very antithesis to the egocentric self-aggrandizing striving of Goethe's Faust, as interpreted by Turgenev in his study of *Faust*. Schütz is right: "Turgeniews Tat unterscheidet sich demzufolge von der Fausts, der Selbsterlösungsidee ist sie gerade entgegengesetzt, und weder in der Faustkritik noch späterhin wird die Tat aus Selbstzweck als solche anerkannt" (K. Schütz, *Das Goethebild Turgeniews*, 50).

This is Turgenev's toast to his idealistic youth, to his Romantic period. Though his paths led him away from the Romantic world, he still knows himself to be a "last Mohican," a "last Romantic," in the innermost recesses of his being as man and artist. Nor is it difficult to recognize the representatives of that "new generation" which is moving toward goals that are not Turgenev's. They are, of course, his declared opponents Chernyshevski, Dobroliubov, and Pisarev,* who denigrate Turgenev's Romantic world, the world of Goethe, and rouse in him the determination never to betray the memory of his idealistic enthusiasms. As an imperishable source of inspiration, though often hidden, these early impressions, these "Romantic enthusiasms and raptures," his love of German poetry and music and his admiration of Goethe, continue to nurture his creative work.

There are two more novellas among Turgenev's works that deserve special attention in our context, the *Faust* novella and the novella *Asia*. Turgenev's *Faust* [128] signals by its very title the pervasive influence of Goethe. In its form it stands in the epistolary tradition and points back to Goethe's *Werther*. Its plot is centered on a sensitive description of the overwhelming effect that a reading of Goethe's *Faust* has on the lives of the hero and heroine. I disagree with the extreme positions Schütz and Bem take in their interpretation of the role played by Goethe's masterpiece in Turgenev's tale. Bem would have us see in Turgenev's novella a Russian re-creation of Goethe's Gretchen tragedy, but he has to do violence to Turgenev's plot to bring it into consonance with his farfetched theory. [129] Schütz goes to the other extreme and would deny any connection of Goethe's Gretchen tragedy with the tragic love and fate of the protagonists in Turgenev's novella: "Die Faust-tragödie wird hier als Ausgangspunkt einer von ihr völlig unabhängigen Liebessgeschichte verwendet. An Stelle des "Faust" könnte hier ebensogut eine andere Dichtung treten." Having taken this extreme position, she hedges: "Allerdings scheinen [!] Veras Fieberphantasien stark an den ersten Teil des "Faust" sich anzulehnen und ihm sogar entnommen zu sein; wahrscheinlich [!] hat Turgenew diese auch unmittelbar aus "Faust" übernommen." [130]

Schütz's argument is untenable. The tragic course of the protagonists' love affair is, in fact, profoundly conditioned by the unsettling impact of Goethe's drama on Vera. Her "Fieberphantasien" are not "probably" but deliberately "übernommen" from Goethe's *Faust*. [131] Nor is Schütz's contention that Turgenev could have used any other work with equal effect for his purpose at all plausible. In fact, the temptation must have been great for the author to

---

*It must be pointed out that Turgenev did accept certain of their socioeconomic views as "necessary for our times" while strenuously objecting to their aesthetics.

introduce into his tale a work of far greater familiarity to his Russian audience—Pushkin's *Onegin*, for example, also a powerful poem of tragic love. He did not do so for decisive reasons.

Turgenev's choice of *Faust* was clearly intentional. Goethe's drama was to play a unique role in his novella as *the* crowning example of Romantic poetry. We will remember that in his *Faust* essay Turgenev had defined Romantic poetry as the "apotheosis of the ego" and *Faust* as the "most extreme expression of Romanticism" [132] and had developed from that definition a highly ambivalent evaluation and characterization of Goethe's drama. Now—some ten years later—having gained objective distance to his intense *theoretical* preoccupation with the enigmatic work, he seeks to give *artistic* form to his ambivalent view of Goethe's drama as the most beguilingly enchanting and at the same time potentially the most dangerous and destructive of poetic works. Clearly, his central intent in this novella is to depict, to *body forth* as it were, the powerful effect of Goethe's poetry on the protagonists, who are irresistibly drawn into the emotional vortex suddenly created by its mighty impact.

Paul Aleksandrovich, the narrator or, more exactly, the correspondent in the epistolary tale, had been abroad for some nine years and during that time had been out of touch with Goethe and his works. Now, on his return to his estate,[133] rummaging through its library, he comes on a copy of Goethe's *Faust*, settles to its reading, and suddenly finds himself caught up again in ardent admiration of the work such as he had experienced in those far-off days of his first uncritical idealization of Goethe—clearly Turgenev's own—when he had "known 'Faust' by heart, word for word." Then he adds revealingly, "Only its First Part, of course." The Second Part of *Faust* is for the hero quite as unacceptable as for Turgenev. Later in the tale, when he reads the drama to Vera, Paul "leaves out certain scenes of the 'Walpurgisnacht' and the 'Intermezzo,'" with the characteristic explanation that they really belong, in their form and supranatural content, to the allegorical Second Part, a clear echo of Turgenev's own slighting in his *Faust* study of the *Walpurgisnacht* scene, of the "Oberon-Titania Intermezzo" and of the entire Second Part as inferior products. On the other hand, Paul greets the Earth Spirit scene with the same enthusiasm with which Turgenev had extolled it in his essay. As Schütz puts it aptly, "Was er [Turgenev] . . . 1845, als er die Faustkritik schrieb, für wahr, damit auch für schön hielt, wiederholt er zehn Jahre später, ohne seine Meinung in irgendwelcher Beziehung geändert zu haben." [134]

With Paul's reading of Goethe's *Faust* to Vera we are at the peripeteia typical for a well-structured novella.[135] Goethe's drama implodes into the life of Vera like a flash of lightning, a stroke of fate not only changing it but ending it abruptly. For Vera, whose deeply emotional nature had been artificially repressed by a one-sidedly rationalistic upbringing eschewing everything that could have stimulated her imagination or stirred her passions, and by a love-less, "safe" marriage arranged by the overly protective mother, this first con-tact with emotionally rousing poetry proves fatal. Turgenev, in a manner typical for him, does not give us a detailed psychological analysis of this lethal effect of Goethe's drama but rather conveys it with extreme economy of means, by symbolic gestures, allusions, subtle hints, and silences fraught with meaning.

Observing Vera's character, we are reminded once again of Turgenev's sweeping generalization in his essay on *Faust* that "Russian women do not resemble Gretchen." One need not agree with Turgenev's surprisingly sim-plistic view of Gretchen to realize that Vera is indeed a far more complex, problematical, and endangered personality. Vera's nature is one whose irra-tional drives are kept in check by her highly—one must say, *one-sidedly*—developed rational powers. To use Freudian terminology, Vera's id is under excessively rigid control of her ego. But for that very reason, let the power of that ego be diminished ever so slightly or the pressures of the id increase by a fortuitous influence, and the pent-up passions would burst forth and the id would overthrow the ego in a most violent and fatal manner. Such an influence on Vera's personality with altogether deadly results proved to be the sudden impact on her of Goethe's drama. Especially the scenes of Gretchen's love for Faust and Gretchen's tragic end gain an all-but-hypnotic power over her, wakening in her forebodings of her own fate. She begins to realize that her own psychic makeup is more akin to Gretchen's than she could have imagined. She is forced to admit to herself that her rational self, her moral principles, the well-remembered warnings of her mother, could all be swept aside, yes, were being swept headlong by the rising passion, just as Gretchen's bourgeois mores, her religious convictions, even her fear of her straitlaced mother had all been swept away in the embrace of Faust.

Vera had been listening attentively while Paul was reading the early scenes of Faust in his *Studierzimmer*, but "after Faust's first meeting with Gretchen, she [Vera] leaned forward away from the backrest of the chair, folded her hands, and in that posture remained to the end of the reading." She sits transfixed, quite at a loss at her reaction to Goethe's words, unable to understand the storm of feelings roused in her. The reading over, she utters not a word, and when pressed by Paul for her reaction she merely asks him to "let [her] have the book," which she then takes to her room. Shortly afterward her husband finds her there in tears. She does not know why she is crying. "Per-haps," she says to Paul, "this was the reason my mother forbade me to read such books, perhaps she knew. . . ." Vera leaves the phrase unfinished; we can readily supply her unspoken thought. Her mother had warned her, "You are like ice as long as you do not melt. You will be strong as stone, but should you melt, then not a trace will remain of you." The ice that had kept her passionate self in its unyielding grip was melting in the glow of the emotions radiating from Goethe's poetry. Vera felt its liberating power but also its destructive force. Groping for an answer to the drama's hold on her, she complains to Paul, "In that book of yours there are some things I cannot get rid of. It seems to me it is they that so inflame my head." It is not her head alone that is inflamed, it is her heart as well. As she reads and rereads the Gretchen scenes, Vera begins to realize, horror-struck, that Gretchen's ineluctable attraction to Faust, driving her into suffering, insanity, and death, is a poetic prefiguration of her own impending fate.

Her unacknowledged, repressed love for Paul surfaces into her consciousness. Mephisto, defined by Turgenev as "reflection" and self-analysis, enters her being and throws a mercilessly revealing light into the dark depths of her subconscious. As Paul says of her, she knew *réflexion* only in that term's French meaning of scientific, analytical, rational thought and "had grown accustomed to think of it as useful." Now she learns to know "reflection" as the torturing process of self-analysis reaching down to the secret depths of her emotional life. "Reflection" forces Vera to review and to revise her image of the cool, calm, composed, rational self, to question suddenly her moral code, which she thought to be so unproblematical and secure. Under the spell of Goethe's tragedy, she is compelled to confess to herself and then to Paul the unimaginable fact that she, the wife of a loyal if innocuous husband, the mother of his children, has fallen desperately in love with the man who had asked for her hand in marriage but had been rejected by her mother as not the "proper partner" for her.

Paul, as he comes on Vera sitting at the window with Goethe's *Faust* in her hand, detects the fatigue of inner torment on her face. He sits down facing her.

She asked me to read aloud the scene of Faust with Gretchen in which she asks him whether he believes in God. I took the book and began to read. As I finished I looked at her, leaning her head against the back of her chair, with hands crossed on her breast, she kept looking at me with an intense gaze. I do not know why my heart began to pound.

"What have you done with me!" she said in a low voice.

"How?" I exclaimed, taken aback.

"Yes," she repeated, "what have you done with me."

"You mean to say," I began, "why I convinced you to read such books?"

She rose without a word and was leaving the room. I looked after her. At the threshold she stopped and turned to me.

"I love you," she said, "that's what you have done with me."

The blood rushed to my head.

"I love you, I am in love with you," repeated Vera.

This is the peripeteia of Turgenev's novella. Vera's fate is sealed. All safeguards, so painstakingly erected by the mother, prove ineffectual. The Italian grandmother's passionate nature, the grandfather's moodiness, imagination, and proneness to hallucinations—all these inherited traits now overwhelmingly assert themselves. In the embrace of Paul, Vera suddenly "sees" the vengeful apparition of her mother as a messenger of death. In torment she cries out, "My mother. . . . This is insanity. . . . This is death!" In the delirium that follows she mistakes Paul for Faust-Mephisto and bursts out at him with Gretchen's words: "Was will er an dem heiligen Ort, Der da . . . der dort." We are told by the narrator that during the entire course of her fatal sickness Vera was raving in her fever fantasies "of 'Faust' and of her mother, whom she would take now for Martha, now for Gretchen's mother."

Is it possible, in view of such close interweaving of Goethean motifs with Turgenev's narrative, to speak here of a "love story completely independent of the *Faust* tragedy?" [136] The opposite seems to be closer to the complex truth. To me, Turgenev's novella appears to reexamine and reenact a central theme of *Faust*, the painful process of self-cognition, the tragedy of star-crossed love—with different protagonists, to be sure, and a very different setting in space and time.

Can Paul, the modern hero of Turgenev's novella, be compared with Goethe's Faust? Yes, if due regard be given to difference in milieu and in *Zeitgeist*. Paul, like Faust, experiences love's imperviousness to the corrosive acid of Mephistophelian, nihilistic cynicism. Of course, Paul's Mephisto is utterly internalized, but is not Mephisto in Goethe's drama also a part of Faust's very nature? Paul, feeling the irresistible power of his love for Vera overwhelming him, exclaims despairingly, "O Mephistopheles, you too are failing me. . . . Intentionally I had excited in me the ironic vein, intentionally I have recalled to my mind how ludicrous and cloyingly sweet all these love plaints and effusions would strike me within a year, within half a year. . . . No, Mephisto, you are impotent, your tooth has lost its sharpness. . . ."

There is another parallel. Like Faust, Paul has been in search of an answer to the "secret meaning of life." Like Faust, Paul ultimately finds his answer in his own way, an answer in keeping with his personality, his Russian surroundings, and his times. Having destroyed his beloved, Paul is plunged into profound suffering, withdraws from the world, and in solitude and pain culminates his twenty-year-long search for life's secret meaning in a philosophy that is as typical for Turgenev as Faust's ultimate unriddling of life's meaning was for Goethe. Recognizing the utter futility, vanity, even immorality, of striving for one's personal happiness, Paul becomes convinced that "life is not a joke and not amusement; life is not pleasurable self-gratification . . . life is hard labor." Life demands of us ceaseless renunciation: "Entbehren sollst du, sollst entbehren." [137]

This is the motto of Turgenev's novella, and though it is once again a "borrowing" from Goethe, it was not the German poet who inspired the Russian's deeply pessimistic world view. Goethe's "Entbehren," or rather his "Entsagen," differs fundamentally from Paul-Turgenev's self-effacing, "smirennyi" acceptance of fate-ordained renunciation. Goethe's "Entsagen" is a freely willed, creative act of self-limitation in socially beneficent, specialized activity in the altruistic spirit of the thoroughly modern hero of *Wilhelm Meisters Wanderjahre*.

During the work on the novella, Turgenev found himself under the influence of Arthur Schopenhauer.[138] Unquestionably it fortified the Russian poet's inborn pessimism. Yet Turgenev's *Weltanschauung* differs fundamentally from Schopenhauer's. It lacks altogether the latter's transcendentalism. Turgenev's eye is turned not to nirvana but to the black soil of Mother Russia. He shares in the activism and the social consciousness of the more progressive among the Russian liberals.

As in his *Faust* essay, so also in his *Faust* novella, Turgenev subjects the traits of egocentricity and egoism to sharpest criticism. Both protagonists of the novella assail selfishness as an inexcusable failing in a mature person. "What sense is there in daydreaming of personal happiness?" asks Vera, and Paul condemns even love as an egoistical emotion: He confesses, "I am ashamed, after all, love too is egoism. But at my age to be an egoist is not permissible. At the age of thirty-seven one cannot live for himself, one must live usefully, with a purpose on this earth, fulfill one's duty, carry forward one's work." This modern-day Russian Faust discovers the "secret meaning of life" "not in furthering one's favorite ideas and fantasies, no matter how lofty those may be, but in the fulfillment of one's duty." And with "duty" Paul-Turgenev means socially beneficent activity in the spirit of Belinski's "sociality."

With this unriddling of "life's secret meaning," Turgenev stands closer to Goethe than he would admit. We will remember how he slighted in his essay Faust's socially dedicated activity in the fifth act of that hated "allegorical" Second Part of Goethe's drama. And yet how close is Faust's "der Weisheit letzter Schluss" to Turgenev's final answer to "life's secret meaning," how kindred are Faust-Goethe's and Paul-Turgenev's concepts of "duty": "Eröffn' ich Räume vielen Millionen, / Nicht sicher zwar doch tätig-frei zu wohnen."[139] "Tätig-frei zu wohnen"—was that not the ultimate goal of Turgenev, of Belinski, of Herzen, and of the other Russian liberals in their valiant efforts to end serfdom and dark reaction in their country?

I have sought to demonstrate the central role of Goethe's influence in the composition of this novella. Many more instances in proof of this role could be adduced. Let two suffice: In contemplating Vera's kind and noble character, Paul is moved to quote Goethe's famous lines from the "Prologue in Heaven" as the most fitting description of his beloved: "Ein guter Mensch in seinem dunklen Drange / Ist sich des rechten Weges wohl bewusst." [140] In the tragic course of Vera's love these lines take on a profoundly ironic connotation.

On a boat ride with Vera, Paul suddenly recalls Goethe's poem "Auf dem See." He writes to his friend: "All at once there came to my mind the poem by Goethe (for some time now I am altogether infected with him). . . . Remember the lines: 'Auf den Wellen blinken / Tausend schwebende Sterne,' . . . and I recited aloud the entire poem. When I reached the line ' "Aug," mein Aug, was sinkst du nieder,' [141] she [Vera] slightly raised her eyes . . . and for a long time gazed into the distance. . . ." Thus Goethe's poetry interweaves with the emotional life of the lovers. In composing his *Faust*, Turgenev must have been "altogether infected with Goethe" much as was the hero of his novella. [142] The German poet's works—and not only his *Faust*—must have been vividly present in his mind.

If the essay on *Faust* must be seen as the *locus classicus* of Turgenev's theoretical preoccupation with Goethe's personality and work, then his *Faust* novella must be adjudged the culmination of Goethe's influence on Turgenev the *poet*. None of Turgenev's belletristic works preceding or following this novella exhibits the same degree of interplay of Goethean motives, dramatic or lyrical, or such a heavy preponderance of Goethe's influence as does this novella. The next work, *Asia*, [143] appearing a year later, shows that interplay much diminished and Goethe's influence relegated to a peripheral role.

Turgenev used some vivid impressions gained during a brief stay in the German town of Sinzig on the banks of the Rhine for a detailed description of the locale of his novella, its "ancient encircling walls," "the cockerel atop the steeple of its Gothic church," and, on the steeply rising riverbank, the picturesque ruin of a medieval castle. This extract of German Romanticism evokes in the hero a precious memory: "The word 'Gretchen'—was it as an exclamation, was it as a question?—insinuated itself on my lips."

It has been argued on the basis of "evidence provided by manuscript variants and an 'unpublished draft' " that it was "not merely the Romantic setting of the German medieval town that caused the author [Turgenev] to recall Goethe's heroine but rather more profound associations." This interpretation makes much of the fact that "the name of Gretchen occurs to the narrator at the very moment he observes the comely German girls of the town standing before the half-opened doors of their dwellings as if wanting to hide . . . while something flits past in the dusk crossing in front of the well in the center of the triangular marketplace." These descriptive details, which we find in the final version of the novella, together with evidence from the "unpublished draft," are supposed to "suggest the remote juxtaposition of the tragedy of love as given by Goethe in his drama with the experiences awaiting the hero and heroine of [Turgenev's] tale," and are even claimed to "bespeak a degree of kinship between the conception of 'Asia' and Turgenev's novella 'Faust.'" [144] I have not been able to examine the "evidence provided by manuscript variants" or by "the unpublished draft." The extant text, however, leaves the "juxtaposition" of Gretchen's and Asia's love tragedy "remote" indeed, and the claim of kinship between Turgenev's novellas *Asia* and *Faust* by way of the supposedly "common link" of Goethe's drama is decidedly farfetched, especially in the light of the well-established fact that the novella *Asia* and specifically its central theme of tragic love have their origin in far more personal and painful experiences of the author than in the influence on him of Goethe's *Faust*: the birth, upbringing, love, and marriage of his illegitimate daughter Pauline, events that were the cause of continued vexation and anxiety to Turgenev. These found a reflection in the novella, particularly in the descriptions of Asia's upbringing and tragic love. [145]

Examining the characters of the star-crossed lovers of this novella, I find not the least resemblance, in any of their aspects, to the personalities and tragic love of Goethe's Faust and Gretchen. The hero of the novella, Mr. N.N., has been compared to Rudin as another of Turgenev's "superfluous people." [146] I agree with the critic N. M. Gut'iar, who blames P. V. Annenkov, a close friend, confidant, and earliest critic of Turgenev, for having "misled the reading public and even the literary critics and historians by having been the most influential voice to have initiated the erroneous identification of the hero of 'Asia' with Rudin." [147] To be sure, the theme of empty loquacity, that characteristic of the "superfluous people," is briefly touched on with reference to N.N. His conversation with his friend Gagin is characterized as the kind of "idle talk" in "which the Russian so readily dissolves [razlivaetsia], speeches now impassioned, now profound, now rapturous but always unclear and confused." But this Russian weakness is here simply stated as a fact, not analyzed, not traced to its source, the "kruzhki," those hothouses of German idealistic philosophy and the cult of Goethe, as it has been traced in *Hamlet of the Shchigry District* and the novel *Rudin*. [148]

In drawing the figure of Asia, Turgenev associates her with Pushkin's Tatiana; he speaks of her fascination with the arch-Romantic figure of fairy tale and folklore, the famous Lorelei. He even has her, in her love of role-playing, identify believably with the domestic and staid heroine of Goethe's *Hermann und Dorothea*, which made a strong impression on her receptive imagination. But nowhere does Turgenev so much as hint at a similarity or affinity of Asia to the German Gretchen. They are, if anything, true antipodes, as sharply contrasting in their natures as Asia's raven locks contrast with Gretchen's flaxen braids.

In Asia's mercurial moods, changing in a wink from childlike gaiety to pensive sadness; in the unpredictable, chameleon-like[149] behavior of this "wilding" (dichok); in the lightness, sureness, and grace of the motions of her supple body; in Asia's love of song and dance; quite especially, in the enigmatic, even frightening impression this "self-willed being" (volnitsa) produces on N.N., Asia would seem to be akin not to Goethe's Gretchen but to that other "strange creature," to the "Russalka," to the heroine of Mikhail Lermontov's *Taman'*. Reading the following description of Asia, one cannot help but be reminded of Lermontov's portrayal of his smuggler girl. Even Turgenev's lyrical prose seems to take on, suddenly, the crispness and verve of Lermontov's rhythms, which alas are lost in a translation: "I had never seen a more restless being. Not for a moment would she sit still; she would get up, run into the house, return, hum in half voice, burst into laughter. . . . Her eyes looked straight ahead, brightly, boldly, but then all of a sudden her lids would slightly lower and then her glance would suddenly grow deep and tender." It is surprising that none of the critics known to me has pointed to this kinship,[150] even though they have drawn a far less likely comparison between N.N. and Pechorin.[151]

It should be obvious why I dwell on this kinship of Asia to Lermontov's heroine. If it could be firmly established, Asia's literary lineage could be traced to Goethe's Mignon. Lermontov's narrator of the *Taman'* tale "imagines he has discovered [in the smuggler girl] Goethe's Mignon."[152] Of course, there is the distinct possibility that Turgenev went directly to that most Romantic of all Goethe's female figures for the model of his Asia. Unfortunately, no supporting autobiographical evidence or buttressing critical opinion seems to exist, and in their absence my hypothesis must remain just that.

In sum, Goethe's influence on the novella *Asia*, though undeniably present, is superficial, peripheral, and problematic. It is the last important work in which Turgenev looks back to his experience of "Romantic Germany." Already in this novella, Turgenev's Berlin days, his immersion in the world of German Idealism, has ceased to be a challenging, disturbing, and as such an artistically productive past. With the *Faust* essay, with the *Shchigry Hamlet*, with *Pasynkov* and *Rudin*, and with the *Faust* novella, that past had been "bewältigt." It no longer cries out for exteriorization and sublimation in essay form or in a work of art.

In his next novel, *A Nobleman's Nest* (1859),[153] Turgenev takes a last, nostalgic backward look not at Germany but at his own "dvorianskaia Rossia" (aristocratic Russia) as it recedes irrevocably into the past.[154] To be sure, in the touching figure of the old German composer-musician Lemm, Turgenev did draw once more on his German experience to erect an unforgettable monument to the musical genius of the German nation, to its soul, its "Seele."[155] It may also be granted that in Panshin, the "Westerner" in the novel, Turgenev

placed before us a recognizable portrait of the "lishnyi chelovek," akin to
Rudin but drawn now at an ironic distance, almost as a caricature of the hero
of his first novel. The author takes actual delight in showing Panshin in all the
shallowness and hollowness of his unsubstantial personality, an easy mark for
the withering attacks by the arch-Russian hero of this novel, Lavretski, the
first Slavophile in Turgenev's works and the last "dvorianin" to occupy the
"nobleman's nest" in a rapidly changing Russia.[156] Henceforth Turgenev will
no longer ponder, analyze, and depict the problematical character and sad fate
of the "superfluous people"; henceforth he will envisage and shape with
imagination and perceptiveness *"consciously* heroic" figures,[157] Insarov,
Bazarov, Solomin, and their helpmates Elena, Odintsova, and Marinna,[158]
strong, forward-looking women dedicated to social reform, to the eradica-
tion of serfdom, and to a new and better life for their country. Essentially,
Turgenev's *past*, whether spent in Germany or in Russia, lies behind him. His
artist's eye will henceforth be focused on Russia's *present*; he will dedicate his
pen to the task of helping shape his country's *future*.

One would expect that with this drastic reorientation Turgenev's attitude
toward Goethe would have also undergone a drastic change, but this was not
the case. In fact, compared with the sharply critical attitude of the early *Faust*
essay, Turgenev's view of Goethe, if anything, grows more balanced. The
sharpness of Turgenev's attack on Goethe's aloofness and egocentricity softens
and grows less frequent as Belinski's influence on him diminishes.[159] With
growing maturity, Turgenev comes to see more clearly the strength and wholeness, the balance, harmony, and vitality, of Goethe's nature, which enabled
him to outgrow the excesses and to avoid the aberrations to which so many of
his contemporaries, the Sturm und Drang and the Romantic poets, fell victim.

References to and quotations from Goethe continue undiminished in
Turgenev's correspondence and persist in his belles lettres,[160] often in quite
incongruous contexts. Thus, in his novella *Brigadier* (1867) Turgenev compares his hero (an officer) with Werther and his heroine with Lotte: "Thus
there appeared Werther. I thought to myself, A strange name for 'Lotte'—
'Agraphina.'" Not only is the Russian name a "strange" one for the German
Lotte, but the entire comparison is farfetched in the extreme.[161] Or again, in
his last novel, *Virgin Soil* (November 1876), Turgenev has the radical revolutionary Paklin quote Goethe's famous lines "Wer den Dichter will verstehen, /
Muss in Dichters Lande gehen,"[162] only to pervert them in his radical spirit
and to his aggressive purpose: "Wer die *Feinde* will versteh'n / Muss in
Feindes Lande geh'n."[163] Even in his late Paris years, Turgenev continued his
"systematic studies" of Goethe, and in the intimate circle of French writers
composed of Gustave Flaubert, Alphonse Daudet, Guy de Maupassant, Émile
Zola, and the Goncourt brothers, he would frequently entertain his friends by

translating from Goethe's works *à livre ouvert*. On the occasion of his last public appearance, in a speech [164] delivered at the unveiling of Pushkin's monument in Moscow on May 26, 1880, he paid once again his respects to the German poet.

In 1845, in his *Faust* essay, Turgenev had celebrated Goethe as the great German *national* poet who expressed with his personality and works the very essence of that nation's character. Now, some thirty-five years later, he strikes the same note: "Goethe, Molière, and Shakespeare are popular poets in the true sense of that word, that is, they are *national* poets. . . . It is not in vain that Greece is called the native land of Homer, Germany that of Goethe, England that of Shakespeare." And Turgenev poses the question, "Can we call Pushkin a national poet in the sense that we call Shakespeare, Goethe, and Homer national poets?" Surprisingly, to the dismay and anger of many in his audience, Turgenev hedged: "We are not prepared to give him [Pushkin] the appellation of a national poet of world eminence, but we also dare not take it from him." As to Goethe, there is no doubt in Turgenev's mind that he does indeed belong in the august company of national poets of world fame.

Affinities and Contrasts

What was it that kept Goethe's star from fading for Turgenev? Surely it was more than merely Turgenev's "systematic studies" of Europe's leading authors. It was an elective affinity, a genuine *Wahlverwandtschaft*, which Turgenev believed existed between Goethe and himself, especially between Goethe, the artist, and his own artistic temperament and tastes. I have referred to some of the aspects of this kinship: the immediacy and intensity of these poets' contact with life, so poignantly expressed, for example, by the *Lustige Person* in Goethe's "Vorspiel auf dem Theater": "Greift nur hinein ins volle Menschenleben! . . ." [165] or again, Goethe's "gradualism," which was essentially Turgenev's own preference for evolution rather than revolution in mankind's cultural, social, and political progress. [166]

Like Goethe, Turgenev was an *Augenmensch*, an artist gifted with an ever-observing eye that caught the subtlest nuances and shadings in human characters and in nature's moods. He admired in Goethe that "all-embracing power of observation" which he cultivated in himself. [167] Turgenev shared with Goethe the penchant for *Bekenntnisdichtung*. He recognized much of his own writing for what it was: "fragments of a great confession," acts of coming to grips with his own past, or "objectifying" traumatic experiences and thus liberating himself from their oppressive weight. Goethe's conviction that a person in his development cannot escape his own preestablished law was fully shared by Turgenev. Lines in Goethe's poem "Dämon"—"Wie an dem Tag, der dich der

Welt verliehen, / Die Sonne stand zum Grusse der Planeten, / Bist alsobald und fort und fort gediehen / Nach dem Gesetz, wonach du angetreten" [168]— express Turgenev's deep personal conviction. I might also mention the aristocratic bearing common to both poets despite Turgenev's "liberal" democratic leanings and his frequent protestations of a well-developed sense of "sociality." Goethe and Turgenev, sons of the German patriciate and Russian landed gentry, could not deny their forebears.

In matters of aesthetics there were many correspondences between them. Both favored the *Gelegenheitsgedicht*,[169] both thought little of "invention" in their art, both were wary of the artist who would use his art to demonstrate and broadcast a preconceived idea, a dogma, or a rigid program, be it philosophic, aesthetic, or sociopolitical.[170] Turgenev subscribes to the view of poetry, of the "Wahre Darstellung" as Goethe defines it in *Dichtung und Wahrheit*: "Sie [wahre Darstellung] billigt nicht, sie tadelt nicht, sondern sie entwickelt die Gesinnungen und Handlungen in ihrer Folge und dadurch erleuchtet und belehrt sie." [171] Both were critical of heavy-handed naturalism in art. Goethe's words to Eckermann can serve as a succinct paraphrase of Turgenev's attacks on the materialist aesthetics of the Radical Democrats: "Man will Wahrheit, man will Wirklichkeit und verdirbt dadurch die Poesie." [172] And again, "Die Wirklichkeit soll die Motive hergeben . . . ; aber ein schönes belebtes Ganzes daraus zu bilden ist Sache des Dichters." [173] Turgenev greets Goethe as a mighty ally in his battle for a "higher poetic truth," which the talented artist achieves by stripping reality of its nonessential, fortuitous features and elevates it to the "typical." [174] He considers Goethe to be chiefly preoccupied in his art with "raising reality to the ideal of poetry ('die Wirklichkeit zum schönen Schein erhoben,' as Goethe expresses it)." That preoccupation is Turgenev's as well.

Turgenev shares with many writers a characteristic weakness: a tendency to view and represent one's admired and emulated predecessors in one's own likeness. Turgenev's image of Goethe has this flaw. Thus Turgenev, for whom the sensitive portrayal of the human being was the "Alpha and the Omega of [my] calling as a writer," [175] extols Goethe as the unrivaled "Menschenbildner" but has nothing to say of his *Farbenlehre*, for example, to which Goethe devoted so much of his time and energy. Or again, he claims that Goethe had an intense hatred for all "Systemzwang," a hatred far more characteristic for the Russian than for the German poet. This was undoubtedly one reason Turgenev preferred the "spontaneous disorder" of Goethe's Sturm und Drang creations [176] and could never come to terms with the "classical Goethe" and his "artfully" structured works.[177]

But these are minor flaws in Turgenev's Goethe image, indicative of discrepancies in the tastes and sensibilities of the two poets. There is, however, one profound difference in their temperament, their outlook on life, their life's philosophy: Goethe's basically optimistic and Turgenev's incurably pessimistic world view. That pessimism finds its expression in Turgenev's works and letters, early and late, most poignantly in that darkest of his poems-in-prose *Enough* (*Dovol'no*), that "legacy" with its subtitle "Fragment from the Notes of a Deceased Poet" and with this gloomy message:

Art, at a given moment, may well seem more powerful than nature, because in nature there is no symphony of Beethoven, no painting by Ruisdael, no poem by Goethe. . . . And yet in the long run nature proves irresistible; she is in no hurry, and sooner or later she will be victorious. Unconsciously and persistently following its immutable laws, she does not know Art, as she does not know Freedom or Goodness. Forever moving, forever on her way, she does not tolerate anything immortal, anything changeless. . . . She creates and destroys, and she is completely indifferent to what she creates—just as long as life continues and death does not lose its rights. And that is why she calmly covers with mold the godlike image of the Jupiter of Phidias, just as she does a simple pebble, and lets the lowly moth devour the most precious lines of Sophocles.[178]

Turgenev could never have joined in Goethe's unwavering celebration of life—"Wie es auch sei, das Leben, es ist gut"[179]—or written:

> In unseres Lebens oft getrübten Tagen
> Gab uns ein Gott Ersatz für alle Plagen,
> Dass unser Blick sich himmelwärts gewöhne:
> Den Sonnenschein, die Tugend und das Schöne.[180]

Turgenev's eye was fixed on this troubled earth. He lacked the faith in a benevolent God, and while he yearned for "sunshine, virtue, and beauty," he could not escape the overwhelming darkness and ugliness surrounding him.

The thought of death preyed on his mind, evoking terrifying visions that he seemed to experience as palpably present with all his senses:

That something was all the more terrifying not having a definite shape. Something ponderous, glowering, speckled yellow-to-black like the underbelly of a lizard. Not a cloud, not smoke, it moved slowly, snakelike over the earth, in regular up-and-down sweeping movements like the threatening swoop of the wings of a bird of prey searching for its victim, and now and again hunching down to earth, a spider hunching over the fly it caught. Who are you? What are you, threatening mass? Under its influence— I saw it, I felt it—everything was numbed, destroyed. . . . It exuded the cold breath of decay and putrefaction, and that cold breath sickened your heart, blinded your vision, made your hair stand on end. That power moved forward, inexorably, a power against which there is no resisting, to which all is subject, which has no vision, no shape or meaning, yet sees and knows everything and like a bird of prey chooses its victims, like a snake strangles them, licks them with its icy tongue.[181]

This fear of death is surely the deep source and impulse for Turgenev's fascination with the twilight world of the occult, with telepathy, hallucinations, revenants, and vampirism, as in his macabre tale of *Klara Milich* (1883) in which the suicide Klara, a gypsy in temperament and looks, casts from her grave a spell on her lover and draws him into insanity and death.[182] Surprisingly, tales that make the supranatural strangely and frighteningly real are numerous in the works of this "objective realist": *Phantoms*, *The Dog*, *The Dream*, *Knock . . . Knock . . . Knock*, among others. With all these, Turgenev stands far closer to Heinrich von Kleist, to that writer's *Bettelweib von Locarno*, for example, or *Die Marquise von O . . .* , or even to the tales of Edgar Allan Poe than to Goethe.

Nor could Turgenev find release from his inborn pessimism and fear of death in contact with and in the contemplation of nature. The Russian landscape that he loved and knew so well and that he evoked with such empathy and perceptiveness in his *Notes of a Huntsman* and in so many of his best works could not illumine the inner darkness, free him from his fear and hopelessness. Goethe could apostrophize nature as his "Königreich." He had been given "die Kraft, sie zu fühlen, zu geniessen . . . in ihre tiefe Brust, / Wie in den Busen eines Freunds, zu schauen." [183] For Turgenev, nature remained the "cold-eyed" goddess Isis, who moved according to her own inscrutable laws and cared not a whit for human hopes or despair, joy, or suffering. In his openly autobiographical narrative *A Ride into the Forest Region* (1857) he gives chilling expression to this pessimism: "It is difficult for man, this creature of a day, . . . to endure the cold stare of the eternal Isis fixed on him with utter indifference. Not only the impudent hopes and dreams of youth are humbled and extinguished under that staring gaze, no—your very soul cowers and grows numb; you feel that the last of your brethren could vanish from this earth and not a needle would so much as tremble on the branches [of the vast primeval Russian forest]." [184]

His profound pessimism drew Turgenev to Schopenhauer's philosophy; it attuned him to the pessimism prevalent in intellectual circles of post-1848 Europe. He shared it with his admired German friend Theodor Storm. But that pessimism was also the salient facet of his personality, and this prevented Turgenev from entering fully Goethe's world, in which the "classical" poet strove to establish and to maintain, against contrary currents of the day, harmony of spirit and balance of form. Turgenev was never to share in the humanistic optimism of Goethe's *Iphigenie* or in the Classico-Romantic harmony of the "wedding" of Helena and Faust in Goethe's greatest masterpiece.[185]

In conclusion, let me retrace in essential outline Turgenev's ambivalent view of Goethe. There was a brief period of unambiguous, uncritical adulation of Goethe during his student years at Berlin University, 1838–1841. This brief period, in which Turgenev tried his hand at translating Goethe's lyrics and also produced the remarkable rendering of the dungeon scene from *Faust*, was followed by a critical reexamination of his idol carried out primarily under the influence of Belinski. It was inextricably interlinked with a review of Turgenev's attitude toward the entire sphere of German Idealistic philosophy and Romantic poetry, the "unbewältigte Vergangenheit" of his Berlin experiences, a review and revision that found its fullest theoretical expression in the *Faust* essay (1845) and its artistic form in the novellas of the late 1840s and 1850s, centrally in the *Hamlet of the Shchigrov District*, in *Iakov Pasynkov*, in the *Faust* novella, and in the novel *Rudin*. The resultant attitude of Turgenev toward his Idealistic, Romantic German past and specifically toward Goethe was characterized by an ambivalence that remained typical for the Russian poet throughout his life.

Much in the manner of Herzen and Belinski, Turgenev criticized Goethe the man for his egocentricity and antisocial attitude. At the same time he held Goethe the artist in high esteem, praising him as the supreme realist, a poet of extraordinary intensity and immediacy in such inimitable creations as his Sturm und Drang lyrics, his *Werther*, *Götz*, and *Faust*, Part One, while refusing to acknowledge the greatness of the "artful" author of *Iphigenie*, *Tasso*, and especially of the "allegorical" Second Part of *Faust*.

With growing maturity and independence, with the gradual waning of Belinski's influence, Turgenev's criticism of Goethe the man diminished in its sharpness, while Goethe's importance for him as the incomparable poet and the wise "teacher of us all" clearly increased, a development also observed by Erich Hock: "Immer bewusster stellt Turgeniew den Künstler Goethe in den Vordergrund, je intensiver er sich selbst dem eigenen dichterischen Schaffen widmet." [186]

And yet the ambivalence in Turgenev's attitude toward Goethe remained basically unchanged. He continued to reject the creations of the "classical" Goethe and remained indifferent toward Goethe's achievements in the natural sciences. He faulted Goethe for lack of "sociality," though that criticism grew less frequent and less strident with his advancing years. On the other hand, Goethe did remain for him the incomparable artist. His knowledgeable, empathetic, perceptive appreciation of the German poet as the "objective realist," as the *Menschenbildner*, was not equaled by any of his Russian contemporaries. Turgenev could rightfully call himself to his dying day the "sworn follower of Goethe," a "zakliatyi Gëteanets."

CHAPTER TWO

Crosscurrents of Opinion

The Liberal Democrats: Vasili Petrovich Botkin (1811–1869)
and Aleksandr Vasilievich Druzhinin (1824–1864)

Vasili Botkin and Aleksandr Druzhinin are generally regarded as the two outstanding figures among the Liberal Democrats. Their rapidly and radically changing attitudes toward Germany, its philosophy, and its literature, and specifically toward its greatest poets, Schiller and Goethe, strikingly exemplify the shifting currents of opinion generated by the spirited confrontation of the moderate, radical, and conservative groups—the Liberal and Radical Democrats, the Slavophiles, and the "Pure Poets"—in the cultural and political life of Russia in the second half of the nineteenth century.

Botkin began as a youthful admirer of Germany's culture, grew critical of it, but soon recaptured his early enthusiasms and rekindled his love of Goethe to extol him as the incomparable exemplar of "pure art." In a letter written in his "declining years" (August 28, 1862) from Berlin to his friend, Afanasi Fet, he recalls the signal role played by German philosophy, music, and poetry in his early development:

Yes, here [in Berlin] wird es mir behaglich zu Muthe. The main reason for this is that my entire spiritual development is tied to Germany. Not to mention its philosophy and poetry, even its humor is after my own heart. . . .
   Stankevich, Granovski, my entire youth, incline me toward Germany; all my best ideals have developed here, all my first enthusiasms for music, poetry, philosophy, all have their origins here. And this is not to be blamed on me or my education. To be exact, I had no education. On leaving boarding school (a very poor one), I literally had not a single clear idea about anything. Everything around me was hazy as in a fog. From that early period I only remember having read Schiller's *Fiesko* and his *Räuber* and some of Zhukovski's translations of that poet. And it was that impression which formed from the very earliest beginnings and for my entire life a bond of kinship with Germany. . . . Is it my fault that the ballads of Schiller excited my heart a thousand times more than the Russian fairy tales and the ancient tales of Prince Vladimir? And now, in my declining years, I once again greet this land which was first to awaken in my soul all that to this day I hold dear.[1]

Botkin shared with his friends Nikolai Stankevich, Mikhail Bakunin, and Vissarion Belinski their early Romantic enthusiasm for the Olympian Goethe, the sage of Weimar. But he also shared Belinski's reorientation in those critical years of the early 1840s, "furious Vissarion's" revulsion against Hegel's once-

47

admired "reconciliation with reality," his disavowal of the philosopher in whom he suddenly recognized a dangerous guide into the blind alley of a pernicious status quo, his curt dismissal of his idol Goethe as a "poet of the past," as a "king dethroned."[2]

Botkin embraced Belinski's critical view of Germany's philosophy and poetry and of their greatest representatives, Hegel and Goethe. He too turned abruptly from Hegel to become an ardent admirer of Ludwig Feuerbach and in the realm of belles lettres replaced Schiller and Goethe with George Sand. Now Botkin criticizes Germany's backwardness, comparing it unfavorably with the progressive stance of *la belle France*. In German literature he now misses the liberal spirit of French letters, the lively social and political consciousness of a Sand, a Pierre Béranger, their fervent strivings in the service of mankind and womanhood.

In his essay "German Literature in the Year 1843,"[3] Botkin develops his contrasting view of France and Germany. He represents France as a country that has perfected the art of analysis and criticism. On the other hand, he sees Germany as merely groping toward analytical self-cognition, only beginning to develop a social and political consciousness. Botkin finds this backwardness mirrored in Germany's literature. He is particularly critical of those German writers who in their vapid, stilted prose and verse indulge in self-adulation and the philistine cultivation of their private emotions. He accuses these pseudo-poets of being totally unable to forget their petty egos, their "feelings wrapped in thick swads of cotton," and to dedicate themselves to high ideals and worthy causes. In particular, Botkin points an accusing finger at the German "erotic" prose and poetry, which in contrast to the progressive French has not even begun to celebrate those noble emotions and aspirations kindled in the modern woman which raise her to equal status with man in dignity and freedom.

Still, Botkin must admit that a gradual awakening of a progressive spirit can be detected in German life and letters. "It took much time . . . before the principle of moral dignity and worth of women could manifest itself in [German] society. The newest love poetry—especially Goethe's—is the expression of that principle. . . . Hand in hand with the modern development in [Germany's] day-to-day life and in its education of both sexes there went the development of its love poetry, which finally reached its full power in the songs of Goethe."[4] To be sure, Botkin finds this new "principle" of an emancipated spirit in only a small fraction of Goethe's lyrics. He divides Goethe's poems into two contrasting groups: "One group, by far the largest, belongs to an earlier period and deals with the Dorilis and shepherds [obviously, Goethe's Anacreontic poems]; the other, not at all numerous, presents genuine, poetically inspired expression of the emotions of love. To this small group belong such poems as: 'Hand in Hand und Lipp an Lippe' ["An die Erwählte"], 'Es schlug mein Herz: Geschwind zu Pferde!' ["Willkommen und Abschied"], 'Einschränkung,' and some others."[5] Botkin finds it "important to note, that the love poetry of such poets as Goethe is the inspired presentation of real and profound interests of the human soul, of rational and real moments of life." Not satisfied with merely noting this extraordinary quality of Goethe's best poems, Botkin elaborates: "In the love poems of Goethe and of the other great European poets there predominates some kind of a mighty fullness of sensation; their lyrics are the very essence of profound and irrepressible interests, of crucial moments in the course of human life, not the vacuous babble about personal amorous sentiments."[6] How Botkin could miss the predominance of "personal amorous sentiments" in the enumerated poems is difficult to understand.

Such was Botkin's view of Goethe the lyricist in the early 1840s. He places Goethe among the "other great of European poets," that is, he elevates Goethe to the side of Béranger, of Sand, and of other socially conscious writers. He does this because he finds in Goethe's best lyrics the essence of the crucial moments in human history and not merely the "babble" of a lovelorn heart. All this was soon to change. The "babble" was to become the only message worthy of a true poet, of all great art, of "pure poetry."

After Belinski's death, with the appearance on the literary scene of such radical champions of a new materialistic aesthetics as Chernyshevski, Dobroliubov, and Pisarev, Botkin entered a period of intense reexamination of his views on art and the artist. He found himself in ever sharper disagreement with the Radical Democrats and ever more attracted by the aesthetics developed and vigorously propagated by the Pure Poets, with Afanasi Fet and Apollon Nikolaevich Maikov in their lead. This was an aesthetics deeply rooted in the traditional Romantic glorification of *l'art pour l'art*, but carrying this tradition to an extreme that the founding fathers of Russian Romanticism, Vasili Zhukovski, Nikolai Stankevich, Dmitri Venevitinov, and Stepan Shevyrëv, would hardly have espoused. The Pure Poets demanded of the artist total insulation in his art from all mundane interests; they emphasized the function of art as a medium of expression for purely private emotions and esoteric concerns. Analytical thought became suspect as a dangerous interference with the unconscious or, rather, supraconscious mysterious processes of artistic creation.

Botkin came to share these views. In his spirited defense of his brother-in-law Afanasi Fet against the attacks of the Radical Democrats who demanded a poetry of social and political commitment, he held high the banner of a "poetry of feeling," the banner of "Pure Art." He now proclaimed categorically:

The depth, power, and purity of emotion . . . that is the only true source of all poetry! No matter how lofty your thought, if it has not turned into your flesh and blood, has not become the life of your soul, in a word, if it has not become your personal feeling and has not filled your heart, then that thought will remain forever a generality, an abstract ratiocination without poetry, no matter in what lofty phrases you express it. Basically, there have not been and cannot be poets of thought.[7]

This is Botkin's most uncompromising attack, which he could not and would not sustain. In the very essay in which he denies the existence of the "poet of thought," he admits, upon reflection, that "all great poets are also great thinkers." Adducing striking examples, he asks, "Who looked at life more unerringly and penetratingly than Shakespeare, where would you find more of life's wisdom than in Goethe's works? One and the same mental power is active both in the spiritual world and in the material world, i.e., in the practical world of action. The only difference is in the degree of that energy and in its specialization."[8]

Botkin's self-contradiction is more apparent than real. While accepting intellect as a component of a poet's endowment, he nevertheless remains true to his basic conviction: a poet's thoughts, in order to be artistically effective, must have turned into his very flesh and blood, must have "become the life of [his] soul." To prove his point, Botkin turns to Goethe. In this "true poet" this process has taken place. In his greatest creations, thought has become his "personal feeling and has filled [his] heart." "Granted, there are many poems of Goethe expressing his views on nature, man, and the world in general, and yet these lyrics are filled with genuine poetry because these thoughts are not mere products of cerebration; on the contrary, they have become his innermost convictions and faith, the very life of his soul. He not only thought in this manner, he actually felt that way."[9]

Botkin accepts the *thinker* in the poet, the *thought* in Goethe's poetry; he even extols Goethe's extraordinary analytical faculties as a critic and interpreter. He singles out Goethe's famous interpretation of Shakespeare's *Hamlet* for highest praise. According to Botkin, "Goethe has presented us in his *Wilhelm Meister* with an interpretation of *Hamlet* which can truly be called a key to all the works of the English bard." For Botkin these few pages represent

a model of art criticism . . . As soon as Goethe's interpretation appeared, at that very instant all that seeming chaos [which Voltaire had seen in Shakespeare's works] revealed itself as a harmonious world filled with marvelous order. He [Goethe] had pointed out for all to see the consistent inner logic that unified all those seemingly disparate scenes and characters. He had discovered the central thought motivating every persona and every action.[10]

All those puzzling strangenesses in [Shakespeare's] characters suddenly had an explanation, every apparent fortuitousness of role and action was suddenly revealed as an inner necessity, every extraneous episode as a scene interlinked with the whole.[11]

Having thus lavished his praise on Goethe's mighty intellect, Botkin rises in defense of the German poet and at the same time of Fet against the injust accusation of both by the Radical Democrats for alleged indifference toward the social and political events, toward "contemporaneity [sovremennost']." "The author of *Werther* has been accused of complete indifference toward his contemporaneity. Such accusations are made either out of malice or in utter ignorance of that type of contemporary life for which Goethe always had shown the liveliest of interest and a profound understanding." For Botkin,

there are *two* faces to contemporaneity. One face consists of fanaticism and extremism; it is filled with hatred of antagonistic parties moved by rapidly changing demands and desires, each striving to impress its mark, the symbol of its aims, on contemporaneity. But there is also another face, which transforms all this hostility of the parties and their special interests and which pronounces its weighty, irrefutable judgment. Alas, this face, together with the thought that motivates it, remains almost always hidden to us. We know and understand it only in retrospect, as *history*. Goethe was the mighty poet for the very reason that he did not let himself be carried away by the cotidal events but kept his gaze firmly fixed on the eternal aspects of nature, on the eternal origins of the human soul.[12]

It is from this point of view that Botkin would have us understand Goethe's lack of sympathy for history, or rather for historiography, the ephemeral record of time-bound events. Drawing on Goethe's famous conversation with historian Heinrich Luden, he emphasizes Goethe's irritation with those glib generalizations about human life, with those abstractions about human nature which are the joy of German scholars and which so successfully obliterate the individual personality. Botkin quotes at length from the conversation, in complete agreement with Goethe's critique of historiography as a mere shadow of actual human life:

How limited is even the most extensive historical account in comparison with man's existence in its full living expanse. After you have probed and interpreted all the historical sources—what do you finally have? Nothing but the great truth, long since discovered and most readily ascertained, that people have always and everywhere irritated and tortured themselves and others; that they have poisoned with all possible means for themselves and for others the pitifully brief span of our existence, unable to value or to enjoy the beauty of the world and the sweetness of life. That is how it has always been, how it is, and how it will always be.[13]

Botkin considers these words to be most revealing of Goethe's conciliatory nature attuned to harmony rather than to discord. Goethe would rather extol the "sweetness of life" than dwell on its tragic conflicts. He teaches us how to rise above party bickering and ideological strife, above the clash and chaos of fleeting events. In Goethe's works we find lasting enjoyment of harmony and beauty, of the "eternal aspects of nature" and the "eternal origins of the soul."

Thus Botkin enlists Goethe, his name and his fame, as a mighty ally in his fight for "pure poetry" against politicized pseudo-art propagated by the Radical Democrats. The closing words of Botkin's essay are a most apt, albeit unacknowledged, verbatim quotation from Goethe's essay on Johann Winckelmann:

When the human being feels himself in the world as in a unified beautiful whole, when a feeling of inner harmony rouses in him pure, free enthusiasm, it is in such moments that the entire universe, if it could become conscious of itself, would be astounded and happy at having reached its ultimate goal of existence. What other purpose could all these marvelous suns, planets, and stars, all these rising and vanishing worlds, have if man would not in the end rejoice instinctively [bezotchetno; Goethe's "unbewusst"] in his existence.[14]

Thus Botkin's attitude toward Goethe had come full circle. After a period of criticism, his early enthusiasm for the German poet was rekindled on a more mature plane of agreement with Goethe's basic philosophy, his conciliatory stance in life. There is no evidence that Botkin's admiration for Goethe ever changed again.

In sharp contrast to the Germanophile Botkin, his fellow Liberal, Aleksandr Druzhinin, in his early years, viewed Goethe with the critical eyes of an admirer of English culture and judged his works with the "deeply practical mind of England's great thinkers," who had helped him escape the sad fate of those continental Europeans who had been "led astray by their pernicious enthusiasms for false theories."[15] Among these "false" theories Druzhinin included the Romanticists' "insane idolatry of the sage of Weimar."[16] His own initial evaluation of Goethe's works was to be most carefully measured in censure and praise. He called for a judicious separation of Goethe's successful creations from the many failures: "The truly great works will not separate on their own accord from the weak, strange, and unsuccessful ones,"[17] he warns. There is much work to be done, and he intends at least to make a beginning with it.

In one of his earliest essays, "The Greek Versifications" (1850), Druzhinin rejects Goethe's "Achilleis" and even his *Iphigenie auf Tauris* as products of "excessive apathy on the part of the poet"[18] and characterizes Goethe's talents in less than flattering terms:

In witness of Goethe's profound understanding of ancient life and of his ability to depict it in an original manner can stand his "Prometheus" and other excellent poems.

However, how next to these, he [Goethe] could write an "Achilleis" and other slavish anthological imitations—that question must remain one of the secrets of this Olympian Sphinx. . . . It was Goethe's fate to be a most uneven writer, his works ranging from the false to the lofty, from failure to artistic success, from the Second Part of "Faust" to the "Braut von Korinth," from Dorothea [of *Hermann und Dorothea*] to Mignon.[19]

Two years later Druzhinin subjects *Wilhelm Meister* to an equally critical review. He compares the novel to a "strangely constructed building supported by two caryatids in the persons of Mignon and Philine." Were it not for these two successful creations, *Wilhelm Meister* would long have shared the fate of the "Achilleis" and of the Second Part of *Faust*.[20] Clearly, the opinion Druzhinin held of Goethe's novel at that time (ca. 1852) was anything but favorable. He found himself in wholehearted agreement with a highly critical piece on Thomas Carlyle's translation of *Wilhelm Meisters Lehrjahre* by the Scottish Lord Jeffrey, editor of the *Edinburgh Review*.[21] He translated Jeffrey's review and published it in shortened form in the *Library for Reading*,[22] a journal of which he was editor at the time. Evidently he considered the Scottish lord's views of Goethe's masterpiece worthy of dissemination among Russian readers.

Jeffrey's views are remarkable for their parochial bias. He is quite unable to enter into the spirit of Goethe's novel. "After the most deliberate consideration," he finds it "eminently absurd, puerile, incongruous, vulgar, and affected . . . almost from beginning to end, one flagrant offence against every principle of taste, and every just rule of composition."[23] Jeffrey recognized in the novel a distinguishing quality that he considers typical of all German belles lettres, "a peculiar type of vulgarity" that he is at a loss to describe "except by saying that it is the vulgarity of pacific, comfortable Burghers, occupied with stuffing, cooking and providing for their coarse personal accommodations."[24] The novel, and with it most of German fiction, offended the lord's sensitive nose. "It smells, as it were, of groceries—of brown papers filled with greasy cakes and slices of bacon, and fryings in frowzy back parlours."[25] Goethe's thoughts on the theater as an educational institution the critic dismisses in cavalier fashion: "Such is the sublime of German speculations! And it is by such sheer nonsense as this that men in that country acquire a reputation of great genius—and of uniting with pleasant inventions the most profound suggestions of political wisdom! Can we be wrong in maintaining, after this, that there are diversities of national taste that can never be reconciled, and scarcely ever accounted for?"[26] Nothing in the review is more indicative of this critic's total inability to establish a rapport with Goethe's creation than his treatment of so central a chapter as the "Bekenntnisse einer schönen Seele." The first part he finds "full of vulgarities and obscurity—the last absolutely unintelligible." [27] Here is how this critic sees fit to conclude his plot-sketch of the "Confessions": "After this the fair Saint and Narzissus are betrothed. But she grows Methodistical, and he cold,—and their engagement flies off;—and then she becomes pious in good earnest, and is by turns a *Hallean* and a *Herrnhutter*, and we do not know how many other things, and raves through seventy or eighty pages of which we have not courage to attempt any analysis." [28]

In fairness it must be said that Jeffrey does scatter throughout his review some approbations of Goethe's "mind capable of acute and profound reflections," [29] of his "warm and sprightly imagination";[30] he does credit the poet with "touches of bright and powerful description" [31] and singles out for special praise Goethe's interpretation of *Hamlet* "as the most able, eloquent, and profound exposition . . . that has ever been given to the world." But he finds himself at a complete loss how to explain the presence of so splendid a piece among so much rubbish; to him "it is inconceivable that such an exposition should have been written by the chronicler of puppet-shows and gluttonous vulgarities." [32] And he closes his scathing review "with some feelings of mollification toward [the novel's] faults, and a disposition to abate, if possible, some part of the censure we were impelled to bestow on it at the beginning." [33]

I have cited Lord Jeffrey's critique in some detail because it not only reached a large reading public but—what was far more injurious to the Russian image of Goethe—influenced many a Russian critic in his view of the German poet. Druzhinin's criticism, for one, is clearly modeled after it. Druzhinin confidently predicts:

Wilhelm Meister will never become popular outside Germany—all these Laertes, Jarnos, and other personages with their inhuman names will forever repel modern readers. . . . No matter how much the interpreters [such as Carlyle in England and assorted critics in Germany] prattle, the non-German audience will never grow accustomed to those oceans of mysticism and allegory, to those confessions of beautiful souls, to those events that take place not on this earth but somewhere beyond space and time, not in the human sphere but in some strange world of twilight visions. Particularly the Russian reader, by his very nature inclined to the jocose and the jesting, nursed as he is by poets, satirical, semisatirical, and tenderly ironic, will not be able to suppress a smile reading *Wilhelm Meister*. Everything will seem to him ludicrous and barbarous: the actors' philosophical disputes ending in vulgar drunkenness, women who without the least apparent need change into men's clothes, those mystics [members of the *Turmgesellschaft*] who treat the hero of the novel as if he were their lackey, that harpist resembling a halfwit, and the concluding scenes in the count's castle, scenes that resemble nothing so much as a puppet play. . . .[34]

All this and more amuses or repels Druzhinin.

With such opinions on the novel, Druzhinin seemed committed to a hostile attitude toward its author. Yet only a short time after publishing his own and Jeffrey's reviews, Druzhinin experienced a radical change of mind. He realized that the lord's review "was no way to judge him [Goethe], who is admired by a whole generation." [35] Now, according to Druzhinin, "Jeffrey, from his British point of view, had failed to understand Goethe's intentions and had made of Goethe's work a laughingstock for the thoughtless who had long been led to see in every German a queer fellow and a dreamer with a slightly fractured mind." Druzhinin finds, to his surprise, that "repeated reading of the review" had a positive effect on him. "It roused the desire to familiarize myself with the thoughts of Goethe, to immerse myself in the limitless ocean, of which only such a small part has been opened to us." [36] He is now convinced that the life and work of a poet such as Goethe must be studied in its full scope:

One must know a poet such as the author of "Faust" fully or not at all, because everything that Goethe did, both in literature and in life, is one indivisible, logically consistent, unprecedented mighty creation altogether consciously achieved and instructive in every one of its minutest details. Goethe is great as a poet, as a thinker, as an experienced man of affairs, and yet all these accomplishments are but parts of an indivisible whole: Goethe is an entire philosophy. Goethe is the spirit and embodiment of an epoch, a firm link binding the *past* to the *present*, a marvelous monumental structure built on the very spot where only recently mere fragments lay scattered. Is it possible [Druzhinin asks] to comprehend such a being in the same manner as one would understand a less mighty personality? Who would dare speak of Napoleon merely on the basis of acquaintance with only a single year in his life? Who would dare judge Goethe having read only one of his famous works? In fact, were we to study all the works of the Weimar poet, we would still know him only in part. Every newly discovered letter by the great personality, every one of his conversations . . . opens up a whole world, entire systems of life science [zhiznenoi nauke], explains dark passages in his works, moves us to admire this all-comprehending mind, this all-sentient heart! [37]

For Druzhinin, as for Botkin, Goethe gradually became *the* Pure Poet, "*the* representative of *l'art pour l'art*, of aesthetics in all their contemporaneousness." [38] And again like Botkin, Druzhinin welcomed Goethe as a powerful ally in his battle against the selfsame enemy, the Radical Democrats and their materialistic aesthetics. He saw the attack against pure art being carried forward not only by the Russian radicals Chernyshevski, Dobroliubov, Pisarev, and their cohorts, but by a host of German writers as well, whom Druzhinin assigns to what he calls the "neo-didactic school":

The poets of *Young Germany*—alas, how pitiful and senile are these young poets at the present moment—Heine, Börne, Herwegh, Freiligrath,[39] together with some representatives of the new (now very old) philosophical systems,[40] lightheartedly set out to do battle with Goethe in the name of a new didactic beginning. . . . Never before had the ideas of the artistic school been subjected to such violent persecution; never had more acid derision been poured on the motto of "*l'art pour l'art*"; never had the personality of Goethe, of that leading poet following the road of pure art, provoked such furious attacks. One agreed not to mention his name; his best works were denounced as senile babble; one addressed to him the words of his own Prometheus ["Ich dich ehren? Wofür?"]; one avoided him and prophesied for him Lethe[41] and eternal oblivion.[42]

Instead it was the neo-didactics who grew old and were forgotten: "What has become of these bombastic poetasters and all those philosophers of the neo-didactic school? . . . What have these dwarfs, these pygmies [liudikarliki], created, who dared throw mud at the statue of him who had created 'Faust'? The mud they threw did not reach even halfway up the pedestal of the statue and fell back straight on their own heads."[43] "Goethe, that Napoleon in the realm of thought, the mightiest genius of poetry, the greatest representative of our century,"[44] had conquered them all.

Nor had they been the first and only ones to attack him. The great Olympian had had to endure vituperation and vilification before these attacks. During the War of Liberation (1812–1813) he had to face another group of vociferous detractors, who falsely accused him of a lack of patriotism. Actually, Goethe's sympathies were with the fighters of his native land, but he would not join in their chauvinistic frenzy, would not prostitute his poetic gift in songs of hatred for the enemy. Goethe remained faithful to his calling of the pure artist and in so doing proved to be far wiser than the chauvinistic poets Theodor Körner, Ernst Moritz Arndt, Friedrich de la Motte-Fouqué, and others of similar persuasion.

Druzhinin, now that he had become the enthusiastic champion of *l'art pour l'art*, is full of admiration for Goethe's wisdom and artistic integrity and full of scorn for the political pseudo-artists. "Goethe appears to us to have been absolutely right. With his penetrating mind he had perceived the impotence of his compatriots . . . their childish arrogance, their readiness to strike up songs of triumph even before victory had been won." Goethe knew the proper role for the poet in times of war:

Either he should be a silent fighter for his native land, or he should quietly observe the unfolding of events without interrupting his artistic activities. . . . To strike up the Romantic song where bullets whistle and armies clash, *that* he should leave to shallow dreamers. . . . The renaissance of ancient Germany was close to his noble heart. However, a Goethe could sing, could carry on his work and complete his task in any Germany, no matter how constituted.[45]

Obviously, Druzhinin was striving, much like Botkin, to put forward the name and fame of Goethe in support of "pure art" of which he had become an ardent proponent. For this purpose, he sets up an imaginary scenario, a confrontation between Goethe and his detractors. A condescending Goethe doubts the ability of his myopic critics to ever understand the true mission of an artist, of a poet. He has Goethe ask: "Is there any hope of ever convincing them that a seer does not take up a broom to sweep the refuse from noisy streets? . . . Can they ever be convinced that a poet's task is not to dry the tears of his contemporaries or to teach them the newest philosophy, which within ten short years is sure to turn into a dated, pitiful, wrinkled theory?" Druzhinin's fictional Goethe is convinced that there is indeed no hope. They will never understand! "That is why Goethe kept silent, and keeping silent triumphed in the end. His enemies, old and new alike, have vanished, but Goethe and his works stand before us in all their beauty and grandeur." And what is most remarkable for Druzhinin, "what constitutes the moral of this tale is the fact that even for the *education* of his contemporaries, for their immediate, practical benefit, one page written by the Weimar giant proved to be of greater value than all the work of both the didactic schools [the Romantic patriots and the Young Germans] who raised their banners against the singer of 'Faust.' " [46] Druzhinin triumphantly extols Goethe's life and work as incontrovertible proof of the absolute superiority of "pure art." The poet who remains faithful to his calling not only enriches mankind with the imperishable beauty and the transcending loftiness of his creations, but at the same time proves to be of supreme practical benefit as mankind's unfailing guide through the trials and tribulations of day-to-day existence.

My examination of the changing attitudes of the Liberal Democrats toward Goethe reveals a basic pattern. Their respect and admiration for Goethe the poet and thinker grew in proportion to their growing opposition to the materialistic aesthetics and political activism of the Radical Democrats. As the battle mounted in intensity they sought to enlist Goethe as a most powerful ally in their cause. He was put forward, with more or less effect, as the examplar of the uncommitted artist, faithful only to his art, as the unchallengeable guarantor of the superiority of "pure art" over time-bound pseudo-art servile to politics and ideologies.

The Radical Democrats: Nikolai Gavrilovich Chernyshevski (1828–1889) and Dmitri Ivanovich Pisarev (1840–1868)

Nikolai Chernyshevski is generally regarded not only as the leading Radical Democrat but also as the most extreme one. [47] Dmitri Chizhevski, for instance, considers him "the champion of the most extreme enlightenment" and his aesthetics "the crudest materialism." [48] He gives this characterization: "The Russian 'Feuerbach,' Chernyshevski, is more consistent than the real

Feuerbach"; and he quotes Chernyshevski's "contention that a real apple is aesthetically more valuable than the 'painted' one, than the picture representing an apple."[49] With such views on art, Chernyshevski could hardly be expected to have much sympathy for or understanding of Goethe the man and artist. Yet a detailed examination of his works does reveal a surprisingly appreciative attitude toward the German poet. My study supports Anatoli Lunacharski, who in sharp contrast to Chizhevski recognizes in Chernyshevski "the most gentle and responsive of readers in whose rich and noble soul the call of poetry resounded with an intense fervor."[50] Surely this is an excessive, ideologically motivated praise of a fellow revolutionary, and yet I too have found young Chernyshevski responding with "fervor" to Goethe's poetry, especially to the Sturm und Drang lyrics ("Mailied"!) but also to Goethe's "classical" ballads, particularly "Die Braut von Korinth." This does not mean that he idolized Goethe as an incomparable model and guide. B. I. Bursov correctly points out that "neither Schiller nor even Shakespeare and Goethe served him for norms and examples."[51] Early in his career Chernyshevski had "completely freed himself of the Romantic adulation of Goethe characteristic of Russian literature at the end of the 1830s, when—in Chernyshevski's words—'the young enthusiasts all but lost their minds over the Olympian Goethe.'"[52] Not being hostile or indifferent toward Goethe, he granted him only limited relevance to his time or to the democratic future extolled by him as his ideal.

Chernyshevski's early and very personal attraction to Goethe can be traced in the refreshingly frank and animated pages of his diary recording his university years (1848–1850). There he discusses his ambitious literary projects, his day-to-day readings, his experiences in the lecture halls, and his intense discussions and debates with his professors and fellow students. He enumerates his favorite authors: "The people who interest me greatly at present are Gogol', Dickens, and George Sand."[53] His list of "classical authors" is brief and disarmingly honest: "Of the dead I am unable to name anyone except Goethe, Schiller, and Lermontov."[54] He has heard of Byron but has not read him yet. Goethe, Schiller, and Lermontov, however, have won him completely. "These people are my friends!" he exclaims, and on second thought adds modestly, "Or rather, I am their devoted friend."[55]

Young Chernyshevski is fascinated with Goethe's personality and life as they unfold before him in *Dichtung und Wahrheit*, which he reads in the German original. For one of his favorite professors he writes a paper in defense of Goethe "about the accusation against him for his egoism and coldness." He considers these accusations quite as unjust and uncalled for as those leveled "against Gogol's supposed hypocrisy and cant."[56] He argues that the personality and life of a genius are not to be measured with our conventional moral standards. The interests of a genius, his loves, are concentrated on general not on personal matters, and especially his love for women is not of the type characteristic of ordinary men. Whoever accuses Goethe of coldness and egocentricity is merely proving his inability to grasp the true nature of genius and the true meaning of his life.[57]

The earliest plans for this paper date back to 1848, Chernyshevski's first year at the university. At the same time, he was planning a "tale the size of a novel" on Goethe's love for Lilli Schönemann, with the revealing title *Understanding (Ponimanie)*.[58] "I will write it," he exclaims in youthful enthusiasm, "in such a way that nobody, but nobody, would ever dare write on the same theme again!"[59] Alas, he soon discovered that a Russian translation of Goethe's biography was being published in the widely circulating journal *The Contemporary (Sovremennik)*. Discouraged, Chernyshevski gave up his grand design: "And now," he notes sadly, "there is hardly a need any longer to write on the episode of his [Goethe's] love for Lilli."[60] A few pages of his draft have been preserved. Unfortunately, they contain only a sketch of Goethe's mother, father, and sister and not a line on Goethe, for the fragment ends at the very moment Goethe appears on Chernyshevski's stage: "After three days Goethe arrived. Everyone was happy to see him, especially his sister, who had nothing more urgent to do than to converse with him. . . ."[61] Here, tantalizingly, the manuscript breaks off abruptly, leaving us without even a glimpse of Chernyshevski's intended portrayal of Goethe.

Goethe's *Faust* fascinated the budding critic. He examined in detail the extant Russian translations of Eduard Ivanovich Huber (Guber) and Mikhail Pavlovich Vronchenko and defended the Second Part of *Faust* against Vronchenko's less-than-perceptive comments on its "excessively obscure allegory."[62] We can gather how deeply personal an experience *Faust* had become for young Chernyshevski from the following diary jotting:

As I was writing down from memory Gretchen's song, my heart was strangely moved as it had not been for a long time. I had read the lines "officially" and nothing had happened. But now I *felt* especially the last strophes, that yearning for a strange love. When I now read them, there always comes to mind Vera's words [from Lermontov's novel *A Hero of Our Times*], "You men are materialists and cannot understand the voluptuous joy of a glance, of a handshake. But I, when I hear the sound of your voice, I feel such a deep, strange bliss as not even the most passionate kisses can rouse."[63]

Goethe's "Mailied" became the very expression for Chernyshevski of a love he yearned for: vibrant, vital, natural, uncorrupted by artifice or convention, a love that was to be his with Olga Sokratova Vasilieva, his wife-to-be. In his *Saratov Diary* we find lines from Goethe's poem addressed to Olga: "O Mädchen, Mädchen, wie lieb ich dich! . . ." but with the following characteristic variation. For Goethe's lines "Die du mir Jugend / Und Freud und Mut / zu neuen Liedern / und Tänzen giebst" Chernyshevski writes, in German: "Die du mir Leben / Und Freud und Mut / zu neuem Glück / Und *Taten* giebst." Goethe's carefree enjoyment of life has given way with Chernyshevski to a more purposeful, activist mood. The diary continues: "Oh my dear one, most bright, most blessed apparition of my life! Oh may you be happy, as you deserve it! If only I could add: 'Wie du mich liebst!' " [64]

Thirteen years later, in 1863, when writing his novel *What Is to Be Done? (Chto Delat'?)*, Chernyshevski again turned to the poem, quoting and paraphrasing it to lend color and lyricism to his description of the ideal love experienced by the hero and heroine of his tale, by the "new people" Kirsanov and Vera Pavlovna. Chernyshevski could not have found in Goethe's poem the social theme that is so prominent in his own work. What he did find was a poetic expression of an experience of nature, of youthful life and love that was totally new in its immediacy, exuberant intenseness, and uninhibited naturalness. He found here that capacity of "a pure enjoyment of life" characteristic of "the new human being" which he sought to portray in his novel. This liberating message enthralled Chernyshevski and moved him to weave the verses of the "Mailied" into his novel. They run as a leitmotiv through the "Fourth Dream of Vera Pavlovna," a chapter in which Chernyshevski's utopian vision of that "new" love reaches its poetic climax. His adaptation of Goethe's verses deserves quotation:

And Vera Pavlovna has a dream. She seems to hear a voice—oh how familiar a voice!—a voice from afar, coming closer and closer—

> Wie herrlich leuchtet
> Mir die Natur!
> Wie glänzt die Sonne,
> Wie lacht die Flur. . . . [65]

Having thus set the mood with the help of Goethe's poem, Chernyshevski develops a vernal setting for his love idyl, which again consists of a paraphrase of and variation on the verses of the *Lied*:

The field ["niva," an exact rendering of Goethe's "Flur"!] sparkles with a golden gleam; . . . hundreds, thousands of blossoms unfold on the bushes ["es dringen Blüten / Aus jedem Zweig"] . . . birds flutter from branch to branch and thousands of voices rise from the branches ["und tausend Stimmen aus dem Gesträuch"] . . . the far-off mountains, covered with forests, lit up by the sun, and above them here and there, . . . bright, silvery, golden, crimson transparent clouds ["wie Morgenwolken / Auf jenen Höhn"] . . . the sun has risen, . . . pours light and warmth, aroma and song, love, tenderness, and contentment into our breast, and from our breast there pours forth a song of joy and tenderness, of contentment, love, and benevolence ["Du segnest herrlich / Das frische Feld— / Im Blütendampfe / Die volle Welt!" and "Und Freud' und Wonne / Aus jeder Brust"].

This paean to nature, to love and happiness, rises in intensity to culminate in an all-but-verbatim translation of Goethe's lines "O Erd! O Sonne! / O Glück, O Lust / O, Lieb, O Liebe, / So golden schön, / Wie Morgenwolken / Auf jenen Höhn!" The Russian lines are followed by the original German verses, obviously intended to form the ultimate climax of the whole scene.[66] Whatever one may think of this type of pastiche, and one may well have one's reservations, it does attest to the lasting impression of Goethe's poem on Chernyshevski.

Nor is this the only instance of such borrowing. In another chapter of the novel, Chernyshevski describes Vera's thoughts of her beloved in the words of Gretchen at the spinning wheel: "And his sweet speech / His caressing voice / His smile / And, oh, his kiss!"[67] Or to give still another example, the lines "Wie Schnee, so weiss / Aber kalt wie Eis" from the ballad "Die Braut von Korinth" run leitmotiv-fashion through the unfinished tale "Alfieri" and recur as well in the larger context of the fragmentary novel *Tales in a Tale* (*Povesti v Povesti*).[68]

Clearly, Goethe's lyrics echoed and reechoed in the Russian's mind and entered his work, early and late. Yet Chernyshevski's youthful admiration for Goethe the man and poet was soon to change to a more reserved attitude. In his "Sketch of the Gogolian Period in Russian Literature" ("Ocherki Gogolevskogo Perioda Russkoi Literatury") the main thrust of his argument is to draw a sharp line between the patriotic, socially conscious artists—among whom Chernyshevski counts the great Russians Mikhailo Lomonosov, Gavriil Derzhavin, Nikolai Karamzin, Pushkin—and "cosmopolitan" writers such as Shakespeare, Ludovico Ariosto, and Goethe, whose "names remind us of aesthetic achievements in the service of pure art but not of any special outstanding efforts in the service of national welfare."[69] In contrast to poets deeply involved in the social and political questions of the day, such as George Sand, Béranger, and others who roused strong emotions of love and hate, "Goethe never warmed or chilled anyone; he was equally friendly and exquisitely tactful toward everybody. Goethe could be approached by anyone, no matter what that person's claim to moral respect. Obliging, soft, and basically quite indifferent to everything and everybody, Goethe was a host who would never insult with outright rudeness, not even with a touchy insinuation. But he who strokes everybody's fur, loves nobody but himself." Such a person was Goethe. He tried to please everybody and ended up by doing no one any good, because, according to the Russian critic, "genuine philanthropy is impossible without insult to evil. Nobody owes any thanks to him whom nobody hates."[70]

Chernyshevski has also many a harsh comment on Goethe's failings as a writer. He regards Schiller as superior to Goethe, because nowhere in Schiller's works did he find the type of sentimentality that repelled him so violently in Goethe's *Hermann und Dorothea*. Schiller's "poetry is not at all sentimental. There is no play in it of a dreamy fantasy. The pathos of his poetry is a flaming sympathy with all that ennobles and strengthens the human spirit. The time for such poetry has not passed and will never pass as long as man continues to strive for something higher than is offered by the reality surrounding him."[71]

Such praise Chernyshevski never bestowed on Goethe, never called his works "timeless." Even *Faust* appeared to him "time-bound." In his strongly autobiographical tale "Alfieri," Chernyshevski has one of the protagonists characterize Goethe as a writer "out of step with modern times" and dismiss his *Faust* as "dated." Admitting that there are "outstanding passages, marvelous ones," this speaker nevertheless maintains that the work's "general point of view is really passé; it strikes us moderns, you and me, as downright funny."[72] We are safe in assuming that this character in Chernyshevski's tale is speaking for the author. Years later, in one of his last letters from his Siberian exile to his children, Chernyshevski emphatically repeats this negative judgment of Goethe's masterpiece: "If you want to know," he writes on that occasion, "not only what I think but also what I feel, then do *not* read Goethe's *Faust*, no, that work is written from an extremely dated point of view—instead read his 'Braut von Korinth.'"[73]

One can cite many another critical appraisal of Goethe's talents. Thus, in his essay on Lessing, Chernyshevski boldly claims that Goethe had written "but one successful novel [*Werther*]" and that "all his other works in the epic genre are failures."[74] Moreover, even in that one successful effort Goethe created a very dangerous hero-idol. Chernyshevski then quotes at length and with his full approval from Lessing's letter to Johann Joachim Eschenburg, in which Lessing predicts the detrimental influence *Werther* would have on modern youths, who, mistaking the work's formal beauty for moral perfection, would embrace its weak and sentimental hero as their ideal. The Russian critic is convinced that Lessing "correctly divined the pernicious influence on the young by a novel that presents in such a positive light the sickly faintheartedness of its hero."[75]

Chernyshevski mounted his sharpest attack against Goethe's verse-epic *Hermann und Dorothea*. In his essay "On Sincerity in Criticism" ("Ob Iskrennosti v Kritike") he uses Goethe's work as an example of the type of harmful writing by a famous author that deserves the most severe censure. He

places before an imaginary German critic Goethe's "supreme artistic achievement" together with "an idyllic poem of some mediocre scribbler" and asks,
"Which of the two should you attack most furiously if you believe (as every
intelligent person does) that sweetly sentimental idealization is a sickness that
is most harmful to the Germans?" The answer seems obvious to him. The idyl
of the scribbler will pass unnoticed and will do little harm if any. But Goethe's
poem "of a saccharine sentimentality" has been delighting the German public
for some fifty-seven years:

Therefore you as a German critic would be well advised to pour all the gall of your
indignation on that destructive poem. . . . You should not fear criticism for lack of
proper respect for the great name. . . . Attack as openly and as sharply as you can the
harmful sentimentalism and the vacuity of the poem's content. Strive to prove with all
the force at your command that Goethe's poem is indeed a pitiful product with a pernicious tendency and message. To rise up against the one whom you would wish to
praise will surely be a painful experience. But what can you do? Your duty as a critic
demands it of you![76]

There are other negative evaluations of Goethe's works, but they cannot
be taken as characteristic of Chernyshevski's basic view of Goethe the poet.
Even in his scathing rejection of *Hermann und Dorothea* there is respect for
Goethe's artistry. His reference to the poem as a "supreme artistic achievement" is by no means ironic; he stresses that the poem is "indeed well written" and emphasizes that it is precisely its aesthetic excellence that constitutes
its gravest danger, for that very perfection of form seduces the reader to an
acceptance, even love of, the sentimentality and saccharine vacuity of its content. There are a number of Goethe's works which impress Chernyshevski
with the ideas they set forth, especially his classical ballads "Die Braut von
Korinth" and "Der Gott und die Bajadere," which remained Chernyshevski's
lifelong favorites.

In one of his reviews for *The Contemporary* (*Sovremennik*, 1860, no. 6),
Chernyshevski praises Goethe for having discovered in the old tales on which
he based these ballads a "hint of the ideas that preoccupied him." He credits
Goethe not only with this discovery but also with eminent success in developing "these hints into a meaningful message for his contemporaries." [77] According to him, this "message transcends the moral sphere and reaches up into the
social," that is, into the very sphere that had become the chief concern of the
"Radical Democrat" Chernyshevski. "Die Braut von Korinth" is singled out
for special praise because in it Goethe celebrates the "healthy" attitude of the
heathen Greeks toward life while condemning the hypocritical cruelty of
Christianity which is quite prepared to sacrifice the human being on the altar
of its faith. Chernyshevski repeatedly quotes the lines "Opfer fallen hier, /

Weder Lamm noch Stier, / Aber Menschenopfer unerhört" as the most poignant expression of his own criticism of the Christian dogma, which denies and destroys man's natural instincts, his love of life in the here and now, for an illusory promise of a blessed life in the hereafter.[78] Nor is Chernyshevski's criticism of *Faust* unequivocally negative. While rejecting the work's transcendental idealism, he nevertheless singles out Goethe's masterpiece as the "only work in German literature superior in its colossal importance to Lessing's *Nathan der Weise*," high praise indeed from this fervent devotee of Lessing. He extols *Faust* as "one of the most dramatic creations known to [him]; it is the most flawless in form: not a word too much, not one out of place." He marvels at the "terrifying inevitability with which the dramatic action unfolds before us" and admires the lifelike characters "who act in keeping with their nature and not in accordance with some whimsical plan of the author." [79]

Moreover, Chernyshevski's extensive "Notes to a Translation of *Faust*" by Alexander Nikolaevich Strugovchikov[80] clearly indicate that even the *central message* of Goethe's work held more attraction for him than his scattered negative comments would suggest. The "Notes" clearly indicate that Chernyshevski found its message to be basically an optimistic one with which he could fully sympathize. He believes that Goethe's central aim in his *Faust* is the demonstration of the eternal truth that the dialectical spirit, that skepticism, doubt, and negation, were in essence positive forces acting as a goad and a challenge to man in his constant striving toward ever more profound insights. "Skepticism [Mephisto] rises up against reason [God], boasting that it can deprive man of all noble striving if only it can gain access to him. But reason does not fear this trial because it knows human spirit to be such as to triumph in the end, no matter how much it is tortured. . . . Man's nature leads him to goodness and truth." To be sure, skepticism is evil and causes suffering, but it does not destroy a strong personality. "Negation merely leads to new, purer, and truer convictions. . . . Reason is not hostile to negation and skepticism; on the contrary, skepticism serves reason to attain its goals, leading man by way of uncertainty to pure and clear convictions."

It is Faust's self-doubt and despair about man's limited powers of cognition which, in Chernyshevski's empathetic interpretation of Goethe's message, opens Faust to Mephisto's advances. Yet these evil-intentioned advances lead to the pact and thus ultimately to Faust's triumph. Chernyshevski is impressed with the dynamic nature of Goethe's treatment of the traditional pact not as an unalterable contract but as a wager: "Such is the nature of the agreement: Man will remain caught up in negation [i.e., in bondage to Mephisto] only if it [negation personified in Mephisto] can satisfy him, but the Prologue has already told us that this is impossible." Those vulgar temptations that Mephisto can serve up to Faust can only repel him. But even the lofty emotion of love cannot still Faust's longings and strivings. Approvingly, Chernyshevski stresses this trait in the character of Goethe's hero: "Love takes possession of him with terrifying force. But will he find in this lofty emotion full satisfaction of all the needs of his nature? Will love force him to reject all his ideal strivings? No, never. One-sided abandonment to passion does not give man complete happiness." Gretchen, in Chernyshevski's view, is introduced chiefly to underscore, by contrast, Faust's insatiable striving for ultimate truth. "She demands that for her sake he renounce the insights he has gained. . . . This is impossible." Wagner performs a similar function. He represents those utterly narrow and vulgar sentiments and thoughts that cannot possibly satisfy Faust, "who is in need of a more profound truth, of a richer life."

While dwelling at length and with evident approval on Goethe's central message, Chernyshevski warns that one must not attempt to reduce Goethe's masterpiece to one single theme:

We would be interpreting Goethe's tragedy one-sidedly were we to see in it only one central idea: to lead Faust (i.e., man in his striving toward truth) through life's temptations. It is important to recognize Goethe's other intent in the selection of the different scenes of his drama: Goethe planned to mirror in his creation all the various tendencies, all the spheres of life. In the First Part he carried out only half his plan—he represented private life. In the Second Part he wanted to depict public, political life and to develop his ideas on the meaning of science and art.

Chernyshevski recognizes in Goethe the supreme poet-philosopher. He contrasts him with Pushkin, who "did not espouse any particular world view. . . . The artistic form of *Faust* was developed to express a profound view of the world; in Pushkin's works we will not find this." It is a mistake to liken Pushkin's *Boris Godunov* to Goethe's *Goetz von Berlichingen*. In his *Goetz*, Goethe had discovered and set forth "the deeper meaning of historical events." Pushkin, while being a master at rendering realistically the psychology of his characters, merely repeated in his *Godunov* views on history as they had been developed by the great Russian historian Karamzin.[81] And again, in his commentary on Strugovchikov's *Faust* translation it is Goethe the poet of ideas, the poet-thinker, that preoccupies Chernyshevski virtually to the total exclusion of the artist. He makes no attempt to convey to his Russian readers an impression of the style and structure that Goethe had lent to the content of his drama even though he was well aware that Strugovchikov's heavy-handed rendering of Goethe's text had all but obliterated the formal elements of the original. Chernyshevski's commentary does not contain a single important reference to matters of prosody, of rhyme, rhythm, and meter, to the novel realism of Goethe's language or to Goethe's choice of metaphor and symbol, although he reads Part One as "the great allegory [!] of man's salvation." To be sure, he had, on another occasion, praised Goethe for "having presented examples of artistic creation, in which the idea was not forced into conventional forms alien to it, where thought brought forth a form altogether its own and totally compatible with it." [82] Surely *Faust*, in both its parts, was such an "example" that could have served Chernyshevski supremely well to prove his contention. Yet in his extensive "Notes" on the work, no attempt is made at structural or stylistic analysis.

This concentration on ideational content we may well ascribe to Chernyshevski's ideological orientation, which became more pronounced with advancing years. We find the most extreme statement of Chernyshevski's materialistic or—as he preferred to call it—his "realistic" aesthetics in his discussion of the dramatis personae in *Faust*. He poses a revealing question: "Who is, in greater degree, the author of Mephisto—Merck [young Goethe's friend, Johann Heinrich Merck] or Goethe? Who is more the author of Gretchen—that servant girl at the inn [in Frankfurt, Gretchen's supposed prototype] or Goethe?" [83] In Chernyshevski's opinion "both [Merck and the servant girl] can lay greater claim to authorship than Goethe can." His reasoning runs as follows: "To write down words is no great wisdom. In some way or other to invent for them, i.e., for the speeches of the personae some kind of setting, is no great wisdom!" The following assertion is even more startlingly revealing of Chernyshevski's aesthetics.

Goethe was mistaken in thinking that Merck and the servant girl were the prototypes of his fictional personae. Actually, that was not at all the case. What really happened is this: He [Goethe] saw literally hundreds of people who resembled his Mephisto and his Gretchen not one whit less than did Merck and the servant girl. Had Goethe not met those hundreds of other characters, he would have remembered the original two but dimly, might never have understood them at all. Those two were the real prototypes only in his imagination; he wrongly imagined them to be the worthy models. Actually he knew hundreds of such "worthy models." All these hundreds were also the authors of Mephisto and of Gretchen.

With this insight, Chernyshevski felt himself to be abreast of his times.

In former days one failed to understand all this clearly. One used to say, "The poet idealizes."—*No, the poet merely sees, understands, and records*. There is no more in the figure of Mephisto than in Merck and in the hundreds of other educated people known to Goethe. In fact, there is in Mephisto actually less than in any one of them— in each of them there was a more flaming spirit of negation, a more titanic insolence, both impudent and cowardly; there were in them all the traits that characterize Mephisto. In each of the many hundreds of tender and pure young girls whom Goethe knew, there was more of tender and pure beauty of heart than in the Gretchen of *Faust*. All these are models or, to be more exact, portraits; they all are authors.

Even this extreme statement does not satisfy our critic. Single-mindedly he drives home his point: "Nor are they [these hundreds of people Goethe had met] the only authors of Goethe's dramatis personae. Surely it could not be a chance meeting with Goethe that determined people's status in the life of German society, their roles in it. No, that *society* was such that people of noble character grew strongly in its milieu—they became Mephistos, and the women, tender but not strong, became Gretchens." Chernyshevski concludes: "The real authors of *Faust* are all these noble people of the Germany of those days."

We have here the canon of Chernyshevski's materialistic aesthetics: The real author of a work of art is *society*. The social, economic, and political conditions in the Germany of Goethe's days shaped the character, the behavior patterns, and the habits of the people. The author's role in the creative process is reduced to the act of "*seeing, understanding*, and *recording*." The free play of his imagination, the creative act of selection, stylization, and interpretation, of "poetization and idealization," have become suspect and must be kept in check. At best they add little to the stuff furnished by life itself, at worst they "debase and distort" reality.

Chernyshevski must be credited with having been the first among Russian men of letters to have recognized the full significance of Gotthold Ephraim Lessing[84] in the cultural life of Europe. He is certainly the first, and to my knowledge the only one in his generation, to have placed Lessing above Goethe and Schiller in the hierarchy of Germany's great writers. One can readily understand why he would have chosen Lessing for his hero. In him he had discovered a kindred spirit, a fellow revolutionary. He sees Lessing as a supremely courageous champion of progress, a thoroughly modern spirit ready for battle with all that is time-worn, petrified, regressive. Lessing "stands closer to our age than Goethe," in Chernyshevski's opinion. "His vision is more perceptive and profound, his concepts are broader and more humane." [85]

Chernyshevski puts forward in his "Lessing" essay the challenging thesis that in Germany *literature* was the prime moving force of its national development. *Poets*, not statesmen, were the real leaders in Germany's cultural as well as sociopolitical growth. He writes: "Milton and Dante may well possess greater poetic genius than Goethe and Schiller, but in the history of [Germany's] progress Goethe and Schiller occupy a far more important place. The former are leaders in their specialty [poetry]; the latter are movers of historical progress, directly influencing the fate of humanity." [86] And to whom do they owe their high and mighty position? To Lessing, because Lessing "was the father of the new German literature. He ruled it with the power of a dictator." In Chernyshevski's view of the German cultural scene, all the most important German writers, even Goethe and Schiller, were Lessing's pupils.[87] Lessing "was the oracle of the young generation. Goethe, Herder, and Merck, by studying him, prepared themselves to set out on the road opened up for them by none other than Lessing." [88] In Chernyshevski's extravagant judgment of Lessing's role as founder and leader,

the achievements of his successors were but the realization of his thoughts. In the great struggle for the rejuvenation of the German people, not only the plan of battle but also the victory belongs to him—Goethe and Schiller only completed what Lessing had already laid out. They had a sympathetic audience because Lessing had forced the German people to accept those ideas expressed by them—all that was sound in their ideas had been suggested to them by Lessing. In him was contained and through him and from him sprang the entire new literature up to the end of the productive period of Goethe's activity. [89]

In Lessing's *Hamburgische Dramaturgie*, Chernyshevski discovered the "codex on the basis of which arose Goethe's *Goetz von Berlichingen* and even his *Faust*." [90] Lessing's *Minna von Barnhelm* "opened up a whole new world to literature, the world of native, national life. . . . National talents spread their wings, and within six years there appeared *Goetz von Berlichingen* and *Werther*." [91] With his *Emilia Galotti*, Lessing "set the standard of excellence for *Goetz* and *Egmont*, for Schiller's *Räuber*, for his *Don Carlos*, his *Kabale und Liebe* and *Wilhelm Tell*." [92]

Chernyshevski was not satisfied with such sweeping claims of Lessing's leadership in life and letters. He adduces specific, detailed proof to his thesis of Goethe's dependence on Lessing's precedent-setting achievements even in the sphere of stylistics. In his *Laokoon*, Lessing had pointed out "that Homer did not describe objects but rather had given the *origins* and *fates* of these objects." As an example Chernyshevski cites the "origin and fate" of the famous shield of Achilles. Everywhere in the works of Goethe Chernyshevski finds "this principle of composition adhered to." Lessing had observed and set forth in his seminal essay the fact that "Homer never presented portraits of the personae. . . . Yet the features of Helena stand vividly before the readers' eye." Homer achieved this effect not by describing Helena's face but by "telling us of the impression it produced on those who saw it." And once again Goethe followed this method of presentation. Confidently Chernyshevski asserts, "There are no portraits in his [Goethe's] works, there are only reports of the impressions produced by his characters." [93]

Having thus emphasized, even belabored, Goethe's dependence on Lessing, Chernyshevski evidently felt the need to explain and justify his view. He warns us not to mistake Goethe's dependence for slavish borrowing from or imitation of the admired teacher. He would have us know that "Goethe . . . was not a slave to rules derived mechanically from Lessing. If details of Lessing's system did find their reflection in Goethe's works, it was only because he had been so profoundly imbued with the *spirit* that determined Lessing's choice of these details." Kinship of spirit, then, not slavish imitation, was the true reason for Goethe's ready acceptance of Lessing's guidance. "As a true genius, Goethe moved independently; he willingly followed in the paths opened up by Lessing, but only insofar as these paths led to goals set by Goethe's own nature." [94]

Chernyshevski was even prepared to admit that in poetic power Goethe "excelled Lessing by far." [95] "Goethe stands incomparably higher than his teacher, Lessing, in point of poetic talent." [96] He concedes that "Goethe's genius was . . . more universal, embracing not only the spheres of knowledge and thought which preoccupied Lessing but also the natural sciences which lay outside the scope of his activity." [97]

Yet having made these concessions, Chernyshevski nevertheless holds to his thesis that Goethe was at his greatest when following in Lessing's footsteps, developing Lessing's ideas and accepting the wiser, more perceptive, more truly progressive guidelines of his mentor. Deviation from these resulted in wasted effort and downright harm. He laments Goethe's and Herder's aberrations: "Herder's weak side was an excess of imagination over common sense, Goethe's (in the period of *Werther* and of his preoccupation with the pseudo-Ossian) was his sentimentalism." Here Chernyshevski locates the "source of Herder's infatuation with Hamann [Chernyshevski's *bête noire*] and Goethe's tolerance of people like Lavater and Jung-Stilling," whom he scornfully dismisses as mystics and sentimentalists, as "obscurantic philosophers of feeling and faith." [98] Lessing had been aware of the "serious errors in the activities of leading members of the young generation and foresaw the bad results." In Chernyshevski's opinion, Lessing in his prognosis was only too right: "Schlegel, Tieck, and others had their origin in the one-sided excesses that Goethe, Herder, and their friends had fallen prey to." [99] These excesses lay at the very root of all the pernicious, antirational elements that Chernyshevski abhorred in the Romantic movement and in Germany's cultural development in general.

Putting forth this negative view of Goethe as a spiritual progenitor of the hated Romanticists, Chernyshevski is equally critical of Goethe the "Classicist's" efforts, together with Schiller, to revive (by way of translations) the French pseudo-classical drama, a "hopelessly dated genre that had been so effectively laid to rest by Lessing in his *Hamburgische Dramaturgie*." Goethe and Schiller, however, "thought the time was ripe to pay their due to the greatness of these works, but Lessing's ridicule of them was still fresh in everyone's memory, and the great poets merely exposed themselves to the just criticism of undertaking a task unworthy of their talents." [100] Chernyshevski is convinced that Goethe and Schiller, and the German nation and all humanity, would have gained much had the poets instead continued to cultivate the vast areas of knowledge and thought opened up by Lessing.

Chernyshevski's comparison of Goethe with Lessing makes it abundantly clear that the "Weimar sage" had lost for him the unchallenged preeminence he had enjoyed with the Russian Romanticists. But it is equally clear on the evidence of my study that Goethe did remain for the Russian critic an artist of genius, a thinker of great scope and profundity. In all of German literature, Chernyshevski could not find any work to equal, in world-encompassing sweep and significance, Goethe's *Faust*. He did declare that he would "discard as inferior nine-tenths of all of Goethe's works," but the rest he valued as "immeasurably loftier than anything written in the German language." [101]

Chernyshevski began as Goethe's admirer and remained throughout his life if not his sympathetic critic then certainly his responsive critic. He did not take part in the Romanticists' adulation of the sage of Weimar, but neither did he join Belinski in his abrupt dismissal of Goethe as a "king dethroned." [102] For a Radical Democrat and "consequent realist," Chernyshevski proved to be a surprisingly moderate critic of the German poet, far more circumspect and just than his fellow materialist and revolutionary Dmitri Ivanovich Pisarev.

In Pisarev we meet the most rigorous of Russian materialists. [103] He took great pride in his contempt for the arts. "For a long time now," he writes, "our antagonists have reprimanded us frequently and harshly for our not understanding and not respecting art. The accusation of our not understanding art is totally unjust; however, that we do not respect art—that is indeed the case." [104] The uncompromising rigidity of Pisarev in his judgments on poets and all their works have rarely, if ever, been equaled in their ruthlessness. According to him, "the poet has to be a mighty fighter, a fearless knight, or else he is a pitiful parasite amusing other pitiful parasites with picayune tricks of unproductive jugglery. There is no midway position [serediny net!]." [105] As to Russian poets, Pisarev states categorically: "There are none. Russia has only poets in an embryonic state or parodies of poets. Embryonic poets are Lermontov, Gogol', Polezhaev, Krylov, and Griboedov; among the parodies of poets we place Pushkin and Zhukovski." [106]

It will be well to remember this rigor of Pisarev's standards—or should we rather say, his wrongheadedness—when we examine his criticism of Goethe. In fact, only an acquaintance with his basic world view, and specifically with his total rejection of traditional aesthetics, will enable the reader to set in proper perspective Pisarev's denigrations of the German poet. I therefore introduce my discussion with a succinct presentation of the philosophy of this "consequent" realist, as Pisarev liked to call himself.

Pisarev recognized only one aim in life worthy of a thinking person: to improve the lot of people, especially of the poor. He was convinced that this overriding need was being accomplished far more effectively by natural scientists than by speculative philosophers or artists. Fine arts were to him "parasitic plants that have always fed on luxury" [107] and have rarely, if ever, brought tangible benefits to mankind. "The consequent realist hates everything that does not bring substantive benefits. . . . We insistently demand that the poet as poet and the historian as historian contribute, each in his own specialty, *actual* benefits." [108] If the arts are to be tolerated at all, they must mirror in the most meaningful way the important phenomena of life that could be of interest and educational value for a thinking person, that could be "useful" in a pragmatic way. In Pisarev's view, art's existence can be justified only "as an auxiliary cog in the general mechanism of productive labor or as an interlude between the end of work and the beginning of a new task." [109]

Usefulness is Pisarev's highest standard of value. "The realist," he assures us, "constantly strives to be useful and denies himself and others all types of activity that do not produce useful results." [110] He demands that all those who by their natural gifts and social station can and wish to perform intellectual work employ their energies with the greatest of circumspection, that they practice what Pisarev calls "economy of intellectual energies." Such "economy" will increase, in Pisarev's pragmatic calculation, "our intellectual capital, and this increased capital invested in useful production will in turn increase the amount of available bread, meat, clothing, footwear, and all the other products of labor." [111]

Pisarev certainly practiced what he preached. As a university student he set for himself the most rigid program of reading. He never took a book in his hand without asking himself, "Do I really have to read this for my specialty?" He did permit himself to read Shakespeare, Schiller, and Goethe, "only because these names were mentioned in all the histories of literature." [112] He sternly lectured his followers: "You will read Shakespeare, Byron, Goethe, Schiller, Heine, Molière, and very few other poets, only those who are famous not for having lived at some time or other and for having written something or other, but only those whose fame is solidly based on their success in communicating rational and wise thoughts." [113]

Of philosophy Pisarev has a still lower opinion: "Speculative philosophy amounts to empty waste of mental energies. It is purposeless luxury that will forever remain inaccessible to the masses in need of life-sustaining bread." Philosophy to him is a "cancerous growth that developed when all the vital forces reaching out for practical activity had been forcibly arrested and suppressed." [114]

The central target of Pisarev's attacks is what he terms "aesthetics." "My readers will probably think that aesthetics are my nightmare [koshmar]—and for once they are absolutely right." [115] Aesthetics in Pisarev's definition subsume all the negative and pernicious forces. "Aesthetics that is the uncontrolled subconscious, is routine, is deadening habit—all these are completely synonymous terms. Over against these stand realism, analysis, criticism, and intellectual progress—all these are also synonymous terms diametrically opposed to the former." [116] Aestheticism and Realism are in Pisarev's world view deadly enemies. Realism must extirpate aestheticism if it is to survive. "Aestheticism poisons in our day all the branches of our scientific endeavors and deprives them of meaning." [117] And Pisarev raises his voice in warning: "Should the aesthetic world view gain the upper hand, we shall certainly take a backward step into routine, mental impotence, and deadly obscurantism." [118]

Many a great personality has been led astray in the past by the allurements of aestheticism, and many a powerful intellect is even now being perverted by a harmful cultivation of hyperrefined sensibilities, by a pernicious absorption in narcissistic self-analysis and in the idle game of virtuosic phrasemaking. Goethe and Schiller have been so led astray and debauched by the destructive effect of aestheticism. Pisarev diagnoses their grievous failings as being rooted in their very nature as poets and aesthetes. Pisarev likes to repeat accusations put forward against Goethe by Belinski, Herzen, and many another liberal. His criticism of Goethe often sounds all too familiar. Goethe's "*heart,*" he claims, "*was torn from the world. Fate had not considered him worthy of poetic martyrdom* because he had made peace with miserable reality and thus had remained untouched by the soul-searing torments suffered by such Titans as Byron." [119] This type of criticism merely echoes Belinski and Herzen.

Pisarev's *novel* critique of Goethe is to be found in his spirited if wrongheaded attempt to demonstrate the evil effect aestheticism had on Goethe's mighty intellect. He depicts Goethe as a "moderate and enlightened Epicurean . . . who had chosen for his guiding principle the fullest possible enjoyment of life and who in that spirit lolled in ease on the multicolored, voluptuous cushions of the *West-Östliche Divan.*" [120] This incorrigible Epicurean had convinced himself—so runs his analysis of Goethe's aberration— "that all he needed to do was refine his sensibilities, aspire to ever loftier flights of thought, and coin ever more subtle phrases in order to bring immeasurable benefits to all mankind." What he actually brought was disaster to himself.

Goethe was joined on this disastrous path of self-deception and destruction by Schiller. These mighty luminaries of German letters soon discovered that their sensibilities had been sufficiently elevated, their phrases sufficiently refined. Now all that remained for them was to "admire their own perfection and to feed simpleminded humanity not with honest products of useful intellectual labor but with the hypercultivated elegance of their enlightened personalities." With evident malice Pisarev puts words of self-adulation into the poets' mouths: "Exult over us!" he has them exclaim. "Give thanks to God, that we live among you and that you are privileged to behold such unique beauty of soul and mind!"[121]

Having created this imaginary Goethe figure, Pisarev is amazed at its behavior. He exclaims in disbelief: "How could Goethe, this mighty mind, prefer the narrow sphere of his personal emotions to the stirring life of humanity? How could he consider the subjective longings and the activities of a single organism as being of greater importance than the real drama enacted before the eyes of every thinking observer, at every moment, at every step since the founding of the first human society?"[122] In examining Goethe's paradoxical personality, Pisarev has come to the conclusion that—contrary to the usual explanation—Goethe's "philistine cowardice" and his indifferentism could not possibly be the key to the riddle of this foolish self-adulation by so brilliant a mind. "If cowardice were the only cause, then Goethe could never have so naively respected and loved himself."[123] Pisarev offers an original solution to the enigma: "For Goethe the world of personal feelings was not a mere refuge; for him it was a *temple* in which he took up his permanent residence in the complete conviction that a more beautiful and holy place there did not exist in the whole wide world." But in order to be capable of such gross self-delusion, one had to be an *aesthete*. To see one's personality as a holy temple and the surrounding world as a dirty marketplace, "to grow oblivious of the natural coexistence of one's *ego* with fellow men in their trials and tribulations, it was necessary to lull to sleep and to corrupt one's critical faculties systematically in admiring contemplation of the beauty of exquisite phrases. . . . Goethe had performed this trick." He had actually won it over himself "to raise *picayune thoughts and picayune feelings to a pearl of creation.*"[124]

In performing this "trick," Goethe had done incalculable harm to his nation. Pisarev is prepared to grant Goethe all those virtues habitually ascribed to him by his fellow aesthetes: Goethe is indeed

very clever, very "objective," very "plastic," and so forth. All these qualities will remain to his credit *forever and ever*. Yet [and now Pisarev delivers his *coup de grace*] this Goethe has inflicted on his nation untold injury. Together with Schiller he has adorned—also *forever and ever*—the pig's head of the German philistine with the laurels of immortal poetry. Thanks to the efforts of these two poets, the German philistine can now reconcile the highest aesthetic delights with the most colorless vulgarities of his empty, aimless bourgeois existence. He reads his great poets and is inspired and turns up his eyes like a well-fed tomcat, and remains, with it all, to the end of his days a hopeless vulgarian firmly convinced that he is a human being and that nothing human can be alien to him.

Developing his attack on the high-sounding vacuities of the aesthetes, Pisarev ascribes the pernicious effect of Goethe's works to the complete lack in them of "that lively stream of criticism and negation which characterizes the writings of all great realists and is absent from the writings of all mere aesthetes." That is the reason why the German philistines so eagerly read Goethe's works and why, "adoring and devouring them, they remain forever what they always had been—hopeless philistines. . . . Where there is no gall and no laughter, there is no hope for renewal and progress. Where there is no sarcasm, there also is no real love of mankind." [125]

It is difficult to believe that even so puritanical a recoil from aestheticism as Pisarev's could have produced so distorted a picture of the poet-thinker Goethe, of the creator of the figure of Mephisto, that purest embodiment of "criticism and negation." Surely Pisarev must have heard of, if not actually read, some of Goethe's scientific works. He fails to mention a single one. It must be assumed that these works were unacceptable to him as genuine, productive labors in the realm of "useful" science because they were the products not only of "realistic" observation but also of "poetic" imagination, inspiration, and sensitive empathy, and because they were couched in the language of a poet and an accomplished stylist—unforgivable aberrations in the critical judgment of this "consequent realist." We have not met with so one-sided censure of Goethe and shall not meet with so vehement one again until we come on Leo Nikolaevich Tolstoi's thunderous denunciations of the "amoral aesthete" and "damnable heathen," Goethe.

Yet even Pisarev saw fit to make certain concessions to Goethe's greatness. He did it with grudging reluctance and a great deal of circumlocution. Once he had actually placed Goethe "among the Titans of literature." [126] Such high praise, he was quick to realize, would surely strike his readers as inconsistent with his usual denigration of this "Titan." He is ready with an explanation. He asks us to "look at the problem more closely" and then, to our surprise, introduces his "explanation" with still another *attack* on Goethe. Very much in the manner of Herzen, he draws our attention to Goethe's marked ability and unequaled success in playing up to the high and the mighty and points sarcastically to "the rich assortment of versified almond-sweet dishes and operettas" which Goethe so expertly fashioned to delight that high society he courted. Yet this same Goethe was greatly admired by the "Titan" Byron. How are we to explain that paradox asks Pisarev, and he gives an answer that once again carries a barb: "In the eyes of Byron Goethe's intellectual powers obviously outweighed those flaws of character which, of course, were well known to Byron and with which he could never have sympathized, being a most independent personality." [127]

One would now expect Pisarev to dwell on Goethe's intellectual powers so highly esteemed by Byron. After all, he is trying to explain why he had placed Goethe in the company of Byron as a mighty Titan of thought. Instead we find him delivering still another blow against the German poet. With evident relish he calls our attention once again to Goethe's abject servility: "Whenever Goethe descended . . . into the milieu of the gilded German philistines [i.e., whenever he joined court society], whenever he turned his talents into a milking cow, whenever he chased after the patronizing smiles of the powerful, he suddenly shrank to the size of the smallest insect and fell lower than the lowest of our contemporary lyricists [the Pure Poets, the targets of Pisarev's sharpest criticism], because those puny lyricists sang the best they could within the narrow limits of their abilities, while he, Goethe, intentionally shrank his mighty size and simulated an innocent canary." [128] Having delivered this thrust, Pisarev then offers, as an afterthought, his "explanation" of Goethe's greatness: Whenever Goethe created "with sincerity and firmness born of a deep conviction, unencumbered by any calculations of mundane gain," on those rare occasions Goethe "did satisfy my [Pisarev's] definition of 'usefulness.'" And yet how grudgingly is this praise bestowed! Pisarev hastens to stress that the type of "usefulness" Goethe exemplifies could never be the type characteristic of those gloriously rebellious spirits of a Béranger, a Leopardi, a Shelley, of a Thomas Hood and those other great furtherers of social consciousness and human progress. "Those were poets of the current moment. They awakened the people to the urgent needs of contemporary social life, they loved the people, shared their day-to-day trials, sorrows, and pains. But Goethe loved nobody except himself and his thoughts." [129]

Thus Pisarev is back again on his favorite theme, Goethe's aloofness, indifferentism, and egocentricity. Yet mindful of the goal he had set for himself in his discourse, namely, to justify his inclusion of Goethe among the Titans, Pisarev now takes a novel and unexpected tack. He admits that poet-leaders such as Béranger and Leopardi "are thoughtful and enlightened workers, but not geniuses on a worldwide scale. They are frequently in need of intellectual rejuvenation." And now Pisarev reveals his view of Goethe's "usefulness." Though not a poet of the people, totally incapable of communicating his thoughts directly to the masses, Goethe could nonetheless inspire and rejuvenate those poet-leaders and champions of the masses whose highly developed intellect was powerful enough to grasp and benefit from Goethe's thoughts. For these poet-leaders, exhausted by their unceasing efforts in behalf of the poor and downtrodden, "the works of Goethe represent a huge galvanic battery that constantly feeds their tiring minds with ever-renewed electrical power. . . . And in turn these renewed energies thus generated are transmitted down the current into that vast ocean vibrant with life which we call the masses." [130] Thus, despite himself, along this circuitous route, Goethe, that cold and aloof privy-councilor of Weimar, did benefit the masses by rejuvenating the flagging spirits of their leaders.

This process of rejuvenation, Pisarev would have us know, is a most complex and often unexpected one. Paradoxically, it is sparked and sustained not only by the respect and veneration of the select for Goethe's genius but—perhaps even more frequently and violently—by their very hatred of him and all he stands for. Pisarev cites the example of Ludwig Börne. This flaming Democrat drew inspiration from "his productive hatred of the Cavalier von Goethe." Roused by it, he penned some of his most brilliant pages. This and similar examples constitute for Pisarev proof-positive that "a mighty phenomenon [such as Goethe] could not possibly remain unproductive; he refreshes and rejuvenates life both with all that is good and with all that is evil in him. He benefits people by the love as well as by the hatred he rouses in them." [131]

Pisarev's grudging concessions to Goethe's greatness in labored circumlocutions, his insistent emphasis on Goethe's failings even in his efforts at melioration of his harsh judgment of the German "Pure Poet," are striking evidence of Pisarev's unwillingness to grant Goethe a place among the admired champions of human progress. With far greater consistency and sharpness than Chernyshevski, Pisarev exemplifies the Radical Democrats' critical attitude toward Goethe the man and artist.

The Slavophiles

Nicholas V. Riasanovski, in his scholarly study of the Slavophiles,[132] has stressed the difficulty of establishing the membership of the group. There never was what one could properly call a "Slavophile school." Many of the Slavophiles were close to members of the left or democratic group, to the "Westerners," for instance, to Herzen. Even in the years of their sharpest debates they remained united with their opponents by their common love of Mother Russia. One need but read the following heartfelt panegyric by Herzen of two of the deceased Slavophile leaders—Aleksei Stepanovich Khomiakov (1804–1860) and Konstantin Aksakov (1817–1861)—to become aware of the profound bond of kinship between these warring spirits:

It is painful to people who have known them to realize that these active, noble, indefatigable *opponents* are no longer among the living, *opponents* who were closer to us than many a one of *our own*. . . . Yes, we were opponents, but very strange ones. . . . From the earliest years they and we were possessed by one powerful, unaccountable, physiological, passionate feeling, which they took for reminiscence and we for prophecy: the feeling of a limitless love for the Russian people, for Russian customs, for Russian ways of thought. And thus we looked in opposite directions Janus-like or like the two-headed [Russian] eagle, while *our hearts beat in unison.*[133]

Riasanovski counts among the leading members of the loosely knit group Aleksei Khomiakov, Ivan and Pëtr Kireievski, Konstantin and Sergei

Aksakov, Iuri Samarin, and A. I. Koshelëv. These were joined, more or less peripherally, sooner or later in time, by Apollon Grigor'ev, Stepan Petrovich Shevyrëv, and M. P. Pogodin.

Riasanovski and other scholars[134] have clearly demonstrated that despite their antagonism toward Europe's enlightenment and its progressive, democratic ideas, the Slavophiles had a thorough grasp of the many-faceted cultural and political developments in the West. They were especially interested in Europe's philosophers and theologians, but they also were acquainted with the literary figures, the historians, and the writers on politics, economics, and the social scene. "Opposing all imitation [of the West] and demanding that literature and art be original in order to express the spirit of the [Russian] nation, [the Slavophiles] did mention in their writings almost every contemporary Western thinker of any importance. . . . They discussed all aspects of Western cultural life: from Paganini's concerts and the Dresden Art Gallery to the latest textbook on economics."[135] Riasanovski emphasizes that the Slavophiles "went through a period of intense admiration of Schiller and Goethe."[136]

This admiration of the German poets was certainly characteristic of Ivan Kireievski (1806–1856), Konstantin Aksakov, and especially of Apollon Grigor'ev (1822–1864). On the other hand, it is also true that some of the most representative members did not elaborate on their attitude toward Goethe, if they had formed one at all. Thus, Aleksei Khomiakov, generally regarded as the originator of the movement and a father figure among the Slavophiles, seems to have bypassed Goethe. In his collected works I found nothing that could be considered revealing of this Russian's view of the German poet.[137] The justly famous voluminous *Recollections*[138] of that other important Slavophile, the movement's most articulate and charming chronicler, Sergei Timofeevich Aksakov (1791–1859), contains no references to Goethe, even though frequent mention is made of the dramatist August von Kotzebue, popular at the time, as well as of various second-rate French and English writers. There is also a lengthy reminiscence on a thwarted performance of Schiller's *Die Räuber*, which had been planned, elaborately prepared, and rehearsed by the students of Kiev University only to be called off at the last moment because of an official *ukaz* forbidding the performance.[139] But not a word on Goethe!

Sergei Timofeevich's son, Konstantin, demonstrated his interest for Goethe less by interpretative statements and critical comments[140] than by a considerable number of translations of Goethe's poems. His choice of poems indicates a commendable acquaintance with the vast range of Goethe's lyrics. That choice seems to have been influenced by such Russian Romantic predecessors as Zhukovski and Venevitinov and predominantly by Nikolai V. Stankevich, to whose Circle young Konstantin belonged in the years 1838–1840. Dmitri Chizhevski has aptly characterized his spiritual orientation in the formative years of his life:

From the very beginning he was not a Westler [Westerner]. He resents the criticism that other members of the [Stankevich] Circle leveled against Russia. And yet he is the enthusiastic worshiper of German culture; in the history of the Russian Goethe—and the Schiller cult—he occupies an important position. He is also active as a translator of Goethe and Schiller. His mood around 1840 is that of a Romantic enthusiast, and this at a time when such enthusiasm was beginning to fade among the friends of Stankevich.[141]

Konstantin Aksakov published his translations of Goethe's and Schiller's poetry in such leading periodicals as the *Moscow Observer* (*Moskovski Nabliudatel'*, 1838) and the *Notes of the Fatherland* (*Otechestvennye Zapiski*, 1839) and in the Slavophile organ the *Moskvitianin* (*The Moscower*, 1840). Among his eighteen renderings of Goethe lyrics,[142] I found the perennial favorites "Der Sänger," "Der Fischer," "Der Gott und die Bajadere," the first twelve strophes of "Die Braut von Korinth," and four excerpts from *Faust*, two of which had been translated by Venevitinov and Tiutchev ("Vor dem Tor" and the song of the three archangels from the "Prologue in Heaven"). But Aksakov by no means limited his selection to the Romantics' choice. His renderings of "Auf Kieseln im Bache . . ." and of the "Morgenklagen"[143] were welcomed by Belinski as an overwhelming revelation of a "whole new world of healthy, normal poetry" far removed from Schiller's "abstract idealism erected on thin air."[144] Belinski also admired Aksakov's translations of "Auf dem See," "Neue Liebe, neues Leben," "Meeres Stille," and its ebullient counterpiece "Glückliche Fahrt," as well as "Der Besuch" and the fourteenth Roman Elegy, "Zünde mir Licht an, Knabe!" all of which were to Belinski examples of that "healthy, normal poetry" which captures the human spirit in its ever-changing moods of gaiety and sadness, of a robust, sensuous passion, and of playful love, of the "joys of changing bliss" (die Freuden der wechselnden Lust).

At first contact, Belinski found Aksakov's translations "more than good—superb!"[145] Soon, however, he changed his mind. Scarcely half a year later he wrote this sharply critical reaction in a letter to his friend Botkin: "For the sake of Allah—what makes you think Aksakov's [translations] are really good and not really bad? Can this be Goethe? What makes him [Aksakov] better than, say, Semën Egorovich Raich?"[146]

Such impulsive changes of judgment were, as we know, characteristic for the "furious Vissarion." I would not follow him into either extreme of praise or denigration. Aksakov's renderings I find less than "superb" but a definite improvement over Zhukovski's sentimentalizing and often unnecessarily verbose versions. To single out one typical example for comparison, Aksakov's rendering of "Neue Liebe, neues Leben." Aksakov's version conveys the basic mood of Goethe's original with much greater felicity than

Zhukovski's version, which changes the buoyant gaiety, the touch of irony, even the roguishness of Goethe's verses to an elegiac plaint of sweet torments ending on a note of languor and resignation. Aksakov, in contrast, is able to recapture Goethe's youthful élan, that spirit of resistance to the enthrallment of love: "What has happened to me? Am I still myself? / Oh, love, let me free!" are (in prose paraphrase) the last lines of Aksakov's version,[147] rendering Goethe's "Die Veränderung, ach wie gross! / Liebe! Liebe! lass mich los!" Certainly an improvement over Zhukovski, who had his hero exclaim, "I want to love. Evidently, my dear heart, it must be thus!"[148] changing spirited resistance to an abject surrender of the heart to hopeless love.

Aksakov does lack the great poet's power of imagination and that originality of expression that mark the translations of a Venevitinov or a Tiutchev, but this very lack makes Aksakov a more faithful servant of Goethe's genius. With him we enter a new phase in the history of Russian Goethe translations. Together with Afanasi Fet, Apollon Grigor'ev, and Apollon Maikov, Aksakov strove for the closest possible rendering of the rhyme and rhythm and of all the formal elements of Goethe's poetry while conveying its thought and mood unimpaired by authorial intrusions. There is unquestionably in Aksakov's translations a loss of verve and originality; on the other hand, there is a definite gain in control and literalness in faithful approximation to the original.

It is surprising that Aksakov's preoccupation with Goethe's creations failed to produce any significant interpretative statements. Such references to Goethe as are scattered through Aksakov's essayistic writings[149] fail to define his view of Goethe. In contrast, Aksakov's friend and fellow Slavophile, Ivan Vasil'evich Kireievski, who left no translations of Goethe and whose interest in Goethe seems to have been less intense and lasting, did develop and articulate a characteristic attitude toward the German poet.

As a young man, Kireievski, like Aksakov, had been close to the Stankevich Circle. Moreover, he had been an intimate friend of those two arch-Romantics, Vasili Zhukovski and Nikolai Matveevich Rozhalin, the "Russian Werther."[150] Inescapably he fell under the spell of their adulation and idealization of Goethe the "Olympian." With them he extolled Goethe's works as "the crowning wreath of modern poetry."[151] In a review of Vronchenko's *Faust* translation, which Kireievski wrote some twenty years later (1845), one can still hear the echo of this youthful adulation. Kireievski still marvels at "how much life there is caught up" in Goethe's work, how many genres and poetical modes are embraced "by this creation of genius: *Faust* is part novel, part tragedy, part allegory, part truth, part idea, part dream, part music! Least of all it is a theatrical spectacle."[152]

"Least of all a theatrical spectacle!" Kireievski recalls how one had doubted the effectiveness of *Faust* on the stage. "Everyone thought that *Faust* would be killed by a stage performance, and everyone was mistaken." When Ludwig Tieck put it on the Dresden stage, the piece proved its great power. Kireievski had attended the memorable performance (in 1829) and had come away "greatly surprised to find that its effect actually enhanced the overwhelming impression repeated readings of the play had made on me." [153] On careful consideration, he came to attribute this surprising stage effect of Goethe's lyrical drama not only to the play's exquisite form and profound content but, more important, to its timeliness. He sees in this *timeliness* of Goethe's masterpiece also the chief reason for "the enormous, amazing influence of *Faust* on European literature, an influence that could not possibly be explained by the work's poetic and philosophical worth alone." [154] It was Goethe's uncanny ability to express the spirit of the times, the *Zeitgeist* that produced that worldwide effect: "*Faust*—that *is* the nineteenth century at the moment of its birth. *Faust* is as German as *Candide* is French, as Hamlet is English, and as *Don Juan* is Hispano-Italian." According to Kireievski, "this work could generate its all-human significance precisely because of its thoroughly German character and because it had been Germany that played so important a role in that hour of European life. Germany, as the representative of abstract thought, had roused the West to battle, awakening it to a turbulent, many-voiced life which demanded harmonizing." [155]

Kireievski is amazed at *Faust*'s effectiveness even in a translation such as Vronchenko's so markedly lacking in "poetic fidelity." He and his friends had approached that rendering with many doubts and reservations.

We thought: *Faust* without the poetry of its language would be like a beautiful maiden without the bloom of youth; we began reading in that prejudiced frame of mind. The first pages proved indeed unbearable; almost every word, recalling the original, insulted our memory the more outrageously. But as we read on, what happened? Having perused several scenes, we found it impossible to tear ourselves from the book. The inner poetry of *Faust* had completely captivated our imagination. [156]

One of the very few voices raised in defense of the Second Part of *Faust* is Kireievski's. Shevyrëv had extolled the "Helena act," that magnificent Classic-Romantic phantasmagoria, the central message of which the Russian had grasped to the satisfaction of Goethe himself, [157] but that had been in the heyday of the Romanticists' adulation of Goethe, in 1827. Since then the Second Part, with its supposedly obscure allegory, had become the *bête noire* of Russian critics. Young Chernyshevski had defended it in his youthful admiration of everything from the pen of Goethe but soon joined the chorus of critical voices. Even Ivan Turgenev, this great Goethe enthusiast among the Westerners, had many a reservation about this part. [158] Thus Kireievski stands virtually alone in his defense of Goethe's masterpiece against Vronchenko. He takes him to task for not having known Shevyrëv's famous interpretation and high evaluation of the Helena act. There he could have found a perceptive critical appraisal of Goethe's allegory. Kireievski finds Vronchenko's failing all the more startling since he had properly recognized the symbolic significance of the Faust figure as a representative of modern man in Part One of the drama. How, he asks, could Vronchenko have missed so completely the symbolic import of Part Two? How could he find in it nothing but "an unsuccessful attempt at autobiography," nothing but a "nebulous self-portrait of Goethe"?[159]

Kireievski is quite ready to admit the importance of Vronchenko's discovery of autobiographical elements in both parts of the drama. This discovery he finds "interesting and instructive, both psychologically and aesthetically." But to limit one's analysis to this aspect of the work was to misunderstand and misrepresent its full significance. Vronchenko had misread Goethe's central intention to symbolize in the lofty allegory of Part Two "the all-human spirit or, at the very least, the spirit of our times." Kireievski extends this high praise of allegory in *Faust* to embrace all Goethe's poetry. For him "Goethe's poetry—and quite especially his allegorical poetry—does not represent the recording of some chance happenings devoid of inner meaning." It is "the poetic record of man's spirit in our time, in all of human history."[160] This insistence on the "all-human significance" of Goethe's allegory is rare in Russian Goethe criticism. We will find it again only with the Pure Poets and the Symbolists.

Impressive as these positive evaluations are, they cannot be considered basic for Kireievski's attitude toward Goethe. As he developed beyond his Romantic beginnings, as his philosophy crystallized and he became one of the chief spokesmen of the Slavophiles, his view of Goethe became critical and all but hostile. This critical view was basically determined by his and his fellow Slavophiles' deep-rooted suspicion of the pernicious development of European culture. Goethe was now seen by Kireievski as a victim of as well as a contributor to that development, which in essence Kireievski traced to the "ultimate triumph of formal, naked reason over faith and tradition. . . . This naked reason recognized nothing above and outside itself and appeared in two forms characteristic of it: in the form of formal abstraction and in the form of abstract sensualism."[161]

Goethe's spirit, as reflected in his life and work, was representative of these two pernicious influences. Kireievski was sure he had detected in Goethe's character a debilitating rootlessness, a lack of firmness and constancy. Goethe, "this Talleyrand of literature," as Kireievski called him with doubtful flattery, "changed his concepts of beauty as readily as Talleyrand changed his allegiance to rulers."[162] Unable to resist the disastrous trend of the times, Goethe shared the fate of the artist and of art in the "rotting West." [163] "The arts . . . were possible in Europe as a vital, necessary element of its culture only so long as rationalism, dominant in its thought and life, had not reached the extreme in its development. Now that this had happened," Kireievski sees art degraded to "theatrical decorations, unable to deceive the inner eye of the observer who accepts it forthwith as an artificial lie, amusing him in his leisure hours. Were it to disappear, his life could not lose anything essential." [164]

This cultural disintegration had followed immediately on a period of extraordinary florescence. "The alienation of art from life had been preceded by a general striving toward art." [165] In that period, Goethe had been the foremost genius leading the arts to their climactic development. In his mature works the ideal combination of "imagination with realism, of correctness of form with the freedom of content, of art's plasticity with the depth of nature, in a word . . . *the synthesis of Classicism with . . . Romanticism* had been achieved." [166] But being the greatest artist of the epoch, Goethe was also "the *last* artist of Europe . . . who had expressed the death of art with the Second Part of his *Faust*." [167] The times of great art had passed, and with it Goethe's influence as its foremost representative: "Ten years ago [in the 1830s], Goethe and Walter Scott were the only models for all to imitate; they were the ideal expression of all those qualities the European public demanded of its writers. But now the great majority of readers search for something else, . . . for the kind of writing the enjoyment of which is incompatible with predilection for a Goethe or a Walter Scott." [168]

Kireievski finds the reason for this far-reaching change "in the fact that beauty of form . . . has become a secondary virtue even in poetry and that the masses' foremost demand is that *all writing*, including lyric poetry, be attuned to the current moment." [169] An unnatural hyper-refinement in style, together with a tasteless commonness of thought and generally the ugliness of the talents who now rule in the most enlightened literary circles," are positive proof for him "that the tastes characteristic of our times demand something new, which is lacking in the earlier writers [i.e., in Goethe, Schiller, and Scott] and for which there has not yet appeared a true poet." [170]

But it is not only the decline of taste and the alienation of art from life that have caused the eclipse of Goethe's preeminence as a model and a guide. There is a deeper reason. Kireievski is convinced that the times for *imitation* are irretrievably gone. The present demands complete independence of spirit, a totally indigenous art. "Now is no longer the time when one could be a follower of Voltaire or of Jean Jacques [Rousseau], an imitator of Jean Paul or of Schelling, of Byron or of Goethe. . . . Each one of us must now fashion his own manner of thinking. If one fails to fashion one's own world view out of the totality of one's life experience, then one will forever be left with nothing but bookish phrases." [171] The Slavophile Kireievski now sounds the insistent warning not to submit to alien influences but instead to draw on indigenous spiritual resources. "There is," he argues, "no reason to doubt that the Russian mind can comprehend Hegel and Goethe better than the French or the English. . . . Once we turn away from the basic beliefs and convictions of our people, there are no special blocks or hindrances to our comprehending German philosophy or its literature. . . . We can then freely share in all opinions, acquire all systems, sympathize with all interests, accept all convictions." But, he warns,

Once we subject ourselves in this manner to the influences of foreign literature, we will no longer be able to influence *them* with our pale reflections of their creations and, what is more, we will not even be able to influence *our own literary culture*, dependent as we will be on the overwhelming influences from abroad. And finally, we will be unable to guide the education of our native folk, because between them and us there will no longer be any intellectual ties, no emotional rapport, no common language. [172]

For all these reasons, basic to the Slavophile world view, Kireievski distanced himself from Goethe. Like Belinski before him, he dismissed Goethe as a "poet of the past." But more than that, the Slavophile Kireievski shuns Goethe as an alien and therefore a potentially dangerous influence destructive for Kireievski's personal development as well as for the indigenous growth of his native country. The conservative Kireievski's reasons for dismissing Goethe were basically different from those of Belinski the progressive Democrat, yet the resultant attitude toward the German poet is strikingly similar. For Kireievski, as for Belinski, Goethe ceases to be a guide and a model, an inspiring poet with a message for his native land. Goethe's figure is still visible, but it is receding into a past that is rapidly losing all relevance both for the progressive and for the conservative wing of Russia's intelligentsia, for the Radical Democrats as well as for the Slavophiles.

Of all the poet-critics close to the Slavophiles, it was Apollon Aleksandrovich Grigor'ev who had the most complex, even ambiguous, view of Goethe. Educated in the Romantic atmosphere of the 1830s, he came to share fully in the idealization of Goethe. In retrospect, Grigor'ev recalls how in those early years "only Goethe, in his majestic Olympian calm, had been raised to an idol, while all the other poets had been looked down on and neglected." [173] "That young generation had talked endlessly about the eternal sun of the spirit . . . and in the company of the great Goethe had soared off *ins Unendliche* to enter the life *des absoluten Geistes*." [174] Grigor'ev's friend Afanasi Fet has given us a vivid account in his autobiographical reminiscences (*The Early Years*) of how he had familiarized Apollon with the poetry of Goethe and Schiller and the philosophies of Hegel and Schelling:

I introduced [Grigor'ev] not only to the poet-thinker Schiller but, more important, to the "objective truth," to Goethe. The talented Grigor'ev became at once convinced that serious education without a thorough knowledge of German was impossible and—gifted as he was—immediately took up the study of German authors, turning to me for help with unfamiliar words and idiomatic phrases. After a brief half-year Apollon was rarely in need of my oracular assistance and proceeded forthwith to read independently German philosophical works, beginning with Hegel, whose teachings . . . were the main topic of interest in the extracurricular discussions of the students. I cannot fail to mention these heated debates because their real leader must be considered to have been Apollon Grigor'ev.[175]

In those early years, Goethe had completely captured the student in search of spiritual guidance. In his letters Grigor'ev tells us that he "constantly studied Goethe," that "incomparable poet-philosopher." He began to translate Goethe's poetry and parts of *Wilhelm Meister*. He was quite productive and soon was able to send to the journal *Repertory and Pantheon* (*Repertuar i Panteon*) a "whole cycle of Goethe poems," requesting that they "appear as arranged." To Kraievski, who at the time was editing the *Notes of the Fatherland* (*Otechestvennye Zapiski*), he offered his services as translator of *Wilhelm Meister*, of which he had already completed two books. To make his offer more attractive, he assured the editor that he would "undertake the task . . . without any special demands, for the going rate per page. More I would not want because, in a manner of speaking, this labor would actually be relaxation to me."[176]

Goethe the lyric poet had a special attraction for Grigor'ev. He was to him "the true ideal of the lyricist, without flaw, insofar as anything human can be flawless."[177] In this genre Goethe's "mighty genius, placing its imprint on everything, had expressed itself more fully than in any other." In Goethe's lyrics Grigor'ev hears "the echo of nature and of the human spirit; they respond equally to everything, transforming everything to a pearl of creation." Searching for an explanation of the frequent assertion that Goethe's poetry was difficult to comprehend, Grigor'ev wonders whether it might not be precisely its all-embracing scope that caused this difficulty. He muses: "Perhaps this very comprehensiveness of Goethe in his lyrical creations prevents some readers from experiencing the exquisite pleasure this poet has to offer." But Grigor'ev is certain that "those capable of experiencing this pleasure in any degree whatever will not find the claim paradoxical that [Goethe's] lyrics do contain all the elements, even those of contemporary poetry, and that every one of his followers cultivates, so to speak, only a small fraction of their immeasurable content." He even claims that Goethe in his poetry had reached "the extreme limits of all lyricism. This ultimate poesy has the same actuality and immediacy for us that it had for the contemporaries of the grand old man: there is in this poetry that eternal, imperishable truth of which Goethe speaks." And Grigor'ev quotes his favorite lines from the poem "Vermächtnis" in their original German: "Das Wahre war schon längst gefunden / Hat edle Geisterschaft verbunden / Das alte Wahre, fass es an!" [178]

The range of Grigor'ev's acquaintance wih Goethe's poetry is impressive, especially since it is attested not by theoretical comments alone but also by translations, that show a thorough grasp of plot and theme, empathy into each poem's mood, and a surprising control of its prosody. We find among these renderings such favorites of Russian translators as "Mailied," "Auf dem See," "Erlkönig" and "Der Fischer," "Die Braut von Korinth," and "Der Gott und die Bajadere." But Grigor'ev ranged further. He was also greatly attracted by the philosophical poems of Goethe's old age. His favorite among these was "Das Vermächtnis," which he rendered in a poetic paraphrase remarkable both for its faithfulness to the original and for its subtly unforced assimilation to his own world view. [179]

Grigor'ev justly deserves a place among that small group of Russian translators, alongside Konstantin Aksakov, Fet, Maikov, Viacheslav Ivanov, and a very few others who strove to achieve faithful rendering of a poem's formal elements. He regarded these as organic parts of an artistic creation completely inseparable from its ideational message. In fact, this insistence on the organic fusion of form and content must be regarded as a central canon of Grigor'ev's "organismic criticism" (organicheskaia kritika). He saw in genuine art a living organism "born" of the artist's genius, never a mere construct of abstract reason. According to him, "the creative principle is in its origin an unconscious but firmly rooted feeling, never a mere formula, because theoretical formulas are nothing but 'Schall und Rauch / Umnebelnd Himmelsglut.' " [180]

Much in the manner of Turgenev, Grigor'ev liked to draw on Goethe's works in support of his theories. Thus, he repeatedly compared the "theoretical formulas," those "artificial constructs of cold reason," to Wagner's Homunculus, that product of the laboratory with Mephisto for a godfather. "Ratiocination [rezonerstvo] is an intellectual eunuch, is a product of moral philistinism, is its beloved offspring as laboriously begotten as the Homunculus by Wagner." [181] It is axiomatic with Grigor'ev that "thought must acquire corporeality to be believable" and that, on the other hand, "thought can never gain corporeality if it is artificially produced instead of being born." Driving home his point, he once again invokes the figure of Homunculus, joining it this time with Goethe's figure of Euphorion: "A thought that is mechanically pieced together is akin to Wagner's Homunculus. A thought produced by fortuitous effort, even if it is the offspring of a powerful personality, would still resemble Faust's Euphorion. That, it would seem, is the simplest, basic meaning of these figures in the Second Part of *Faust*." [182]

With such views on art, Grigor'ev found himself in the sharpest possible opposition to the materialistic aesthetics of the Radical Democrats, of Chernyshevski, and, in particular, of Pisarev, who insisted on the preeminence of reason, considered ideational content as all-important, and dismissed formal elements of a work as mere embellishments that obfuscated its intellectual message. Goethe's aestheticism, which Pisarev condemned so stridently as idle self-indulgence in pretty phrase-making, Grigor'ev holds high as the poet's triumphant achievement of a perfect marriage of thought and emotion, of content and form. In Goethe's poem "Auf dem See," "filled with the aromatic breath of Mother Nature's revivifying embrace," the Russian critic finds such an ideal marriage truly achieved: "Granted that this poem stands out [among Goethe's other lyrics] by virtue of the depth, richness, and scope of its thought, yet again its form is inextricably interwoven with its content. That is the reason why this song enters so deeply into our soul, why it satisfies us so completely with that imperturbable bliss of which it is a faithful echo. Never has thought and feeling been lent a more poetic envelopment [obolochka], than in these verses." Grigor'ev finds a comparable symbiosis in Goethe's "Mailied." [183] Whether it be an early Sturm und Drang poem such as "Wanderers Sturmlied" [184] or the ballad "Die Braut von Korinth," typical of Goethe's "classical" period, Grigor'ev traces their power to the same ultimate source, to that perfect, inseparable fusion of form and content. Interpreting the "Sturmlied," he challenges us to remove the form from these half-articulated images and thoughts that seem to rush headlong upon one another in their precipitous dash. "Remove the form, and images and thoughts will at once disappear! It cannot be otherwise. Such lyric inspiration was born of the moment—it is inconceivable without precisely these words, without these very sounds." The powerful impression produced by "Die Braut von Korinth" depends again "quite as much on its form as on its content. The very meter and the choice of every word cooperate in creating a certain kind of nervous emotional state in us." [185]

Despite this insistence on fusion of thought and emotion and of form and content in the perfect poem, Grigor'ev's response to Goethe's poetry and to art in general was predominantly sensuous. He relishes nothing so much as the powerful mood, the inimitable *Stimmung* with which the poet has charged his verses. In the words of Faust, Grigor'ev extols emotion as superior, in poetry at least, to conceptual expression: "Gefühl ist alles; / Name ist Schall und Rauch, / Umnebelnd Himmelsglut." [186] Admitting that a poem such as "Nachtgesang" [187] has nearly nothing to offer by way of action or ideational message, Grigor'ev nevertheless singles it out for special praise as a foremost example of Goethe's greatness as a lyric poet endowed with the magical power to transmute words into bewitching music, to charge his verses with the vitality of imperishable life. He asks, "What is the content of this poem by Goethe? . . . It is simply the sound of a guitar in a summer's night, a musical *roulade*, melodious sounds imbued with an indefinable longing, with a yearning for love. It is, in a word, a *serenade* in which the musical element plays the dominant role. And yet what fullness of life does this poem breathe! How vivifying it is! How wholesome!" Grigor'ev thrills to the "mysterious darkness of Orphic hymns," which he discovers in the "Wanderers Sturmlied," and is exhilarated by its "passionate leaps from thought to thought, illusive as the flight of the eagle in the heights beyond the clouds." He is especially impressed with the "marvelous strophe about Pindar," verses that he experiences as "a headlong dash that leaves you breathless." These verses, "like racing horses at the goal, come to a sudden halt on the final words: Wenn die Räder rasselten Rad an Rad rasch ums Ziel weg, / Hoch flog / Siegdurchglühter / Jünglinge Peitschenknall." This, then, is the manner in which Grigor'ev experiences poetry, with all his senses receptive to its acoustic and visual message. This sensitive apperception of the verses' rhythmic and sound effects enables him to recognize them for what they really are, "not vulgar sound imitations so proudly practiced by the rhetoricians and poets of old," but "an inevitable, inspired form created by the poet's genius." [188]

This predilection for the emotional content of Goethe's poetry did not prevent young Grigor'ev from recognizing and appreciating the immense intellect at work in the German poet's creations. He realized that "the power of genius is always a power that is, in the highest possible degree, a conscious one." [189] In a perceptive discussion of Goethe's Sturm und Drang ballads, Grigor'ev traces their effectiveness specifically to the poet's conscious artistry, to his ability to maintain a distance from his creation, an "ironic attitude" toward the "outworn themes" of popular superstition to which he lent artistic form. He asks us to focus our attention on "Erlkönig" and "Der Fischer," because these ballads demonstrate better than any others Goethe's ironic stance. "In both there is to be noticed a certain irony, despite the liveliness of presentation." In developing the tale of the elf-king, Goethe does not demand of us a willing suspension of disbelief. Rather, "we are intentionally left in a state of doubt: we hear the weeping of the boy and the words of the elf-king, but then the father's and, with it, our own disbelief is aroused. Instead of the elf-king we now see the gray mists, and instead of the elf-king's voice we now hear the rustling of the leaves." "It is this irony of the poet that is the ultimate source of the depth and magic of this brief poem." This same irony produces its magic effect in "Der Fischer." As enlightened readers, we know that it is not the water nymph who lured the fisherman into the depths. We realize that "the watery element had gradually taken on for him the palpable, translucent shape of the nymph, 'had sung to him, had spoken to him' [Sie sprach zu ihm, sie sang zu ihm]." And yet Goethe's magic proves irresistible. While not believing the superstitious tale, intentionally left by the author in that disbelief, we find ourselves involved in the fate of the alluring nymph's half-willing, half-resisting victim. Such is the magical spell of Goethe's conscious, "ironic" artistry.[190]

In 1851, Grigor'ev joined the Slavophile periodical *Moskvitianin* as its co-editor and official critic. Taking his duties seriously, he proceeded to set up "two basic demands" that any critic pledged to Grigor'ev's "organismic criticism" was bound to fulfill. First, he must "study and interpret only the truly *procreated* [rozhdennye], organic works of art; second, he must reject the insincerity and untruth of all that is merely *made* [sdelano], cerebrally constructed."[191] Grigor'ev is very suspicious of all "theoretical systems," considering them ruinous to art. He posits as basic to all truly creative activity a sure "historical sense" (istoricheskoe chuvstvo) by which he means the belief in and love for the established, traditional values, an intuitive grasp of the eternal verities. This historical sense he counterposes as a creative force to the West's corruptive "rage for progress."

"The ideal," to Grigor'ev, "always remains the same, always represents the eternal oneness of the soul [vechnuiu dushevnuiu edinitsu]. He is convinced of the basic truth that at all times, in all nations, . . . the human soul had always expressed the selfsame needs, the selfsame aspirations [with the sole exception of China, his *bête noire*]."[192] The same unerring sense for the eternal truth inspired the geniuses of all nations in all epochs: "One and the same profound faith, one and the same lively feeling for the awe of the beautiful you will find in Shakespeare, in Gogol', in Goethe, and in Pushkin. For Grigor'ev, "the same basic note sounds in the tense pathos of Gogol' and in the even, measured, radiant flow of Goethe's creativity." A mysterious instinct for the eternal norm guides genius in his work,

points out to him the outer limits he may not transgress, . . . and protects him from two evils: slavish copying of life's phenomena [i.e., "naked realism" (golyi realizm)] and fawning idealization. One single thought not fully articulated, and Akaki Akakevich [in Gogol's novella *The Overcoat*] would impress us not as a tragic hero but as a sentimental, whining nobody; just one additional lineament, and Goethe's Mignon would turn into an unnatural even if brilliant Esmeralda [heroine of Victor Hugo's *Hunchback of Notre Dame*].[193]

Goethe had that unfailing sense of the eternal verities; he had grasped the "old truths" and had given them expression with a visionary clarity and force in his

"Vermächtnis," a poetic "legacy" that Grigor'ev eagerly and gratefully accepted. "We believe Goethe when we hear from his lips the motto of his life, the firm, calm word of this youthful ancient." [194] And Grigor'ev quotes once again his favorite lines: "Das Wahre war schon längst gefunden / . . . Das alte Wahre fass es an!"

With this intuitive insight, in the wisdom of his old age, Goethe remained aloof from the turmoil threatening to destroy all traditional values in his native land and in all of western Europe. Grigor'ev wholeheartedly approves of this aloofness: "Goethe was completely right in turning from the picayune, one-sided efforts of contemporary society, motivated as they were by political partisan spirit and not by the eternal spirit of life." Goethe, that "wise seeker after the fundamental and inevitable, had the right to seclude himself in the world of art, to disregard all those hectic, forced, unnatural efforts, those feverish outbursts in which he could easily recognize the total absence of the basic, eternal, essential elements." [195] He knew the only permanent solution to the social ills and personal torments ravaging the decaying West: "The reconciliation with reality which Goethe had in mind . . . is both simpler and loftier. It is a reconciliation in activity, in love-discovering greatness in the minute, in the everyday, and in the commonplace. . . . He had sound encouragement for the striving ones: Kopf und Arm mit heitern Kräften / Überall sind sie zu Haus. . . . But, alas," Grigor'ev realizes, "we are not the kind of people who could achieve such simple and healthy reconciliation." [196] "Not everyone can attain that desired resolution which Goethe has offered in a song of his *Wilhelm Meister*: 'Und dem unbedingten Triebe / Folget Freude, folget Rat; / Und dein Streben, sei's in Liebe, / Und dein Leben sei die Tat!' " [197]

Goethe knew the root evil that was causing the decline and disintegration of Western civilization. "The sage of Weimar in his omniscience" had recognized it in Europe's unbridled individualism, its Icarus-like defiance of tradition and of the laws of nature. This attitude Goethe had found personified in the poet and freedom fighter Byron and had given it artistic embodiment in the figure of Euphorion in the Second Part of *Faust*. Grigor'ev would have us remember "how poetically and at the same time from what superior a point of view Goethe had depicted Byron in his Euphorion," and he quotes the line "Ikarus, Ikarus, Leiden [!] genug" as Goethe's heartfelt lament over the self-destruction of so brilliant a talent. [198]

Grigor'ev considers Goethe's understanding of Byron's eccentric personality to have been far more profound than the generally accepted view of Byron as "the manly fighter against people and against fate, as the gloomy, restless wanderer cursing his native land, as the mysterious Lara, whose soul was as deep as an abyss." Goethe's all-seeing eye had unerringly recognized the impetuous adolescent in Byron bent on self-fulfillment at any price, even at the price of self-destruction. He had exposed Byron, that mighty champion of freedom, the poet of passion and beauty for what he really was, "a youthful, untethered, passionate, and in part irrational power, unrestrainable, a brilliant meteor that crumbled into dust." And, a most telling gesture for Grigor'ev, Goethe had denied Byron the role of a Prometheus, of the wise and beneficent Titan laboring heroically in the cause of mankind. Instead Goethe had portrayed him in the figure of Euphorion, as "a youth who had just outgrown adolescence . . . marked by some sort of blindness in the untethered power of his talent."[199]

Why did Grigor'ev dwell so insistently on these negative features of Goethe's interpretation of Byron's personality? Clearly because he wished to emphasize Goethe's conservative stance. He wanted to enlist Goethe's immense authority in the cause of his own battle against libertine subjectivism, the "rootless progressivism" that he found embodied in the person of Byron. By showing the self-destructiveness inherent in the Euphorion-Byron temperament, Goethe had demonstrated a central thesis of the Slavophile Grigor'ev, who thought he recognized in western Europe another Euphorion, "that brilliant meteor, crumbling into dust," plunging headlong to self-destruction because of its unchecked subjectivism, its "Protestant" spirit, that term taken in its broadest meaning as the spirit of protest against all traditional values and eternal verities.

Undeniably, Grigor'ev did base his interpretation of Goethe's critical attitude toward Byron on solid textual evidence. However, his one-sided emphasis, his evident eagerness to stress Goethe's conservativism by insistently quoting Goethe's conservative statements, all this would seem to betray his basic uneasiness about the true nature of his great ally. He could not but be aware of the enormous complexity of Goethe's personality and of his works, in which conservative traits enjoyed a happy coexistence with markedly progressive, subjective, "Protestant" tendencies. Obviously, Goethe was not only the transcendent seer of those "eternal verities" Grigor'ev so gratefully and eagerly accepted as a precious "legacy." Goethe was also the son of his nation and of his time. Here is the source of Grigor'ev's dilemma: his idol without flaw proved to be flawed indeed, tainted by the "protesting," subjective spirit so repugnant to the Slavophile. Grigor'ev had to admit reluctantly that "Goethe as the representative of individualism in poetry never had been able to free himself, in any of his works, from this subjective point of view,"[200] that "despite his apparent, much eulogized objectivity, Goethe had in fact been one of the most subjective of poets."[201] "No matter how many-faceted his nature, at bottom [Goethe's] is a sanguine personality—he could shed reality like an outer shell, free himself continuously from its influence, establishing ever and again the center solely in himself."[202]

This irrepressible egocentricity introduces for Grigor'ev a false and disturbing note into many of Goethe's works. Though Goethe represents "an all-but-unachievable ideal of the objective lyric-poet," there is in him "a certain surprising artifice, a false note." [203] This false note he detects, for example, in Goethe's portrayal of Egmont, the hero of the historical drama by that name. "Goethe the poet-individualist was unable to suppress his personality in his creation of Egmont; he could not—so to speak—restrain himself from introducing personal and trivial motives into his view of the great national event [the rebellion of the Netherlands against Spain]." [204] In his *Goetz* and his *Faust* Goethe was able, to a degree, to recreate the atmosphere of the German Middle Ages because "Goethe was, after all, a German." But even in these works Goethe's Protestantism prevented him from taking the superstitions of the Catholic world seriously and thus caused him to distort the image of the world of Faust and Goetz. For Grigor'ev "the German Protestant is always evident in the poetic irony characteristic of Goethe's attitude toward the phantasmic realm of medieval superstitions." [205]

Grigor'ev had discovered "poetic irony" in "Erlkönig" and "Der Fischer" and had extolled this irony as the very source of the powerful artistic effect of these ballads. But in striking self-contradiction he can also single out that irony as one of the reasons why Goethe, this modern "subjective" poet, was unable to create a faithful image of bygone ages. He can blame Goethe's ironic temper for producing an artificial sleight of hand instead of a genuine work of art. He censures the poet for not maintaining the illusion of myth in his "Elf-King": "The voice of the elf-king intermingles with the sound of the wind so as to produce confusion in the reader's mind and with it an unartistic effect. One is constantly forced to take the one for the other." [206] Goethe has failed in recreating for us the world of legend and myth.

With this criticism, Grigor'ev denies Goethe the power of ubiquitous empathy ascribed to him by the Romanticists, the poet's Protean identification with the spirit of all the ages. [207] The destructive influence of Goethe's pronounced subjectivity, the Russian critic finds particularly active in his "classical" works. Thus, the "Braut von Korinth" clearly mirrors for Grigor'ev the temperament of Goethe, the *Protestant*, despite Goethe's avowed yearning for the *alte Götter* and his professed hatred of the *Nordens schauerlichen Wahn*. He finds "the hectic tension and the feverish tone" of the poem totally out of keeping with the "sensibilities characteristic of the ancient world." Moreover, the abstract philosophical and historical generalizations, those "intellectual formulae" which Goethe sets up in his ballad, are for Grigor'ev "completely incompatible with the ancients' apperception of the world, which was concrete, naive, and quite incapable of divorcing itself from reality (at least as far as the poets were concerned)." That same faulting subjectivity Grigor'ev finds

in his other favorite, the much-praised ballad "Der Gott und die Bajadere."
Here Goethe had permitted his Spinozistic pantheism to intrude on the Indian
scene, even though "it had little if any kinship with the pantheistic religions
indigenous to India." This intrusion totally destroys for Grigor'ev the ethnic
authenticity of the ballad.[208] Nor does Goethe's "classical" drama *Iphigenie
auf Tauris* escape censure. Grigor'ev puts it down as a work marred by "artistic coldness, as a . . . masterful study but one lacking flesh and blood." [209]

Grigor'ev levels his sharpest and most insistent criticism at Goethe's *Roman Elegies*. He detects in them "a surprising artifice, a hyper-refined plasticity." They represent for him "the Achilles' heel" of the German poet. Here
Goethe tried desperately to recreate the antique spirit and failed dismally. "He
strove, in accordance with a preconceived notion, to recapture the feelings
and ways of classical antiquity. These efforts strike us at times as awkward,
even as antipoetical." [210] Goethe is accused of having misled his fellow poets
into "unnatural efforts" by having raised before them this false model. "With
his *Roman Elegies* and with some few odes à la Pindar in which the artificial
Pindarism is warmed up—*sauf le respect*—only by means of a chaotic disorder, Goethe set up an enticement for other poets to exert unnatural efforts." [211]

Especially the much-quoted verses of the fifth Roman Elegy, in which
Goethe describes himself as tapping out the hexameter rhythms on the back of
his beloved sleeping by his side,[212] meet with Grigor'ev's sarcastic censure:
"They affect us unpleasantly," he argues, "because we see here not a Roman,
much less a Greek, but a modern man, a German to boot, *preoccupied*, me-
thodically and self-consciously, with the business of enjoying himself." [213] Repeatedly, Grigor'ev returns to these verses to point out their unnaturalness and
unintended comicality: "No matter how hard one tries, one cannot imagine,
without bursting into laughter, this antique personage, drumming with his finger the hexameters on the back of his paramour. Involuntarily one asks oneself, What if all this is not for real? What if the very love and those classical
sensibilities had been consciously coaxed into being for art's sake?" [214] And
delivering still another critical barb, Grigor'ev exclaims, "What can be more
prosaic and crude than the basic content of the famous Roman Elegy in which
the poet taps out the hexameter beat on the back of his love! That is not the
naive bliss of antiquity; that is a *philistine* enjoyment, an enjoyment arranged
consciously and according to plan, a kind of enjoyment that repels the spiritual part in man." [215]

I have quoted the last passage despite its repetitiveness because it contains
a key term basic to Grigor'ev's criticism of Goethe, the term "philistine."
Grigor'ev argues that "even the greatest mind in Germany [Goethe] proved
incapable of overcoming and freeing himself of that inborn failing of philistinism," which he finds to be characteristic of all Germans. To be sure,

Goethe could rise above it, but only "when looking through the prism of phil-osophical thought"; in his everyday existence he remained hopelessly caught up in the narrow smugness of his "isolated, little Weimar world." [216]

One reason why Goethe could not free himself from his philistine sur-roundings and why he was unable to conquer philistinism in himself was a lack of humor, which Grigor'ev detects in the overwhelming majority of Goethe's works. It led Goethe into many a grievous error of taste and judgment. It caused him to write "the immoral utopia of his *Wahlverwandtschaften* and in this utopia to *attack* . . . the *sanctity of marriage* instead of merely making fun of the philistine aspects of German married life as our humorists had done when pillorying the marital abuses and abominations of our native land." [217] Grigor'ev defines "humor" (komizm) as the "attitude toward untruth which uses laughter to attack it in the name of a truth firmly believed in by the humorist. Thus, when Gogol' denounces corruption one need not fear that the laughing humorist has anything to do with corruption or with vice; but Goethe, while being hostile toward philistine morality, nonetheless often suc-cumbs to it in his *Wilhelm Meister*." [218]

Following in the footsteps of Lord Jeffrey and young Druzhinin, [219] Grigor'ev discovers in Goethe's *Wilhelm Meister* the *locus classicus* of the German poet's philistinism. He questions the greatness of Meister's idealistic striving: "Is Meister in any way superior to Laertes and Philine?" he asks. "Admittedly, he is more *articulate* than they are (and even that not always); he fantasizes more sweetly than they, that is, *they* simply surrender to all kinds of animal instincts, while *he*, artfully spinning out his fantasies and closing his eyes to reality, is a typical Manilov [a character in Gogol's *Dead Souls*]. Meister is an archphilistine from head to foot." [220]

Having delivered himself of this sharply critical characterization of Wilhelm Meister, Grigor'ev hastens to offer his explanation of why Goethe could not avoid creating an archphilistine in this hero of his "unsuccess-ful comedy [*sic*]" *Wilhelm Meister*. The reason: "German pauperism," the "Deutsche Misere" that Goethe could not escape in a life tied to the petty Duchy of Weimar [221] and that placed its indelible imprint on Goethe's portrayal of a typical German. Meister, being that typical German, thus had to be a philistine. Not only Meister but even Faust, that lofty representative of man-kind, could not escape the taint of philistinism. To be sure, Goethe had his hero "meet death at the moment of creative activity." But what is the true nature of that activity? Is it the stuff of reality? No! Faust's activity is nothing but a figment of his imagination: While the blind old man fancies his workers to be digging canals, laying dry the swamps, gaining fertile land for a free and ever-striving people—in the "reality" of Goethe's drama the minions of Mephisto, the spectral lemures, are digging Faust's grave. Grigor'ev considers

Goethe's effort to save his hero a dismal failure. There simply was no *realistic* escape from the philistine pauperism imprisoning the poet: "Striving to devise some sort of escape for the unsatisfied yet irrepressible strivings of his Faust, the poet plunged in the Second Part of his tragedy into a lifeless symbolism, far removed from reality and alien to poetry." But Grigor'ev would have us consider the circumstances under which the poet was writing. Considering these, we would realize that Goethe could not do otherwise but dream up a metaphysical solution, a transcendental salvation for his hero. "Where could Goethe have led his hero?" he asks.

Into life, into practical, productive activity? But where could these be found? In real life the German Faust is a Wilhelm Meister, because he [Faust-Goethe] cannot laugh at that pitiable reality with the laugh of a humorist. He is too much of a German to do this! So there remained for Goethe nothing but to send his Faust off into the Middle Ages, to unite him there in marriage with a dead Helena, a Helena conjured up by the tricks of magic, a Helena that is but a lifeless statue to us.

Compared with this dilemma, solving the fate of Wilhelm Meister was an easy matter. All Goethe needed to do was create for Meister "a life in muddled hallucinations amid some kind of half-crazy people who talk about everything under the sun in cavalier fashion, carry on lengthy discussions about the loftiest of goals and productive activities, and in the end fail completely in realizing such goals or in actuating such activities." And with biting irony Grigor'ev adds, "A right fine solution, a most straightforward solution indeed!" As he sees it, "life in its practical, realistic aspects as set forth in *Wilhelm Meister* turns out to be a protracted process of progressive banalization amidst the trivia of a philistine existence, these trivia being warmed up and poeticized by the poet's 'immortal, eternally youthful imagination.'" For Grigor'ev, Meister's life "proves to be nothing but a withdrawal into the narrow circle of the 'elect,' as in the *Wanderjahre* and as in the life of the Weimar Zeus," Goethe himself.

In developing his views of Goethe's masterpieces, Grigor'ev seems prepared to relent in his critique of their creator. To him it appears as if "two different persons had written *Faust* and *Meister*. One was an intellectual giant to whom even a Byron looked like a mere child Euphorion; the other was an author who makes his hero a servant to a tiny circle of people who seem to have escaped an insane asylum—and then fails to find anything funny in such a hero." But having paid this halfhearted compliment, Grigor'ev returns to his attack, directing it against Faust's analytical, idealistic, ever-striving bent of mind and thus, by implication, of Goethe's own mind. Faust's "strivings, carried forward by means of relentless analysis, fragmentize all that is mighty and grand into the miniscule and denude the beautiful in a way that causes us to turn from it in disgust. In a word, Faust *is* Germany, and Goethe in him [Faust] *is* a German."

It is almost as if Grigor'ev, in this critique of Faust, was confusing him with Mephisto, who does fragmentize all that is mighty and grand and does denude all that is beautiful. However, such is not the case. Rather, Grigor'ev cannot accept the protesting, progressive Faustian spirit that soars beyond reality into a utopian future. Faust's life appears to him "conditioned and determined by some kind of unattainable future ideal" which has lost all contact with the reality of the here and now and has become rootless, spectral, abstract. Grigor'ev sees an unintended comedy unfolding before his eyes as he observes those Faustian flights of imagination in Goethe's dramatic masterpiece and then compares them with the philistine reality of the tiny Duchy of Weimar, in which Goethe was fated or actually chose to spend most of his long life. And he finds himself forced to this sweepingly damning conclusion: "The comical result of all the limitless strivings of the German spirit is, inescapably, a theoretico-practical philistinism."

It was Grigor'ev's misfortune to fall victim to one of those very "theoretical systems" that he abhorred and denounced as spiritually confining the artist, as blocking his intuitive grasp of the multifaceted vastness and depth of living reality. The "system" of Slavophilism impeded Grigor'ev's ability to do justice to the depth and breadth of Goethe's personality and the full import of his message. It ultimately caused him to reject Goethe as the representative of progressive Western man, as the creator of the dynamic, restless, ever-striving Faust figure. To explain and justify this negative view of Goethe, Grigor'ev hit on a farfetched, unconvincing stratagem: Against all textual evidence and logic, he twisted Goethe's greatest creations, his Meister and his Faust and with them Goethe himself, into parochially German archphilistines, surely a deplorable and indefensible distortion in the image of the poet, whom he basically admired.

The "Pure Poets"

The general stance of these devotees of *l'art pour l'art* has been aptly characterized by Zhirmunski. Singling out as leading members of this group Afanasi Afanasievich Fet (Shenshin) (1820–1892), Aleksei Konstantinovich Tolstoi (1817–1875), and Apollon Nikolaevich Maikov (1821–1897),[222] he stresses their lifelong sympathies with the idealism of Russian Romanticism, with its cult of the "Olympian Goethe." Zhirmunski credits these three in particular with having "preserved [Russia's] ties to the German poetic tradition of the 1830s and 1840s. . . . [They had] raised the aristocratic standard of 'pure art' against the literary activism of the Radical Democrats, taking for their motto Goethe's lines 'Ich singe wie der Vogel singt' . . . ," [223] which had also been the favorites of the Russian Romanticists, the *Liubomudry*. Of course, these were not the only Goethean lines that we find in the writings of the Pure Poets. Like so many Russian writers before them, whether of liberal, radical, or conservative persuasion, they too were quick to quote extensively from the works of the greatest of German poets as the ultimate guarantor of the un- assailable soundness of *their* view of art and the artist. The motto "With Goethe!" inscribed on their banner, they faced with increased confidence their critics on the Radical Left, Dobroliubov, Chernyshevski, Pisarev, and a host of minor opponents.

The Pure Poets, while acknowledging their indebtedness to Roman- ticism, both German and Russian, and acclaiming Tiutchev as their forebear, were less interested in philosophy and more critical of sociopolitical themes in art than their Romantic precursors had been. Afanasi Fet expresses the group's attitude when he turns in disgust from politics and all petty everyday mun- dane concerns. He feels it debasing "to ponder such questions as poetry's rights to citizenship [!] alongside other human activities, its ethical impor- tance, its relevance in a given epoch, and so forth. All these questions [of such burning concern to the radicals on the left as well as the right] are to me a nightmare from which I have freed myself long ago and forever." [224] Moreover, the Pure Poets no longer extol Goethe as the incomparable exemplar of the *Dichter-Denker*, the philosopher-artist, as the Romanticists had done. Instead they see Goethe's greatness precisely in his ability to exclude from his art all "abstract ratiocinations" as well as all concern with "distracting," "sullying" minutia of everyday life. As Botkin, that great chronicler of his times, ob- served, "Goethe was the mighty poet that he was because he did not permit himself to be distracted by his surroundings but kept his gaze firmly fixed on the eternal verities of nature, on the elemental depths of the human soul." [225]

Being predominantly lyrical poets who developed intimately emotional themes, the Pure Poets were naturally attracted to Goethe's "Lieder." Time and again we find in their collected works translations of Goethe's "Mailied," his "Auf dem See," and of course the "Mignonlieder." They are predominantly concerned with rendering with utmost fidelity not so much the ideational con- tent as the emotional and acoustic qualities, the *Stimmung* of Goethe's lyrics. But they are also impressed with Goethe's mastery of form, with the plasticity of his imagery in his ballads ("Erlkönig," "Der Fischer," "Die Braut von Korinth," "Der Gott und die Bajadere"), and achieved outstanding transla- tions of these. To this day Aleksei Tolstoi's rendering of the "Braut von Korinth," for example, stands unsurpassed, having been acclaimed as a master- piece by many of his contemporaries as well as by modern poets, for example, by Ossip Mandelstam, known for his unyielding high standards. [226] Characteristically, Goethe's *Gedankenlyrik*, such as "Grenzen der Menschheit," "Das Göttliche," "Gesang der Geister über den Wassern," "Harzreise im Winter," or the late "Urworte Orphisch," play a lesser role, though they were among the favorites of the *Liubomudry*.

One particularly important contribution to a more comprehensive and balanced view of Goethe must be credited to this group, namely, their successful effort to place Goethe the "classic" poet into sharper focus. As I have pointed out on many an occasion, Russian writers as well as readers had been slow in developing any appreciation whatever for Goethe's "antikisierende Kunst," for his valiant effort to bring the spirit and form of classical antiquity to his native soil, to create what we now call "Weimar Klassik." The reasons for this are not difficult to determine. One need only recall that Russia had failed to participate in the seminal movement of the Renaissance, which revived, in its fashion, for western Europe the immense riches of Greek and Roman cultures. Russia's subsequent contacts with this tradition by way of such intermediaries as Voltaire and d'Alembert, whose works were assidously read by Catherine the Great, remained limited to a thin strata of the "enlightened" intelligentsia. The classicistic efforts of the leading writers of the time, of Aleksandr Sumarokov, Gavriil Derzhavin, and Mikhailo Lomonosov, failed to penetrate deeply into the Russian culture and, while they influenced budding young talents, foremost among them the great Pushkin, were destined to be all but swept away by the rising tide of sentimental Romanticism initiated and nurtured by such influential writers as Aleksandr Radishchev and Nikolai Karamzin. Moreover, it must be remembered that Goethe was introduced to the Russian reading public as a sentimental Romanticist. For a long time he remained for them the author of *The Sorrows of Young Werther*, a novel that they read as still another *Nouvelle Héloise* or a Karamzinian *Poor Liza*. Small wonder that Goethe's turn to a classical form and content in his drama *Iphigenie* or his effort to introduce classicistic style and spirit into the bourgeois setting of *Hermann und Dorothea* surprised his Russian admirers and confused, even repelled, them. This attitude was slow in changing, and when it finally began to give way to one of greater appreciation and understanding, that change was due largely to the efforts of the Pure Poets. Their translations of the *Römische Elegien*, of *Hermann und Dorothea*, of "Die Braut von Korinth," of many of Goethe's "antikisierende Gedichte," for example, "Anakreons Grab" and "Alexis und Dora," introduced in persuasive form this aspect of Goethe's art to Russian readers and prepared the veritable cult of the "classical" Goethe which the Symbolist Viacheslav Ivanov and his enthusiastic followers were to develop.

Of all the Pure Poets it was Afanasi Afansievich Fet who was most deeply rooted in German culture and stood closest to Goethe. As a boy he was introduced by his German mother to the history and literature of her native land. German was literally his first language. In his autobiography, *The Early Years of My Life*, he tells us that in his seventh year his "knowledge of German grammar far outstripped [his] Russian literacy." In *Campe's Book for Children* he read "with pleasure various poems that effortlessly remained fixed in my memory. . . . I delighted in the speech rhythms of the German fairy tales that I would learn by heart, so that of nights, when awake, I would suffer sweet pains trying to translate the German tale into Russian." [227] So Fet's skill as a translator had its roots in his earliest youth. To be sure, the fairy tales of *Campe's Reader* were soon to be superseded by lyrics of Heine, Schiller, and Goethe. Heinrich Heine was the first German poet to kindle his admiration. "No other writer exercised over me so compelling a force as did Heine," Fet recalls, looking back to his early impressionable years. [228] Heine's "force" over him was not to be lasting. As Apollon Grigor'ev, Fet's close friend and astute critic, categorically states, "Not Heine's but Goethe's was the preeminent influence on Fet's poetry; the talented student owes to the great old teacher both the inner worth as well as the outstanding success of his poetry." [229] In fact, it was Fet who had introduced Grigor'ev "not only to the poet-thinker Schiller but, more important, to the poet of 'objective truth,' to Goethe." [230] Those were the early years "when a truly terrifying obsession with Goethe's lyrics in particular" had seized Fet. [231] He had recognized in these "intimately personal creations of Goethe's genius" the inspiration his own predominantly lyrical muse was in need of. The grace, the limpidness, the musicality, the inwardness of the "Lieder" had captivated him. Their clear echo can be heard in some of Fet's best poems. [232] Among Fet's translations, the renderings of such Goethean gems as "Mailied," "Auf dem See," "Die schöne Nacht," "Wanderers Nachtlied," and "Neue Liebe, neues Leben" attest a true congeniality in the unforced way they recapture the *Stimmung*, the subtle emotional nuances, the vigor and verve, the rhythms and meters, even some characteristic syntactical details of the originals. [233] Reading them, one cannot help but be impressed by how far Fet had outstripped the best efforts of even such eminently gifted predecessors as Zhukovski, Venevitinov, and Rozhalin. To the Russian ear, at home in German as well, there is here all but total consonance of Fet's voice with Goethe's, of the German original with its Russian rendering.

Next to the "Lieder," Fet's early favorites were the ballads of Goethe's Sturm und Drang period, his "Erlkönig," "Der Sänger," and "Der Fischer." [234] In these he found that "organismic" unity of thought and imagination, of imagery and idea, that he demanded, together with Grigor'ev, of the greatest masterpieces not only of poetry but also of art in general. On "Der Fischer" Fet makes this revealing comment: "Back of the external form of this ballad there is a cosmic feeling, the alluring element, and at the bottom of this feel-

ing the thought of the irresistible, mysterious force enticing man into an unknown world." Thus there is here for Fet "the image followed by emotion, and
following the emotion there radiates thought."[235] First the image generating
emotion, which in turn sparks the thought—a sequence in the creative process
typical of the true artist, according to Fet. The primacy of emotion over
thought, of image over abstract idea, is unmistakable in this concept of
true art.*

This concept of the creative process so typical for Fet, and generally for
the Pure Poets, who have also been rightly called "imagists," determines Fet's
attitude toward Goethe's work, especially his *Faust*. Like the writers and critics of the liberal progressive and radical left, Fet too condemns the Second
Part, but, characteristically, for exactly the opposite reasons. The left-wing
critics had found its shortcomings in an excess of mysticism and "dark" allegory, in a signal lack of realism and social consciousness. For them Goethe in
his old age, laboring over the Second Part, had lost all contact with contemporary life and had become mired in obstruse phantasmagoria. Fet, in sharp contrast, decries the Second Part's excessive abstractness and ratiocination and its
tendency to "philosophizing." He exclaims, "Goethe has ruined the Second
Part of his *Faust* by burdening it with philosophy!"[236] According to Fet,
Goethe had surrendered in that Second Part to the "poetry of ideas," had
"broken faith with his intuitive genius"; he had abandoned with "fatal results
the fountainhead of all great creations, the language of music and song."[237]
And in another central pronouncement, Fet once again emphasizes "music
and song" as the hallmark of all great poetry: "All immortal poetic works
from the Prophets to Goethe and Pushkin are basically musical creations,
songs."[238] The Second Part of *Faust* has thus lost its right for him to be included among "immortal poetic works."

Though critical of *Faust*, Fet nevertheless undertook the stupendous task
of translating the entire *opus*[239]—with predictable results: the lyrical, emotionally charged parts, especially of the Gretchen tragedy, he rendered with
great empathy and skill, as he did those passages of the Second Part which by
dint of their "musicality" and exquisite imagery held special appeal for him,
such as, for instance, the song of Ariel and the "Chorus of the Geisterkreis" in
the first act.[240] With the "philosophical" passages, on the other hand, he failed
miserably, often to the point of all but total incomprehensibility of his labored

---

* Yet Fet, in contrast to the majority of Pure Poets, did not eschew Goethe's *Gedankenlyrik*,
as his translations of "Harzreise im Winter" and "Grenzen der Menschheit" attest. According to
Zhirmunski, Fet "learned, in translating these poems, the use of free verse [volnomu stikhu bez
rifmu], which plays such an important role in [Fet's] creations." (Zhirmunski, *Gete v Russkoi
Literature*, p. 444).

rendering. No small part in this failure must be ascribed to Fet's preoccupation with felicity to the original, especially to its rhythm and meter, to "equirhythmicity" (ekviritmichnost), which was to become a veritable fetish of the Symbolists in their translations. Zhirmunski corroborates my general impression of Fet's unequal effort in his usual concise and precise manner: "Fet, being by nature no master of the ideationally precise word but rather a musical improviser, was capable of adequate translation only where the original contained lyrical elements congenial to his own poetry. For this reason he renders the philosophical monologues [in *Faust*], despite all possible formal exactness, at times with extreme awkwardness." [241]

Fet is one of the few Russian poets who, from their early beginnings to the end of their creative lives, drew on classical antiquity for inspiration and held Goethe's classical works in high esteem. Grigor'ev singles out this characteristic of Fet's development: "Fet's is an original talent," he writes, "which was nourished and formed solely [!] under the influence of antique models and, quite especially, under Goethe's influence. . . . The best of [Fet's] classical poems are those that he creates as a talented student of the ancients and of Goethe." [242] And Fet himself singles out the overwhelming impression the works of the "classical" Goethe had on him: "Goethe, with his *Roman Elegies* and his *Hermann und Dorothea*, and generally with his masterful works influenced by Greek and Roman classical poetry, so captivated me that I translated the first canto of *Hermann und Dorothea*." [243]

Indeed, the *Roman Elegies* did leave their impress on Fet's work, most clearly perhaps on the poems he grouped in the section titled "The Ancient World and the Anthological Poems." [244] Here we find the characteristic mood and tone of Goethe's original: jocose, frankly sensuous, capturing the joyous personal involvement in erotic experience, even such details of plot as the author's flight from bookish pedants to the lighthearted enjoyment of companionship with a "dark-eyed" beloved. [245] There is here that vitality and vigor, that glorying in physical beauty, that is so striking in the *Elegies*, conveyed not with heroic pomposity but with the light touch of playfulness and "loving irony," to borrow from Thomas Mann a term especially apt in this context. Even the alternation of descriptive and narrative passages with introspective lyrical ones, and the author's often roughish banter with the beloved in Fet's poems, are strongly reminiscent of the *Elegies*' content and tone, their rhythms and meter. The locale of Fet's poems is not consistently "classical" but often familially native, the Russian milieu quaintly clashing with the invocations of the Greek divinities, Aphrodite, Eros, Psyche, and all. Moreover, there are stanzas in which the Romantic theme of the beauty and enchantment of night, night's magic power of waking the poet in Fet, [246] distances his "antique" poems from Goethe's more consistently "classical" *Elegies*.

Fet's admiration for *Hermann und Dorothea*, that "immortal idyll," strikes one as all but excessive. Fet can actually argue that "no matter who might try to recreate the very spirit of Germany, no one can possibly give us that full and true image of the country that rises before us so vividly as we attentively read Goethe's *Hermann und Dorothea*." And he even maintains that "only through a close study of Goethe's immortal idyll will one grasp the secret ideal of Germany." [247]

Fet translated the epic poem (not only its first canto but the complete work) and was greatly pleased with and proud of his achievement. He read his translation in the home of his friend Fedor Nikolaevich Glinka before a group of *literati*. In his *Memoire* he proudly records the praise of a critic in his audience who claimed close acquaintance with Goethe's work: "I know *Hermann und Dorothea* well," he quotes this critic as saying, "and all the while I was listening to the reading of your translation I thought I was hearing the German text," [248] indeed a fine compliment of which Fet could rightly be proud.

Fet's high regard of Goethe's idyll and satisfaction with his translation are attested on still another occasion. When famine struck his district in the fall and winter of 1867 and 1868, Fet organized a benefit for the starving peasants and chose as his contribution to the program his translation of the first canto of Goethe's poem. He could not think, he tells us, of a more fitting offering than this lofty statement of high courage and unstinting mutual aid in times of dire adversity. Again he could report with great satifaction "a very favorable reception of the reading." [249]

His translation remains to this day the best and most widely read Russian rendering.[250] It is truly remarkable with what natural ease Fet is able to reproduce the narrative tone of the original which holds in such fine balance the traditional "high" epic style and an all-but-realistic manner of speech. Surprisingly rare are the instances where he yields to the pull of the heroic diction made almost obligatory for an epic poem by such influential classical authors as Sumarokov, Lomonosov, and Mikhail Kheraskov, whose patriotic epics *Vladimir* and especially his *Rossiada* earned for him the sobriquet of a "Russian Homer." Faithfully Fet follows his basic rule of translation, a line-for-line rendering of the original. He masters the hexameter with surprisingly few instances of forced or incorrect stress, flaws which, it must be admitted, can also be found in the original. Goethe's metaphors, intentional archaisms, and the countless participials that ever since Voss's translation of the *Iliad* have stood as the standard device of lending "Greekness" to the German text—all these and other features of the original's syntax and style Fet reproduces successfully. Perhaps most surprising is his ability here to render the philosophical content of Goethe's poem without that strain and outright awkwardness we found in his *Faust* translation. One possible explanation is that the conservative Fet must have found Goethe's conservative stance in this idyll extraordinarily congenial.

Congeniality, fancied and real, is the hallmark of Fet's relation to Goethe. Always conscious of Goethe's unique, unapproachable greatness, Fet nevertheless felt a basic kinship with him. He acclaims Goethe as an admired authority figure, as one of the few unquestioned guides in the realm of art: "Schiller, Goethe, and Pushkin understood their calling clearly and sensitively; to them, as to the ultimate authorities, I would send the doubting Thomases," who dared challenge the rightness of Fet's views on art, that "noblest form of existence granted to man." [251]

Goethe's intimate lyrics, the "Lieder," the ballads of his Sturm und Drang period were for Fet, as I have shown, ultimate examples of transrational, intuitive art which in Fet's view was the only form of artistic creation that could delve to "objective truth." Goethe's pantheism held special appeal for him. He embraced it as the ultimate justification of his own aesthetic irrationalism, as he did young Goethe's glorification of the primacy of emotion: "Gefühl ist alles; / Name ist Schall und Rauch, / Umnebelnd Himmelsglut" could well stand as a fit motto for Fet's aesthetics. Ivan Turgenev, a close friend of Fet, took him to task for this lifelong one-sided adulation of "Gefühl," which, after all, was but a passing youthful phase in Goethe's life. In a letter uncommonly brusque and sarcastic for Turgenev, he challenges Fet, invoking Goethe's authority:

By the way, that is an unending quarrel between us. I say that art is so great a task that the whole man, with all his talents, with his mind as well as with his feelings, is hardly equal to it. You, on the other hand, ostracize mind and see in the products of art merely unconscious babble of sleepers. Such a view I must call Slavophilism, for it carries the stamp of that school: "Here everything is black, there everything is white, truth residing exclusively on one side.". . . But here one is forced to say with Goethe (with the clever or with the stupid one—what is your opinion on this?): "Ja! Wenn es wir nur nicht besser wüssten!" [252]

Fet enthusiastically shared Goethe's view of the world as an "open mystery" (ein offenes Geheimnis), making of Goethe all but a mystic *pur sang*: "For such a profound, all-embracing mind as Goethe's all the world represents an *open* mystery, while for the ignorant and shallow everything appears so obvious, so simple, so easy." [253] On Goethe's authority Fet elevates beauty above the good and the true: "Goethe says, 'Das Schöne ist höher als das Gute, das Schöne schliesst das Gute ein.' He could have said with equal justice the very same about truth as well." [254] Clearly, Fet is not above interpreting Goethe's thoughts with an eye to his own convictions and theories, stretching if not actually distorting Goethe's *dicta* so as to corroborate with them tenets of his own and the Pure Poets' fervently preached aesthetics announced by Fet in the following apodictic fashion: "The true artist values only one aspect of objects—beauty." [255]

As another striking example of such "stretching" by Fet may serve his interpretation of Goethe's concept of the "Eternal Feminine" (das Ewig-Weibliche). Fet is speaking of Raphael's adoration of the Mother of Christ: "It is well known that Raphael felt from his very childhood a special pious devotion to the Madonna. It was this pious devotion, burning in the soul of the greatest artists, that has created those ideal images which even today one cannot contemplate without profound emotion." And then Fet sets up a daring equation: "Here we have it," he exclaims, "*das Ewig-Weibliche*, with which Goethe concluded his apperception of the world [*sic*]." [256] This explication, though surely questionable as a commentary on the famous lines with which Goethe concluded his *Faust* and not his "apperception of the world," does serve Fet's purpose admirably. In equating *das Ewig-Weibliche* with Raphael's inspiring vision that enabled him to create ultimate beauty, Fet adroitly places Goethe's imprimature on one of the central tenets of his *Weltanschauung*, the artist's inspired vision as the ultimate ennobling, uplifting power in human existence.

To make, in conclusion, a balanced statement of Goethe's role in Fet's life, it must be emphasized that Goethe was for Fet not only an admired and respected authority figure, not merely an eagerly sought ally in his struggle with the Radical Left, not only a supreme guarantor of the rightness of his views on art and life. He was all this for Fet and more—a lifelong friend and companion whose genius never ceased to astound and delight him. As Fet tells us in his autobiography, "Goethe remained for me throughout my life a source of unending surprise and everlasting enjoyment." [257] Of Fet, as of Turgenev, it can truly be said that he too, in his own way, was a "sworn follower of Goethe," a "zakliatyi Gëteanets."

Next to Fet, it is Aleksei Konstantinovich Tolstoi who, among the Pure Poets, deserves our special attention. Zhirmunski joins Apollon Maikov with Fet and Tolstoi in a triumvirate of "Goetheists," but he devotes only a few lines to Maikov, merely to point out that his "entire development, like Fet's and Tolstoi's, was influenced by Goethe's philosophy," that as a "classicist" Maikov had an "outspoken predilection for the classicist Goethe," and finally, that Maikov's "translations [of Goethe] were not confined to his youth," but that he, again "like Fet and Tolstoi, kept his interest for Goethe's poetry alive in the mature period of his life." Moreover, Maikov did this "at a time (1850–1870) when the basic orientation of Russian bourgeois and revolutionary-democratic literatures no longer paid any attention to the lyrical creations of the German poet." [258] In sharp contrast, D. S. Mirski rates Maikov as the "least indebted to Goethe" of all the Pure Poets or, as he calls them, the "imagists." According to him, Maikov "has left no critical appraisal of the German writer and has translated relatively few of Goethe's poems." [259] I have been able to find only six Goethe items in Maikov's collected works, [260] and no comments on Goethe worth noting.

But to turn to Aleksei Konstantinovich Tolstoi. Like Fet, he was brought up in a very Germanophile atmosphere. His uncle Perovski took the boy to Weimar in 1827 to visit Goethe. Tolstoi recalls having sat on Goethe's knee, having gazed up at his "majestic features," an occasion he never forgot. [261] Like Fet, Tolstoi developed perfect command of German and, again like Fet, came to know the works of Goethe early and well. But here the similarities end. Fet stood in awe and admiration before his idol, but Tolstoi developed a certain dislike for the man, disdain for his Weimar surroundings, and a critical view of many of his works. He translated few of Goethe's poems, his renderings of "Die Braut von Korinth" and "Gott und die Bajadere" [262] receiving acclaim beyond their just deserts.

In his translations, Tolstoi does not aim at "equi-rhythmicity," as Fet had. He strives for "congruity" of his translation with the original "in the total artistic impression." He wants to "transport the reader into the same sphere in which [he] finds himself while reading the original." His translation is "to play on the same sensibilities [lit.: "nerves," "nervy"] as does the original." He would be faithful to the original, but only "up to the point where faithfulness and exactness of rendering do not detract from the *artistic effect*" and adds, significantly, "I do not believe it is necessary to translate *words* and even to render the *meaning*. Rather, it is important to reproduce the *general impression* that the original creates." Tolstoi is certain that, using his method, he was able to capture the mood and very essence of Goethe's "Braut." He even goes so far as to claim that in his translation he had actually improved on the original. "I have," he tells us, "unceremoniously discarded a considerable number of lines in the 'Braut' which I found to be mere 'fillers.' My Russian strophes have gained thereby and have become better than the German." [263] As some fragments indicate, Tolstoi had also tried his hand at a *Faust* translation but failed to persevere in that effort. All that is extant are a few lines from "Walpurgisnacht" and from the description of Arcadia in the third act of Part Two. [264]

In his original writings, poetical and critical, signs of Goethe's influence are relatively few. We find one noteworthy instance in his drama *Don Juan*, particularly in the "Prologue" to that work, [265] which clearly stands under the influence of Goethe's *Faust*. To be sure, God, "der Herr" in Goethe's "Prolog im Himmel," does not appear on Tolstoi's stage, and the biblical archangels are transformed into "celestial spirits," if only for reasons of the ruthless censorship imposed by the Greek Orthodox church in Tolstoi's days. Also, instead of Mephisto it is Satan himself who, as a "dark angel," interrupts with his taunting comments the hosannas of the spirits in praise of God, his everlasting works and his mysterious ways. The rhythm, meter, and tone of Satan's cynical remarks, contrasting so effectively with the pathos of the spirits' incantations, faithfully echo the contrasting voices of the archangels and Mephisto in Goethe's "Prologue." Tolstoi's Satan, quite like Goethe's Mephisto, introduces himself as the "negation of life," as the "spirit of denial, agnosticism, and darkness," and argues, again exactly like Mephisto in his dialogue with Faust, the ubiquity of evil in the divine cosmos and its importance as a progressive force. Tolstoi's Don Juan, even as a fifteen-year-old youth, exhibits Faust's striving toward "some kind of a goal, illusive and lofty." Even Faust's "zwei Seelen" are shared by Don Juan: "His path is twofold and he himself, it seems, it twofold." Juan's soul, like Faust's becomes the prize in a contest between Satan and the "celestial spirits," with the outcome foreordained. The spirits jubilantly announce: "He [Don Juan] will reach the truth! His turbid sight / Has already spied a ray of the divine light!" In keeping with this prophecy, Don Juan's soul, despite his many transgressions, is saved by his deep love for Donna Anna. An "Epilogue" (Don Juan does not himself appear in it) reports his pious death in a monastery. It seems that Tolstoi felt the inconsistency of the epilogue with the plot and spirit of his drama and cut it.* In the final version, his hero dies when touched by the statue of the commandant. More significant, the final version shows a defiant Don Juan who does not see the "divine light," does not pray to God, and thus is doomed to die a despicable "worm": "The Statue: 'For the last time, pray!' Don Juan (irate): 'I will not. . . .' The Statue (touching Don Juan): 'Then perish, Worm!' " Both versions (with or without the "Epilogue") are basically the products of a thoroughly conservative stance and are an outright negation of Goethe's in his *Faust* as a progressive humanist and vanguard artist.

The most revealing source of Tolstoi's attitude toward Goethe are his letters written on his trip to Germany from Weimar, Karlsbad, and Dresden. During his stay at Weimar, his drama *Death of Ivan the Terrible* was given its premiere on January 30, 1868. Proudly he reports to his bride that "the Grand Duke [Karl August] had invited him to dinner . . . and the next morning had paid him a visit at the hotel. Am being compared to Shakespeare and to

---

*While cutting the "Epilogue," Tolstoi retained the "Prologue" despite the advice of his friend B. M. Markevich to drop it as inconsistent with the play. Goethe's "Prologue" may well have prompted the decision. See *Sob. Soch.* 2:666 for Markevich's comment.

Goethe—in a word, a smashing success." [266] Tolstoi credits the high quality of the performance to an excellent German translation of his drama by a Mrs. Pavlova, to its impressive staging, and "to the unusual conscientiousness of the artists who have preserved the Goethean stage tradition . . . During the rehearsal," he admits, "[he] had been deeply moved by the thought that on this stage some sixty years ago Goethe and Schiller had walked. It took my breath away, and tears came to my eyes." [267]

This is one of the rare remarks in his correspondence that indicate admiration, even love, of Goethe. More frequent are the statements that express a critical attitude toward the poet and some of his works. Thus, in reading Müller's study of Goethe, Tolstoi singles out the fact that despite Müller's respect for the famous poet "[Goethe] is not always presented from his attractive side. . . . Goethe, it seems, is constantly astounded at himself and genuflects before his own greatness." And then Tolstoi confesses that he "much prefers the self-respect of Schopenhauer [whom he had met in Dresden]. It seems to me that I could get along with Schopenhauer, but with Goethe—never!" [268] Again, on reading *Eckermann's Conversations with Goethe*, he vents his dislike of the German poet: "I continue to think that I could not possibly long endure life together with Goethe!" It is primarily Goethe's aloofness, his haughtiness, his self-admiration, that repel him. "Goethe did not have a bad opinion of himself, and Eckermann disgusts me with his constant rapture at every word of Goethe. . . . Eckermann to him: 'Excellence,' but Goethe to Eckermann: 'Instructions,'"—the lordly master's orders to his obsequious servant. But then Tolstoi relents so far as to admit that "after all, he [Goethe] is a very great man, and it is very good to read about him and to know what he thought about every single thing." [269]

In another letter, Tolstoi refers to Goethe's "Selige Sehnsucht," one of the most admired poems of the *West-Östliche Divan*, as "one of the most undigestible creations known to me." [270] To his bride he reports a reading of Goethe's one-act play *Die Geschwister* and comments: "Very nice and nothing more, and yet it seems this is—a famous creation." [271] The note of irony is unmistakable. On another occasion Tolstoi prides himself on having "the courage to find *Wilhelm Meister* meaningless and deadly boring." [272] A rereading of *Faust* elicits the comment "At times this thing [*Faust*] is very fine, at times, however, very simpleminded." [273]

While in Weimar, Tolstoi was invited by Ottilie von Goethe who "was very eager to make my acquaintance."

She at once started to talk about my Ivan [his tragedy, *The Death of Ivan the Terrible*] and said that this was "das einzige Stück, welchem Sie die Abwesenheit der Liebe verzeiht und wo Sie es gern vermisst.". . . She is living in Goethe's house, where nothing has been changed. Thus she is breathing the air of a time some fifty years ago:

the selfsame furnishings standing in the very same place, and she herself belonging to that past and speaks much of Goethe. Everything smells of dust, moths, of coffee and old spinster—it's both saddening and yet somehow pleasant. This house was considered in those days to be luxurious, but as a matter of fact it is incomparably more modest than ours in Krasnogorsk. And the plastercast statues are still standing there, and surely Goethe must have been proud of them.[274]

Once again one cannot help but hear a note of condescension toward Ottilie as well as toward Goethe and his surroundings.

We find the most devastatingly sarcastic reaction to Goethe the dramatist in a letter from Dresden, where Tolstoi had attended a performance of *Iphigenie*. As we read this squib, we must be aware that it aims primarily at the less-than-adequate acting and staging of the play. Yet the ironically critical barbs against Goethe's drama cannot be missed. Here is Tolstoi's pasquinade:

Out of the gates of Druza stepped forth Iphigenie. . . . This was Madame Ziegler come from Munich. She began to speak in a pleasant enough mezzo soprano of how bored she was in the Crimea, and she spoke of this so long and so convincingly that I too became inexpressibly bored. . . . Then came a royal adjutant in a beautiful helmet and a ragged bear skin and announced his majesty's order to tell her [Iphigenie] that he wants to marry her. Her reply: Nevermore! Thereupon Winger* strode forth in a coat of mail of Wilhelm the Conquerer and in a tiger skin, which he had tied around his belly and from behind had stuffed with hay—all of which did not help matters. Iphigenie proceeded to explain that for many reasons she could not marry him, among others because she was a descendant of Tantalus. Winger observed that this was not a valid reason. Thereupon Iphigenie began to tell him of all the dirty tricks the Tantalides had perpetrated so that Winger, who was used to butchering all people who came to the Crimea, was horror-struck.

In the second act there came running on stage, supporting each other, a traveling salesman [commis-voyageur—Pylades] and a hairdresser [Orest]; the hands of both were embellished with long, thin watch chains, which did not hinder them in violent gesticulation. The hairdresser was my friend Dettmer [an actor]. With bulging eyes and head thrust forward, he struggled to express his pangs of conscience for having killed his mother. But the traveling salesman, strongly rouged and with mouth askew, assured him that this was of no importance. After that the hairdresser went off somewhere, and Iphigenie took the watch chain off the traveling saleman's hands and started talking with him about the Trojan war. I had already heard of this war and was therefore not at all interested. I thought the entire drama would go on that way but nevertheless decided to stay to the bitter end. To my great surprise, all of a sudden in the third act it got to be really interesting and good, even very good. This was when Iphigenie recognized Orest, and Orest recounted the tale of Pylade's about Clytemnestra and disclosed his true identity. . . . The fourth act and the fifth, in which both prisoners, though condemned, run freely around in the Crimea and even plot a dirty trick on Toas, were once again boring, except for the very end, which was fine.

---

*The name of an actor who was playing the role of Toas.

Madame Ziegler is very beautiful and pleasant and *almost* a good actress, but the drama, hm-hm, is very boring, although cleverly and artistically planned. All this is not motivated [!], and nothing is made of Toas, though on the basis of Goethe's conception much could have been made of him.

Boring, but good, and Iphigenie is pleasing.[275]

From such evidence as this, one could readily conclude that Tolstoi's attitude toward Goethe the man and artist was, to say the least, negative. It was indeed a critical one. For Aleksei Tolstoi, Goethe was not without his flaws, both as a man and as a writer. Moreover, because of his leanings toward Romantic mysticism and the Greek Orthodox church, Tolstoi tends to exaggerate in Goethe's idealistic humanism the religious and mystical elements, thus anticipating a view of the German poet that was to be characteristic of the Symbolists. Zhirmunski points this up in a perceptive pun: "One may say," he writes, "that in Tolstoi's creative interpretation . . . Goethe's entire *Faust* is, as it were, swallowed up by the 'Epilogue in Heaven,' with its mystical symbolism of the Eternal-Feminine." [276]

Despite these critical elements in his attitude toward Goethe and distortions of his message, Tolstoi must be credited with having recognized Goethe's greatness and, more important, with having helped keep alive the interest of the Russian reading public in the German writer, especially with his popular translations of Goethe's ballads. Moreover, he did this at a time when the attacks of such radical materialists as Pisarev and the growing vogue of the French and English realistic social novels were threatening not only Goethe's preeminence as an influence on Russian letters but his very name with oblivion. This threat was very real indeed, considering that such leading authors of the day as Nekrasov, Ostrovski, Garshin, Saltikov-Shchedrin, and Goncharov either opposed or bypassed him and that the foremost left-wing critic of the day, Dobroliubov, consistently practiced on Goethe what the Germans so aptly call "totschweigen." In his voluminous writings I could not find a single meaningful mention of Goethe's name.

A survey of the collected works of the remaining Pure Poets of note— L. Mei (1822–1862), Y. P. Polonski (1819–1898), and A. N. Pleshcheev (1825–1893)—revealed no new facets of the Russian image of Goethe. Yet by keeping some of Goethe's works, especially his lyrics, before the Russian public in popular translations, they did help strengthen the spiritual ties between the Goethe cult of the Romanticists in the 1820s and 1830s and the Goethe renaissance at the end of the century, when the Symbolists brought Goethe back to the center of the Russian literary stage.

In looking back on the turbulent crosscurrents of opinion in the 1860s and 1870s—Chizhevski has called them the great watershed in the development of Russian thought—one is struck by one basic fact: the power of fervently held ideologies to shape and often distort the Russian Goethe image. While the Radical Democrats were hindered by their materialism and the "Consequent Realism" of their aesthetics in properly appreciating Goethe and his works, the Slavophiles as well as the Pure Poets were certainly not helped by their ideological stance in developing and maintaining a fair, comprehensive view of the German poet-thinker. Botkin and Druzhinin, Chernyshevski and Pisarev, Kireievski and Grigor'ev, Fet and Aleskei Tolstoi came to see Goethe through eyes more or less blinkered by ideology. As their "systems" grew more rigid and more sharply defined in the heat of their spirited confrontations, their attitude toward Goethe became more myopic, prejudiced. They all strove, each in his way, to enlist Goethe's authority on their side, while rejecting as dangerously misleading those aspects of his thought and personality which they found incompatible with their fervently held beliefs. None could avoid distorting a feature and stretching a point. Their opinions, often perceptive, more often biased and sometimes downright wrongheaded, were too narrowly focused to give their contemporaries a faithful likeness of the German poet. And yet they must be credited with having introduced to the Russian reading public Goethe the "Classicist" in an appealingly favorable light, thus adding an important new facet to the Russian image of Goethe.

CHAPTER THREE

Fëdor Mikhailovich Dostoevski (1821–1881)

Dostoevski as Goethe's Antipode

Contraposing Dostoevski to Goethe is a favorite approach not only of the comparatists but also of the Slavists, the Germanists, and the belletrists. I give but a few characteristic examples: Karl Nötzel, in his biography of the Russian writer, speaks of the "inner orientation" of the two poets as being fundamentally different, "grundverschieden." According to him, "Dostoevskij erblickt, gleich von Beginn seiner schöpferischen Tätigkeit an, den Kern des Menschheitsdaseins in bedingungsloser Problematik . . . Goethe war völlig beruhigt über das endgültige Schicksal des Menschen." [1] Comparatist Joseph Matl sees in Goethe the starkest antithesis to Dostoevski: "Für Fëdor Dostoewskij stellt Goethe den Antipoden dar. Schon der geistigseelischen Struktur und Dynamik nach. Dostoewskij ist das Gegensätzliche, Antinomische, Disharmonische, chaotisch-dämonisch Abgründige" to Goethe's harmonious, well-balanced, "classical" being.[2] Matl is emphatically seconded by Slavist Zenta Maurina in the following purple passage: "Goethe und Dostoevskij sind die am weitesten von einander entfernten Sterne im Weltall, deren Bahnen einander nie kreuzen. Wie das Unendliche zum Endlichen, wie das Masslose zum Mass, verhält sich Dostoewskijs Kunst zu Goethes. Goethes Welt ist ein klarer Bergsee, in dem sich die hehren Gipfel und kleinen Kieselsteine mit derselben Klarheit spiegeln. Dostoewskijs Kunst ist ein alles mit sich reissender, wildrauschender Wasserfall." [3] And finally, to underscore the questionable generalizations, unsubstantiated exaggerations, and outright distortions this game of contraposing the two writers can lead to, I add two typical quotations from a "study" by Ilja Kostovski entitled *Dostoevski and Goethe: Two Devils—Two Geniuses*:

Goethe strives for integrity, order. Dostoevskiĭ tends towards atomization, chaos. Goethe disciplined himself to harmony. Dostoevskiĭ took pleasure in lack of harmony.

Goethe strives for unity of personality. In Dostoevskiĭ personality disintegrates. Goethe avoided everything volcanic, demonic, Dostoevskiĭ rushes into the demonic domain.

[In Dostoevski] the seething Russian strength . . . broke forth and destroyed utterly the beautiful objective world of Goethe and raised up the empire of the wildest Russian subjectivism. . . . The Russian man came to have vengeance on Goethe with his wild, unbridled subjectivism. . . . [He] threw himself on Goethe's pyramid and destroyed it with the stone blocks of an avalanche.[4]

As for the belletrists, they were the ones who popularized the view of Goethe as antipode to Dostoevski. Some of the foremost writers, among them Franz Werfel, Hermann Hesse, Stefan Zweig, Alfred Döblin, and Jacob Wassermann, created for countless readers the image of Dostoevski as the writer of demonic intensity of emotion and imagination, struck with the "holy" sickness of epilepsy, endowed with a well-nigh superhuman gift of insight into the deepest recesses of human nature, as a "god-seeker," a "holy sinner," an intuitive genius *in extremis* sustained by an unwavering faith beyond reason in Jesus Christ and in the Russian people. And over against this all-but-mythical figure they raised Goethe as a towering symbol of European culture and tradition, a mighty bulwark, stemming with his calm, harmonious, classical personality the onrushing Eastern flood, the Russian chaos seething in Dostoevski's immortal creations.[5]

This approach to the two writers led quite naturally to the assumption that any significant influence of Goethe on Dostoevski was out of the question; this assumption, in turn, inhibited investigation of Dostoevski's attitude toward Goethe, his image of Goethe. One should have remembered that an adversary stance of two poets can quite as likely result in cross-fertilization of ideas. Fritz Strich, in his comprehensive study *Goethe and World Literature*, offers this acute observation:

Influence from a foreign mind may be one of two kinds. It can take the form of one creative spirit being roused to self-knowledge, and stimulated to further creation, by a kindred one; this reinforces his own nature and gives him the courage to be himself. . . . But the influence may be of a totally different kind when it proceeds not from a kindred spirit but from one which is different or even opposite. . . . This influence need not necessarily confirm or arouse, it may transform.[6]

I would go even further and claim that in the case of Dostoevski the antithetical nature of Goethe, in its influence on him, did not "transform" but rather did much to accentuate Dostoevski's contrasting nature and world view, that it served to encourage, even inflame, him in his opposition to Goethe and thus helped him reach heights of genius which produced his greatest works, foremost among them *The Brothers Karamazov*. This great novel, as well as *The Devils* (*Besy*), are in a fundamental way grand *polemics* against Goethe's basic *Weltanschauung*, as I shall try to show.

The degree to which this possibility of an "antithetical" influence was discounted is surprising. Of all the many studies of Dostoevski I have read, few shed any significant light on the question of Dostoevski's attitude toward Goethe or the nature and extent of Goethe's influence on the Russian writer. Few of them pay any attention to the many clear echoes of Goethean themes and characters in Dostoevski's works. It will be my aim to identify and analyze the most important of these.

In contrast to Ivan Turgenev, Dostoevski left us no articles or essays from which to extrapolate his image of Goethe. Yet an examination of Dostoevski's recently available collected letters [7] and of his *Diaries of a Writer* for the years 1873, 1876–1877, 1880, and 1881 has uncovered a considerable number of relevant statements.

As to the specific nature of Goethe's influence on Dostoevski, that is a most illusive problem. Gene Fitzgerald, in a review of N. M. Lary's study *Dostoevsky and Dickens*, has put the matter aptly:

For the literary comparativist Dostoevsky's works are simultaneously a source of delight and despair. To his delight, he can find and identify numerous echoes, parallels and similarities to a great number of European, English, and Russian literary works. But to his despair, he faces a most difficult task of defining and demonstrating concrete literary influences. Any study purporting to examine influences on Dostoevsky's fiction must be based on a methodological approach that distinguishes literary influences from literary parallels and demonstrates influence through stylistic and textual analysis. [8]

This is probably the reason why Zhirmunski dismisses the problem of Goethe's influence on Dostoevski in a mere footnote. Not being *primarily* interested in demonstrating influence through stylistic analysis, he is content with the following summary statement: "In Dostoevski's creative work there has been identified the influence of [Goethe's] Mignon on the image of Nelli (in *The Insulted and the Injured*); the conversations of Ivan Karamazov with the devil are reminiscent of the dialogues of [Goethe's] Faust with Mephistopheles." [9] That is all.

I, on the other hand, being specifically interested in a stylistic and thematic analysis of Dostoevski's works in their relation to Goethe's, will attempt to identify and explicate some of the evident as well as the more illusive echoes of and variations on Goethean themes and personae and with the help of these will try to develop Dostoevski's image of the German writer.

Goethe in Dostoevski's Letters and in the Diary of 1876

On the basis of the definitive edition of Dostoevski's letters, [10] it can now be shown conclusively that references to Goethe are no fewer than references to other European writers, the only exceptions being Friedrich Schiller and Charles Dickens.[11] There can be no doubt that Schiller occupied a very special place in Dostoevski's affections as the lofty idealist and inspiring poet of the "beautiful and the sublime." Moreover, Schiller had been a deeply personal experience to him, being inextricably interwoven with his latently homosexual friendship with Ivan Berezhedski, a fellow student at the Academy of Engineers, and, when that relationship had come to a very "bitter" end, with Ivan Nikolaevich Shidlovski. With Berezhedski he had shared "a fiery enthusiasm for the noble, inspiring figures of Don Carlos, Marquis Posa, and Mortimer."[12] With Shidlovski he had typically "Russian" night-long discussions of "Homer, Shakespeare, Schiller, Hoffmann, of all those we had talked of so much, whom we had read so much!"[13] Dostoevski's infatuation with Schiller at that time had been so intense that—as he confesses to his older brother Mikhael—he had "learned him by heart, had spoken his very language, had dreamed of him. . . . The name of Schiller has become near and dear to me, a magical sound capable of evoking, ever and again, the fondest, most inspiring reveries."[14]

And yet Goethe too attracted young Dostoevski's attention and made a lasting impression on him early in his life, particularly Goethe's "Faust and his short lyrics," as he wrote to Mikhael in a letter with the early date of August 9, 1838.[15] He urged him to translate Goethe's *Reineke Fuchs*. Such a project would, he assured him, produce at a single stroke a resounding literary effect and would bring in money as well.[16] Alas, this was a farfetched hope! How Dostoevski could have expected this transparently masked, bitter political satire to pass the censorship under the iron rule of Nicholas I can be explained only by the young writer's enthusiasm and lack of experience. Soon, however, there followed a more practical suggestion, a "much needed translation" of Goethe's epic poem *Hermann und Dorothea*. They also discussed a rendering of *Wilhelm Meisters Lehrjahre*. As it turned out, none of these projects was ever completed, but their very mention by Dostoevski sheds light on the young writer's readings in Goethe.[17]

Dostoevski seems never to have gone through periods of violent reaction to Goethe. Never embracing his personality or works as he did Schiller's, always keeping a critical distance between himself and the self-proclaimed heathen, that paragon of the "classical," of that "alien Western culture," Dostoevski nevertheless respected Goethe's humane wisdom, and, more than that, he envied Goethe his sure sense of his own worth and position in life, his ability to live life to the full, that "living life" (the "zhivaia zhizn'") which Dostoevski always longed to experience and cherished as his highest ideal. In his *Diary of a Writer* (1876) we find a passage entitled ". . . on the prayer of the great Goethe." Here we read: "The suicide Werther, as he is ending his life, in the last lines written by him, laments that he will never see again the 'splendid constellation of the Great Bear' [!] and bids farewell to it." Dostoevski exclaims, "Oh how this small detail reveals the spirit of young Goethe at the very outset of his career!" and asks, "What was it that made this constellation so dear to Werther?" Dostoevski's revealing answer: "It was the fact that everytime he [Werther] contemplated [the constellation] he realized that he was by no means a mere atom, a nothingness before it, that all this limitless vastness of God's creation was not beyond his thought, not beyond the ideal of beauty held fast in his breast, but that he was the equal of it and kin to the infinity of being. . . ." Dostoevski has Werther exclaim, "Oh mighty spirit, I thank you for the human form you have given me," and he concludes: "Such must have been Goethe's prayer all through his life." [18] Throughout the quotation it is of course not Werther who is speaking [19] but Goethe, a Goethe as envisaged by Dostoevski, a young, vigorous, self-assured Goethe certain of his powers, of his personal worth, of his rightful place in the universe. Sparked by Goethe's life- and self-affirming personality, this is Dostoevski's rapturous encomium to the human being as God's creation, endowed by the Almighty with a sure sense of his inalienable right to his proper place and worth in God's cosmos.

Dostoevski never failed to appreciate Goethe's greatness as man and artist even while he sharply differed with Goethe's world view. He was quick to rise to the defense of Goethe. When a correspondent dares place Victor Hugo on a level with Goethe, Dostoevski rebuffs him in no uncertain terms: "I see," he writes, "that you are still very young, since you place a Victor Hugo on the same plane with Goethe and Shakespeare." [20] And in several letters to parents seeking advice from the famous writer as to the proper education of their children—a common practice in the Russia of those days—he does not fail to include Goethe in the list of authors he considered to be required reading, usually alongside Shakespeare. [21]

These and similar references scattered throughout the correspondence corroborate my impression, gained in an examination of Dostoevski's belles lettres, that Goethe was never altogether forgotten by him, that Goethe's personality, his world view, and certain central themes and characters of his works often rose before Dostoevski as inspirations and even more frequently as a *challenge* that called for spirited rebuttal.

Instances of Goethe's Early Influence

Dostoevski made his literary debut with the highly successful novel *Poor Folk* (1846). Like Goethe's *Werther*, *Poor Folk* is a novel in letters. Its un-heroic hero suffers a fate that—in its basic plot line—is not unlike that of

Werther.[22] As Victor Terras observes, "Like Werther, Devushkin [the unheroic hero] loses his love to a rival and is broken by that blow. Like Werther, he is also humiliated socially. Like Werther, he philosophizes much but lacks the energy to rise against the ills which he observes and which he suffers. He does not commit suicide, but threatens to do so. Of course," Terras continues, "the middle-aged, timid, ignorant Devushkin is in many other respects quite different from the young, fiery, brilliant hero of *Werthers Leiden*." [23] He is indeed, for Devushkin derives in his character as well as in his circumstances—he is a *chinovnik*, a lowly clerk—from Gogol's Akaki Akakievich, that grotesquely "unheroic hero" of the supremely seminal short story *The Overcoat*. *Poor Folk* is Dostoevski's original contribution to the so-called "Natural School," which at that time was in the ascendancy in Russian letters in great part due to Gogol's genius. "Retaining the 'naturalism' of detail and decor associated with the comic tradition of the portrayal of the *chinovnik*, Dostoevski unites it with the tearful strain of Russian sentimentalism that goes back to Karamzin; and this fusion created an original artistic current within the Natural School— the current of sentimental Naturalism." [24] There is in this mode of narrative no surge of lofty thoughts or emotions, of ecstatic passion, of searing longings, of despair leading to suicide, such as we find in Goethe's *Werther*. Dostoevski's tale is told *sotto voce*. To make a comparison from the point of view of German literature, Dostoevski's epistolary novel is far closer in mood and style to Wilhelm Raabe's work, for example, to that author's *Die Chronik der Sperlingsgasse* (1857), than to Goethe's Sturm und Drang novel. Nevertheless, Goethe's work, which as we know was admired by the Russian writer, may well have been one influence among many, if not on the general mood, the atmosphere of Dostoevski's first successful creation, then on its epistolary form and certain episodes of the plot line of his hero's tragic fate.

We find another early instance of Goethean influence in the novella *The Landlady* (1848), with which Dostoevski sought (unsuccessfully) to recoup his sinking fortunes on the literary scene and to satisfy his irrepressible longings for Romanticism which he was never able to fully overcome. This short story has for its hero a "dreamer," Vasili Mikhael Ordynov, whose lofty idealism, otherworldliness, and intense, ceaseless strivings for the achievement of his "system" (a visionary utopia) has been all too farfetchedly compared with those of a Faust. I prefer to accept Ordynov's far less lofty self-characterization as the Sorcerer's Apprentice. At "the sad moment" of the total collapse of his creative powers there comes to Ordynov's mind, rather incongruously, Goethe's famous ballad "Der Zauberlehrling," and he "involuntarily" identifies himself with "that boastful student [!] of the sorcerer who, having stolen the magic word from his teacher, ordered the broom to carry water and all but drowned, having forgotten how to say 'stop.'" [25]

Toward the end of 1859, not long after his release from Siberian incarceration, Dostoevski made the following jotting on a loose piece of paper: "In 1860 to be developed, 1.) Min'ona [Mignon], 2.) Vesenniaia liubov' [Spring Love], 3.) 'Dvoinik' (peredelka) [*The Double*. To be revised] 4.) Zapiski katorzhnika (otryvok) [Notes of a prisoner. A fragment]." [26] The "Mignon" plan was never developed into an independent work, but was fused with others to form the novel *The Injured and Insulted (Unizhennye i Oskorblennye)*. [27]

The heroine of that work, dark-eyed, dark-skinned Nelli—the author emphasizes her "non-Russian" appearance (253)—is generally seen as an offspring from Goethe's Mignon. [28] I agree that in Nelli we do have before us a striking example of Dostoevski's characteristic method of "borrowing." With him such borrowing is never a mechanical montage, but rather a thoroughgoing assimilation of another poet's personae and themes to his own master plan, in content and style, by way of his uniquely personal psychological motivation, by his method of portrayal and plot development. Thus his transformation of Goethe's Mignon is considerably more deep-reaching than her adaptations by Lermontov in his *Taman'* or by Turgenev in his *Asia*. To be sure, Dostoevski's Nelli exhibits much the same instability of character, similar rapid and unpredictable changes of mood, as does Mignon (373, 378, and passim). She too is a poor orphan, surrounded by an aura of dark mystery as to her parentage. [29] In her childlike defenselessness she likewise arouses our sympathy and compassion. But there is in Nelli hardly a trace of Mignon's vitality, vivaciousness, and lovable roguishness. She is a pitifully weak, consumptive child, suffering frequent attacks of epilepsy. And small wonder, for she has been far more deeply injured and insulted by life than Mignon; she has been ruthlessly abandoned by her Mephistophelian father, [30] cruelly maltreated by a malicious, half-insane grandfather, and viciously and obscenely abused by a sadistic, greedy procuress and her lecherous customers.

Dostoevski departs most drastically from Goethe's portrayal in his insistent delving into the pathological psyche of the deeply traumatized Nelli. His first-person narrator senses "something uncanny ripening in her soul. . . . She feels insulted, her wound cannot heal, she tries, as if on purpose, to irritate and exacerbate her wound by her secretiveness, by her lack of trust toward all of us, as if she delighted in her pain, in that *egoism of suffering* . . ." (385–386; italics in the original). We would not find this type of explicit, all-but-Freudian pathology, carried to extreme with obsessive insistence, in Goethe's portrayal of Mignon.

There are, however, obvious echoes from Mignon's life in Nelli's. Thus, Nelli's jealousy of the narrator's love for Natasha is reminiscent of Mignon's jealousy of Wilhelm's flirtation with Philine, and in an epilogue we find Dostoevski's prose rendering of several motives of Mignon's *Italiensehnsucht* in her famous song: the forbidding mountains with their snow and ice and raging waterfalls that Nelli meets on her way to the lovely valleys and lakes of beautiful Italy. *"There"*—and the author italicizes and repeats that key word *"Tam"* (there) in the manner of the haunting "dahin, dahin!" of the song—*there*, as Nelli wistfully recalls, she had spent halcyon days with her mother and her mother's paramour, whose first name just happens to be Genrikh, that is, Heinrich, the first name of Faust (432).

Another scene must be mentioned in this context—the opening scene of the novel, the appearance of the impressive figure of Nelli's grandfather together with his inseparable companion, a sort of alter ego, the ancient dog Azorka. This scene is striking proof of Dostoevski's empathetic reading of Goethe's *Faust* with a special sensitivity for its atmospheric effects, for Dostoevski's description is charged with that poignant atmosphere we find in Goethe's scene of Faust's meeting with the poodle at the end of the *Osterspaziergang* [31] with its aura of magic, mystery, and ominous foreboding. Dostoevski has his narrator describe his intense reaction to the scene, thus providing the opportunity of pointing explicitly to its derivation from Goethe's and specifically to the filiation of the dog Azorka to Goethe's poodle. The narrator had hardly caught sight of the dog when a thought flashed through his mind: "This dog cannot possibly be an ordinary dog. . . . It has, unquestionably, about it something fantastic, something bewitched. This dog is perhaps some kind of a Mephistopheles in the guise of a dog, its fate being linked in some ineluctable way with that of its master" (171). There we have it, explicitly: "des Pudels Kern" is Mephistopheles in Dostoevski's scene as it is in Goethe's. [32]

Having said this much about Goethean echoes in this work, one is well advised to stress that these echoes and thematic parallels, though often obvious enough, are nevertheless at best peripheral to the central plot and message of *The Injured and Insulted*. [33]

Goethe's *Faust* and *The Brothers Karamazov*

Of all Goethe's works, it was *Faust* that made the most profound impression on Dostoevski. There is ample evidence that Dostoevski knew and appreciated both parts of the work, in contrast to many of his fellow Russian writers, who—as we will recall—rejected the Second Part as darkly allegorical or even as downright stupid. [34] All three chief protagonists of the drama—Faust, Mephisto, and Gretchen—had a lasting and productive impact on Dostoevski, contributing significantly to the creation of central characters and to important episodes of two of Dostoevski's masterpieces, *The Brothers Karamazov* and *The Devils*.

Ivan Karamazov has been called a "Russian Faust." [35] He should more properly be called a "Russian *anti*-Faust." I contend that Dostoevski's portrayal of Ivan's tragic fate is a profound *polemic* against Goethe's apotheosis of Faust, against Goethe's glorification of Faust's hubric self-reliance in his "eternal striving." [36] Dostoevski refused to accept Goethe's Faustian "correction" of the first line of the Gospel according to John. One will remember that Goethe had Faust, in his translation of the "holy original" (das heilige Original), substitute "deed" (Tat) for "word" (das Wort) [37] to read "in the beginning was the *deed*." [38] This Faustian glorification of the self-assertive "Tat" is anathema to Dostoevski. He recognizes in it the very root source of the decline of Western civilization, the devil's temptation leading mankind to its doom. It is significant that one of the books that had made the earliest and deepest impression on Dostoevski was the Book of Job. To his wife he wrote: "Am reading the Book of Job and am seized with a veritable paroxysm of rapture. I stop reading and pace the floor by the hour all but weeping. . . . This book, dear Ania, strange to say, is one of the very first to have overwhelmed me. I was at the time almost a child." [39]

Job is, of course, the antithetical figure to Faust. He is the supreme personification of humility, submissive suffering, and boundless faith in God's inscrutable wisdom and justice. Such self-effacing suffering in complete trust in the Almighty is, according to Dostoevski, worthy of God's blessing and ultimate salvation, while Faustian limitless striving and Luciferian, godless pride are doomed to damnation. Katharina Schütz is right when she asserts: "Dostoejewski [machte] das faustische Menschentum verantwortlich . . . für die Zersetzung der westlichen Kultur. Es war für ihn der Ausdruck menschlicher Überheblichkeit, menschlichen Hochmuts, frevlerischen Vertrauens in die eignen, begrenzten Kräfte." [40]

Dostoevski does see in Goethe's Faust *the* personification of this hubric self-reliance, of vaulting arrogance. Faust, in his view, would force the cosmos into his grasp exclusively by means of his intellectual and emotional powers without the divine assistance and blessing from above. He sees Faust as the figure Goethe has drawn in Faust's speeches of proud, Promethean self-assertive disdain of the transcendental:

> FAUST: Der Erdenkreis ist mir genug bekannt.
> Nach drüben ist die Aussicht uns verrant;
> Tor, wer dorthin die Augen blinzelnd richtet,
> Sich über Wolken seinesgleichen dichtet!
> Er stehe fest und sehe hier sich um;
> Dem Tüchtigen ist diese Welt nicht stumm. [41]

This arrogant, self-centered, atheistic Faust figure presents to Dostoevski a supreme challenge. It rouses him to a powerful rebuttal. He delivers this rebuttal with his unique intensity and psychological penetration in the figure of Ivan Karamazov. By means of his inspired portrayal of Ivan's tragic life and collapse in insanity, Dostoevski delivers, he literally "bodies forth" his answer to Goethe's glorification, in an apotheosis, of Faustian, "terrestrial," self-assertive "eternal striving," which the Russian author, a devout Greek Orthod, condemns as an impious, hybric affront to God.

Ivan, like Faust, is "ein Strebender." He too seeks to unriddle the most profound problems of existence: man's relation to fellow men, to the universe, and to God. But—and this is the crucial difference—this striving is experienced by Ivan as an ineluctable curse that leads him to self-destruction not to a Faustian apotheosis. Ivan suffers cruelly from a tension between his irrepressible desire to believe in God and immortality—a desire, according to Dostoevski, indwelling in every human—and his inability to embrace such faith because of a total domination over him by his "Euclidian," [42] "terrestrial" mind. In soul-searing conversations with his brother Alësha he confesses to him: "My mind is Euclidian, terrestrial, and therefore how can I possibly decide about matters that are not of this world. . . . Even if parallel lines were to cross [a 'miracle' against Euclidian 'proof'] and I were actually to witness this crossing and to say that they have crossed, even then I would still not accept it. Such is my very being [sut']." [43] Ivan's "Euclidian," Faustian mind—as Dostoevski sees Faust's atheistic intellect—blocks out the faith his soul craves for. He will not, he cannot, admit God's existence: "I do not accept God, understand this, Alësha. I do not and cannot accept the world as God's creation, I do not and cannot agree to accept it." [44] And yet he knows, to his utter horror, that his denial of God, and of God's creation and of immortality, means the destruction of ethics, of morality: "Once mankind arrives at total denial of God and immortality . . . then, automatically, his entire world view and, most important of all, his entire former ethics will collapse. Man will usurp God's place, will become Man-God, and everything will be permitted," [45] including murder and patricide.

Dostoevski's portrayal of Ivan's terrible fate is the vivid demonstration of this very process. Ivan's morality, the very basis of his existence, is shown as being undermined by his Euclidian-Faustian mind far more profoundly and inexorably than by the pressures of external events, by the impact of milieu. He does not find the inner strength to resist the temptations of selfish impulses, of greed, and of hatred toward his bestial father. In fact, he confesses to Alësha that he "never understood [with his "Euclidian" mind] how one can love one's fellow men." [46] Ultimately, he finds himself incapable of resisting the devilish temptation—abetted by the Mephistophelian Smerdiakov [47]—to conspire, in thought if not in deed, in his father's murder, a self-admitted crime that drives him into insanity.

My linkage of Ivan to Goethe's Faust might well appear fortuitous, even forced, were it not for that central chapter of the novel aptly entitled "Ivan's Nightmare." Here Dostoevski clearly stands under the influence of Goethe's drama. Like Faust in Goethe's work, Ivan is confronted by the devil. Yet here again, Dostoevski's adversary stance is operative, this time against Goethe's basic concept of the Faust-Mephisto confrontation. The entire thrust of Dostoevski's argument in this scene presents the "Russian *anti*-Faust" as being totally in the devil's power. He is, as it were, *inside* Ivan, in total command of Ivan's perturbed mind. There is no hint here of possible escape. In Goethe's presentation of the encounter, two equals face each other and conclude a wager that is foreordained in heaven ("Prolog im Himmel") to be won by Faust. It is precisely this change of *contract* in the medieval chapbook between Faust and Mephisto into a *wager* between them that constitutes the originality and very essence of Goethe's drama, rooted, as it is, not in Catholic Orthodoxy or in the Reformation but in the spirit of the Enlightenment. Goethe's Faust, that self-reliant, modern man, knows himself to be superior to that "arme Teufel." He is convinced that Mephisto will never be able to comprehend, much less satisfy, Faust's yearning for ideal beauty, his lofty ambition to gain suprahuman omniscience, vital contact with nature, total involvement in human existence. Faust is absolutely certain that Mephisto will never put to rest his unquenchable striving. Confidently he challenges Mephisto: "Werd' ich beruhigt je mich auf ein Faulbett legen / So sei es gleich um mich getan. . . . Werd' ich zum Augenblicke sagen: / Verweile doch! du bist so schön! / Dann magst du mich in Fesseln schlagen, / Dann will ich gern zugrunde gehn." [48]

The Faust-Mephisto confrontation develops in Goethe's work on a spacious stage, encompassing the Nordic and the Mediterranean worlds with hellish and celestial vistas. The confrontation between Ivan and the devil takes place in Ivan's mind. Dostoevski offers us one of the most brilliant displays of depth psychology or, more exactly, of depth pathology in world literature. The chief burden of Dostoevski's argument in this scene—and not in this scene alone—is Ivan's excruciating, literally deranging effort to solve the riddle of his conversation partner's discrete being or his existence only as a figment, a hallucination, of Ivan's overwrought psyche hovering on the brink of insanity. Ivan's "Euclidian" mind denies the existence of the Evil One and refuses to accept an irrational, supranatural phenomenon, while Ivan's subconscious, his "soul," yearns for proof of the palpable presence of the devil. [49] Why this yearning? Because such proof of the devil's concrete existence, once established, would offer incontrovertible evidence of the existence of a metaphysical realm, of God's existence, would rekindle faith in Ivan's heart, release him from the fetters of his "terrestrial" mind and vouchsafe him his salvation.

Ivan's ultimate inability to reach this proof, to break the iron bonds of his disbelief in metaphysical Evil and, with it, in the existence of God, is Ivan's most profound tragedy and clearly contributes to his ultimate collapse in insanity. Such is the starkly antithetical "variation" on Goethe's apotheosis of Faust which Dostoevski presents in his masterpiece *The Brothers Karamazov*.

Goethe's Mephisto in Dostoevski's Works

Let us now examine Goethe's Mephisto as he reappears in typical "variations" in Dostoevski's works. He proves to be a challenging figure for Dostoevski, stimulating his imagination and intellect from his early beginnings as a writer to his late works. It is specifically Mephisto's self-characterization in Goethe's drama as "Ein Teil von jener Kraft, / Die stets das Böse will und stets das Gute schafft"[50] that rouses Dostoevski's opposition and sparks his creative urge. In his *Diary for the Year 1876/77*, Dostoevski observes with pointed irony that such a characterization may befit a demonic spirit but that it is totally contradicted by everyday, realistic experience. Quoting Goethe's lines, he exclaims, "Alas! Man could answer to the contrary speaking of himself: I am a part of that whole which eternally wishes, desires, yearns for the good but as the result of his activity produces nothing but evil."[51] In the same year of the diary entry, Dostoevski set about writing a "brief tale," *The Meek One* (*Krotkaia*).[52] This "fantastic tale," as the subtitle ironically announces, is actually a highly realistic rendering of the stream of consciousness of a pawnbroker at the lifeless body of his wife, a suicide. The central thrust of the "tale" is to transpose into *narrative* form the *theoretical* observation of the diary entry.

A pawnbroker with the unmistakably Mephistophelian trait of studied sadism courts a young girl of sixteen who is blond, blue-eyed, naive, and pure—very much a Gretchen type. He courts her according to an "honorable plan" as a "gentleman." "Partly as a joke, partly in mystification," he introduces himself in words that clearly echo those of Goethe's Mephistopheles. "You see," he says to her, "I am a part of that part of the whole that wishes evil but creates the good"[53] and quickly adds: "Please do not think me of such poor taste as to want to hide my true role as pawnbroker by introducing myself as Mephisto. . . . You see, my dear, one can do good in any profession." The macabre irony of this "joke and mystification" is promptly and most drastically revealed. Having overcome the young girl's instinctive fear of the "strange" behavior of her suitor—reminiscent of Gretchen's instinctive fear of Mephisto—the pawnbroker gains her hand in marriage and drives her into suicide. Following his "honorable plan" with "the best of intentions," he succeeds in killing his young wife's budding love for him and in undermining her health. As he sees her wilt, "suddenly the veil falls from his eyes," his Mephistophelian tortures of his wife according to his "honorable plan" cease abruptly, and love flames in his heart for her. But the very excess of his passion, which she cannot honestly reciprocate, drives the "meek one" into suicide. His newfound love no less than his sadistic "honorable plan" carried on with the "best of intentions" produce in the end "nothing but evil." He laments in his bereavement, "Now I realize that I have erred in some way or other, that something has gone very wrong in that plan of mine that had seemed 'clear as the sky.'. . . Paradise was in my soul, and I would have surrounded you [his dead wife] with paradisiac bliss." And yet what had he actually done? "I have tortured her to death, that's what I have done!"

Mephisto appears in another "brief tale," this one in the *Diary of 1873* with the title "Vlas." [54] Vlas is the name of a peasant youth who is tempted by the "village Mephisto" into shooting at the consecrated wafer and thus to commit what to the Russian faithful was the most horrible of sacrileges. As Dostoevski comments, "To besmirch such a sacred object . . . and thus to break with all the world and to destroy oneself for all eternity, . . . the Russian Mephisto could not possibly have thought of anything more dastardly than that." And continuing his revealing commentary, Dostoevski would have us recognize in this "Russian Mephisto" the ultimate personification of perverted evil, a sadist who in cold blood observes the soul torments of his victim "merely from a craving for another's pain and humiliation," a portrayal of Mephisto far more drastic in its unrelieved malevolence than Goethe's. There is still another brief mention of Mephisto in the *Diary for 1876*. Tongue-in-cheek, Dostoevski denies the existence of devils while at the same time crediting them with extraordinary astuteness. They are, he tells us, creating disorder, yet doing it so subtly that they deceive mankind about their ultimate goal, namely, to create a tabula rasa on which to erect their devilish domain (an interesting anticipation, *in nuce*, of the central theme *The Devils*). These devils are led by "some kind of immense evil spirit of terrifying power and of greater intelligence than Mephisto, who had made Goethe famous—according to Yakov Petrovich Polonski." [55] The ironically critical barb against Goethe and Polonski, "the most romantic of the mid-nineteenth-century eclectics," [56] cannot be missed.

The *locus classicus* of Dostoevski's portrayal of the Mephisto figure is that central chapter of *The Brothers Karamazov*, "Ivan's Nightmare." The "Notes" to the novel contain Dostoevski's plan for a conversation of Satan with the archangel Michael and the Lord, "Satana and Mikhael" and "Satana and God," indicative of a scene not unlike Goethe's "Prologue." The conversation was to have been about the meaning of "Logos" ("Slovo") in the Gospel according to John, an echo of Faust's translating that Gospel line in

Goethe's play.[57] Because the plan was discarded, one cannot tell how much of Goethe's argument would have appeared.

In portraying his devil, Dostoevski follows the Russian tradition initiated by Pushkin in his "Scene from Faust" (1825) and developed by Gogol' in "The Night Before Christmas" (1832), by Lermontov in his "Fairy Tale for Children" (1842), and by Turgenev in his narrative poem "Parasha" (1844). Dostoevski's devil has nothing in common with Milton's Satan or Byron's Lucifer nor, outwardly at least, with Goethe's "edlem Junker . . . in rotem, goldverbrämten Kleide, / Das Mäntelchen von starrer Seide, / Die Hahnenfeder auf dem Hut. . . ."[58] Dostoevski's devil is "merely . . . a petty devil, not Satan with 'singed wings.'"[59] He appears to Ivan in the guise of a "prizhival'chik," that is, a Russian aristocrat fallen on hard times who lives on his more fortunate fellow aristocrats' and landowners' estates and pocketbooks, a sponger, a not uncommon, pathetic figure in Dostoevski's Russia. This thoroughly demythicized "contemporary" devil takes issue with Goethe's Mephistopheles by singling out the very lines in Mephisto's self-characterization that sparked Dostoevski's creative imagination more than once. He recalls to Ivan's mind Mephisto's introduction of himself to Faust as one "who intends evil but produces nothing but good. Well, let him have his say," Dostoevski's devil smirkingly remarks, "but as for me, I am his very opposite. I am probably the only being in all nature who loves the truth and wishes nothing but good." He bitterly laments his tragic fate or, more precisely, the loathed duties imposed on him by his "office" and "status in society," which demand that he eschew the good and do "his dirty work . . . destroy thousands that one person may be saved." The total destruction of life, which Goethe's Mephisto would if he but could accomplish gleefully as his deepest desire, his Russian counterpart performs under duress, with "bleeding heart." Clearly, this Russian Mephisto is conceived by Dostoevski, in a sharply ironic vein, as the very antithesis to Goethe's devil, that "Geist, der stets verneint."

The Faust-Mephisto Pair in *The Devils*

Another typically Dostoevskian "variation" on Goethe's Faust-Mephisto pair has been recognized in the chief protagonists of his novel *The Devils*[60] in Nikolai Stavrogin and Pëtr Verkhovenski. Stavrogin is a most complex character,[61] even when compared with the long list of Dostoevski's extraordinarily multifaceted protagonists.

It has been established that an acquaintance of young Dostoevski, a radical revolutionary named Nikolai A. Speshnev, "unquestionably furnished Dostoevski . . . with some of the inspiration for the character of Nikolay Stavrogin."[62] It is equally certain that Dostoevski's conception of the figure of

Stavrogin reaches well beyond the biographical and the topical[63] into the realm of religion, myth, legend, and world literature. Interpreters of the novel are all but unanimous in recognizing in the character of Stavrogin demonic (Mephistophelian) traits, and at least one critic compares him with Lucifer, the fallen angel.[64] The title of the chapter that deals with Stavrogin's mystifying relationship to Maria Timofeevna Lebiadkin refers to him as "the subtle serpent" who tempts Eve into losing paradise for mankind (127ff.). Stepan Verkhovenski attempts to excuse Stavrogin's youthful excesses by comparing them with those of Shakespeare's "young Prince Harry" (36),[65] while his adoring mother sees in him a Hamlet whose fate is all the more deeply tragic in that Stavrogin "never had a faithful Horatio or an Ophelia at his side" (151). He is also likened to Lermontov's Pechorin, the "hero of our time" (84). Pëtr Verkhovenski, in turn, extols him as "Ivan the Tsarevich," as a "born leader" (319).

Into this tapestry of resemblances and associations Dostoevski has woven many a strand from Goethe's *Faust*.[66] There are too many scenic echoes and "verbal signals," too many clearly related themes, to leave room for doubt that Goethe's masterpiece was very much in Dostoevski's mind while writing *The Devils*. A careful reading of the novel reveals Stavrogin's life as a tragic "inversion" of Faust's heaven-bound career. We first meet Goethe's Faust in his study, that "verfluchtes, dumpfes Mauerloch," an old man despairing of his quest for knowledge along traditional lines. At the end of Goethe's work we witness Faust's apotheosis. *Inversely*, Stavrogin begins his life as an idealistic youth buoyed by his Orthodox faith, his love of the Russian people, his belief in "Russia's sacred mission," only to fall into the snares of the Mephistophelian Pëtr Verkhovenski and to end his life by hanging himself in a sordid attic room, a suicide described by Dostoevski in starkly realistic terms.

To my knowledge, it was Viacheslav Ivanov, a foremost Symbolist poet and empathetic reader of Goethe,* who first explicitly identified Stavrogin with Faust, and Pëtr Verkhovenski with Mephistopheles. In his essay "The Basic Myth in *The Devils*" he writes: "Nikolai Stavrogin is the *negating* [otritsatel'nyi] Russian Faust, a negating one because in him the flame of love has been extinguished and with it that eternal striving that saves Faust. The role of Mephisto is played by Pëtr Verkhovenski, who—in all the important moments—rises up behind Stavrogin with all the gestures and all the grimaces of his prototype."[67]

Points of similarity and contrast between Stavrogin, this "*negating* Russian Faust," and Goethe's preponderantly "affirmative," ever-striving hero are

---

*See my discussion of Viacheslav Ivanov's image of Goethe on pp. 190–203, below.

many and significant. Like Faust, Stavrogin stands at center stage, a role assigned him already in an early plan for *The Devils*: "The entire pathos of the
novel is centered in the prince [Stavrogin]. He is the hero. Everything else
moves alongside him, like in a kaleidoscope." [68] The same can be said of
Faust. In him too the "pathos" of the work is "centered." Both Stavrogin and
Faust suffer tragic tensions between the "two souls," the one clinging to the
material world, the other "thrusting from the dust upward to the spheres of
lofty forebears." [69] Stavrogin is, much like Goethe's hero, at once a sensualist
and an idealist with highest aspirations, a "übersinnlicher, sinnlicher Freier,"
as Mephisto so aptly characterizes Faust. [70] And yet there is a most characteristic difference in their complex natures. Dostoevski exaggerates the "bestial
sexuality" of his protagonist to the pathological. In contrast to Goethe's depiction of Faust, he portrays Stavrogin as capable of sexual perversions worthy
of a Marquis de Sade. Though Goethe's Faust does participate in the sexual
orgy of the *Walpurgisnacht*, dancing with the young witch, he never sinks to
the depths into which Stavrogin plunges when he commits the loathsome
abomination of raping a child. [71] At the same time, Dostoevski imbues his hero
with the loftiest idealism. Through the eyes of Shatov we see young Stavrogin
as the apostle of the ideal closest to Dostoevski's heart, as the champion of
"holy Russia" in its mission as savior of mankind. [72]

Stavrogin had converted his friend Shatov from a revolutionary to a devoted patriot, a lofty Slavophile. Then their ways had parted: Shatov left for
America, Stavrogin for St. Petersburg. [73] In that "Western" capital of Russia,
Stavrogin had fallen in with a gang (vataga) of questionable characters with
Pëtr Verkhovenski, that "chief devil," at their head. He had plunged with a
will into a life of debauchery and savage "mockery." For the perverse thrill of
it, he had stolen a month's salary from a starveling of a clerk, had dishonored
women and destroyed their lives, had committed murder by poison, had married a cripple, Maria Timofeevna Lebiadkin, "not merely on a bet after a
drunken party but moved by an irresistible desire to commit an act of supreme
shameless ugliness by taking to his lawful wife the lowliest of creatures." To
crown all this, he rapes a girl of fourteen, innocent Matrësha, then gloats over
her suicide, not lifting a finger to prevent it.

Immediately after her rape, Matrësha heaps blame on herself, insistently
repeating that she "had killed God." But then she turns on Stavrogin. She had
instinctively understood that it had been he who had "killed God" by violating
her. Forever afterward Stavrogin feels compelled to conjure up that dreadful
image of the accusing girl. And every time that image was inextricably linked
with the chilling apparition of a "malevolent being, mocking and 'intelligent,'
in all sorts of shapes and forms yet always one and the same." He could never
be certain "whether this was I or, in truth, the devil!" [74]

Such is the form of Stavrogin's pact with his devil, an outright "inversion" of Faust's wager with Mephisto. This devil, unlike Faust's Mephisto, takes complete possession of his victim. This devil does not only "*wish* evil, he *does* evil." Bishop Tikhon, with whom Stavrogin has a most revealing conversation and who has read Stavrogin's "confession," is "horrified at the intentional transformation of [Stavrogin's] wasted, aimless powers into abominations." In a state of clairvoyance he sees Stavrogin standing at the brink of disaster and fervently pleads with him to humble himself in sincere repentance: "Thus you will put to shame all your pride and the devil [!] within you! You will gain freedom, you will end in triumph." In Tikhon's urgent pleading we recognize once again Dostoevski's firmly held belief in Job's way to grace through humility and unquestioning faith in God's inscrutable justice, a belief that stands in stark contrast to Goethe's celebration of "eternal striving" as man's way to "freedom and ultimate triumph [apotheosis]."

Stavrogin does not find the inner strength to respond positively to Tikhon's pleading to overcome his "Satanic pride," to control the "outbursts of demonic irony." On his return to his hometown after four years in St. Petersburg and Europe, he startles everyone with his changed appearance. There is an aura of demonism about his imposing, handsome, brooding figure. With dark, piercing eyes, a "subtle serpent," he proves irresistible to women, young and old.[75] He is compared to the "devourer of women's hearts [serdtseed]," to Lermontov's Pechorin.[76]

In my section on Lermontov in volume I[77] I demonstrate the Russian poet's dependence, to some degree, on Goethe's Faust figure in his depiction of Pechorin.[78] Faust had the seduction and death of Gretchen on his conscience, Pechorin suffered pangs of remorse over the ruined lives of Bela, Princess Mary, Vera—all of them sisters in suffering to Gretchen. Stavrogin too is tormented, at moments of soul-searching, by the tragic fate of all those innocent victims who, like Gretchen to Faust, had been irresistibly drawn to him: Maria Timofeevna Lebiadkin, Liza Drozdov (Tiushina), Daria Pavlovna, and Shatov's wife.[79] Yet there is an important difference between Pechorin and Stavrogin. Dostoevski's Stavrogin figure stands one further remove from Goethe's Faust. Pechorin shared Faust's intensity of striving (though it proved futile), his *élan vital*. Even after his "fall," Pechorin still felt a "boundless strength in his soul."[80] Stavrogin, after his years of debauchery and mockery, has lost all "strength of soul" and become a cynic incapable of love or of a firm faith in "holy Russia's" mission. As Shatov, in his bitter disillusionment with his former idol, reproaches Stavrogin, "You have become an atheist because you have turned into a snob, a snob of snobs. You have lost the distinction between good and evil because you have lost touch with your own people" (202). As an atheist, Stavrogin has joined company with Goethe's

Faust as *Dostoevski sees that figure*. But for this "*negating* Russian Faust" there is no escape from the devil's grasp, no magic potion of rejuvenation. At the end of his tragically short life, "a man prematurely weary" (150), he plans to return to Switzerland,[81] where he had bought an isolated cottage in a "very gloomy gorge" closed in by glowering mountains (513). In his description of Stavrogin's refuge, Dostoevski makes use of the Russian term "ooshchelie," best translated "mountain gorge," "Bergschlucht." His choice of this term is deliberate. With it he introduces one of the "verbal signals" liberally scattered throughout his texts which are meant to alert us to his use of a literary allusion, in this case quite obviously to Goethe's scene "*Bergschluchten*: Wald, Fels, Einöde," in which Faust's apotheosis is celebrated.

But what a contrast of imagery, atmosphere, and message there is in these two scenes! In Goethe's we feel and see throughout a thrusting upward to ever-loftier spheres; there is joy, jubilation, and ultimate transcendence for the hero, made worthy of it by his eternal striving and the grace of "love from above." [82] In Dostoevski's scene there is but utter gloom, boredom, a blighted life, complete hopelessness. The "Bergschlucht" is confining and confined: "The mountains hem in one's vision and one's thoughts" (513). Stavrogin's flight to it is not an escape to freedom, to salvation. He plans to go there "without any hope, expecting nothing of the place," merely because he "is estranged from Russia more than from any other place" (514). Total alienation is *his* fate.

As his sole companion he chooses Daria Pavlovna—his faithful confidante, a "great and tender heart," blessed with Gretchen's "inner beauty," with *Seelenschönheit*. But Stavrogin warns her not to harbor any hopes of saving him from his blighted existence by "giving me so much love and lavishing on me so much that is beautiful from your beautiful soul." She will be merely an attendant [sidelka] to a broken man with feelings "feeble and petty, too weak to give [him] guidance" (514). Daria's role is not to be Gretchen's. She will not lift this Faust to loftier realms ("zu höheren Sphären"). The "Eternally Feminine" (das Ewig-Weibliche) is powerless to save this "negating Russian Faust," to "draw him heavenward." [83]

And Dostoevski intensifies the hopeless gloom of Stavrogin's fate by denying him even this forlorn refugium. Stavrogin never leaves for his "Bergschlucht." Instead he retreats to "his wing" of his mother's estate, Skvoreshniki, there to commit suicide. Dostoevski records in precise detail Stavrogin's final moments. He has him climb "a long, very narrow and terribly steep wooden ladder" to a dingy attic room "almost under the very roof." Are we perhaps to recognize in this "ascension" Dostoevski's intentionally macabre parody of Faust's apotheosis? In the attic room Stavrogin hangs himself with a "heavily soaped strong, silken cord," having first placed on a table "a suicide note, . . . a hammer, soap, and a spare nail in case of need. . . . Everything pointed to a premeditated act and consciousness up to the last moment. At the autopsy, our medics rejected absolutely and insistently all idea of insanity" (515).

This is Dostoevski's brutally explicit, "realistic" way of emphasizing the inescapable, "logical" fate—recognized as such by the protagonist himself— of the "*negating* Russian Faust" who had abandoned his Orthodox faith and his love of "holy Russia" and its people, had plunged into a "life of mockery and abominations," and thus had concluded his pact with the devil.[84] We have once again before us a typically Dostoevskian "variation" on a central Goethean theme, this time an even more pessimistic "inversion" of Faust's salvation than that portrayed in the tragic fate of Ivan Karamazov.

As I focus now on Pëtr Verkhovenski, the Mephisto of *The Devils*, we will have many other opportunities to observe Nikolai Stavrogin in his role as a "negating Faust," for these two, Pëtr and Nikolai, are at least as inseparable a pair in Dostoevski's novel as Mephisto and Faust are in Goethe's drama. As Ivanov has put it so aptly: "Mephisto [Pëtr] . . . rises up [in all important moments] behind Stavrogin with all the gesturing and all the grimaces of his prototype." This Mephisto had sought out Stavrogin in St. Petersburg, had followed him to Europe, and had been his best man at Stavrogin's fateful marriage to Maria Timofeevna Lebiadkin. He and Stavrogin return together to Moscow and are seen by us—for the first time *in person*—again together, in the salon of Nikolai's mother. There is no hint here that Pëtr, this archdevil, could possibly be a vision, a hallucination of an overwrought mind, as Ivan's devil certainly is. Nor is Pëtr even close to an allegorical figure, as is Mephisto in Goethe's supranaturalistic drama. Pëtr is drawn by Dostoevski with utmost psychological realism. He possesses no magical powers, as does Goethe's Mephisto. And yet there are more than enough "verbal signals" in Dostoevski's description of Pëtr to identify him as a diabolical Mephisto, his diabolism even exceeding in its consistency that of Goethe's counterpart, who tends time and again to depart from his role as "der Geist, der stets verneint" and to identify himself in his demeanor, in tone and gesture, with Faust's speech and manner, as has been persuasively demonstrated by a most perceptive student of Goethe's drama, Kurt May: "Merkwürdig und fragwürdig," he points out as one striking example among others, "ist das mephistophelische Pathos, in dem der verführende Dämon das Geheimnis der Mütter auf Faust überträgt." He asks, "Gehört es zu Mephistos Art, dass er sich erschüttern lassen kann?" and answers, "Nein . . . Mephisto spricht hier die Sprache der religiösen Erschütterung wie mit völliger Auslöschung seines eigenen Wesens."[85]

Dostoevski's introductory description of Pëtr Verkhovenski multiplies physical characteristics that are strikingly serpent-like, Mephistophelian: "He

spoke rapidly and hurriedly. . . . His articulation was remarkably clear—
words poured out of him like small, even grains, carefully selected and always
ready to serve. At first the effect of this was pleasing, but after a while one
began . . . to imagine that the tongue in his mouth had something special
about it, that it was very long and thin, very red, and exceptionally pointed,
with a constantly flickering tip." He has "black, darting eyes," restless movements. He "whirled about the room and seemed to be everywhere at once"
(147). Guile, unfeeling brazenness, and ruthless cynicism are Pëtr's salient
character traits. A "malicious scandalmonger," he at once sets about spread-
ing disorder in the private and public lives of people. He drives the weak,
irresolute governor of the district, the "Russified German" von Lembke, into
a mild case of insanity and gains with fawning guile the blind confidence of
ambitious Mrs. von Lembke, only to inflict on her utter humiliation and disgrace and to drive her into despair and ruin. He treats his father with haughty
condescension, humiliating him.

Pëtr's father, deeply shocked, calls him a "monster" to his face, but then
his conscience stirs uneasily, for he had sorely neglected his son's upbringing
and had sent him off to St. Petersburg to be rid of him. The full realization of
his fateful sins of omission break on him at the moment of approaching death.
In near delirium he sees himself, Pëtr, and Pëtr's fellow conspirators as the
devils in the famous passage of the Gospel according to Luke who enter the
Gadarene swine, cast themselves into the sea, and are drowned. Besides himself, he bemoans his fate: "All these devils," he exclaims, "large and small,
they are we, we, and those . . . and Petrusha and *les autres avec lui* . . . and I
myself perhaps at the head of them, and we shall cast ourselves down, possessed and raving, from the rocks into the sea and we shall all be drowned,
and that is our destined way for that is all we are good for" (499).[86]

Of course, Pëtr does not cast himself down, nor does he drown. Very
purposefully he concentrates his pernicious activity on Stavrogin, fawning
on him guilefully, repeating insistently Mephisto's phrase "I am absolutely at
your service, I am your servant here and now, in every circumstance," this
being another set of those effective "verbal signals" alerting us to Pëtr's
Mephistophelian role (179, 181, 298). He is, quite like Mephisto, the cunning
go-between, the arranger of events with dire consequences. Thus, at Stavrogin's
wedding to Maria Timofeevna he is far more than a passive participant.
Dostoevski subtly hints that his was an important part in instigating the wedding. Gleefully Pëtr reports the macabre scene to the horrified mother of
Stavrogin. One seems to hear Mephisto's malicious laugh: "Hab' ich doch
meine Freude dran!"[87] Moreover, he is the resourceful planner of Stavrogin's
tryst with Liza, which leaves her in complete despair and leads directly to her
brutal murder. In unbearable exasperation the authorial narrator challenges

Pëtr: "It's all your doing, you scoundrel! . . . You helped Stavrogin, you came in the carriage, you helped her [Liza] into it, . . . it was you, you, you!" (384).

In devious ways Pëtr manages the murder of Maria and of her brother Lebiadkin, who block Stavrogin's urgent desire to marry Liza and thus to gain "a chance at a new life" (401, 402). In his murderous plan this Mephisto enlists the help of the jailbird Fedka, who is only too willing to remove the annoying pair for a fee. Stavrogin sees through the diabolical scheme yet cannot extricate himself from this devil's snare because of his uncontrollable desire to be rid of Maria. He rages at Pëtr, "I know you think I want to have my wife murdered too. You think you can tie my hands by this crime and thus surely have me in your power" (320, 322). Pëtr gains his end, the Lebiadkins are murdered, and Stavrogin finds himself a self-confessed accomplice in the crime: "I did not kill and was against it [the murder]," he declares, but he has to admit that he "knew that they would be killed and did not stop the murderers." These words of Stavrogin are a free prose paraphrase of Faust's on the occasion of Baukis and Philemon's murder by Mephisto and his three helpmates ("die drei Gesellen"), words that also were both an attempt at self-justification and at the same time a confession of his guilty involvement in the crime: "Faust: 'Dem unbesonnenen wilden Streich, / Ihm fluch' ich; teilt es unter euch,'" followed by the conscience-stricken self-accusation "Geboten schnell, zu schnell getan!" and again, ". . . mich im Innern, / Verdriesst die ungeduld'ge Tat." [88]

There are other striking similarities between Dostoevski's description of the Lebiadkin murder during the Zarechiia conflagration and Goethe's Philemon-Baukis scene. In both scenes there is arson linked to murder. In both the perpetrators offer flimsy justification of their vile deed, Pëtr Verkhovenski's glib-tongued remonstrances of his innocence echoing, in Dostoevski's rhythmic prose, the staccato stream of Mephisto's and his accomplices' callously lying self-justifications.[89] In both scenes there is a victim whose death had not been planned: in Goethe's, the "Wandrer," who happens to be visiting the old couple; in Dostoevski's, a servant living with the Lebiadkins. Even Mephisto's accomplices—"die Drei"—find their counterparts in the "three scoundrels" by whom the Zarechiia fire had been set.

Clearly, we have here another of those Dostoevskian "borrowings" that reveal the Russian writer as a most receptive, creative reader, a reader of genius who unfailingly selects visual, acoustic, atmospheric, and thematic elements of a scene that can serve most effectively in reinforcing the central thrust of his own narrative—in this instance, the portrayal of Stavrogin-Faust as the half-willing, half-resisting, guilt-ridden, self-confessed accomplice in a dastardly crime, caught in the snares of a lying, scheming, devious devil, Pëtr Verkhovenski.

For his "services," Pëtr expects, Mephisto-like, service in return. To be sure, Stavrogin is to repay not in a transcendental hereafter but here and now as the charismatic leader in Pëtr's "cause." Here Dostoevski succeeds in a masterstroke of tragic irony. It is Pëtr himself who foils his own doggedly pursued plans of enlisting Stavrogin in his revolutionary venture. No matter how much Pëtr fawns, doglike (324), on Stavrogin, he fails to sway him. And not because Stavrogin resists him with a show of resentment or by cogent argument. Stavrogin has simply lost all interest in any "cause," in any purposeful action. Why this? Precisely because of Stavrogin's association with Pëtr's world of "mockery and abominations." This Russian Mephisto is no goad to active striving, as is Goethe's devil—"despite himself." This devil is a corrosive agent who destroys Stavrogin's youthful enthusiasms, his capacity for decisive action, and leaves him a "hollow man." Under his influence, Stavrogin, having lost contact with the Russian people and the Russian soil, has lost all "his gods and, with it, all his aims" (514).

Faust's soul escapes Mephisto (scene: "Grablegung"), Dostoevski's Mephisto blights Stavrogin's soul. "I have tasted the great lewdness," Nikolai confesses, "and have exhausted my strength in it. . . . Everything within me has turned petty and spiritless." This is why he "cannot be companion to them [to Pëtr and his co-conspirators], because I cannot take part in anything" (514).

Thus Pëtr had foiled himself, had been left with a mere husk of a man instead of the hoped-for leader. In this respect he reminds one of Goethe's duped dunce of a devil who had let Faust's soul slip through his fingers: "Ich habe schimpflich missgehandelt, / Ein grosser Aufwandt, schmählich! ist vertan. . . ."[90] All the more striking is Dostoevski's "inversion" of Mephisto's role. His Mephisto does not leave the stage a cheated dunce but stands before us in full triumph, having accomplished his devilish designs of driving Stavrogin into suicide, of murdering Shatov, creating chaos and destruction and setting his country's course to bloody revolution.

We last see Pëtr Verkhovenski in the Moscow railroad station dismissing his most devoted accomplice, Erkel, with truly Mephistophelian deceit and coldness and gleefully accepting an invitation to a game of cards with rich Muscovites in the first-class compartment of an express to St. Petersburg (476–479).

Dostoevski's choice of St. Petersburg as Verkhovenski's escape hatch to the West is highly symbolic. For Dostoevski, St. Petersburg is the unholy city, the realm of the Antichrist on Russian soil. We will remember that St. Petersburg was where Pëtr lured Stavrogin into his snares in a life of "debauchery and mockery." Now, escaping to St. Petersburg, this Russian Mephisto is symbolically escaping to his native realm, returning in full triumph to his hellish domain, where he knows himself to be completely safe from secular as well as from divine retributive justice.

There are no redeeming traits in Dostoevski's portrayal of his Mephisto.

Pëtr Verkhovenski remains to the end an unregenerated "scoundrel," male-factor, cynic, nihilist, a part of that great "power that always wills evil and always does evil," "ein Teil von jener Kraft, / Die stets das Böse will und stets das *Böse* [!] schafft," to quote with one significant change Goethe's famous characterization of Mephisto.

Goethe's Gretchen in Dostoevski's Works

In the "Handwritten Editings" to *The Brothers Karamazov*, we come on one of the infrequent explicit references by Dostoevski to a work of Goethe, to his *Faust*. He writes, "The highest beauty is not external but emanates from *within* [izvnutri]," and continues, "See Goethe. Second Part of *Faust*." [91] He is obviously referring here to the "Hochgebirg" scene (Act IV, Scene I), in which physical beauty and beauty of soul are extolled in verse so rich in imagery and charged with such lyric intensity as even Goethe has rarely if ever surpassed. The glorification of classical beauty of form (personified in Juno, Leda, and Helena) is followed by that inimitable paean to *Seelenschönheit* personified in Gretchen and is cherished by the poet as his everlasting, most precious possession, transcendent and transcending: "Wie Seelenschönheit steigert sich die holde Form, / Löst sich nicht auf, erhebt sich in den Äther hin / Und zieht das Beste meines Innern mit sich fort." [92]

With this glorification of beauty of soul Dostoevski could fully empathize. And small wonder! Had he not glorified *Seelenschönheit*, beauty "from within," early and late, in female as well as in male characters, in his Prince Myshkin, in the "Seraphic Pater" Zosima, in Alësha and in Sonia Marmeladova, to name but the outstanding figures? And it was Goethe's Gretchen who in no small measure served Dostoevski as an ideal and inspiration. This figure and all it stands for he embraced as fervently as he rejected and condemned the figure of Faust and its symbolic import.

In Dostoevski's earliest works we had found Goethe's *Mignon* as a prototype for his heroines. But by the time he turned to his first masterpiece, the novel *Crime and Punishment*, Gretchen had replaced Mignon as model and inspiration, Gretchen the injured and insulted innocent, the self-sacrificing victim of a selfish lover to whom she gives herself body and soul. Sonia Marmeladova, the heroine of *Crime and Punishment*, [93] is Dostoevski's Gretchen—of course, not as a mechanical copy of Goethe's figure, but as a typically Dostoevskian "variation" on and amplification and intensification of salient traits of the model. Gretchen's naiveté reappears in Sonia as a child-likeness belying her eighteen years, as an innocent girlishness that Dostoevski explicitly singles out as an "especially characteristic trait" (183). Sonia's love of Raskol'nikov and her willingness to share his fate, to "follow [him] everywhere—into exile I will go with you" (316), are a typical "Steigerung" of Gretchen's self-surrendering love for Faust.

Still, such similarities as these, including such a physical trait as Sonia's Gretchen-like "blue eyes, lending her face an expression of kindness and open-heartedness" (183), could all be considered mere coincidences if Dostoevski had not introduced those "verbal signals" that are clearly intended to alert the knowledgeable reader to the author's intent of fashioning a link between his Sonia figure and Goethe's Gretchen: At her first appearance, Sonia is wearing "a straw hat with a fiery-colored feather" (solomennoi shliapke s ognënnogo tsveta perom) (121). Here we may not as yet attach special significance to the "fiery-colored feather," but when it recurs in a telling variation in Raskol'nikov's description of his meeting with Sonia, we cannot fail to recognize Dostoevski's symbolic use of the device. Raskol'nikov, semi-delirious, recounts to his friend Razumikhin how he had stood at the deathbed of Sonia's father, how he had given the family all his money, had been kissed by Sonia and had seen, at that moment, "another being standing there with a fiery feather" (drugoe odno sushchestvo . . . s ognennym perom) (150).* In a flash we realize the association of the "fiery-colored feather" on Sonia's straw hat with the lurking figure of Mephisto with the "fiery feather" on *his* hat or, in Goethe's version, "die *Hahnenfeder* auf dem Hut." [94] Sonia as a prostitute, and as such in Mephisto's realm even if not in his power, must carry his sign and symbol though undefiled in her innermost being, as Raskol'nikov is quick to realize: "All this disgrace had touched her only mechanically; not even a drop of corruption had penetrated her heart" (247). We remember Mephisto's words about Gretchen: "Über die hab' ich keine Gewalt." [95]

Dostoevski develops this motif in a highly dramatic scene. The dying Marmeladov catches sight of his daughter Sonia "standing in a corner, in its shadows. 'Who is it? Who is it?' he cries out in a hoarse, breathless voice, pointing with terrified eyes toward the door where his daughter was standing" (145). He had never seen her in a prostitute's attire, with that "fiery-colored feather," and in his feverish ravings had mistaken her for the devil. His terror-struck exclamation "Who is it? Who is it?" in its rhythmic effect is once again

---

* Mephisto, that "other being standing there," reappears linked to Swidrigailov, who exhibits many Mephistophelian traits—Mephisto's lewdness, slyness, guile, and brutality—and uses phrases that echo Mephisto's words so often cited by Dostoevski, as, for example, "I certainly did not claim the privilege of *doing nothing but evil*" (233) or "After this man *can do only evil* to fellow men and has not the right *to do the least bit of good* and this because of accepted empty formalities" (ibid., italics added). At times it seems to Raskol'nikov that his meetings with Swidrigailov are but fantasies of his distraught mind, that he is but the apparition of "that Evil One who pulled him into his crime" (225, 321, 322), a theme to be fully developed in "Ivan's Nightmare" in *The Brothers Karamazov*.

a "signal" that links this scene unmistakably to the dungeon scene of *Faust*, where Gretchen catches sight of Mephisto and cries out in insane terror, "Der! Der! Schick ihn fort! / Was will der an dem heiligen Ort? . . ."[96] Once again we have here not a mechanical duplication but Dostoevski's subtle variation on the Goethean scene: Gretchen is confronted by evil incarnated in Mephisto, Marmeladov by the figment of his overwrought imagination triggered by the sight of the "fire-red feather," that symbolic *requisite* of Mephistopheles. Both victims remain beyond the devil's grasp: Gretchen in her total surrender to God's justice—" '. . . dir hab ich mich ergeben!'. . . Stimme von oben: 'Ist gerettet' "—Marmeladov in the sheltering embrace of Sonia, that personification of all-redeeming love.

As always with Dostoevski, the character traits and fate of a Goethean figure are intensified, carried to the extreme of stark realism. Sonia's determination to help her beloved family drives her into prostitution. With this intensification of Gretchen's self-sacrificing love for Faust, Dostoevski has created a figure that was destined to become an inspiring model to German authors at the turn of the century, especially to the Expressionists. Walter Sokel, in his perceptive study of the movement, points to this influence: "The degradation to which Sonya submitted in order to save her family resembled the self-sacrifice of the Saviour. For her act of love, mankind ostracizes and crucifies her. But a healing power radiates from her [as it does from Gretchen] and nurses Raskol'nikov from spiritual sickness slowly back to spiritual health and rebirth. . . . Throughout Expressionism the Sonya-Raskol'nikov relationship is repeated in many variations."[97] Thus a circle of literary influence is closed: Goethe's Gretchen, an inspiration to Dostoevski, reappears as the saintly prostitute in the creations of modern German writers inspired, in their turn, by the Russian author.

In Dostoevski's work, Goethe's Gretchen reappears in an all-but-grotesque variation as the cripple ("Khromonozhka," literally "the lame one") Maria Timofeevna Lebiadkin, a central figure of his novel *The Devils*. Association of this figure with Goethe's Gretchen might seem farfetched if Dostoevski had not characterized her, explicitly and implicitly, as another personification of "beauty from *within*," of *Seelenschönheit*. Maria is "gifted with a wonderful and luminous soul" (XII, 255), a characteristic stressed time and again by the author. Moreover, Dostoevski has placed his injured and insulted heroine in situations that closely resemble those in Gretchen's life, though again in greatly intensified form: Maria is viciously abused by her lover, Stavrogin, and is brought to a violent death by the *agent provocateur*, the Mephistophelian Pëtr Verkhovenski. Other parallels have been pointed out by that perceptive reader of Goethe, Symbolist poet Viacheslav Ivanov. He compares "the relationship of Gretchen to the Mother Gloriosa with the cripple's relation to the Mother of Christ [bogomateriia], the cripple's horror at Stavrogin's appearance in her room [X, 214–219] to Margareten's insane reaction in the dungeon scene." [98] Moreover, and most tellingly, Ivanov identifies Maria Timofeevna's "daydreams about her child [with] Gretchen's nightmarish recollections" [99] of murdering her infant. While the first two comparisons are of a more general nature and thus might be discounted, the third removes any lingering doubt of Dostoevski's use of the Goethean model. We have here before us an all-but-verbatim rendering of the German original. We remember in the dungeon scene Gretchen's ravings to Faust about how she had carried her newborn child through the forest to a pond where she drowned it: "Immer den Weg / Am Bach hinauf, / Über den Steg, / In den Wald hinein, / Links, wo die Planke steht, / Im Teich." [100] Dostoevski's Maria follows Gretchen's very path in her distraught fantasizings. Breathlessly she recounts, "I carry him [the infant] through the forest, am afraid of the forest, am terrified, I carry it to the pond" there to drown it (X, 117). Dostoevski would seem to imply that Maria had read Goethe's powerfully evocative scene and is now identifying herself, consciously or subconsciously, with Gretchen, whom she both pities and enviously admires. To be sure, in Maria's case both the child and its murder are figments of her imagination or, more exactly, a wish-dream of a childless woman who would take on herself the crime of imagined infanticide if she could thereby partake of the bliss of imagined motherhood.

A contrasting figure to Maria Timofeevna in *The Devils* is Lizaveta Nikolaevna Drozdov. She is as beautiful as Maria is ugly, as self-assertive as Maria is meek, as admired as Maria is injured and insulted. Liza might well be considered at first glance the very paragon of physical, "external" beauty, in contrast to Maria's "beauty of soul" or "beauty from within." And yet both suffer the same fate, Gretchen's fate. To be sure, there is a significant difference in Stavrogin's attitude toward the two women. His marriage to Maria was a mock ceremony, a dastardly humiliation of the poor woman. His desire to marry Liza, to "start a new life" with her, is profoundly sincere. And yet Liza, like Maria, is also destroyed by her infatuation with Stavrogin. Pëtr, the Mephisto, uses Liza's infatuation, that love-hate to the point of insanity, and Stavrogin's love for her as snares in which to catch and destroy his victims. Thus Stavrogin finds himself guilty, though against his will, of the violent end of his beloved. In this tormenting guilt he shares the fate of Faust.

Alfred Bem, in one of the few substantive studies of *Faust* in the works of Dostoevski [101] that have come to my attention, has linked Liza most convincingly with Goethe's *Faust* by a feat of literary sleuthing that deserves to be reproduced in full. He is speaking of Liza's last meeting with Stavrogin, a central scene of the novel entitled "A Romance Ended" (X, 397–402):

I have frequently wondered, trying to penetrate into the meaning of this scene, why in its dialogue Dostoevski has placed the words "moment" [mgnovenie] and "hour"

[chas] in quotation marks. Now it has become clear to me. Strugovshchikov's translation of *Faust*[102] . . . provides the key to the puzzle. It was this translation that was most
familiar to Dostoevski, and it is this text that translates the German "Augenblick" with
"mgnovenie" and with "chas."

Then Bem quotes the famous lines "Werd ich zum Augenblicke sagen / Verweile doch du bist so schön! . . ." in Strugovshchikov's translation, which
does, in fact, contain "mgnovenie" and "chas," the latter word twice. Then he
continues:

If according to Dostoevski's conviction "one can find among jurors at times very literate persons who ponder the fate of Margarete" [Bem is quoting here from Dostoevski's
Diary of a Writer for the Year 1876], if the simple girl in his novella "The Meek One"
["Krotkaia"] could shine with her knowledge of "Faust," then surely our provincial
heroine of "A Romance Ended" could in her conversation with Stavrogin quite naturally play with allusions to the famous pact in "Faust." The discovery of these allusions
indicates to us that she [Liza] was subconsciously comparing her fate to Gretchen's and
that she recognized in Stavrogin a sort of Faust [svoego roda Faust].[103]

What a striking instance of Dostoevski's manner of signalization! Not
only are words deliberately used as "verbal signals" but, beyond that, they are
here placed in quotation marks, surely a signaling device that could hardly be
topped in its effectiveness in revealing Dostoevski's source of inspiration, the
central theme of Goethe's *Faust*. And once again Dostoevski polemicizes
against this central theme: Faust's denigration of the "Augenblick" that he
would overleap to reach his ultimate goal of self-fulfillment. Dostoevski has
Liza chide Stavrogin for having "left the moment behind." "Listen," she addresses Stavrogin, "I have told you already. I have put all my life into one
single hour [chas] and am at peace. Now do the same with yours. . . . Oh, but
of course, that's not for you. You will have many different 'hours' and 'moments'" (X, 401). Stavrogin, she knows, will never put all of himself into a
"single hour," never endow a "moment" with ultimate meaning, will not keep
faith with his love for her, but instead will "leave the moment behind," will
remain to the tragic end of his life the "negating Russian Faust."

It is impossible to enumerate, let alone interpret, all the subtle, illusive
instances of Goethe's influence on Dostoevski by way of his Gretchen figure.
Nor would such an effort be at all called for in the context of this study. I am
aiming not at a comprehensive compilation of such occurrences but rather at
illuminating, with the help of a limited number of the most characteristic and
revealing instances, Dostoevski's method of "borrowing" from Goethe, his
relationship to the German writer, his *creative response* to him.

There is one more highly revealing appearance of Gretchen in Dostoevski's
work, this one in *propria persona*. We find it in Dostoevski's late novel *A Raw*

Youth (*Podrostok*).[104] Dostoevski introduces this Gretchen scene in a light, almost humorous vein to build it to a most powerful climax. He presents a minor character, Trishatov, with a touch of irony and humor, yet with that same inimitable precision of realistic detail we admire in the portrayals of central personae in his novels. He has Trishatov, a dilettante and dreamer, a would-be composer who has not put a note to paper, give a sketch of an opera he is "carrying in his head" which has Gretchen for its tragic heroine and takes place in a cathedral.

As we follow this "sketch," we grow aware that Dostoevski is using Trishatov as his mouthpiece to articulate a deeply felt desire to glorify Gretchen, clearly his favorite among all Goethe's figures. We find Dostoevski passionately involved as he presents his "correction" of Goethe's cathedral scene. Dostoevski begins by setting the locale and action exactly as Goethe has it: "The Gothic cathedral, the choirs, the hymns. Gretchen enters, and medieval singing, so that one can hear the fifteenth century in it. Gretchen overwhelmed with grief . . . at first the recitative, *sotto voce*—but terrifying, torturing, and the choirs thunder forth, darkly, sternly, unfeelingly, 'dies irae, dies illa!' " Then Dostoevski introduces, in place of Goethe's "Böser Geist," Satan himself, "invisible, only his song, mingling with the hymns, almost melting into them, and yet so different from them. . . . It begins softly, tenderly: 'Do you remember, Gretchen, when you were innocent, when you came with your mother to this cathedral and lisped your prayers from an old prayer book?' "—words that are a close paraphrase of Goethe's: "Wie anders, Gretchen, war dir's / Als du noch voll Unschuld / Hier zum Altar tratst, / Aus dem vergriffenen Büchelchen / Gebete lalltest. . . ."[105] Satan's song grows louder, more intense: "There are tears in it, hopeless longing, unceasing, inescapable, and finally despair. 'There is no forgiveness, Gretchen, no forgiveness here,' Satan's voice intones."[106] "Gretchen wants to pray, but only agonized cries break from her, you know, when the breast is convulsed with tears. But Satan's song does not cease, it pierces deeper and deeper into the soul like a dagger, it rises higher and higher—and suddenly breaks off almost in a shriek: 'The end to all, you cursed one!' "

I have quoted at length to illustrate how Dostoevski recreates, up to this point, Goethe's text, intensifying it in parts, especially the descriptions of Gretchen's agony, transposing it from the dramatic to the operatic genre but in the essential plot line remaining faithful to Goethe's original. Then, abruptly, there follows Dostoevski's "correction." Gretchen had swooned at the last note of Satan's song. But as she falls senseless, she is caught up and raised on high by the angels—"and at that moment suddenly the choir thunders forth like a storm of voices, an inspired, victorious, overwhelming chorus, something like our 'Borne on high by angels,' so that everything trembles to its very foundations—and all is transformed into a triumphant cry of celebration, 'Hosanna!' as though the entire universe had joined in a joyous shout—and they carry her, carry her aloft" (XIII, 352, 353).

Such is Dostoevski's glorification of Gretchen, that paragon of *Seelenschönheit*. It is not in the spirit of Goethe. Goethe's laconic "Sie ist gerettet" fails to satisfy Dostoevski. Nor is it in the spirit of the Roman Catholic church. Instead it is celebrated by Dostoevski in the full splendor of the majestic Greek Orthodox ritual so dear to Dostoevski's heart. This is *his* apotheosis of Gretchen, an apotheosis he had denied in such dramatic fashion to his Faust figures, Ivan Karamazov and Nikolai Stavrogin.

Summary and Conclusion

What then are the results of my study, or rather, what is it striving to accomplish? Its main purpose is to lay to rest the simplistic notion that Dostoevski had "bypassed" Goethe or that he had seen in his work a world view totally unacceptable to him, one to be simply ignored. What my study hopes to have revealed is an attitude of Dostoevski toward Goethe that is far more complex and differentiated. To be sure, his interest in Goethe's vast work was limited. For instance, he "bypassed" completely the contributions of Goethe the natural scientist, remained surprisingly unimpressed by his lyrics, and had only superficial contact with the stage plays of Goethe other than *Faust*. But that masterpiece had the most profound and lasting influence on him. In it Dostoevski found central figures, scenes, and ideas that roused him to creative opposition or again, less frequently, to empathetic agreement. He could not leave unchallenged Goethe's glorification of Faustian self-reliance and self-assertion, Faust's atheistic *superbia*, as he saw it. Strich does not indulge in glib generalization when he argues that "the Faustian striving which Goethe's western European mind saw as an effort to reach God seemed to the Russian mentality the exact opposite. It saw in the Faustian spirit the determination to win spiritual power in the same way that Napoleon embodied the determination to win temporal power." [107] Dostoevski was the great representative of that "Russian mentality" and became its most forceful spokesman with a voice that had a worldwide resonance.

Ivan Aleksandrovich Goncharov, that great contemporary of Dostoevski, had also written an *anti*-Faust in his famous novel *Oblomov*. In this work he has Andrei Stolz, that Faustian-Mephistophelian foil to Oblomov's passivity and lassitude, lament that the Russians had "no Titans." "Unlike the Manfreds and Fausts, we shall not do serious battle on the major issues; we shall not accept their challenge; we shall bow our heads [smiritsia!], live calmly through difficult moments, and then life and happiness will smile on us once again." [108]

Dostoevski is living proof to the contrary. In him Russia has *her* Manfred and *her* Faust. He did not "live calmly through difficult moments"; he *did* "accept their challenge" and *did* do "serious battle on the major issues." Such a major issue for Dostoevski was Goethe's apotheosis of Faust, in whom he recognized the hated atheistic Man-God. He obviously paid no heed whatever to the words of Goethe that so explicitly make Faust's salvation depend on God's blessing, on the "love from above": "Und hat an ihm die Liebe gar / Von oben teilgenommen, / Begegnet ihm die selige Schar / mit herzlichem Willkommen." [109] He sees only Faust's arrogant, self-assertive striving, a Promethean spirit, the stance of Nietzsche's superman, and launches his attack against him. In the tragic life of Raskol'nikov, of Ivan Karamazov, of Nikolai Stavrogin, Dostoevski has set his impassioned *menetekel* for everyone to be warned whither such *superbia*, such God-denying hubris, inescapably leads—to "logical" self-destruction. To be sure, Raskol'nikov is granted expiation for his wish-dream to be a second Napoleon, whose greatness would justify any crime, including murder, in the fulfillment of his grandiose mission (VI, 199ff., 320ff., 378, 417). This "Russian Faust," [110] under the influence of *his* Gretchen, Sonia, humbles himself, willingly accepts his cross of the Siberian exile, and is "drawn heavenward" by identifying "in some measure at least [with Sonia's] convictions, feelings, and yearnings" (VI, 422), thus partaking in her "beauty from within," in *Seelenschönheit*: "They both were pale and haggard, yet in these sick and pale faces there shone already the dawn of a renewed future, of complete resurrection [polnogo voskreseniia] into a new life" (VI, 421). Such is Dostoevski's realistic rendering of the apotheosis of the reborn "Russian Faust" Raskol'nikov. Ivan Karamazov and Nikolai Stavrogin, in stark contrast, would not humble themselves, could not rekindle their faith in God, remained in the snares of the devil, found no salvation, and were doomed to self-destruction—in insanity for Ivan, in "logical" suicide for Stavrogin.

Joseph Frank has placed Dostoevski's message in its ideational perspective: "When such characters [as Ivan and Stavrogin] reject God and Christ, they invariably engage in the impossible and self-destructive attempt to transcend the human condition and to incarnate the Left-Hegelian dream of replacing the God-Man by the Man-God." [111] In Ivan and Stavrogin, Dostoevski has metamorphosed [112] Goethe's Faust into the Hegelian Man-God, who leads all who would follow him from the path of salvation to damnation.

The other figure with which Dostoevski takes issue is Goethe's Mephisto. Dostoevski refuses to accept Mephisto's self-characterization as the "Teil von jener Kraft, / Die stets das Böse will und stets das Gute schafft." This kind of dictum, he argues, might be all well and good for an allegorical figure such as Goethe's devil; in real life, however, in our everyday experience, we find the very opposite to be true, namely, that *evil* in its workings, even if it should aim at the good, inescapably creates evil: chaos, destruction, death. From this *realistically psychological* point of view, Dostoevski repeatedly recasts the Goethean Mephisto figure, as I have attempted to show in my analyses of his sketch "Vlas'," of his novella "The Meek One," and, on a large scale, of the two novels *The Brothers Karamazov* and *The Devils*.

With this "correction" of Goethe's Mephisto, Dostoevski carries forward his polemic against one of the basic tenets of Goethe's far more optimistic world view, against Goethe's often expressed conviction that evil, despite itself, contributes to the positive upward thrust of life, that—metaphorically speaking—the devil creates the good precisely by aiming at wholesale destruction.[113] In the figure of Pëtr Verkhovenski of *The Devils*, Dostoevski bodied forth his counterargument, introduced his realistic portrayal in Pëtr of a Mephisto who *wanted* evil and *accomplished* evil, who wrought no good "despite himself," but spread chaos, destruction, and death and left the scene of his crimes in triumph.

The third figure whom I have singled out as having been of special influence on Dostoevski is Gretchen. The Goethean apotheosis of Faust which Dostoevski had "taken back" he bestows on Margarete, that innocent sacrifice to selfish passion, this paragon of *Seelenschönheit*, impregnable to evil, beyond Mephisto's grasp. With his damnation of his Faust figures (Ivan and Stavrogin) and with it of Goethe's Faust, and with his glorification of Gretchen, Dostoevski became a powerful influence for a reversal of our attitude toward the self-reliant, assertive, ever-striving Faust from a positive, approving one, initiated in the age of Enlightenment by the great Ephraim Gotthold Lessing,[114] to a negative one, which has become the prevalent attitude in present-day life and letters. One need but think of the problematical Faust figure in Thomas Mann's novel *Doktor Faustus*, of his composer Leverkühn, to become forcefully aware of this basic reorientation. There is no apotheosis here, only a tenuous "hope beyond hope" of an unearned salvation. Through his profound influence on modern literature and philosophy, especially on the French and German Naturalist and Expressionist schools[115] as well as on existentialist philosophy, Dostoevski unquestionably contributed his full share to this crucial reorientation. He bodied forth our modern *Zeitgeist* over against that of the hopeful eighteenth century. His influence may be regarded as problematical insofar as it diminished the impact on our culture of Goethe's optimistic world view. Certainly it was beneficial for having curbed, if not canceled out, the disastrous cult of Nietzsche's "superman" and the *Wille zur Macht*.[116]

In his famous "Speech on Pushkin,"[117] Dostoevski had extolled the Russian poet's great power of empathy with the character of nations, his ability to portray their idiosyncrasies without distortion. This gift Dostoevski considered to be typically Russian, a national trait that destined Russia to be the future founder of panhumanism, of a universal brotherhood of men living in the peace and freedom of mutual tolerance and Christian love. Dostoevski shared in this power of empathy, but he also possessed to a greater degree than did Pushkin the emotional and intellectual power of a fiery adversary, fully capable of taking his unyielding stand against a nation, a society, a person, no matter how great, how powerful, whose *Weltanschauung* he deemed to be a dangerous aberration and to condemn it in unforgettable scenes and characters. Thus he could empathize with certain aspects of Goethe's message while condemning others. Hence his celebration of Gretchen, that symbolic figure he recognized as the very embodiment of his most profound convictions and heartfelt sympathies. Hence, also his equally intense and uncompromising condemnation of that facet of Goethe's comprehensive world view which received its artistic expression in such figures as Prometheus[118] and Faust, utterly alien to Dostoevski's "Russianness" and to his deeply held Greek Orthodox faith.

In the light of my study, then, Dostoevski's attitude toward the German author is seen to be at times affirmative, more frequently sharply critical, but always receptive to that challenge and inspiration that radiate from the life and work of so great a fellow artist and thinker as Goethe.

CHAPTER FOUR

Leo Nikolaevich Tolstoi (1828–1910)

In Tolstojs Lebensdrama ist die Kollision Tolstoj-
Goethe eine der Leitlinien.

—Lev Kopelev

Summarizing the insights gained in her searching study of Tolstoi's relationship to Goethe, Marina Matveievna Chistiakova gives a precise and concise characterization of that relationship between these two Titans of world literature. "Throughout his entire creative life," she writes, "Tolstoi read and reread and rethought Goethe, submitted to his aesthetic influence in the period of his artistic searchings, and fought him on the ideological battleground in the days of his philosophical and public activity, being all the while afraid of not dealing fairly with him, that is, of not understanding him and of undervaluing that essential quality which explains the secret of his aesthetic magic."[1]

This fear of undervaluing the secret of Goethe's "aesthetic magic" is but a part of Tolstoi's torturing quandary: "*What is art?*" His lifelong involvement with Goethe the man and artist faithfully reflects the inner struggle of this genius with "two souls in his breast," the ever-intensifying struggle between his ethical self and his aesthetic self, between the religious man within him and the artist who would not be denied. Tolstoi's "conversion" affected his view of Goethe as deeply and drastically as it affected and transformed his entire life. "Er wollte die Kunst absoluten religiös-sittlichen, d.h. ausseraesthetischen Kriterien unterwerfen. . . . Der Schriftsteller für den das Wort—das lebenschildernde und lebenschaffende Wort—der Sinn seines Lebens war, sagte sich von ihm los im Namen strenger Gesetze eines spartanischbäuerlichen Christentums."[2] Once the "religio-ethical," the "extraaesthetic," criteria had been adopted and rigidly applied, Tolstoi's earlier, predominantly positive view of Goethe changed into a ruthlessly critical one. Yet while he furiously struck out against the once-admired poet, he could not free himself of his influence and returned again and again to his works, to *Faust, Werther, Hermann und Dorothea, Dichtung und Wahrheit*, to Goethe's *Gespräche mit Eckermann*. One can truly speak here of a fatal fascination, a love-hate relationship that had its roots deep in Tolstoi's existential dilemma as the born artist who would deny art in the name of a "spartan-peasant Christianity." As Lev Kopelev sees it: "Für Tolstoj war es der Nahkampf mit einem Gegner, der irgendwo neben ihm, ja in ihm, in seinem eignen unüberwindlichen Schaffensdrang, seinen Gedanken und Zweifeln lebte."[3]

The Young Tolstoi and Goethe

Leo Nikolaevich Tolstoi grew up in an intellectual, cosmopolitan milieu. His mother spoke fluent French and knew German, English, and Italian. His father was well read in French literature. As was the custom in Russian aristocratic families, Liovochka (young Tolstoi's pet name) was placed in the care of tutors at a tender age. His first tutor was a German, Fiodor Ivanovich Rössel, who proved short on erudition but long on genuine affection for the Tolstoi youngsters. He soon won the sympathy and trust of Liovochka, who readily took to his guidance and quickly acquired considerable expertise in the one subject in which his tutor had any degree of competence, the German language. Later, in his entrance examination to Kazan University, it was German in which Tolstoi excelled. For the rest of his life he never lost that proficiency, even though, like Mark Twain, he "could not help but see something funny (du ridicule) in the German language."[4] In his conscientiously kept program of instruction, Goethe's *Faust* is the only work of belles lettres mentioned by title and singled out for systematic study.[5] In the library of some 1,400 volumes which he collected at Iasnaia Poliana, German volumes ranged third in number among foreign books, yielding only to English and French and including a forty-two-volume edition of Goethe's collected works, which, according to Tolstoi's repeated assurances, he "had taken the trouble of reading three times" in his long life.[6]

Tolstoi developed early a truly voracious appetite for literature. As a young boy he "devoured" French novels by Eugène Sue, Alexandre Dumas, and Paul de Kock. Still in his teens, he "grappled" with Hegel and "worshiped" Rousseau, even to the point of wearing a medallion of his idol in place of the Orthodox cross. Rousseau's *Confessions*, *Nouvelle Héloise*, and *Émile* made a tremendous impression on the budding author. Among other works that had a "huge influence from his twentieth to his thirty-fifth year," Tolstoi singles out "Sterne's *Sentimental Journey*, Schiller's *Die Räuber*, and Goethe's *Hermann und Dorothea*,"[7] which was to remain, together with *Werther*, his favorite work by Goethe.

An early entry in his diary mentions his reading of Goethe's *Leiden des jungen Werther*. On March 25, 1851, he notes: "Have read *Werther*."[8] That very year Tolstoi was working on the fictional autobiography *Childhood*. By Tolstoi's own account, the chief model for the beginner had been Laurence Sterne's *Sentimental Journey*.[9] But might he not also have received a measure of inspiration from Goethe's profoundly autobiographical, subtly introspective novel? It is striking to find him returning to that work several years later to reread it with great admiration: "Read *Werther* again. Wonderful." [10] It would seem unlikely that, on first encountering Goethe's *chef d'oeuvre*, he would not have been impressed and influenced by it.

References to Goethe grow more frequent in Tolstoi's diary, beginning with 1854. In July of that year he records: "Read all day, Lermontov, then Goethe," [11] and again, "Read Goethe, Lermontov, Pushkin," adding dejectedly, "The first one [Goethe] I understand poorly." [12] But the very next entry sounds more optimistic: "Read La Fontaine, Goethe, whom I understand better with every passing day." [13] The reading of Goethe seems to have become habitual with Tolstoi during these months, as the following jotting indicates: "In the morning . . . my *usual* reading of Goethe." [14] He makes special mention of "finishing the reading of *Faust*" [15] with evident satisfaction. And to his sweetheart of those days, Valeria Vladimirovna Arsenieva, he reports an "astounding" discovery: "Have just read an astounding piece by Goethe, his *Iphigenie*, and have experienced that indescribable delight that only he who truly understands and loves poetry can appreciate." [16]

The entries continue on this positive note. While in Lucerne amid all kinds of distractions, Tolstoi reads the "*admirable* Goethe" and singles out the poem "Willkomm [!] und Abschied" as having made on him a particularly strong impression. [17] A few days later he records "reading Goethe's *Wilhelm Meister*, despite oppressive heat." [18] Tolstoi's interest in the "admirable" Goethe and his *Meister* must have been compelling. But then we come on an unexpectedly critical entry, in which Tolstoi finds "Goethe *cold* in his *Faust*," the thoughts and strivings of Faust not fully developed, and concludes: "Had Goethe developed all of Faust's thoughts and strivings, he would not have compressed [!] them into this form." [19] It would seem that the epic writer Tolstoi had grown critical of the "compressed," that is, the "dramatic" form of Goethe's masterpiece. But there is also another possible explanation of this cryptic entry with its negative tone. In it Tolstoi characterizes Goethe not only as "*cold* in his Faust" but also as old and feeble. This leads one to assume that Tolstoi is speaking here not about the entire *Faust* but only about its Second Part. In that case the term "compressed" most likely refers to that part's allegorical and symbolic form, a style Tolstoi always disliked.

The year 1860 and the first four months of 1861 were a particularly hectic and trying period in Tolstoi's life. In retrospect he attempts to recapture the rush of stirring events during his journey through Italy, France, Belgium, and England in the following staccato notation in his diary: "What has not passed in those four months?! Difficult to record it now. Italy, Nice, Florence, Livorno, Naples. *A first lively impression of nature and antiquity. Rome—return to art*"—words that could have been set down by Goethe on his Italian journey. Tolstoi continues his recollections: "Paris—closer acquaintance with Turgenev. London—nothing; disgust with civilization. [!] Brussels—peaceful feelings of family life . . . Eisenach—the road—thoughts of God and immortality. God reinstated, hope and eternal life." [20]

Tolstoi's "thoughts of God and immortality" had been roused by the heartrending loss of his adored older brother Nicolai,[21] who died in Italy of tuberculosis, literally in the arms of Tolstoi. Those were indeed overwhelming, soul-searching, mind-testing months. Small wonder that diary and notebook were neglected and references to Goethe ceased during that period.

The above-quoted diary entry was made by Tolstoi in the comparative calm of a brief stay in Weimar[22] on his way back to Russia. Although the Goethe house had been closed for inventory purposes, Tolstoi was determined to visit it. He turned to the Russian envoy von Maltitz with an insistent request and through his influence was given special permission for a guided tour of the house and its surroundings. In his diary I found the following jotting: "Goethe's house. Yellow—Vernunft; green—Sinnlichkeit; red—Phantasie; blue—Verstand." Tolstoi is describing here the "pyramid made of cardboard" that had attracted Vasili Zhukovski's attention during that Russian Romantic poet's repeated visits to the Goethe house in September 1838.[23]

Goethe's works, especially his *Faust*, continued to hold Tolstoi's interest. On March 8, 1861, he writes to Aleksandr Herzen: " 'Faust' is the greatest drama of the world. . . . Even in the revision of the French libretto [for Gounod's opera *Faust*] it remains great." [24] And in his diary he gives a characterization of Goethe's drama as "poetry of thought, a poetry that has for its subject matter that which no other art can possibly express," [25] a definition that amounts to the highest praise Tolstoi can bestow on a work as being inimitable, *sui generis*. *Faust* is indeed much on his mind during these early years, as evidenced by frequent references to the drama in his letters, diary, and notebooks, jottings that often are startling in the originality of Tolstoi's approach to the work. One characteristic example for many is his letter to friend and future biographer N. N. Strakhov: "*Die Sorge* has overwhelmed me. Remember in Part Two of *Faust*? That *Sorge* which does not at all depend on any particular action, on the external world, but rather is an inner sickness—a lack of élan [slabost' poryva]." [26]

In the collection of "Thoughts of Wise People," [27] which Tolstoi carried on for many years for his own and his friends' and followers' edification, Goethe is given a place, even if not a prominent one. In number of quotations he ranges behind such German "wise people" as Kant, Lessing, even Lichtenberg, and well behind Tolstoi's favorite among philosophers, Arthur Schopenhauer.[28] I have located seven Goethe quotations, all of them carrying either a philosophical message or a psychological message, none of them concerned with problems of aesthetics.[29]

A revealing light is shed on Tolstoi's predilections among philosophers and poets by an account we find in the "Notes" of I. M. Ivakin, a visitor to Tolstoi at Iasnaia Poliana. He records:

Osmidov, L'vov, and a student were with him [Tolstoi]. They were selecting from an English catalog a hundred books which "could help a person dispel the darkness surrounding him." I listened as they were setting up the list: "Epictetus" the student would read and Tolstoi would answer: "He belongs into the first category"—[the student again]: "Horace," [and Tolstoi]: "That one to be left out"—"Shakespeare"—"Him too I would gladly leave out, but that is impossible."—"Goethe"—"Let me confess, him too I would leave out."—"Kant"—"Him we need. Whoever wishes to achieve the highest philosophical point of view cannot get along without him. And I would also add Schopenhauer." [30]

Characteristically, Goethe is coupled here with Shakespeare as one whom Tolstoi would not include among the guides to true wisdom if only prevailing opinion would tolerate such an omission. [31]

As the year (1889) of Ivakin's account indicates, this selection was made by Tolstoi well after his immersion in religious thought, which did not mark a complete break with the world of Goethe, the "self-assured heathen." [32] Chistiakova is right in pointing out that during his "most intense creative periods" Tolstoi always sought contact with Goethe's works. "Tolstoi's return to Goethe," she writes, "always marked periods of the most passionate search for new paths and of intense theoretical conceptualizing." [33] This was true for Tolstoi before as well as after his "conversion." Thus, while pondering the plan for his greatest novel, *War and Peace*, Tolstoi records in his diary: "Am reading Goethe—and thoughts are astir." [34] There is textual evidence that Goethe was indeed in Tolstoi's thoughts as he was working on his masterpiece. Among the "rough drafts and variants to *War and Peace*" [35] we find the following revealing exchange on Goethe's ballads between Andrei Bolkonski and Pierre Bezukhov: ·

"Do you remember," Andrei asks his friend, "you also gave me Goethe's ballads and told me to read them? I did." Pierre responds, "Well? Are they not marvelous?" But Andrei does not agree: "That's not my kind of a book, that's not for me. I find all this untrue, exaggerated. And moreover, comme dit Voltaire, tous les genres sont bons hors le genre ennuyeux—and all this is boring." Pierre is stunned. "'How can this be boring!' he exclaimed, and began to recite 'Gott und die Bajadere'—'I simply fail to understand how you, a clever and sensitive person, cannot appreciate it.'" Andrei defends himself vigorously: "'I love Racine, that's poetry! I love Voltaire . . . but these rivulets are to me like sonatas. I can understand how one can adore a man like *le petit corporal* [Napoleon] even though I don't love him and will fight against him with pleasure. But the rest of it all, the Iliads and these Shakespeares and m-me Suza, all that is for ladies' albums. And that 'Gott und die Bajadere' of yours. Was soll das eigentlich bedeuten [*sic*]? And when did it all happen, and what is the purpose of all of it, and why is it not clearly put? After all, the true sign of greatness is clearness." Pierre listens horrified to the heretical speech of his friend: "No, you simply lack it, there is no feeling for it in you. Please do think about it. I, for my part, understand all of them, Goethe as well as Voltaire and *Nouvelle Héloise* and *Contrat Social*. Why is it that you understand only the one kind? You are deprived of great happiness. As I read that poem ['Der Gott und die Bajadere'] tears came to my eyes, and not because I had been drinking. I can drink as much as you want me to and I would never feel that pleasure I experienced reading that poem." [36]

One hears Tolstoi the enthusiastic soldier and inveterate admirer of classical French literature argue with Tolstoi the sensitive, receptive, open-minded artist. At the same time, one realizes that the epic genius Tolstoi stands superior to the debate and embraces with the artist's empathy the idiosyncrasies and tastes of both parties. However, as for the ballads of Goethe, specifically his "Gott und die Bajadere," Tolstoi's impartiality stops short. He clearly speaks to us through Andrei rather than through Pierre. It is Andrei who expresses with fictional exaggeration Tolstoi's own critical attitude toward this type of poetry, an attitude conditioned by his lifelong aversion to "poetic excess," to allegory, and to hyperbole and by his demand of realistic verisimilitude, of the "simple truth" clearly stated in a great work of art. He will not be lured into flights of poetic fancy; he insists on a clear statement of "how, when, where, and why it all happened."

In his next novel, *Anna Karenina*, Tolstoi again introduces a Goethean work into its plot, this time that "affective" masterpiece *Die Leiden des jungen Werther*. He has Vronski's mother object to her son's affair with Anna primarily on the ground that the affair is, in her words, "a *Wertherian* one, *a desperate passion* . . . that could lure him [Vronski] into all sorts of foolishness." [37] The mother speaks here for Tolstoi, who according to a confessional jotting in his diary had himself experienced that "Wertherian passion" as "poetic love, the sufferings of love." [38]

Anna Karenina has been linked to *Werther* on ideological grounds. It has been argued that in his novel Tolstoi criticizes the Russian society of the nineteenth century in a spirit and from a point of view characteristic of Goethe's critique in *Werther* of the German society in the eighteenth century. [39] I find this comparison farfetched. More convincing and instructive is Masaryk's comparison of Tolstoi's Levin, one of the two heroes in *Anna Karenina*, with Goethe's Faust. The author argues that "Levin is neither Faust nor Manfred, but rather Musset's Octave or Lenau's Faust" and goes on to explain:

Goethe's Faust and Byron's Manfred and Cain each tries in his own way to overcome [morbid subjectivism and individualism]; they are able to objectivize themselves by their own inner strength, are capable of enduring as Levin cannot. Instead, Levin turns backward, as he must in order to save himself; he finds his savior and ideal in the *muzhik* [peasant]. Faust and Manfred push onward, while Levin retreats. Faust and Manfred do not abdicate, they do not give up their activities or the direction of their work, while Levin reverts to complete passivity, since his lifesaving *muzhik*'s faith is nothing but passivity.[40]

Further on in his argument Masaryk points up the similarity of Tolstoi and Goethe in their uncompromising, ceaseless search for truth: "Tolstoi . . . looks for truth everywhere and proclaims it irrespective of the consequences. He agrees with Goethe: 'Schädliche Wahrheit, ich ziehe dich vor dem nützlichen Irrtum: Wahrheit heilet den Schmerz, den sie vielleicht uns bereitet.'"[41] Masaryk contrasts this fearless quest after truth characteristic of both Goethe and Tolstoi with Dostoevski's stance, which he believes harmonizes far more with Bernard Fontenelle's attitude expressed in that philosopher's maxim "Si j'avais la main plaine de vérités je me garderais bien de l'ouvrir sur le monde."[42]

It is surely claiming too much when Chistiakova singles out Goethe's *Hermann und Dorothea* and his *Faust* as the "first stimulants of his [Tolstoi's] creativity in the period of his initial work on *War and Peace*."[43] However, her suggestion that Tolstoi's interest in the drama after he had completed *War and Peace* may well have been kindled by his reading Goethe and Shakespeare[44] is corroborated by Tolstoi himself. To his friend and confidant Afanasi Fet he writes, "How much I want to talk with you about Shakespeare, about Goethe, about the drama generally. All this winter [of 1870] I have been preoccupied with the drama."[45] Tolstoi's enthusiasm for this new preoccupation was to prove shortlived. He soon recognized the spirit of the times as most un-propitious for the tragic genre. Already in February of that year he puts down in his "Notes": "Tragedy is terrifyingly difficult in the conditions of modern psychological development. That is the reason why today one can only talk, in school texts, about [Goethe's] *Iphigenie*, about *Egmont*, about [Shakespeare's] *Henry the Fourth*, *Coriolanus*, and so forth. But to read or to perform them is impossible nowadays."[46] Tolstoi considers "Goethe's efforts to imitate the Greek methods in their dramas completely futile." The social and economic conditions having drastically changed, the dramatis personae of Greek theater have lost the basis and very substance of their existence. Thus "the speech of Poverty in Aristophanes's comedy, *The Plutus*, proving her indispensableness was surely very convincing for the Greeks of the fifth century. For us with our concepts of the wealth of nations[47] and general economic laws, that speech is not only deprived of all meaning, but the very personae of the play do not really exist for us."[48]

Tolstoi's Goethe Image After His "Conversion"

Goethe's works continued to challenge and irritate Tolstoi as the religious prophet in him was gaining ascendancy over the artist without ever quite subduing him. We recall the young Tolstoi's admiration for Goethe's *Iphigenie* as an "astounding" masterpiece. Now, Tolstoi's "conversion" having taken place in the late 1870s, he not only considers Goethe's efforts to emulate Greek art "futile" but is actually repelled by Goethe's Grecophilia. He finds its roots in Goethe's "deplorable lack of 'religiosity.' " To art historian and literary critic V. V. Stasov he writes: "For irreligious people, for people who believe that our world, as they perceive it, is truly existing and that there does not and cannot possibly exist another, for people like Goethe and our good Herzen, for such people Greek art was indeed the manifestation of the greatest and highest art." Tolstoi, on the contrary, cannot but agree with his friend, Prince A. I. Urusov, "who looks at everything Greek in literature and sculpture with aversion and loathing."[49]

Thomas Mann, in his study "Goethe and Tolstoi," had characterized Tolstoi's growing hatred of Mediterranean culture as a proto-Russian trait [urrussisch], "in diesem Protest bekundet sich die Richtung seines [Tolstoi's] Blickes nach Osten, sein Asiatismus mit einem Wort, der anti-petrinisch, urrussisch-zivilisationsfeindlich, kurz: bärenmässig ist. Was wir vernahmen, war die Stimme des russischen Gottes auf dem Ahornthron unter der goldenen Linde."[50] Lev Kopelev has taken exception to this view as lacking historical perspective: "Mit diesem Wort engt der Dichter Thomas Mann . . . den objektiven Historiker [Tolstoi] ein. Denn in der Kritik am griechischen Erbe hatte Tolstoi Vorläufer." And Kopelev identifies these predecessors as the "byzantinische Bilderstürmer und die altrussischen Gegner des 'Lateinertums' " and foremost among them "die katholischen Christen des ersten Jahrhunderts unserer Ära und die Sektierer des späten europäischen Mittelalters." He reminds us that "im Volksbuch über den Schwarzkünstler Faust, der seine Seele Satan verkauft, Helena—die Personifizierung des antiken Schönheitsideals— ein Mittel teuflischer Verführung ist."[51] Thus, Tolstoi's Grecophobia can properly be seen as belonging to a tradition reaching back to the early Christians, to medieval Europe, and, in Russia, continuing in the teachings of Pëtr Iakovlevich Chaadaev, author of the famous *Philosophical Letters*.[52]

Goethe's *Gespräche mit Eckermann* were a special challenge to Tolstoi. They both attracted him and roused his protest. Tolstoi the Christian felt challenged by many a thought recorded in this compendium of Goethe the "heathen's" worldly wisdom. He singles out for comment the following typically Goethean assertion: "If a person does not cease being active, he cannot die; his activity is bound to continue, even though with death it does change into a different form." Tolstoi's reaction is highly revealing. He admits that this thought is basically "correct," but it is "turned inside out" (vsiata na vyvorot). According to him, "it is not the will of the person that produces his activity; rather, it is the indwelling divine spirit which is ever active."[53] The same typical reaction is sparked by Goethe's contention that "alles Vergängliche ist nur ein Gleichnis": "Goethe maintains that everything transitory is but a simile, a metaphor, a symbol. *Not so!* In reality everything special, everything temporal, is a manifestation of the divine, of the spiritual." [54] Here it is, the head-on collision of the religious prophet with the aesthetic man, with Goethe the artist, and that collision is the more intense because Tolstoi feels within himself the unresolved conflict of the aesthetic with the ethical, with the religious element in his complex personality.

In the spring of 1909 the publisher of the *Goethe-Kalender auf das Jahr 1909*, Theodor Weicher, sent Tolstoi a complimentary copy. Tolstoi took the time in his busy life to thank him in the following letter, which he wrote in German:

Danke sehr für die Sendung Ihres Goethe Kalenders auf 1909. Ich habe ihn mit grossem Interesse durchgesehen. Was mich besonders interessiert sind Goethes Gespräche mit verschiedenen Personen. [Ich] habe in diesen Gesprächen vieles für mich neues und wertvolles gefunden, so wie z.B. was er mit Falk über die Wissenschaften, die zu weitsichtig geworden sind, äussert, [1] oder mit Riemer über die vegetabile [!] [2] . . . oder dass die Natur eine Orgel ist, auf die [!] unser Herrgott spielt, und der Teufel tritt die Bälge dazu. [3]

Besonders bemerkenswert ist sein Gespräch mit Müller, 1823, 3. Febr. [4] Auch was er von den Schäden, die die Journale und Kriticken [!] beibringen, schon im Jahre 1824 sagte, und was besonders in unserer Zeit so wahr ist. [5]

Aber es wäre zu lang alles tiefsinnige und geistvolle, was ich in dem Buche gefunden habe, aufzuzählen.

Nehmen Sie es mir nicht übel, dass ich Ihren Wunsch mich über Goethes Werke zu äussern wegen meinen vielen Beschäftigungen nicht erfüllen kann.

Danke noch einmal für das Buch, das mir so wertvoll war. [55]

Clearly, Tolstoi's "conversion" did not cancel out or even significantly diminish his interest for Goethe's *thoughts*. It did, however, bring about a drastic change in his earlier positive attitude toward the "*admirable* Goethe."

The onset of Tolstoi's "conversion" can be traced to the "end of the 1870s, when Tolstoy took a full reckoning of himself and of his relations to culture." [56] Most deeply and painfully he pondered his relation to art, which was so much part of his innermost self that he could not abandon it lightly but had to justify its existence, define its true nature. [57] For fifteen years, as he tells us in the conclusion to his tract *What Is Art?* (1897), he wrestled with that bedeviling problem. [58]

In this stubborn effort to define the nature of "true" art, Tolstoi rejects all previous definitions: "Art," he maintains, "is not, as the metaphysicians say, the manifestation of any mysterious idea, beauty, God; it is not, [as] the physiological aestheticians maintain, a play in which a person expends the excess of his accumulated energies; it is not the manifestation of emotions by means of external signs; it is not the production of agreeable objects; above all, it is not enjoyment." Contemptuously Tolstoi brushes aside Hegel's aesthetics, "that unbelievably stupid Hegelian teaching, according to which such activities as building a house, singing a song, painting a picture, and writing stories, comedies, and lyrics would appear to be saintly actions in the 'holy service to beauty,' standing but one step below religion." [59]

The more intense and all-embracing Tolstoi's religious fervor grew, the narrower and more dogmatic became his view of art. "Religious consciousness" [60] became Tolstoi's highest, if not the sole, standard by which to judge art and the artist. The simple laboring man and peasant boy came to constitute for him the blue-ribbon jury whose verdict on art was final. In all seriousness Tolstoi compared their "uncorrupted taste" in matters of art with an animal's sure instinct for palatable food.[61] Speaking of one of his favorite peasant-pupils in his Iasnaia Poliana school, he unabashedly claims that "a sense of measure [chustvo mery, i.e., of artistic form] was stronger and surer in him than in any of the writers known to me" and that this boy "possessed an unconscious artistic power, which Goethe at the height of his immense development [as an artist] could never achieve." [62] Tolstoi's demand that pupils be let out of the "school benches" is common knowledge. It is less widely realized that he also wanted artists, especially writers, to escape the "school bench" of formal rules, thus to gain the freedom of serving "truth," of painting and sculpting, of writing about life in all its palpable reality. In Goethe's formal control of language Tolstoi saw not a virtue but a deplorable shortcoming. He would have us believe that "Goethe tried but could not free himself of the rules of grammar in order to be able to write freely." [63] Goethe would not have agreed. To him only complete mastery of formal rules assured the artist ultimate freedom in his creative work.

Tolstoi was convinced, or rather strove to convince himself, that he had discovered the true mission of art. "Art," he tells us, "should evoke a feeling of awe before the dignity of every man, before the life of every animal, and shame in the presence of luxury, violence, vengeance, the acquisition for one's own pleasure of such objects as are indispensable to other men." Art should seek "to make people freely and joyously, without noticing it, sacrifice themselves in the service of men." In short, art should place itself wholly in the service of Tolstoi's moral code, his religious philosophy, of his "spartanisch-bäuerliches Christentum."

For his sharpest criticism Tolstoi singles out the concept of *kalokagathia*,[64] that "heretical interlinking of beauty and goodness." This concept had been evolved by the Greeks, "that half-savage, slaveholding little people who," Tolstoi has to admit, "knew how to represent the nude human body and to build pretty buildings." Having gone out of fashion in the Middle Ages, it was revived in the Renaissance and "evolved and canonized into the triad: 'Das Schöne, das Wahre, das Gute,' 'Le Beau, le Vrai, le Bon' with capital letters, worshiped by modern philosophers and artists." For Tolstoi this triad is pure heresy: "The arbitrary union of these three incommensurable, mutually alien concepts results in the complete loss of the ability to distinguish good art from bad art." Under its evil influence, he sees the greatest of modern artists, Beethoven and Shakespeare, Dante and Raphael, Bach and Goethe, all of them rushing headlong to their perdition and luring after them an ever-increasing, disoriented, debauched public: "If there is a constantly growing audience listening to the late works of Beethoven, it is because more and more people are being debauched [razvrashchaiutsia] and are turning away from normal working [trudovoi] life dedicated to honest labor. For exactly the same reason the number of readers of Goethe's *Faust*, Part Two and of the *Divine Comedy* of Dante is constantly growing."

Yet Tolstoi does not lose hope, for "as long as there are healthy, laboring people, the creations of a Beethoven, the Second Part of *Faust*, Dante, and all the present-day poems and paintings and musical compositions will fail to evoke in those people an artistic response." [65] "The overwhelming majority of people," according to him, "is completely disinterested in the poems of Virgil, Dante, Tasso, and Milton, and in a great part of Shakespeare's and Goethe's works, in the late compositions of Beethoven, and in a part of Bach's music." [66] That vast majority will turn elsewhere for their uncorrupted pleasure and solid spiritual nourishment. They will seek and find it in the words of the great religious thinkers of all ages and all lands. "We offer the people Pushkin and Gogol', and we are not the only ones to offer them such poets: the Germans offer them their Goethe and Schiller, the French offer Racine, Corneille, Boileau, . . . but the people do not accept them because that is not solid nourishment but merely hors d'oeuvres or desserts. The nourishment we live by is not of that sort; the real nourishment is the revelations of lofty minds by which all mankind lived and is still living and on whom a Pushkin and a Corneille and a Goethe were raised." [67] To be great art, as judged by Tolstoi, a work must be "universally comprehensible." Works of that "highest order are the *Iliad*, the *Odyssey*, the histories of Jacob, Isaac, Joseph, the Jewish prophets, the Psalms, the Gospel parables. All these convey lofty sentiments and elevated thoughts and yet are comprehended by everybody." Striking is the total absence from this list of modern artists and belles lettres. But in fairness it must be stressed that Tolstoi did not include in his listings of outstanding achievements any of his own masterpieces. In fact, he condemned them out of hand, save for two minor works, *God Sees the Truth* and *The Prisoner of the Caucasus*,[68] both of which are marked by that all-important quality "religious consciousness." As examples of "higher art which arises from love of God and of our neighbors," Tolstoi cites "Schiller's *Räuber*; Victor Hugo's *Les pauvres gens* and *Les Misérables*; Dickens's stories and novels, *Tale of Two Cities*, *Chimes*, and others; Stowe's *Uncle Tom's Cabin*; Dostoevski's works, especially his *Dead House* [*House of the Dead*], and George Eliot's *Adam Bede*."

Tolstoi was also much impressed with Jean Paul Richter. "I have read about Jean Paul Richter," he notes in his diary. "The purity of his character and his Platonism are astounding. Wonderful are also his maxims. That is a good sort of writer. Compared to that egoist Goethe." [69] Less surprising is Tolstoi's preference of Schiller over Goethe. With it Tolstoi stands in a long tradition of Schiller worship among Russian men of letters and the intelligentsia generally. [70] With his usual forthrightness Tolstoi confesses, "Schiller, him I love, he is one of us. Goethe is a dead German." [71] Heinrich Heine is another German poet whom he accepts as "one of us." He feels him to be "near and intimate to myself despite his pathos. Goethe is alien to me." And again he lashes out against Goethe's *Faust*. "Faust, Part Two—an old man's love affair. What could be more disgusting than that?!" [72]

Tolstoi recognizes one of the signal defects of modern art in its derivative nature. Abject dependence on sources, wholesale "borrowing," is a cardinal sin of modern artists. Goethe is singled out as having committed that cardinal sin with his *Faust*: "A product based on 'borrowing,' as, for example, Goethe's *Faust*, may be beautifully fashioned and replete with sallies of wit and all kinds of embellishments, but it cannot produce a genuine artistic impression because it lacks the chief characteristics of a work of art—completeness, organicism [*organichnost*'], that is, unity of form and content expressive of the sensations experienced by the artist. By borrowing, the artist conveys no other sensations than those impressed on him by the production of some previous art." Can Tolstoi be seriously claiming that Goethe by "borrowing" conveyed no other sensations than those impressed on him by products of some previous art, by the chapbook of Johannes Spiess, for instance, or by any of his numerous other sources? Alas, our answer must be in the affirmative. Tolstoi was indeed in dead earnest. Nowhere in his thoughts on Goethe's works were we able to find a disclaimer of this startling assertion.

"Religious consciousness" being, as we have seen, Tolstoi's primary prerequisite for the creation of "true" art, *simplicity and directness of expression* stand second in his aesthetic canon. He distrusts pathos and despises bombast and every sort of "poetic excess," namely, rhetorical devices calculated for effect, everything that is "artful," intentionally symbolic, allegorical, fancy, and farfetched. Such devices are particularly offensive to him when used to express a great thought. Again Goethe is singled out as having committed that grave offense. He has treated the grand theme of Faust's salvation "in poetical, artistically dramatic form." And Tolstoi, with his accusing finger pointed at the German poet, lays down his law. "Concerning such [religio-philosophical-ethical] questions [as Faust's salvation], it behooves one either to remain silent or else to speak of them with the greatest of tact and caution without rhetorical phrases and—God forbid—without rhymes."

With his criteria thus firmly established, Tolstoi surveys the forty-two volumes of Goethe's *Gesamtwerk* in his Iasnaia Poliana library and passes stern judgment: "Goethe has written forty-two volumes. From among these one can select at most three genuine creations of art; all the rest of his writing is very clever and subtle, but it is not art. Some pieces are interesting and intelligently written; some, however, such as his dramas, comedies, and novels, are so bad that if they had been written by some unknown author nobody would ever read them. *Werther*, even though an immoral [!] work, is nonetheless a highly affective creation; so are his small versifications. . . . But his *Faust*, that *non-plus-ultra* of intellect and language [!], is a stillborn, coldly reasoned product that has never moved anyone. And yet the critics, mindful that *Faust* is the creation of famous Goethe, proclaim not only the First Part of *Faust* but also its Second Part as a model of art. And promptly imitators appear." [73]

It is interesting to note that Tolstoi did not include this sweeping critique of Goethe's works in the final version of his essay on art. In fact, Goethe generally escapes direct attack, though his name often appears, as we have seen, among the artists whom Tolstoi would condemn as aberrant, as being without "religious consciousness." Goethe, in fact, fares better at the hands of the stern puritan than, for example, the French and Dutch Symbolists whose poetry Tolstoi sweeps peremptorily aside as mere "gibberish without rhyme or reason." Goethe is accorded gentler treatment than Wagner or even Beethoven and is let off easier than Shakespeare. Nevertheless, we do find Goethe's name linked closely with the hated English bard's. To Gol'denveizer, a friend and much admired pianist, Tolstoi confides that he had "three times in his life . . . studied all of Shakespeare and Goethe from beginning to end and had never been able to understand what was so magical about them." [74]

In his essay "On Shakespeare and on the Drama" (1903),[75] that massive, wrongheaded diatribe,[76] Tolstoi singles out Goethe as the chief villain among the misguided proselytizers of the English author. There were, he tells us, various reasons for Goethe's promotion of Shakespeare's fame, "in part his wish to give more freedom to his own dramatic activity, but chiefly because his world view coincided with Shakespeare's." [77] Goethe's praise of Shakespeare had great weight, for "at the beginning of the past century he was the dictator of philosophical thought and aesthetic laws." [78] As soon as Goethe's authoritative voice had proclaimed Shakespeare's greatness, "critics who understood nothing of art descended on Shakespeare like crows diving on carrion and began to search in his works for nonexistent beauties and to praise them" [79] They wrote their "long, nebulous, quasi-scholarly articles, and a vast European public began to admire Shakespeare. . . . And once it had been established that Shakespeare's dramas were indeed the height of perfection and that one had to write as he wrote, not only without religion but even without any moral content whatever, then all dramatists, imitating him, began to write those vacuous works such as the dramas of Goethe, Schiller, and Hugo and, with us, of Pushkin, Ostrovski, Aleksei Tolstoi, and that host of more-or-less well known dramatic creations that fill all our theaters." [80] And all that insidious insanity had been initiated and promoted, according to Tolstoi, by that Pied Piper Goethe.

Tolstoi unmasks the much praised "objectivity" of Shakespeare and Goethe as a reprehensible lack of a serious, empathetic attitude in their works, their egocentric indifference toward art and life alike: "That which is called their objectivity, Goethe's Olympian stance, Shakespeare's soaring flight above mundane events, turns out to be merely a sure sign that they are not serious, *are not in earnest* [Tolstoi uses the English phrase]; they indulge themselves with their writings, that is, they fail to express that which painfully grew in their souls and set forth [in their works] only what they deem to be of use to themselves." [81] Here Tolstoi could have quoted one of his favorite Goethe lines: "So fühlt man Absicht, und man ist verstimmt." [82]

And Tolstoi continues his invective: "Those efforts of theirs to be 'objective,' that is, to be indifferent to goodness and evil (nowadays we would say 'beyond good and evil' [83]) . . . far from attaining their goal, accomplish—for any attentive observer—the very opposite. You cannot hide an awl in a sack. In Goethe's objectivity we recognize without the least effort his very pronounced traits of a bourgeois conservatism, his *Fürstendienertum* [pridvornost'], his egocentric indifference to the current of human life." [84] It is startling how the religious prophet, Tolstoi, echoes here the very words of such materialist radicals as Chernyshevski and Pisarev. Ideological fervor surely makes for strange bedfellows. [85] Of course, in his criticism of the absence of Christian humility and of "religious consciousness" in Goethe's works, Tolstoi stands at the opposite ideological pole from these Radical Democrats.

Sharp as this critique of Goethe certainly is, Tolstoi kept his most violent attacks on the German poet out of his published works [86] and confided to his diaries and letters. We find the earliest attack directed at Goethe's *Faust* in a letter to Strakhov. It clearly marks Tolstoi's alienation from his early idols and the world of art. "I am happy to know," he writes, "that your essay is progressing and beg you to work more on your main task and not on trifles such as translations and especially not on such supreme nonsense [drebeden iz drebednei] as Goethe's *Faust*."[87] On May 28, 1896, the year of his intense work on *What Is Art?* we find the following outburst:

Goethe? Shakespeare? All that appears under their names, all of it, must be ipso facto great and *on se bat les flancs* in order to discover in their stupid, miserably flawed works the marks of beauty—and in the process one perverts taste. But the fact is that all these great geniuses, the Goethes, the Shakespeares, the Beethovens, the Michelangelos, have created, alongside some very beautiful things, not only middling works but utterly abominable stuff. Middling artists produce middling works and never the very bad. But the acknowledged geniuses create either the truly great or absolute trash [drian']: Shakespeare, Goethe, Beethoven, Bach, and others.[88]

And again on December 20 of that year: "There are many creations of famous artists that are below all criticism and many spurious reputations that gained their fame by mere chance: Dante, Shakespeare."[89] Here Tolstoi does not name Goethe, but we can be sure he is thinking of him.

A decade passes, and Tolstoi is again reading Goethe's collected works only to discover "the full extent of the harmful influence of that vain and empty, wretched, egoistical bourgeois and talented [!] person [Goethe] on the generation that preceded mine—especially on poor Turgenev with his admiration for *Faust* (an absolutely bad creation) and for Shakespeare (also one of those creations of Goethe[90]). . . . How much I suffered when—having grown fond of Turgenev—I tried to love whatever he valued so highly. I tried with all my might, and could not. What terrible harm is caused by authorities, by famous people, particularly by those fake reputations."[91] The most sweeping denigration of eminent artists in the pages of Tolstoi's diary lumps together "the Greek tragedians, Shakespeare, Goethe, Bach, Beethoven, Raphael," all of whom, according to Tolstoi, "receive the plaudits of a debauched public on the strength of spurious reputations established and sanctified by ignorant, sycophantic critics vying with each other in mindless adoration of these so-called greats."[92]

We have it on the authority of Tolstoi's physician, Dushan Petrovich Makovitski, that in his old age Tolstoi spoke frequently of Goethe, and almost without exception disparagingly. Thus, in his "Notes [Zapiski]"[93] Makovitski records on September 6, 1905: "In the evening we spoke of Goethe. Lev Nikolaevich said: 'In my youth I admired his disgusting [otvratitel'nye] dramas.'" Yet on another occasion[94] Tolstoi could not but praise Goethe for his "faithful" reproduction of the life of the Middle Ages in his *Goetz von Berlichingen*. The realism of that Sturm und Drang drama continued to appeal to Tolstoi into his old age, while the "classical" form and style of such masterpieces as *Iphigenie* and *Tasso* had become "disgusting" to him.

But to return to Makovitski's "Notes." On May 7, 1906, he records: "Lev

Nikolaevich praised some of Schiller's works, also some of Goethe's, among them his 'Introduction' [Vvedenie. (*sic*) "Zueignung"? "Vorspiel auf dem Theater"?] to *Faust*. Of the Second Part of *Faust*, he said that it was nonsense [chepukha], that he does not understand it even though he is now in the very years in which Goethe had written it. He said that now in his old age he likes to see it all expressed more clearly, more simply, and not mystically." On being asked by literary critic Victor Anatolievich Lebren whether he should read *Faust*, Tolstoi, according to Makovitski, replied in the negative, again stressing "the mystical and mystifying nature of that drama." He then counseled Lebren to read instead Goethe's *Hermann und Dorothea* and *Die Leiden des jungen Werther*, thus once again confirming his lifelong predilection for these two works. To be sure, the "wonderful" *Werther* had been relegated by the "converted" Tolstoi to those "affective" but "immoral" works which his stern puritanism could no longer approve. But *Hermann und Dorothea* continued to enjoy his wholehearted acceptance. In that work he found expressed those very ideals and attitudes he never had to renounce: the patriarchal virtue of frugality, industry, steadfastness in adversity, the helpful hand extended to neighbor and stranger alike, that heartfelt brotherhood of men growing out of mutual trust, respect, and love.

Continuing his "Notes," Makovitski recalls the occasion when Tolstoi had asked him for a copy of *Dichtung und Wahrheit*. He was "interested to see how the old Goethe had written his [recollections]." Not that he liked Goethe's autobiography. Its very title, he told Makovitski, "is a phantasm [vymysel], and a poor one at that." As Tolstoi recalled it—and he had read the work more than once—there was in it "no sincere rendering of feelings and impressions." Sure, he had found in it "much that is well written, that is interesting." But it all seemed to him so "artificial and untrue." And he gives vent to his irrepressible dislike of this "artificial" work. He calls it "boring, pedantic, bourgeois." He chides Goethe for having recorded such trivia as his "acquaintances with dukes, which he [Goethe] considers important," and adds disapprovingly "—as he does art!"

Tolstoi's late remarks on Goethe in his diary and letters underscore his violent aversion to Goethe's "self-assured heathenism [samouverennoe iazychestvo]" [95] and to his "dated Hegelian aesthetics." [96]

In retrospect it seems to the old Tolstoi that he had always disliked Goethe. To Makovitski he asserts, "Goethe was always unsympathetic to me. I was afraid to be unfair to him and kept rereading him—no, I have not changed my opinion of him. . . . He is a man with great talents, to be sure, but with a total lack of one of the most important human feelings—the religious." [97]

There is no reason to question the sincerity of these statements. Clearly, the aging Tolstoi's dislike, yes, even hatred, of Goethe were genuine enough. But the nature of and reasons for this violent reaction are complex, not to say pathological. In his diary Tolstoi records a dream that affected him deeply. He writes, "I saw in my sleep that L. [probably his son Lev L'vovich] somehow does not understand [Goethe] or is intentionally telling something about Goethe, and this is unpleasant to me. Afterward someone [!] said that my activity is that of a fly. Both the former and the latter [statements] insulted and depressed me." Chistiakova and Kopelev both cite this passage. Kopelev follows it up with a concise comment: "So drang Goethe bis in Tolstojs Träume, verletzend und kränkend. Ins Unterbewusste verdrängt, wirkte der nicht auszutragende Streit weiter." [98] Chistiakova offers a perceptive interpretation:

In this note there is revealed a secret subconscious sphere of battle between two Titans. In the undeviating intensity of his nature, Tolstoi would not accept compromise. His battle with Goethe was being fought under the rallying cry "He or I, Weimar or Iasnaia [Poliana]!" This was a battle not only of ideology but also of ambition, and the feeling of uncertainty in final victory may well have stirred in Tolstoi. The unknown, vague "someone" of the dream, calling Tolstoi's activity that of a "fly," may well be nothing other than his own outward-projected doubts in the rightness of his position vis à vis Goethe. Together with the innate aesthetic attraction Goethe exerted on Tolstoi, it is precisely this sense of uncertainty that explains Tolstoi's return, again and again, to Goethe's works in the last years of his life. [99]

In the light of this penetrating analysis it is surprising that Chistiakova fails to quote Tolstoi's full notation, the following portion of which not only supports her interpretation but offers an opportunity to expand on it. Tolstoi continues: "In my sleep I cannot rouse in myself that consciousness of the law which governs my life [togo soznaniia zakona svoei shizni] and which I know would free me of that unpleasant reaction [to the voices of Lev and the 'someone']. That impossibility of [rousing] that highest religious consciousness represents the difference between sleep and waking." [100]

One need not be a professional psychoanalyst to read the message of this revealing dream. The "highest religious consciousness" which Tolstoi tries and cannot rouse in his dream is that artificially developed stance of the ascetic prophet of Iasnaia which is not an essential part of his subconscious, his "dream" self. In his dream he cannot but confront Goethe as his innate artistic self, as that challenging "someone" who compares Tolstoi the artist and his works with Goethe and adjudges them to be a mere "fly." Tolstoi struggles to escape from this self-denigrating nightmare into the safety of "highest religious consciousness" but finds himself blocked—naturally so, for in his dream he can exist only as the artist that he natively is, as his "dream" self. Only when "awake" can he activate the "highest religious consciousness," can he assume the stance of the "converted," religious Tolstoi.

What this dream reveals is not merely an "unpleasant, insulting," and "depressing" confrontation of Tolstoi with Goethe but, in its deepest meaning, the inner struggle between Tolstoi's innate artistic self with his consciously and strenuously cultivated religious self, so arduously striven for and never fully realized. His violent denunciations of Goethe's libertine sensuality (*Römische Elegien*), of Goethe's glorification of beauty—be it sensuous or spiritual, pagan or Christian—of Goethe's lack of humility, of his hauteur as the "darling" of the gods, were all the more relentless and fierce for being an attack on Tolstoi's own unquenchable sensuality, on that beauty-loving and creating artist-self, on his own ineradicable hauteur of the born aristocrat, the Russian "Barin."

All this is not to deny the deep-seated differences between these two Titans in their temperaments, their life's philosophy, and above all in their aesthetics. Tolstoi, scion of a proud, unbending clan of noblemen who stubbornly defied the tsar's authority, felt nothing but contempt for Goethe's all-too-ready compliance with the codes and mores of the Weimar court. He, Tolstoi, would never be a *Fürstendiener*! Also, Tolstoi's outlook on life had always been more deeply conditioned by "religious consciousness" than the world view of Goethe, the "dezidierte Heide," had been. Moreover, as an artist, Tolstoi was from the beginning to the end of his creative life a far more consistent epic realist than was Goethe. We have no noteworthy lyrics from the pen of the young Tolstoi or from the mature and aging artist. The German poet's soaring flights of imagination were alien to Tolstoi; he greatly disliked what he called the "rhetoric," the "poetic excess," the "mystifying mysticism," the allegory and hyperbole in Goethe's work, above all in the Second Part of his *Faust*. Like his Andrei Bolkonski of *War and Peace*, Tolstoi demanded to know the whys and wherefores, the exact place and time, the inner logic of the plot and the characters in a literary work. He valued the products of clear-eyed, penetrating observation and reproduction of "real life," not visionary creations of untrammeled imagination. Tolstoi's genius was earth-rooted, time-related, truly Homeric in its realistic sweep and vitality. This innate artistry more fundamentally even than Tolstoi's "religious consciousness" ultimately determined his attitude toward Goethe. He related with the German poet in his vital, vibrant "realism" and rejected with growing violence Goethe's poetic afflatus, his proteic imagination, the poet's triumph over time, space, and causality so inimitably realized in the Second Part of *Faust*.

In the encomiums upon Tolstoi's death he was frequently compared with Faust. "A second Faust" became all but a standard formula both in the Western press and the Russian press.[101] In his extraordinary study of Tolstoi, Fëdor Stepun has the aged seeker-after-truth die with "Suchen, immer suchen" on his lips and expresses the hope that "er [Tolstoi] im Sterben denselben Chor der Engel gehört hat wie Faust: 'Wer immer strebend sich bemüht, den können wir erlösen." [102] Soviet critic Iaroslav Ivoshkevich, faithful to the Marxist-Leninist line, stresses Tolstoi's likeness to Faust, the liberator of the masses, "who placed the happiness of other people above beauty and above the striving for personal perfection." [103] All these voices, from the past as well as from the present, are agreed that Tolstoi did live a Faustian life of striving and questing. He lived it with greater intensity and self-abandon to the ultimate depths of despair and to the heights of transcendent hopes and yearnings than did the far more harmonious, self-controlled, balanced, "classical" Goethe. Romain Rolland, ardent admirer of both the Russian and the German poets, has felt this difference intensely: "Qu'il [Tolstoi] est loi," he exclaims, "à ses derniers jours, de la sérénité volontaire d'un Goethe!" [104]

Goethe the consummate artist and profound thinker created the image of the modern Faust, ever striving and in his striving found worthy of celestial apotheosis. Leo Nikolaevich Tolstoi, in whom the artistic drive and the religious yearnings could find no harmonious resolution, strove and suffered with truly Faustian energies for his moral utopia here on earth only to end his life a lonely pilgrim, at the forlorn railroad station of Astapovo.

Goethe and Tolstoi! Janus-like their heads were turned in opposite directions—Goethe's predominantly to the cultural treasures of the West, Tolstoi's to the religious wisdom of the East. Yet their hearts beat in unison for a common ideal, a nobler humanity. Goethe, as the eloquent champion of humanism, contributed his full share to furthering human dignity, justice, and freedom, just as did Tolstoi as the "mirovoi posrednik" (world mediator)* with his gospel of human brotherhood united in "religious consciousness," mutual trust, and love. Tolstoi denied ever more violently Goethe's contribution through his art and life to a higher humanity, sensed the unfairness of that denial, and strove to change his views of Goethe, returning again and again to an examination of the German genius' personality and work, but "could not change his mind." Resenting the absence of rigorous moral commitment, as he saw it, in Goethe's life and work, he could not accept him as "one of us" and in a fit of revulsion even called him a "dead German," [105] thus echoing, probably unconsciously, the impetuous words of "furious Vissarion" Belinski, who as we recall dismissed Goethe as "a poet dead for our generation." Such is the nature and tragic fate of fervent prophets. They preach mutual understanding, tolerance, and love, but rarely are they able to achieve these in their own lives. [106]

---

*Also a designation of an office in the Russian legal system, most closely approximated in ours by "justice of the peace."

CHAPTER FIVE

The Russian Symbolists

At the turn of the nineteenth century and during the early decades of the twentieth, there was a welter of movements, schools, circles, and coteries in every one of the European literatures, but none could boast of as many as Russian literature. Aleksandr Blok, looking back at the years between 1897 and 1907, is "amused by the tiny swarm of the Russian intelligentsia who managed in the course of a decade to acquire and shed a plethora of world philosophies and in the process to split into fifty hostile camps."[1] To give a glimpse of the veritable Tower of Babel, I reproduce the program of a poetry reading held under the chairmanship of one of the leading Symbolists, Valeri Briusov.[2] Here is its membership exactly as listed:

Neoklassiki: M. Gal'perin, O. Leonidov
Neoromantiki: Argo, A Mareev
Simvolisty: A. Belyi, V. Briusov, I. Rukavishnikov
Neoakmeisty: Adalis
Futuristy: I. Aksenov, S. Budantsev, K. Kamenski, V. Maiakovski
Imazhinisty: I. Gruzinov, S. Esenin, A. Musikov, A. Mariengof, M. Roizman,
                V. Shershenovich, N. Erdman
Prezantisty: A. Navzorov, D. Tumannyi
Nichevoki: B. Zemenkov, R. Ron, S. Sadinov
Eklektiki: A. Apukhtin, N. Benov

Of all the many schools and movements, none was more deeply involved with Goethe the man and artist both in praise and in criticism than the Symbolists.[3] What the Pure Poets with all their devotion to Goethe had failed to accomplish the Symbolists achieved. They moved him out of the wings of the Russian literary stage back to its center, a position he had lost ever since the cultural revolution of the 1860s. Goethe's name once again appears in the leading journals of the day, in *Mir Iskusstva* (*The World of Art*), in *Vesy* (*The Scales*), in *Apollon*, in *Novyi Put'* (*New Path*), in *Zolotoe Runo* (*The Golden Fleece*), and in *Trudy i Dni Musageta* (*Labors and Days of Musaget*), among others. In 1913, *Trudy i Dni*, edited by Goethe admirer Emili Metner even introduced a special section of "Goetheana."

Goethe is now ranked in importance with Dante and Leonardo da Vinci, with Michelangelo and Shakespeare, as well as with the newly anointed patron saints of the Symbolist movement, Schopenhauer, Wagner, and Nietzsche. He outranks in influence the coryphaei of the French Symbolist school—Baudelaire, Mallarmé, Verlaine, Rimbaud—a ranking that is not as surprising as may appear at first glance. Oleg Maslenikov is right when he points out, "Spiritually the Russian Symbolists [especially the "young generation," Aleksandr Blok, Andrei Belyi, Viacheslav Ivanov] stood closer to the German Romantics (Schleiermacher, the Schlegels, Novalis, Schelling) . . . than they did to the French Symbolists (Verlaine, Rimbaud, Mallarmé). They felt their Russian temperament incompatible with the 'Gallic rationalism.'"[4] Blok speaks not only for himself when he characterizes the Russian Symbolist as a "mystic of a special kind. . . . He wants to pluck the 'blue flower' in the blue midnight hour," a clear reference to Novalis's famous symbol of Romanticism. "Russian Symbolism," declares Blok, "is more deeply rooted in German and Russian Romanticism than in any other movement." Goethe is seen by Blok and his fellow Symbolists as a poet of Romanticism par excellence, as the creator of *Faust*, which to them is the "high song," (das hohe Lied) of German Romanticism. According to Blok, "the French, by dint of their national character . . . are furthest [!] removed from Romanticism."[5] He is seconded by Andrei Belyi, in whose opinion French Symbolism is but a "pseudo-symbolism" when compared with the "profoundly revelatory" German Romanticism and neo-Romanticism.[6] Viacheslav Ivanov, another member of the "younger generation" that by 1905 had taken over the leadership of the movement, is the first among Russian poets who, to my knowledge, had recognized the true greatness of Novalis in all his many-sided originality and creative power. He extols him as a true "theurgist," a "demiurge," a "creator of myths," the "organ of secret traditions." The Russian Symbolists are also the first to reach back to German medieval literature, there to welcome "as kindred spirits" not only Wolfram von Eschenbach and Gottfried von Strassburg but also Hartmann von Aue, in whose novella *Der Arme Heinrich* they found the celebration of the redemptive power of selfless love, a central theme of their *Weltanschauung*. Briusov calls Hartmann "our brother" because he too "expressed his ideas in symbols, that is, in the only possible adequate manner."[7] As to Goethe, he is for the Symbolists, as he was for the Russian Romanticists (the *Liubomudry*), the teacher and guide, the exemplary "modern" poet, the "prophet and inspirer of almost the entire present-day aesthetics." [8]

Yet there is a characteristic difference between the Russian Romanticists' approach to Goethe and that of the Russian Symbolists. The Romanticists admired in him "the Olympian," his all-encompassing genius, his Apollonian balance and measure. The Symbolists, in contrast, seek to discover in his life and works the more essential "Dionysian" strata that they divine below his harmonious Apollonian personality. Viacheslav Ivanov has summed up this probing search in the Latin motto "A realibus ad realiora. Per realia ad realiora." [9] The Symbolists, he tells us, "seek to discover the irrational, mystical depths of Goethe's creative spirit below the Olympian clarity of his classical art." [10]

Thus it is not surprising to find among the plethora of Goethe references in the Symbolists' writings a preponderance of quotations from Goethe's late works. Zhirmunski points to the "exaggerated attention paid by Ivanov, Merezhkovski, and Sergei Solov'ev to the pronouncements of the old Goethe on religion, on the immortality of the soul, on Christianity, on the old man's superstitions and his fear of death." [11] They single out the mythopoetic ballads, especially "Erlkönig" and "Der Fischer," for frequent quotation and incisive discussion. On the other hand, references to *Werther*, to the Sturm und Drang dramas (*Goetz*, *Clavigo*, *Egmont*), are conspicuously rare and insignificant. Characteristically the Symbolists draw on *Wilhelm Meisters Wanderjahre* rather than on the *Lehrjahre* and pay special attention to the *Wahlverwandtschaften*. The esoteric "Die Geheimnisse, ein Fragment," [12] with its symbolism of "cross and roses" ("Es steht das Kreuz mit Rosen dicht umschlungen . . . ," Christ's death and resurrection) and its message of "a union of all religions taken in their pure idea, cleansed of all temporal, historical impurities and distortions," [13] attracts their attention, as does Goethe's late poetry, especially the cycle *Gott und Welt* and the *West-Östliche Divan*; the poems "Weltseele," "Selige Sehnsucht," "Symbolum," and "Epirrhema" are their special favorites. They draw on the *Novelle* (1828), with its mystico-magical ending, as an example of an arcane evocation of the healing, pacifying powers of music which harmonizes with their own celebration of that "supreme art." *Faust* is of course again an important source, particularly its Second Part, the lines "Alles Vergängliche ist nur ein Gleichnis" and "Das Ewig-Weibliche zieht uns hinan" [14] being cited repeatedly to buttress with Goethe's authority central ideas developed by them in prose and poetry. In the First Part it is the "Erdgeist" scene in which they find expressed the very essence of their own life's philosophy, that mighty symbol of a transrational, vital force, eternally procreating and destroying: "Geburt und Grab, / Ein ewiges Meer, / Ein wechselnd Weben, / Ein glühend Leben. . . ." [15] Clearly, the Symbolists' choice of Goethe quotations and their selection of his works for interpretation serves to create the image of Goethe as a predominantly intuitive, irrational, mystic poet.

Toporkov, the Metner Brothers, and Bal'mont

Aleksei Toporkov, a philosopher by profession, wrote rather extensively on Goethe. His essay on Goethe's ballad, "Erlkönig" [16] is a prime example of the predominantly irrational, mystical thrust of Toporkov's *Weltanschauung*, very typical not only of him but also of a number of his fellow Symbolists. As a faithful member of the movement, Toporkov perceives the personae of the ballad as "symbols." Thus, the elf-king *symbolizes* the demonic forces of nature, the child symbolizes our consciousness, and the father symbolizes our reason. The death of the child is to Toporkov "the natural and inescapable outcome of the confrontation in our 'soul' between 'reason' denying the existence of demons and the demons who, asserting their power, triumph over 'reason' despite reason's efforts to declare them for mere phantoms." He is certain that "Goethe created his poem out of the dark chaos in his soul. Deep inside himself he heard the call of the Erlkönig."

Toporkov's analysis of the ballad is but a springboard from which he launches an extensive discussion of Goethe's entire development. In this discussion, his sympathies are altogether with the *young* Goethe, who could empathize with the demonic world, which is for Toporkov the "real reality." Young Goethe participated in that reality; "he heard the call of the Erlkönig," communed with the demons, and conveyed their inescapable sway over human life in powerful poetic statements. Toporkov sees the life of young Goethe as a unified, vital, organic whole. Then there came his fateful Italian journey that disrupted the wholeness. In Italy, Goethe surrendered to the Apollonian spirit of Greek civilization and "transformed the demons from vital, mysterious, dark, elemental forces into mere luminously beautiful artifacts." Toporkov interprets this transformation as an act of treason for which Goethe was to pay a terrible price. Henceforth "Goethe's life loses its passionate intensity, becomes dependent on the [Apollonian] laws of balance and measure, and ends in 'Entsagung,' in renunciation." But the demons prove more powerful: "The heathen gods come alive and, like the Panthers of Dionysus, fall on the grand old man."

Having delivered his encomium to the irrational, dark, Dionysian forces whom Goethe had supposedly betrayed, Toporkov concludes his essay with an altogether unconvincing "Rettung" of the "grand old man" by claiming that "music" had helped Goethe triumph over the "heathen gods": "Goethe held his own—he was helped by music." Unfortunately, Toporkov fails to offer even a shred of biographical evidence to buttress his argument.

Toporkov makes another noteworthy contribution to the Symbolists' image of Goethe in his essay "Goethe and Fichte."[17] Here he moves with far greater assurance, being in his own special field, and achieves a more lifelike portrayal of the poet-philosopher Goethe, one better substantiated by biographical facts and revealing salient aspects of Goethe's world view generally overlooked or misunderstood by the Russian Symbolists. And yet even in this more successful essay the Symbolists' eagerness to delve below what they consider to be a facade in Goethe's life, namely, his Apollonian balance and measure, remains operative. Toporkov dismisses "the usual epithets applied to Goethe, such as 'Olympian,' 'Superman' [sverkhchelovek], and 'darling of fortuna,' etc., as being utterly misleading." He would accept them if applied to some of Goethe's works in which he does find "much harmony, balance, serenity, objectivity, much Hellenism and little barbarism." Yet he would argue that all these qualities of Goethe's "classical" works were but products of Goethe's powerful will and determination, not products of his natural self, his inborn creative gifts: "Goethe wanted to be a Greek, but he was not. By heroic effort he sought to assimilate his nature to ideal antiquity; he writes elegies *almost* like the Romans, tragedies *almost* in the Greek style. . . . Yet all this," Toporkov insists, "is but external, put on. In his classicism Goethe is, more than anyone else with the possible exception of Hölderlin,[18] a Romanticist." Toporkov shares the opinion widely held, and not only among Russian Symbolists, that "in his innermost self Goethe led quite another life than the one he felt duty-bound to simulate outwardly for show. . . . Goethe yearned for those passions of which the Sturm und Drang poets spoke, yet recognized in his wisdom the impossibility of attaining the bliss of rapture. . . . Hence the grief-stricken renunciation 'Entbehren sollst du, sollst entbehren. . . .' Goethe mastered his emotions, brought measure to his excessive passions, well aware of the dangers facing him [the 'heathen gods,' 'the Panthers of Dionysus']."

Up to this point we hear clear echoes of the "Erlkönig" essay, yet there are in this essay other themes, the most important of which I consider to be Toporkov's observations on Goethe's relationship to nature. Unlike many of the Symbolists who tended to stress mystical, even orthodox Christian elements in Goethe's world view, Toporkov recognizes and stresses the Spinozist in Goethe. "Goethe was a Spinozist," he states categorically, and then gives us his reasons: Like Spinoza,

Goethe felt and understood nature as an organic whole embracing all potential elements, forms, all divine intentions and inspirations. For Goethe [as for Spinoza], nature was not merely *natura naturata*, i.e., something created once and for all, something inert, something deprived of self-unfolding powers, of creativity. Rather nature was to him, first and foremost, *natura naturans*, an actively procreative nature. Its innermost essence Goethe understood by way of an analogy to his own personal creativity: "Ist der Kern der Natur / Menschen im Herzen. . . ." His own genius was for Goethe analagous to nature's genius. Hence the highest wisdom for Goethe was not the *conquest* of nature as it was for Fichte, but rather *self-surrender* to it (Ganymed): "sich hinzugeben ist Genuss. . . ." Goethe was truly Ganymed, Zeus' lover. He partook of the "bliss of the Gods." Yet this blissful blessedness of his nature, of his genius, was bought at the cost of renunciation of his "I" [Fichte's "Ich"] in which Goethe seemed to sense the inception of evil, of a Promethean challenge to the gods. His "I" he relinquished in sacrifice to his genius. . . . That is the deepest reason why, for Goethe, Fichte's doctrine was the ultimate absurdity.

I have cited this passage extensively not only because it is the central message of Toporkov's essay but, more important, because it presents novel lineaments in the Russian image of Goethe. Other writings of Toporkov available to me contained many references to Goethe, but none of them added anything of significance to his attitude toward or view of the German poet.

The Metner brothers, Emili (1872–1936) the philosopher and Nikolai (1880–1951) the composer, can justly be called Goethe's apostles on Russian soil. There was in both of them a kindred affinity, a genuine *Wahlverwandtschaft*, to Goethe. Nikolai set numerous poems by Goethe to music.[19] Andrei Belyi, a perceptive critic, characterized Nikolai's compositions as "spiritually kindred to Goethe's poetry." He found in them that "immortal, joyful seriousness" that was Goethe's. That is why, for him, Nikolai's music "is not just haphazardly written but drawn from the very songs of Goethe."[20]

In his theoretical works, Nikolai frequently invokes Goethe's authority. Thus, in his central theoretical effort, *The Muse and the Fashion: In Defense of the Fundamentals of the Art of Music*,[21] he uses as a leitmotiv of his argument the symbols Goethe offers him in his poem "Spiegel der Muse."[22] The "true mirror of the muse" is the still surface of the lake, the false, distorting mirror, the ripples of the rushing brook, that is, eternal verities over against fleeting fashions and fads. Goethe defended the eternal verities in poetry as he, Nikolai, defends them in music against the passing fads of contemporary composers.

In the Metners' home a special room was set aside for their rich collection of Goethe memorabilia. It became for them a veritable "sanctuary" in which to "pray" to their patron saint.[23] Emili had joined the *Goethe-Gesellschaft*. His library was crammed with the literary products of that society and held an impressive array of Goethe editions, including the *Sophien Ausgabe*, which, he insisted, anyone aspiring to a true knowledge of Goethe would have to own and study diligently, "all ninety volumes of it!" He even dreamed of a "church of Goethe worshipers."

For Emili, Goethe was "a being *sui generis*, organized in a completely unique manner," [24] an "incomparable master of comprehensive self-knowledge, endowed with the ability of continuous and detailed analysis of his cognitive process." [25] With this unparalleled insight into human nature, Goethe is the "born healer of the modern artists from their ills and vices, from all the aberrations typical of the quasi-Naturalists, the Impressionists, the Expressionists, the neo-Academicians, the Retrospectivists and Futurists, the Decadents with their mysteries and deviations with their 'abysses' and their 'Demonisms,' " [26]—if only they would look up to Goethe, that "teacher of true wisdom." But alas, in Metner's opinion, "Goethe has remained incomparably more alien to us [the Russians] than to the English and the Germans." And yet, he argues, "despite that very alienation from Goethe (or perhaps precisely because of it), Goethe is all the more essential to us, and especially at this time [1913]." Modern man needs Goethe, whose wisdom is "*true* wisdom being the result of that special Goethean ability to experience and to contemplate life exhaustively."

Above all, Goethe is to Metner "the supreme artist, the first Symbolist." Goethe's "mature creations are altogether inimitable because in them the function of style has reached such impersonal vitality as to become akin to the organizational activity of *nature itself*. Thus, Goethe has forever secured himself from all and any imitation by any school or individual, has made his creations *unique* to a degree never attained by any artist—not by Dante, not by Shakespeare, not by Nietzsche, not by Pushkin or by Tolstoi, nor possibly by any artist whatever in whatever specialty other than literature"—clearly an extreme, perhaps altogether untenable claim, yet one sincerely held by this apostle of the German poet.

The earliest panegyric to Goethe by a Russian Symbolist was delivered by Konstantin Bal'mont (1867–1943) on the occasion of the 150th anniversary of Goethe's birth in 1899. [27] Bal'mont depicts young Goethe as "a fairy-tale prince." This portrayal of a "handsome, clever, gifted" Goethe "in *total harmony with his surroundings, adored by all*" is quite as far off the mark as that by the Radical Democrats, who, we will remember, presented him as a "Fürstendiener," self-indulgent, antisocial, withdrawn "Olympian." Bal'mont idealizes Goethe to the point of idolatry. He paints his childhood "illuminated by the golden rays of sunshine all the more luxuriant for falling on silk and velvet." For this idealized Goethe "there blossomed smiles and blushes on every female face. His genius awakened early and died together with him, developing richly, effortlessly without pathological aberrations and bitter declines."

Bal'mont, quite in keeping with his general style, cannot avoid embellishing his eulogy with a flourish of grandiloquence. He extols Goethe as the "chosen one of this earth" (izbrannyi zemli), whose heaven-storming striving it was "to comprehend, to experience everything." That kind of striving Bal'mont proclaims to be "a worthy motto for an *Übermensch* [sverkhchelovek]." He raises Goethe to the side of Leonardo da Vinci as a "demigod" who shares with Leonardo "that thirst for omniscience, that unerring development in accord with inborn laws, that indifference to traditional concepts of good and evil, those hallmarks of true genius." Their all-encompassing natures were blessed with "a harmonious consonance of inner and outer beauty, with an inborn love for the earth together with complete victory over everything merely terrestrial."

Bal'mont concludes his panegyric by contrasting Goethe's harmonious nature and sunlit life with the torn and troubled inner and outer existence of the Russian Symbolists, tracing this difference to the fact that "in Goethe's personality all that is hostile to human nature, all that enters into fratricidal battle within him creating those lyrical thunderstorms, is always resolved into the harmonious radiance of a rainbow." Not unlike Metner, Bal'mont advises "the overwrought moderns, overrefined and sick with our overrefinement, . . . to return periodically to the balanced, harmonious Goethe, escaping from our aromatic and smothering hothouses to offer up to him the sacred gifts of our best sympathies."

In their discussions of Goethe and his works, the Symbolists often place fulsome praise alongside vitriolic criticism. Bal'mont's treatment of Goethe offers a striking example of that attitude toward the German poet. In his panegyric, as we have seen, Bal'mont had raised Goethe to the status of a demigod. In sharp contrast, a review by him of Goethe's *Faust* written but a few weeks prior to the panegyric subjects Goethe to withering criticism.[28] His argument runs as follows: Choosing the medieval legend of Faust for his drama, Goethe empties the legend of all its meaning. The legend's "demonism" being utterly alien to his harmonious nature, Goethe is completely unable to empathize with its tragicness as could, for example, Marlowe or Goethe's contemporary Lenau, that "somber genius." Bal'mont accuses Goethe of totally miscasting the figure of Faust by saving him from the devil's grasp. "A Faust," he argues, "just like a Don Juan or a Prometheus, born as they are under a dark star, must come to one and the same fated end; they must die tragically or else cease to be true to themselves." And he underscores his argument with a categorical assertion clearly echoing Dostoevski: "Whenever man transgresses the limits set to us humans and chooses the culpable madness of crime to accomplish his ends, his soul is forever poisoned, there is no salvation for him." Goethe, true to his conciliatory nature, could not but cancel out the deepest meaning of the meeting between the human soul and evil incarnate so powerfully symbolized in the legend's fateful pact of Faust with

Mephisto. In Goethe's version Mephisto is "merely a sharp-witted scoffer and clever cheat . . . who serves Faust as a procurer, assisting him in the seduction of a most ordinary lass [Gretchen] and prodding him into a chance murder [of Valentin]." In Bal'mont's interpretation these tragic events become "everyday paltry happenings completely devoid of a deeper spiritual meaning." Goethe's Mephisto "does not *poison* Faust's soul, does not even *touch* his *soul*."

And as to Faust's penance? To Bal'mont it is a laughable, even embarrassing, penance. In disdainful exasperation Bal'mont accuses Goethe of having completely failed to realize that "a spiritual transgression can never be atoned for by a material benefaction," that is, by a socially helpful act of "draining a stretch of seashore and of digging canals as means of commercial intercourse." Despite some unconvincing-sounding complimentary asides (i.e., "Goethe's creation will forever remain one of the most brilliant products of the human mind, thanks to vivid details of its plot [!?]"), Goethe's masterpiece remains for Bal'mont "a gigantic, chaotic accumulation of facts and scenes totally devoid of organic structure and poetic harmony."

It is tragically ironic when in his panegyric Bal'mont urges his contemporaries to "offer up [to Goethe] the gift of their best sympathies." Bal'mont himself, as one of the "hothouse poets with overrefined sensibilities" is neither willing nor able to offer that gift. He is quite incapable of "sympathizing" with Goethe's optimism, with his activism, with Goethe's ideal of socially oriented striving to control nature in the service of mankind. Draining swamps and laying out canals "as useful means of commercial intercourse" are to the decadent aesthete Bal'mont meanly materialistic activities unworthy of a Faust, utterly inadequate as a redemption of his spiritual transgressions. If we were to carry his argument to its logical conclusion, the very concept of Goethe's "eternal striving" as a precondition for ultimate salvation would become suspect and would have to be condemned, as it actually was by Dostoevski.[29]

Valeri Briusov and Andrei Belyi

Valeri Briusov (1873–1924) yields to none of his fellow Symbolists in his admiration of Goethe. Calling Goethe his "close friend,"[30] he praises him literally to high heaven: Goethe is "godlike,"[31] he is the "divinely blessed guest on this earth,"[32] he is the "king and God of German poetry."[33] For Briusov, Goethe is one of the very few "elect, endowed not only with the heavenly gift of poetic genius but equally with a powerful intellect and will."[34] He is "doubly dear" to Briusov "precisely because he was not only the greatest poet of the nineteenth century but also the mightiest scientific mind of his time."[35] "Without his scientific erudition, without the daring of his analytical thought, Goethe could not have become the greatest German poet of the nine-teenth century." [36]

In a poem "To the Beginner" (Nachinaiushchemu) [37] Briusov continues in an original way the Romantic tradition of extolling Goethe as the "Olym-pian." The neophyte in the poem is put to a test when he is asked, "Did you tremble with the ineffable thrill of presentiment / Once you had compre-hended Goethe's secret and sacred message? / You did not?—Then remove your wreath / You will forever remain a stranger to Polyhymnia." Briusov's evocation of the muse is by design. He expects his readers to recognize her as one of the nine daughters of Zeus standing in service to Apollo, living on high Olympus. Thus, linking Goethe's name to Polyhymnia's he bestows subtly, perhaps too subtly, the status of an "Olympian" on the German poet.

Many more of such extravagant encomiums to Goethe could be culled from Briusov's pages. More revealing, however, of his attitude toward Goethe and his works are the many adoptions and adaptations of Goethe's scenes and personae in Briusov's poems, early and late. Thus, in his poem "Faust" [38] we have a powerful evocation of the fate of Faust and Gretchen as Briusov sees it and, from his point of view, "corrects" Goethe's version of it.

Briusov's poem is structured on the stark antithesis of hellish darkness and celestial light, of guilt and innocence, of lust and childlike purity, of Faust as "thief," as "horror, shame, and ruin" and Gretchen as a "luminous spirit." He achieves in his poem a high degree of dramatic tension and extreme the-matic compression, a typically Briusovian tour de force. He sets the scene in Goethe's "Cathedral" (Dom), Gretchen "kneeling in a dark niche" and Faust, assuming the role of Goethe's "Böse Geist," announcing her eternal damnation but also, in contrast to Goethe's version, assuring her that "here she is not alone," that in his guilt he, Faust, is with her. There follows as a soul-searching monologue, in part reminiscent of Faust's monologue in Goethe's "Forest and Cave" scene, the retrospective evocation of central events in Faust's life: his rejuvenation in the "Witch's Kitchen," his seduction of Gretchen, his vain effort to rescue her from dungeon and execution—all this compressed into seven four-line stanzas. Striking is the total absence of such central themes as Faust's striving, which would make him worthy of salvation, Faust's apotheo-sis, and Gretchen's "Rettung." Instead, Briusov emphasizes the irrepressible attraction of Faust to Gretchen, "like steel to magnet" that leads both to a tragic end. Their "flight is not to heaven / But to the abyss of sadness and of gloom." [39]

Such is Briusov's characteristic "correction" of Goethe's optimism, strongly reminiscent of Dostoevski's damnation of Faust but going even fur-ther in its nihilistic mood of gloom and doom by canceling out Gretchen's apotheosis, so powerfully celebrated by Dostoevski.[40] In stark contrast to

Goethe as well as to Dostoevski, Briusov closes his poem by consigning *both* his Faust and his Gretchen to the realm of darkness: "You [Gretchen] ascended in radiance from the dark! / But behind me [Faust] shades ominously rose / *And in darkness we are both.*" [41]

It is characteristic of Briusov, who was the first to introduce into Russian poetry the cityscape as a powerful symbol, to place such figures from Goethe's works as had particularly impressed him into the locale of a modern metropolis. Examples abound. In the poem "On the Square" (Na Skvere) [42] with the subtitle "Erlkönig," couched in rhymes and rhythms of Goethe's ballad, Briusov presents the mythological "king" on the square of a modern city and engages him in a spectral dialogue: "Why are you tarrying here in your fading crown? Another moment, and the factory whistle will challenge you to mortal combat. Your time has passed!" In answer the "king" accuses the poet of treason: You have betrayed nature for the slavery to the machines and mobs of modern monsters of "glass and steel." And like Goethe's elf-king, who enticed the feverish boy to follow him to his realm, Briusov's "king" entices the poet to return to the realm of primal nature, its freedom and vitality, there to "refresh the breast, to submerge yourself in nature's wild, indigenous strength." [43] In Briusov's version of Goethe's ballad a timely, "relevant" message is delivered, a quasi-Rousseauistic call for a return of aberrant modern man, "that slave to stone and mobs," to his roots in native soil.

Another example is a poem written immediately after the aborted Revolution of 1905 with the original title "Revolution" that was renamed "Dukh Zemli: Erdgeist," probably for reasons of censorship. [44] In this poem Briusov presents an amalgam of two Goethean themes, of the "Erdgeist" scene from *Faust* and of the ballad "Der Zauberlehrling," using them to express in Aesopian language his view of the Revolution of 1905: Like Goethe's sorcerer's apprentice, Russia had ineptly conjured the *Erdgeist*, that spirit of birth, death, and rebirth, that "untamable spirit" that would not be exorcised once it had been called and had appeared to play out its regenerative role if not in 1905 then in the near future. This is a powerful, truly prophetic poem and at the same time another striking example of Briusov's variations on Goethean themes, emphasizing explicitly their philosophical, ideological, and historical import, linking them to the *Zeitgeist* of Briusov's turbulent days.

There are numerous other occurrences of Goethe's name and other references to Goethean themes in Briusov's poems, regularly in mythological, philosophical, or historical contexts. There is the poem with the German title "Klassische Walpurgisnacht," [45] for which Briusov borrows the mythological creatures of Goethe's "classical" Walpurgisnight: the sphinxes, griffins, the stymphalides and the centaur Chiron, to have them roam the streets of revolution-torn Moscow playing their part in the "mythological upheaval," as

Briusov interprets the October Revolution. There is the "Ultima Thule" poem with its epigraph "Es war ein König in Thule." [46] Here Goethe's theme loses its power, no longer being Gretchen's expression of fervent longing for faithful love and of her dire forebodings.[47] In the fragmentary poem "Germany" [48] we find a critical view of Goethe. Accusing Germany of having started the First World War, Briusov speaks as much in sorrow as in anger, lamenting mankind's thwarted hopes that "Germany's greatest son," the "Godlike Goethe," would have truly enlightened his nation, set it on a course of the highest moral and intellectual achievements, and instilled in it the spirit of harmony and peace. Alas, "the Godlike" had failed his nation, and once again it had plunged the world into chaos, destruction, and death. Briusov breaks off his poem, leaving unspecified the reasons for Goethe's failure. Thus he initiates a theme that was to be developed by Aleksandr Blok in that Symbolist's important essay "On the Destruction of Humanism," in which Goethe's shortcomings are unsparingly spelled out.[49]

Surprising by their total absence in Briusov's poetry and prose are echoes of Goethe's intimate nature—and love lyrics. I searched in vain for instances of influence on Briusov of such favorites of Russian writers as Goethe's "Mailied," [50] "Auf dem See," "Gefunden," "Auf Kieseln im Bache," [51] or "Ganymed" with its mythological setting. Goethe's uninhibited empathy with nature, his joyous celebration of love's delights or unfeigned expression of love's torments, are alien to Briusov, whose *Poems About Love* [52] are not so much "about love" as about love's perversions, lust, sadism, masochism, voyeurism, about pain and death in exotic, mostly tenebrific settings. These poems are much closer in their mood, locales, and themes to the poetry of the French Symbolists, especially of Baudelaire and Verlaine, or to verses of the German *Jugendstil* and Symbolism [53] than to Goethe's Sturm und Drang lyrics. As a perceptive biographer-critic puts it: "In Briusov's *Chef d'oeuvre* [title of an important collection of Briusov's poetry] the *Flowers of Evil* [Baudelaire] flourish with a typically Moscovian richness." [54] Clearly, the chief source of inspiration for Briusov in his love poetry was not Goethe but the French Symbolists. He imitated their most decadent themes—eroticism, amoralism, demonism, necrophilism—and did this with a chilling, calculated purposefulness. His aim is only too obvious: to become the leading vanguard poet, to achieve the total triumph for his program of Decadent/Symbolist poetry.[55]

Always his own most severe critic, Briusov is quick to admit his failure as a poet of intimate love. Looking back on his collection, which contains four poems "To my Mignon," a Mignon that has so little in common with Goethe's as to be an outright parody of it, Briusov minces no words in self-disparagement: "Have read my *Chef d'Oeuvre* and have come to see clearly how pitiful all that I am now writing really is. 'The devil take it!' and out of this 'The devil take it' have come those poems 'to Mignon' (that is, to Plavochka [a passing passion of his])."[56] This is drastic, forthright self-criticism by any standard.

Mention must be made of Briusov's novel *The Fiery Angel*,[57] set in the Germany of the sixteenth century and dealing with Dr. Faustus and Mephisto. In this work the Symbolist Briusov has chosen a style that can only be characterized as the most consistent Naturalism, as "konsequenter Naturalismus." This is what the author himself has to say of this style: "In my novel . . . appear Faust and Mephisto. Everything they do and say is strictly consistent with the account of Mephistopheles and Doctor Faustus as given by Johannes Spiess. . . . It is but natural that Spiess, living in the sixteenth century, created his heroes in the image of the people of that time." And Briusov defends himself vigorously against a critic (Georgi Chul'kov) who dared criticize the "Mephisto of my *Fiery Angel* . . . for not speaking as cleverly as Goethe's Mephisto." "Is it possible," he asks, "that this critic did not know that Goethe had written his *Faust* at the end of the eighteenth and the beginning of the nineteenth century and not in the sixteenth?"[58] Unmistakably, Briusov sought to give in his novel the most consistently realistic picture of Faust and his age. Insofar as he was successful in his design, he debarred himself from structuring a perspectivistic, multileveled narrative such as, for instance, Thomas Mann achieved in his *Faustus* novel, that is, a type of narrative that could take into itself by way of allusion, symbol, or authorial comment, events, personalities, works of art, and science and philosophy lying outside and beyond the chronological limits (the sixteenth century) he had set for his fictive world. In consequence, all references to Goethe, his *Faust*, *Goetz*, or any other of his works related in theme to Briusov's novel had to be rigorously excluded, thus depriving us in this work of any way to gain insight into Briusov's view of Goethe.

Briusov was not completely successful in his goal. I detect fleeting echoes of Goethe's scene "Rittersaal"[59] in Briusov's description of Faust's conjuration of Helena,[60] and of Goethe's "Kerker" scene[61] in his account of the hero's (Ruprecht's) vain efforts to free his beloved (Renate) from the clutches of the Inquisition.[62] Though these echoes are too indistinct to establish intentional "borrowing," they are sufficient indications that Goethe's *Faust* was intrusively present in Briusov's mind, especially when we take into consideration that at the very time he was working on the novel he was also preparing his *Faust* translation.

Turning to Briusov's translations from German, I found among them a flawed rendering of Goethe's "Willkommen und Abschied."[63] In it Briusov loses much of Goethe's immediacy and youthful intensity of lyrical feeling in artfully conceived, complex imagery. He is more successful in matching his skill with Lermontov's in his translation of "Wanderers Nachtlied: Über allen Gipfeln ist Ruh."[64] Yet Briusov's reputation as Goethe's translator rests on his Russian version of both parts of *Faust*. He is the only Russian Symbolist (excluding Boris Pasternak from the school) who took up that formidable challenge. He was very conscious of the difficulties facing him. In an eloquent little essay[65] he writes, "The translator must have, in addition to a thorough knowledge of the language, that fine sense for its secrets which alone enables him to understand the poet's mere hints to their ultimate depth." It seems to Briusov that "such a fine sense can be developed only in one's own mother tongue." Why then did he undertake such a hopeless task, especially since his German, by his own admission, was "rather poor"?[66] Briusov is ready with an altogether disarming answer: "To translate the creation of a poet from one language into another is impossible. But it is equally impossible not to dream that impossible dream."

Briusov's determined labors on his "dream" resulted in a rendering that, in its prosody, is at least as faithful to the original as Fet's earlier effort without Fet's distortion of the ideational context, which, as I have pointed out,[67] at times amounts to all-but-complete incomprehensibility of Goethe's thought.[68] I agree with Wilma Pohl that Briusov's main shortcoming is his inability to render the colloquial diction of many dialogues of Part One. A prime example is the almost total loss of Gretchen's naive simplicity of speech. As to Faust's part, I find Pohl's comment particularly apt: "In Fausts Versen," she writes, "ist der Sprachstil des Originals vor allem durch die Kompliziertheit und Gewähltheit der Brjusowschen Bilder und Ausdrücke verändert, die Empfindung verfeinert und ihre Stärke vermindert."[69]

The review by N. Vil'mont deserves quotation as a statement of an informed and judicious critic. Vil'mont writes: "Though highly erudite, an excellent philologist, a wonderfully subtle expert on classical antiquity and the Renaissance, Briusov was nonetheless unable to reproduce the pointedness, the terseness, the ironic sharpness, the ease of Goethe's language in his *Faust*. Even the ironic intonations of Mephisto, which had become the common property of Russian poetry thanks to Pushkin's 'Scene from Faust,' . . . did not enter into and become part of Valeri Briusov's poetic style."[70]

One of the most critical voices is that of Victor Zhirmunski. Summing up his criticism, he states categorically, "Briusov's translation does not solve the problem of a Russian *Faust*," and continues with this sweeping generalization: "The epoch of Symbolism was incapable of providing an adequate poetic translation . . . not being attuned, ideologically, to the problems and images created by Goethe in the epoch of the ascendancy of bourgeois culture."[71]

While Zhirmunski's critique is too harsh in many of its details and couched in a Marxian jargon rare for this critic, it does shed light not only on Briusov's *Faust* translation but beyond it on the Russian Symbolists' entire relationship to Goethe the man and artist. Zhirmunski is right when he characterizes the Symbolists, and with them their leader, Briusov, as "not being attuned to the problems and images created by Goethe." The simplicity, the immediacy, and the vitality of Goethe's verse are unattainable to Briusov. He is quite unable to empathize with Goethe's vigorous, rapturous enjoyment of nature and of love's delights. To repeat, there is nothing akin to a "Mailied" in the entire corpus of Briusov's poetry nor, it is safe to say, in his personal life. Briusov was constitutionally incapable of appreciating nature. By his own admission he was left totally unimpressed amid the grandeur and beauty of the Caucasian mountains.[72] He experienced love through literature, not through life. He wanted to be a Don Juan, a seducer, and was only an "experimenter with love." His biographer states categorically: "Feelings are not part of Briusov's makeup. He knew about love only from books. . . . His virtues are a cold attentiveness and lack of emotion; the world and his personal life are to him but materials from which to fashion 'combinations of words [sochitaniia slov], brilliantly melodious verses [iarko pevuchikh stikhov].'"[73]

It is still more significant that Briusov is unable constitutionally to share in Goethe's optimism. As we have seen in his "Faust" poem, he characteristically consigns Goethe's hero and with him Gretchen, that "luminous spirit," to the realm of gloom and doom.[74] There is no salvation, no liberating sense of apotheosis, in Briusov's world, only gloomy forebodings and tentative hopes of a poet living at the "great divide," "na rubezhe." He may assert that "Goethe is near to [him]," that he feels him to be a "close friend." In fact, Goethe's world remains largely closed to him. Briusov could admire and celebrate Goethe as the "king and God of German poetry,"[75] but only across a gulf separating them because of irreconcilable differences in their personalities and in the *Zeitgeist* of their days.

Andrei Belyi (pen name of Boris Bugaev; 1880–1934), one of the leading members of the "young generation" of the Russian Symbolists, had been prepared for an encounter with Goethe's world earlier than Briusov, who had been born to an all-but-illiterate peasant and had to educate himself by sheer willpower, shrewd calculation, and unquenchable thirst for culture. Belyi was the son of a renowned professor of mathematics and dean of the faculty of science at the University of Moscow who had broad intellectual interests. Belyi's mother was a gifted amateur pianist with a predilection for composers of the Romantic school. As was customary in well-to-do families of the Russian intelligentsia, the boy's early upbringing was placed in the hands of governesses. In a characteristically lively autobiographical sketch, Belyi tells us that as a boy "of five and six [he] spent [his] days with governesses; first they were German, then came the French." One of these, a hexlike creature, insisted on reading to him the fairy tales of Andersen and of the Grimm brothers. She would single out for "vivid and cozy [!] commentaries" the various witches in the tales so that they became the boy's favorites.[76] But such appeal as that witchlike person had for young Andrei could not compare with the love he felt for his first German governess, Raisa Ivanovna. Belyi recalls: "I am three years old, am locked away together with Raisa Ivanovna in the nursery, and she is reading to me the poems of Uhland, Heine, Goethe, and Eichendorf (she is really reading them to herself). The poems' plot I understand poorly, but with my heart I grasp the verses and for the first time there rises before me the sound of 'music' thrilling me to the very core of my being: my mother plays Beethoven, Chopin, and Schumann."[77]

Such is Belyi's initiation into the world of fairy tale, music, German poetry, and in a most modest way, Goethe's poetry. For the sensitive, precocious boy with an unusually active imagination, this initiation becomes a very emotional experience. On having Uhland's "Das Schloss am Meer" read to him, his fantasy conjures up "a vision of a mysterious blind king. I was completely enthralled by my vision."[78] The reading of Goethe's ballad "Erlkönig" had a traumatic effect. He identifies with the dying boy in the ballad; he too had experienced the boy's terror in a terrible nightmare during a life-threatening illness. He had "the sensation of being rescued as by a miracle from a wild pursuit by what I felt had been death itself. That is why Goethe's 'Erlkönig' was such a shocking experience for me; it evoked the memory of the wild chase I had endured. After all, the child whom the elf-king entices to his realm was having a nightmare too."[79]

At sixteen Belyi was taken by his mother on the obligatory European tour: Germany, France, Switzerland, the entire route prescribed by inviolable custom. In school the young man promptly developed into an eager auto-didact. Habitually skipping the regular courses, he struck out on his own into the world of letters. "Think of it," he exclaimed in retrospect, in disbelief of his own feat, "think of what I mastered in those early days: Ibsen, Hauptmann, Sudermann, all of Dostoevski, all of Turgenev, Gontcharov, the 'Aesthetics of Hegel,' Schopenhauer, Goethe's *Faust*."[80] As a freshman at the University of Moscow, Belyi became fascinated with the theory of evolution. He set about tracing the history of that science "from its early beginnings with Francis Bacon by way of Jean Baptiste Lamarck, Geoffroy Saint-Hilaire, and Goethe to Darwin and Heckel."[81] Goethe the natural scientist moves into his ken. And yet Belyi feels that his contact with Goethe's personality and work would have remained "purely emotional" or "merely academic" had it not been for the influence of the Metner brothers, those "apostles of Goethe on Russian soil,"[82] especially of the older of the two, Emili. Belyi met Emili Metner in the fall of 1902, in Moscow, and "their stormy friendship began."[83] In Emili he found what he was searching for, a masterful interpreter of Goethe's personality and works, especially of Goethe's lyrics and of his *Faust*. Belyi literally sat at the master's feet, as he charmingly recalls in this delightful vignette, done with that touch of irony so characteristic of him: "Having selected some volume of Goethe, [Metner] would most deliciously [!] recite at tea with equally delicious biscuits reams of fascinating details from Goethe's life. There he would sit before me in his chair, coiled like a spring, precise, meticulously articulate, holding that dainty volume with gold-cut in his dainty hand." Thus proceeded Belyi's comprehensive initiation into Goethe's world by a truly knowledgeable and inspired mentor. It was Emili who brought Goethe to life for Belyi, Goethe the man, the poet, the savant.

Some two years earlier, in the spring of 1900, Belyi had experienced another "initiation," not so specifically focused on Goethe yet bringing him into contact with one of Goethe's important ideas, more precisely, with Goethe's *ideal* of *Das Ewig-Weibliche*. That spring he met Vladimir Solov'ev (1853–1900) and came under the spell, together with such other leading members of "the young Symbolists" as Aleksandr Blok and Viacheslav Ivanov, of that great philosopher-poet's cult of "Saint Sophia, the Blessed, the All-Wise," that embodiment for Solov'ev of the "Eternal-Feminine."[84]

Solov'ev's cult of Sophia had its inception in a truly mystical event, an epiphany. A beauteous figure clothed in celestial radiance had appeared to him during a Greek Orthodox mass when he was a boy of nine. Much later in his life the vision reappeared at a most unlikely place, the reading room of the British Museum, speaking to him and sending him to the Egyptian desert near Cairo, where—as she had promised—she rose before him, full-figure, for the third and last time.[85]

Compared with events of such psychic power, literary influences, no matter how impressive, could play only a secondary role,[86] yet there is clear evidence of Goethe's influence on Solov'ev. It is no accident that Solov'ev gives the German title "Das Ewig-Weibliche" to one of the two most important poems on his Sophia cult. It is Solov'ev's testimonial to his indebtedness to Goethe's ideal, expressed in the final two lines of his Faust ("Das Ewig-Weibliche / Zieht uns hinan"[87]) and portrayed in the "Makarie" chapters of *Wilhelm Meisters Wanderjahre*.[88] Throughout his life, Solov'ev drew inspiration from his celestial vision of the "Eternal-Feminine," of Sophia the "Most Wise" ("Premudraia").[89]

For Belyi, Solov'ev's Sophia cult was an experience he never forgot. It runs as one of the central motifs in his work, and insofar as it is also a celebration of Goethe's "Eternal Feminine," the German poet's ideal appears and reappears in Belyi's prose and poetry, early and late. Thus in his essay "Apokalypsis in Russian Poetry" (1904) he prayerfully entreats the "Holy One" to descend unto this earth "ripe as a golden fruit filled with sweetness" for her coming. And she does descend and actually appears to Belyi incarnated in the beautiful Liubov Dmitrievna Mendeleieva, the lawfully wedded wife of his friend Aleksandr Blok. As was to be expected, this incarnation could not withstand the vicissitudes of the real world, and Belyi's worship of beautiful Liubov was doomed to a tragic denouement.[90] And yet the ideal of the *Ewig-Weibliche* lived on for Belyi. In the aptly entitled essay "The Crisis of Life,"[91] Belyi is sustained by that ideal in his optimism during the devastating years of war and revolution.[92] He sees himself standing at the very threshold of a new world. He knows that "Sophia the Wisest is lighting the heavenly lights in the darkness, and wreathed in that light she is approaching." Belyi closes his essay with the verses of Solov'ev that had inspired him in his youth: "Know thou! The Eternal Feminine is even now descending to this earth in her immortal body." And finally, one of Belyi's late poems, entitled "The First Meeting," is clearly a poetic answer to Solov'ev's Sophia poems ("Das Ewig-Weibliche" and "Three Meetings") and as such another late echo of Goethe's ideal.

After the Metners and Solov'ev there entered into Belyi's life still another Goetheist whose influence on him proved far less beneficent, in fact, outright tragic. It was Rudolf Steiner, the anthroposophist,[93] who drew in his teachings most liberally on Goethe's works, especially on his *Faust* and on his writings on the natural sciences. The meeting with Steiner had a tremendous effect on Belyi's mystically inclined mind.[94] He records his first impression of Steiner: "His beardless, sharply cut, hard face seems . . . that of a youth of nineteen and not that of a mature man, and yet from that face radiate streams of an invisible maelstrom . . . shocking you to your very depths." Belyi felt as if he had been "torn from his normal body."[95] He followed Steiner to Leipzig, where he attended his lectures. He describes their impact on him in words that echo the anthroposophist's argot: "In the impact of these lectures on me there transpired the mystery of the *cleansing* of the soul; the profound shock to the astral body [Astralleib!] is transformed into a shock to the soul, tearing it from the body. That cleansing was preceded by indescribable explosions of purely spiritual love for all mankind."[96] Belyi had given himself "body and soul to the worshiped, incomparable teacher."[97] He follows him to Dornach, that "theosophic Bethlehem."[98] There he joins in the labors on the "Goetheanum,"[99] a temple dedicated to the sanctified poet, attends Steiner's seminars, and wrestles with the master's turgid teachings, driving himself to the brink of insanity.[100] In retrospect, Belyi gives an account of those harrowing years still throbbing with the horror he had experienced.[101] Belyi finally left Dornach in

1916, but not until 1919 could he free himself from Steiner's overwhelming influence.

Belyi's thralldom [102] to Steiner placed its indelible imprint on his attitude and view of Goethe, thus greatly complicating the task of presenting his personally authentic image of the German poet, especially since much of the relevant evidence is contained in the volume *Rudolf Steiner and Goethe*, written in the Dornach years.

Following is Belyi's image of Goethe expurgated, as far as possible, from Steiner's obfuscations and distortions: Like many of the Russian Symbolists, Belyi sees in Goethe the forebear of their movement. "Goethe's pronouncement 'Alles Vergängliche ist nur ein Gleichnis' has found its ultimate confirmation in the works of the Symbolists," [103] and "Goethe is not only a 'Classicist,' he is also a Symbolist. . . . Plato is the philosopher of Symbolism, Goethe is the 'Symbol' of that philosophy." [104] "Goethe the classicist has crowned his *oeuvre* with the deeply symbolical Second Part of *Faust*. The symbolism of *Faust* is profoundly contemplative; it speaks all-embracingly of the symbolic development of mankind." Continuing, Belyi aptly observes that "Goethe frequently obscured the profundity of his symbols with the veil of everyday triteness, as he did, for instance, in *Wilhelm Meisters Lehrjahre* and in the *Wahlverwandtschaften*, among other works." [105] It is significant that Belyi does not include the *Wanderjahre*. He places that part of the Wilhelm Meister novel second only to *Faust* in the directness and richness of its "contemplative" symbolism.

Belyi tends to exaggerate the religious element in Goethe's life and work, tries to make of him a poet in the Christian tradition. He traces the "religious consciousness" of the Russian Symbolists [106] to Goethe's influence: "The new religious consciousness of my generation," he writes, "is providentially linked in its secret origins to Goethe. . . . In Goethe's life and work there is an immortal, evangelical, joyful seriousness. . . . In all his writings we constantly hear the divine annunciation of the inexpressible, which is celebrating its resurrection in our souls and becomes objectified in religious forms, images, and symbols." [107]

Surprisingly, this "religious," this "Christian" Goethe is closely linked by Belyi to Nietzsche, that atheist among philosophers who had declared God as dead and had condemned the Christian spirit of Wagner's *Parzifal*. For Belyi, "Goethe and Nietzsche are bound together by the very essence of their creativity." [108] He insists that "Goethe and Nietzsche frequently speak of the same," the only difference being that "Goethe raises, as if by chance, only a small corner of the veil hiding the mysterious depths, while Nietzsche strives to throw the depths up to the surface and forcefully emphasizes this act of phenomenal exposure." [109] In this difference of Goethe's and Nietzsche's basic approach and style, Belyi recognizes the reason why his contemporaries, so greatly enamored with "mystical depths," readily recognized these "depths" in Nietzsche's *Zarathustra* verses which break the contours of images and logical consistency of thought" while they remained blind to the "theosophical depths of Goethe's *Faust*." [110] For Belyi, Goethe's *Faust* is no less profound than Nietzsche's creations, even though Goethe does not go as far as Nietzsche in breaking with the laws of traditional prosody.

A word of caution here: One should not expect consistency and logic in Belyi's "arabesques." Freewheeling imagination, inconsistencies, outright contradictions, and erratic leaps in reasoning are typical for him. Thus, having linked Goethe and Nietzsche "through the very essence of their creativity," having proclaimed "Nietzsche's *Zarathustra* the lawful successor of Goethe's lyrics," [111] he can blithely maintain soon after in the same essay that "Nietzsche not only stands as an outsider to the world of Kant, Beethoven, and Goethe [!] but also has nothing whatever in common with Schopenhauer, Ibsen, and Wagner." [112]

The most extensive document of Belyi's view of Goethe is his study *Rudolf Steiner and Goethe in the Contemporary World View*," [113] a product of the Dornach years of toil and torment. It is a turgid eulogy to Steiner [114] and a vicious polemic against his quondam friend and teacher Emili Metner, who had dared to attack Steiner in his challenging volume *Thoughts on Goethe*. [115] Still, Belyi manages to devote a considerable portion of the volume to an esoteric interpretation of Goethe's *Farbenlehre*, [116] from which it was possible to extract a substantive statement of Belyi's understanding not only of that particular work but also of Goethe's basic method and approach as a natural scientist. [117]

Belyi is fully aware of the importance of Goethe's theory of colors as a bold departure from the generally accepted Newtonian. It is precisely in comparing and contrasting Goethe's theory with Newton's that Belyi sheds the most revealing light on his view of Goethe the natural scientist. In simplest terms, Belyi sees Newton as the "mechanist," Goethe as the "organicist." This characterization of Goethe is not new in the Russian's image of him. It had been adumbrated by the Russian Romantics and explicitly stated by Apollon Grigor'ev. [118] Yet Belyi develops it in a way that buttresses central tenets of the Symbolist movement. "Goethe," he argues, "looked into the future over the heads of his contemporaries; many of his basic insights were not a rehash of obsolete metaphysical notions but a *symbolical vision* of the future." Belyi presents his argument in great detail. The following is but an excerpt of essentials: "Light in Goethe's sense was not known to contemporary physics. Newton had tried to explain the phenomenon of light in the spirit of the mechanistic concepts of his time; Goethe's aim is to explain the ethical and aesthetic effect of colors—Newton's prism is not Goethe's prism." Newton starts with the concept "color" and proceeds to measure and to weigh the colors green, blue, red, etc., considering them to be static entities. Goethe, in contrast, "proceeds from the concept 'kolorit' [hue, shading], a concept far less tangible, more illusive, flowing, more organic, alive; it is both more concrete and more ethereal than Newton's mechanically conceived color." "Newton's color is abstract and heterogeneous to nature; Goethe's color is alive . . . ; Newton's color is quantitative, Goethe's qualitative, it is a given in our experience, illuminated aesthetically, profoundly conceptualized philosophically. . . . Darkness is for Newton 'nothingness'; for Goethe it is 'something,' namely, matter." For Goethe, "light and darkness are not juxtaposed, they are fused; they are not (as they are for Newton) analytic concepts or even synthetic ones, they are *symbols*." Belyi places greatest importance on Goethe's insistence that, contrary to Newton's thesis, "white light is not a composite of the rainbow of colors but an indivisible whole, and that this indivisible oneness is *spiritual*."

Belyi is intent on the sharpest possible differenciation between Goethe's theory of color and light and Newton's. And yet it would be a serious error to present Belyi's contrapositing of Goethe and Newton as absolute. Actually, Belyi sees their theories as interrelated. He visualizes them as "two comets whose tails intertwine." Goethe "expanded his method to interact with Newton's mechanistic approach, while Newton had expanded and refined his mechanistic theory so as to anticipate, to some degree, Goethe's metaphysical approach." Goethe the poet knew how to value the scientific methods of Newton in his study of color and light. "He was abreast of the experimental physics of his time; in his experiments his motto was circumspection, many-sidedness, inventiveness. . . . Goethe's opposition to Newton was not the opposition of a 'dilettante poet.' Goethe was a serious opponent of Newton, quite capable of meeting him on his own ground."

Belyi argues that Goethe "freed himself from the methods of mechanistic physics" by developing the concept of the protophenomenon (Urphänomen). Goethe's pioneering approach, Belyi insists, was made possible by his unique gift of what Goethe himself had called "empathetic exact imagination." This gift enabled him to recognize the important "milestones" in the formation of nature that surround us, "to discover nature's 'secret laws.'" It enabled him to discover the intermaxillary bone in man, to recognize the source of a sheep's skull to be four vertebrae of the spine, to conceive the proto-plant (Urpflanze), to establish the principle of metamorphosis. To that same special endowment of an "empathetic exact imagination" Belyi traces Goethe's abhorrence of all heavy-handed mechanistic experimentation with nature, of "any method that tethers nature to the Procrustean bed and subjects it to tortures of the Inquisition." Early in his career as a natural scientist, Goethe had realized that nature could not be forced to reveal its secrets, would not yield them except to the empathetic investigator endowed with that special gift of an observant eye and an "exact imagination." And Belyi concludes: "Goethe's methods do not violate nature; they are a realistic communion with it, never its torture, never its rape." Goethe the sensitive, imaginative artist worked hand in hand with Goethe the scientist. "The poet's divinations became with him the scientist's exact, logically reasoned knowledge." Goethe is for Belyi an "empirical idealist" (an apt term he borrowed from Steiner) who combined in his experiments reasoning with sharp-eyed, empathetic observation of nature's phenomena.

With all these insights, Belyi follows a well-trod path in Goethe research and rehearses generally accepted facts, some of which he found developed in Rudolf Steiner's writings, lectures, and seminars. However, Belyi takes a problematical tack when he etherealizes Goethe's scientific message and baptizes Goethe the scientist into a religious, even orthodox, Christian priest and prophet. We had occasion to observe this characteristic bias in Belyi's view of Goethe, which can be traced partly to his inborn mystico-religious tendencies reinforced by these same tendencies in many of his fellow Symbolists and partly to Steiner's anthroposophic preachments, which dangerously exaggerated Belyi's mystical leanings.

Examples of this bias in Belyi's emotion-charged volume are many. For instance, he seriously maintains that "with Goethe's concept of 'light' we stand for the first time at the very threshold of the insight that 'light' is the light of transubstantiation of our body, that light *is* indeed *transubstantiation*" and that "Goethe's light" is possible only in the ray of the light of Christ, his concept of color only as the hierarchical rainbow! Goethe's color descends as a rainbow from heaven to earth; angels and archangels hold their discourse on it. The world of color is the creation of angels, realizable only in their battle with the spirits of darkness. . . . Color poured throughout the world sends us the message that the soul of man is following its ordained path from darkness into the light." With this passage Belyi is intent not only on proving that Goethe's message is a religious, Christian one, but also on demonstrating the productive interaction in Goethe's work of the poet's vision (*Faust:* "Prologue in Heaven") with the scientist's, the "empirical idealist's," observations and deductions. I find his effort in both respects less than successful.

Belyi frequently waxes darkly oracular, obfuscating rather than clarifying Goethe's message. Such is the case when he grotesquely departs from any conceivable textual evidence in the *Farbenlehre* and paints for us a mythological picture of the interaction of darkness and light to produce the clair-obscure effects. He presents it as a "fierce battle between some kind of Ormuzds and Arimans [gods of Eastern mythology]; under the mighty blows of their swords there flows, like some kind of ethereal blood, the clair-obscure color." Or again, when summing up, he grandly makes the arcane announcement that "with Goethe we stand at the threshold of macrocosmic physics and mathematics conceived as sciences about freedom." This, Belyi claims, "is the thrust of Goethe's thinking: Philosophy, science, and art are combinable not within their unique, discrete spheres but only in the most concrete truth." One is tempted to ask "What freedom?" and "What is the nature of that most concrete truth?" For the answer to the first question, Belyi sends us to Nietzsche's *Die fröhliche Wissenschaft*, for the answer to the second he sends us to the "Discourses" of the Bhagavad Gita, that depository of Eastern wisdom.

Such, in its essentials, is Belyi's image of Goethe, traditional in many of its features, startling in some original flashes of insight, disconcerting in many of its inconsistencies, obfuscations, and distortions, a great number of them the result of the overwhelming influence of Rudolf Steiner. Yet whatever our evaluation of Belyi's contribution, there can be no doubt that with it he has added a number of new facets to the Russian image of Goethe, especially of Goethe the natural scientist. No Russian author before him has delved so deeply into the complexities of Goethe's *Farbenlehre*.[119] A comprehensive study of Russian Symbolists in their use and theory of colors has yet to be written. Belyi is certain to play an important role in such a treatise.

Aleksandr Blok and Sergei Solov'ev

In Konstantin Mochul'ski's empathetic and informed biography of Aleksandr Blok (1880–1921) we read: "He dreamed of 'Das Ewig-Weibliche,' . . . but he also had a second mother-country—Russia. . . . Thus in the soul of Blok the Romanticism of the German West collided with the 'Shamanism' of the Russia of song and legend [pesennaia Rossia]. The tension and fusion of these opposites is the true source of Blok's lyrics," [120] a perceptive observation that aptly defines the productive dualism in this poet with a twofold heritage: from the father the Mecklenburger, from the mother the "pure Russian." [121] Blok's parents were divorced when he was very young, and contacts with his father were sporadic and overshadowed by fear, even horror, of him. The boy grew up in his mother's family, the Beketovs, who were pronouncedly Anglophile and Francophile. His mother, a writer of considerable talent and a prolific translator, preferred French and English literature.[122] Thus Blok's acquaintance with German letters was slow in developing. When he did establish contact, it was the Romantic poets that became his favorites—Novalis, the young Tieck, E. T. A. Hoffmann, and especially Heine—a fascination that never faded. In his last years Blok was busily preparing a Russian edition of that poet.[123]

Blok was introduced to Goethe, as were so many of his fellow Symbolists of the "young generation," by Vladimir Solov'ev, specifically through Solov'ev's cult of "*Das Ewig-Weibliche*" in the mystical figure of "Sophia the Most Wise." Blok recalls this event in his autobiography: "Together with intense mystical and Romantic experiences, my whole being was overwhelmed by the poetry of Vladimir Solov'ev." [124] And in the *Diary of the Year 1902*, he notes: "There appeared as one of the brightest mystical constellations on the blue heavens of poetry—*Das Ewig-Weibliche*, the Eternal-Feminine [Vechnaia Zhenstvennost']." [125]

This was the spark that helped ignite Blok's lyric genius. [126] In his first important collection of poems, *The Verses About the Beautiful Lady*, [127] Blok celebrates this ideal. Originally he had intended to give the collection the title "About the Eternal Feminine" because, as he wrote to Briusov, "basically this is the theme of all my verses." [128] Of course it would be an error to claim that Goethe was a decisive influence on Blok. To be sure, Blok did call Goethe "a gigantic and legendary figure," [129] yet basically Goethe's world remained distant for Blok, except for his *Faust*, [130] with its glorification of *Das Ewig-Weibliche*. That ideal unquestionably helped the budding poet create the image of the "Beautiful Lady," which was to grow in his verses and change into a very different, far more complex self-contradictory persona or, rather, into a long sequence of personae at once mythical and real. [131] Blok set out to "correct" his predecessors' vision of the Eternal Feminine, to present its true appearance as he perceived it and experienced it in joy and suffering, despair and hope.

In response to Andrei Belyi's request to define for him the essence of the Eternal Feminine, Blok replied in a letter of July 1903, that is, at the very time he was setting out to develop his vision of that ideal: "She [the Eternal-Feminine], if she be 'Good,' she is that only in aesthetic embodiments, as, for instance, in the poetry of Afanasi Fet or in Baudelaire's verses ('À la très bonne'). The conception of her true being has hardly become more profound since Goethe's time; at most it has grown more extended." [132] It is precisely Blok's central mission as a poet to make more "profound," more "true," and more "realistic" his predecessors' visions of the "Eternal Woman."

It is not difficult to recognize in Blok's "Beautiful Lady" many traits of Solov'ev's Sophia and of Goethe's *Ewig Weibliche*. She does "draw [the poet] heavenward," does uplift, inspire, and ennoble him. Yet in contrast to Goethe's and Solov'ev's conception of her, she also rouses in the poet fear and despair, causes him torment and anguish by her remoteness, inconstancy, aloofness, coldness, and even cruelty. He feels himself "slowly losing his mind at the door of her for whom he is yearning." [133] He is demeaned by her to the role of a "slave," an "altar boy [otrok], lighting the holy candles and tending the sacred fire, while she is laughing on that other shore [i.e., her unapproachable

world] without a thought, without a word" for him (I, 204). In Blok's embodiment of the Eternal-Feminine "are secreted, waiting for their release, both a
mighty light and a ferocious darkness" (I, 190). Her illusiveness is wonderfully caught in the laconism of the lines "I know: You are here. You are near. /
You are not here. You are—there" (I, 237).

Blok was soon to "betray" his role as "prophet" to his "Beautiful Lady"
and to turn into a poet with his eyes fixed on the realities of the modern
world.[134] The world of Russian medieval legend dissolves, the Beautiful Lady
"departs into the snows never to return" (I, 213).[135] Yet the "Eternal-Feminine"
was to remain the central figure in Blok's poetry, appearing in ever-changing
forms as the poet searches for ever more adequate symbols to express his
vision of her. To quote Briusov, Blok's well-informed and sensitive interpreter, "The mystical hymns of Blok to his Beautiful Lady were soon replaced by passionate verses to a 'Beautiful Female Friend' and to the 'Snow
Maiden.'[136]. . . In his dramas, Blok mercilessly ridicules his youthful dream
of the Eternal-Feminine, transforming it into the image of Columbine, who in
the end turns out to be a 'cardboard bride,'[137] or leading his Neznakomka
[Stranger-Woman][138] into the company of soulless and blind people."[139] We
have Blok's own definition of the Neznakomka: "That is not at all simply a
lady in a black dress with ostrich feathers on her hat. That is a devil's alloy of
many worlds."[140] What a far cry from Solov'ev's Sophia or from Goethe's
"Ewig-Weiblichem." And yet this Neznakomka whose "heart is filled with
poison" attracts the poet irresistibly, enthralls, uplifts him, "inspires him to
countless songs" (I, 334). These figures are joined by ever-changing ones, yet
all of them are embodiments of Blok's sharp-eyed, "realistic" vision of the
"Eternal Feminine."

In Blok's poetic world we meet with harlots in saloons, with prostitutes in
cheap brothels, in sleazy taverns with gypsies whose songs enrapture him,
whose "raven-black, snakelike tresses" threaten him with death by strangula-
tion. We follow Faima to the modern metropolis, with its "Universal Palaces
of Art and Culture," with its "Temples of Beauty and Progress where all men
are equal." For Blok these are symbols of a soulless, superficial, money-, sex-,
and 'progress'-crazed civilization, detested by him as the irreconcilable an-
titheses to his concept of true culture.[141] Faima is the ultimate embodiment of
Blok's vision of the Eternal Womanhood, many-faceted, truly an "alloy" of
good and evil. She is a sadistic mondaine whose snakelike whip whistles over
the shoulders of her cowed admirers, who slashes the cheek of her lover; she is
"the lofty thought turned gypsy"; she is "sly and cunning," a "bird in winged,
dancing flight, faithful to none"; she is the beautiful, poisonous snake—
"Hey!" she hisses, "Hey! Take care! I am all snake!" And yet it is she who
promises Herman, her chosen one, an unimaginable freedom, a release from

the shackles of his confining, shallow, lifeless bourgeois existence; she "up-lifts" him to a freedom he both fears and yearns for.[142]

From the magical, lyrical world of the *Verses to the Beautiful Lady*, the poet transports us to the *Terrifying World*, the *Strashnyi Mir* (III, 7–63), into the world of *Retribution and Punishment*, of *Vozmezdie* (III, 64–84, 295–344), a world experienced by him as a palpable reality and as a symbolic realm charged with mystery, magic, and myth. It is in this world of *Retribution and Punishment* that we meet for the first and only time in Blok's poetic work the figure of Faust. "*This* [*Sei*] Faust"[143] had been professor and dean, had had scholarly achievements, had stubbornly pursued knowledge and truth, "der Weisheit letzten Schluss." He had known unforgettable moments of profound insight, of a sense of power, of divine inspiration. He even had been in his youth a radical. But then the darkness of night had descended on him, and now, in his "cold and cruel dreams," he suffers the *Woe from Wit*, that vitriolic message of Aleksandr Griboedov's famous satire on the anti-intellectual spirit in the Russia of his days. Now "*this* Faust" lives in his dank, dark cave of an apartment (the "dumpfes Mauerloch" of Goethe's Faust), cluttered with books and papers, dust-covered, with rags and every sort of object the poet would not name, "forgotten by the people, by God, and by himself, a beaten dog."

Blok's portrayal[144] of "*this* Faust" is no mechanical borrowing from Goethe's *Faust*, yet echoes from the play are unmistakable and obviously intentional (especially from Act I, Scene 1). But what is totally absent in Blok's presentation of the life of *his* Faust is the ultimate salvation, the apotheosis. Instead, this Faust's crushing fate is a "dog's life" to its bitter end, is neglect, loneliness, and tuberculosis brought on by his very "striving," is death in a rundown hospital (III, 255).

Such is Blok's "correction" of Goethe's optimistic vision of Faust's apotheosis, a correction as negative as Dostoevski's yet in Blok's version focused not on Faustian atheistic *superbia* as the cause of his damnation but on the *Zeitgeist* at the "great divide—*na rubezhe*." The darkness of the "iron age" (as Blok likes to call his troublous times) envelopes *this* Faust and destroys him. This Faust is, moreover, the tragic victim of the forces of "retribution" that have grown in the dark ages of Russian history with their injustices, exploitation, and suppression of the Russian people.

There is another "correction" by Blok, this one amounting to an outright criticism of Goethe for his passive attitude in times of crisis. We find it in the essay "The Destruction of Humanism,"[145] in which Blok traces the causes of that destruction to forces within humanism itself, placing in the course of his impassioned argument a substantial part of the blame on Goethe. Thus Blok joins the ranks of the numerous Russian critics of the poet, yet his criticism

differs fundamentally from theirs. Belinski, Herzen, Chernyshevski, Pisarev—
they all had faulted Goethe for his apolitical aestheticism, his lack of "sociality," his Olympian aloofness, his "idealistic humanism," which they so
thoroughly detested. Blok, in sharp contrast, attacks Goethe precisely for his
failure to support "idealistic humanism," as Blok envisaged it,* with the full
weight of his immense authority. Blok is determined to smash the traditional
image of Goethe as the active champion of humanism. He sets out to debunk
the "myth" of Goethe's spiritual kinship with Schiller, that true idealistic humanist, which Blok finds so blatantly symbolized in the famous statue in
Weimar representing the two geniuses hand in hand. "If I were a sculptor," he
assures us, "I would never have sculpted Schiller and Goethe joining hands in
a brotherly gesture. Schiller I would have presented as a youth eagerly and
fearlessly gazing into a mist-shrouded abyss opening up before him. This
youth I see standing in the shadow of another figure, huge and enigmatically
mysterious. That figure is a Goethe who seems to shrink into the protective
shadows of the past, retreating before a blinding vision of a future which his
sharp eyes perceive in the misty depths." In Blok's visionary evocation, Goethe
appears as a fainthearted giant unable to break courageously with the "sheltering past," immobilized by his congenital indecisiveness and ambivalence.

Both these figures, Blok would have us know, "are equally dear and near
to us Symbolists." Yet he cannot hide where his sympathies really lie—with
Schiller, of course, in whom he admires "the last great European humanist,
the last one of the clan of the faithful to the spirit of music." † [146] And he
prophesies, "With Schiller will die the style of humanism. . . . Goethe will
be left alone. . . . He will perceive in the darkness the outlines of the future,
but he will never enter it. Lonely Goethe will watch, motionless, the tongues
of flame flickering eerily in the cathedral," which symbolizes for Blok the
doomed Europe of the Enlightenment. "Goethe listens to the music of these
flames . . . frozen in his immobility, in his mystifying ambivalence toward
everything."

This passage is not only revealing of Blok's view of Goethe and Schiller,
it is also a striking example of the Symbolists' characteristic image-making, a

---

*For Blok, the materialistic, utilitarian humanitarianism of the Radical Democrats, espe-
cially of Pisarev, was anathema. For him it stood in irreconcilable opposition to Schillerian
"idealistic humanism," which, as interpreted by Blok, rejected technological progress dependent
on soulless machines, Blok's *bêtes noires*.

†With Blok the term "music" assumes a special meaning. It is a concept he developed
under the influence of Schopenhauer, Nietzsche, and Wagner. With him the term transcends its
academic connotation and takes on an ontological, noumenal signification. For Blok, "music" is
the very "rhythm of culture, the essence of life." When the rhythm is lost, culture changes to
dead, mechanical civilization. (Cf. *Sob. Soch.* 7:260 and passim.)

type of portrayal more revealing of the portraitist than of the personae portrayed. In his image of Goethe and Schiller as they stand facing the "dark abyss," Blok has symbolically mirrored himself standing at the "great divide," gazing "with sharp eyes" into the "mist-shrouded depths" of a future that holds out a great promise as well as a dire threat.

When Blok wrote this essay the "cathedral" he had seen burning in his phantasmagoric vision had been consumed by the raging flames of war and revolution. Blok not only suffered this tragedy fated to be endured by his generation but also had to bear a truly heartrending loss that he inflicted on himself by betraying the idol of his youth, the "Beautiful Lady," *das Ewig-Weibliche*. He fervently, insistently, and prayerfully entreats her to return: "Return, return, return," he prays, "come back to me when the fated torments have ended. We will pray to Thee amid the terrors and passions that it is our destiny to endure. Once again I will await Thou, always Thy slave, *who has betrayed Thou*, but who has again, again returned. . . . Preserve in me the piercingly sharp memories. Do not assuage my torturing restlessness, do not cut short my torments. Let me behold Thy dawn. Come back, return." [147]

Blok's prayer was in vain. The vision of the "Eternal Feminine," once "betrayed," could never be recaptured. [148] His past lay in ruins before him. The future did not keep its promise of a better world, but it did carry out its dire threat. [149] The October Revolution, so ardently welcomed by the poet and his source of inspiration for his last and perhaps greatest masterpiece, *The Twelve*, [150] was soon to petrify into the "iron" dictatorship of the proletariat. Blok could no longer hear the "music" that was for him the very "essence of life," its "flowing thought," [151] and in the "enveloping silence of the grave" [152] he too fell silent and died at the age of forty, a disillusioned, broken man.

Aleksandr Blok had censured Goethe for his lack of commitment, for his ambivalence in the defense of humanism. His close friend Sergei Solov'ev (1885–1941), nephew of the great Vladimir and a Symbolist deeply rooted in Greek Orthodoxy, attacks Goethe for diametrically opposite reasons, for Goethe's inexcusable preference for humanism over the Christian faith, for his betrayal of the Crucified One to the heathen gods of antiquity. Solov'ev does give Goethe credit for having "pointed the way to the most sacred secrets of Indian theosophy by way of the Samothracian mysteries." He is pleased to find Goethe dissatisfied with Protestantism and seeking "nourishment for his artistically and mystically attuned spirit in Catholicism." [153] He credits Goethe with a "symbolic wisdom." [154] He even admits that Goethe's Hellenism carried "mystical traits that distinguished him from the rationalist-philosophers of the Enlightenment," whom Solov'ev despised. [155] But save for these grudgingly given compliments, his attack on Goethe is unremitting. In Goethe's life and work he detects the "hidden cult of pride and atheistic self-assertion," a "culpable lack of Christian humility." Goethe's entire "well-structured, balanced, logically consistent life's philosophy" is for Solov'ev "an unrelieved affirmation of this world not in the Christian spirit of subordinating it to that other realm which is not *in* or *of* this world" but in the spirit of Spinoza, "establishing the autonomy of nature, equating it to God: *Deus sive Natura*." [156] Summing up, Solov'ev defines Goethe's world view as "an amalgam of atheism and epicureanism, of a classicism incompletely understood, of German optimism [!], of Protestant ethics, and of an almost consistently demonic pantheism." He admits that it is possible to combine, "in some fashion, such diverse elements in one's *writings*, but in *life* one of these must gain the upper hand. Alas, in the life of the great Olympian [!] it was Epicureanism that took precedence above all others." [157]

From his Greek Orthodox perspective, Solov'ev sees the Italian journey as a fateful event in Goethe's life, the *locus classicus* of his tragic aberration: "Worshiping sun and earth, placing his faith in the male and female origin of the heathen Pantheon, Goethe raised the statues of Jupiter and Juno in his Roman cell [!] and 'addressed to them his morning prayers,' having turned in disgust from the church of the Crucified One." [158]

With such a view of Goethe, Solov'ev could not but reject his *Faust*. He condemns Faust's "eternal striving" as being carried out in the devil's name. "Striving," Solov'ev warns, "leads to salvation only when directed toward philanthropy. . . . Passivity is better than activity in the cause of evil." He cannot fathom how Goethe could save Faust. "And this necromancer," he exclaims in rage and consternation, "does not perish, nor is he made to recant." On the contrary, for all his evil deeds, his necromancy, and his sorcery, for his ruthless disregard of human lives, Goethe actually proclaims him a hero of "eternal striving" and celebrates his apotheosis: "Faust is borne aloft by angels and saintly ascetics to the very throne of the immaculate Virgin, the Mater Gloriosa." From this unheard-of sacrilege, Solov'ev dates "the beginning of the Nietzschean transvaluation of all values, the inception of the philosophy 'beyond good and evil.'"

Moreover, Solov'ev makes the Faustian spirit responsible for the destruction and carnage of the First World War: "Germany," he argues, "followed in the footsteps of Faust and plunged the world into a bloody war. Russia, on the other hand, followed Gretchen [!]," in whom he finds personified "the noble spirit of humility and the spirit of Christian Orthodoxy leading humanity to peace and to its salvation."

According to Solov'ev, "Goethe was utterly blind to the fact that this world is caught in the snares of evil, that sin is a very real force. For Goethe, as for Leibniz, this world was the 'best of all possible worlds.' . . . Goethe refused to accept the axiomatic assumption of the Christian world view, the very real existence of the devil and of original sin." These grave errors spelled Goethe's doom. Solov'ev finds "Goethe's tragedy reflected in his face." Goethe's late portraits he judges to be "very characteristic of the man."

His face, furrowed by deep wrinkles, is crude and heavy. The chin grows ever more sensuous. The lower part of the face expresses an astounding stubbornness of physical vitality, of his love affair with the terrestrial sphere, with the phenomenal world. Yet his eyes speak of quite something different. These dark Italian [!] eyes burn ever more fiercely with a mystical fire; in them flicker ever more brightly sudden flashes of terror. It is the nocturnal, chaotic side of Goethe's nature that flickers and flashes here, a deeply rooted trait he could not cure with the healing powers of Christianity and had to suppress and smother artificially by means of the empiricism [!] he had helped create. How helpless that great man, "Solov'ev exclaims," as helpless as all the great Hellens up to Socrates, who trembled before the secrets of the grave.

And Solov'ev imagines seeing "the old, wise man staring terror-struck at a door opening before him into the realm of eternal night, into a nameless chaos."

We cannot be certain which of the "late portraits" Solov'ev refers to, but we can be sure that most of the features and gestures of Goethe he describes are in the eye of this beholder and not characteristic of the late portraits and busts or of the model who sat for them. This is a portrait drawn by a representative of the extreme right wing of the Russian ideological spectrum, an image quite as distorted as the one done by Pisarev, that representative of the extreme left wing of the Radical Democrats. Ideological extremism, right or left, is no reliable guide to a felicitous interpretation of Goethe.

Viacheslav Ivanov (1866–1949)

"In 1903, Viacheslav Ivanov, 'Viacheslav the Magnificent,' spectacularly appeared from nowhere, bedazzled the Russian literary public, and quickly won eminence among the younger Symbolists." [159] The erudition and many-sidedness of this "Wizard of Symbolism" was truly "bedazzling." He was a poet, historian, philosopher, aesthetician, translator, editor, critic, a widely traveled man who knew the Near East, had studied ancient history in Germany with the great Theodor Mommsen, had lived in Greece, Italy, and France, deeply absorbing their culture. Briusov recognized in him "the born eclectic. All times and all countries are equally close to him." [160] Of Ivanov it can truly be said that Goethe and his time and country were "close to him." He can be compared only to the Metner brothers in his grasp of Goethe's aesthetics, in the diligence and empathy with which he delved into Goethe's biography and the vast range of his works.

Goethe's influence is noticeable in Ivanov's poetry, highly supportive in his essays. The most important collection of his lyrics has for its motto the first strophe of his favorite Goethe poem, "Selige Sehnsucht" ("Sagt es niemand, nur den Weisen . . ."). The title of the collection, *Cor Ardens* (*The Ardent Heart*),[161] announces a central theme of the first part of the work: the ardent heart seeks its death in the sacred flame of love and, perishing, is reborn, enhanced into a higher existence, clearly Ivanov's mystical variation on the last strophe of Goethe's poem with its peremptory dictum "Stirb und werde!" Another important collection, *Kormchie Zvëzdy* (*Guiding Stars*),[162] again has a Goethe quotation for its motto, this one from *Faust*: "Du regst und rührst ein kräftiges Beschliessen / Zum höchsten Dasein immerfort zu streben. . . ." In addition, this collection has a number of quotations as mottos for individual poems. All the Goethe lines are uplifting in their mood and message, as if Ivanov had conjured up Goethe's most optimistic, forward-looking, activistic spirit to counterbalance his own generally autumnal, pessimistic, tenebrous verses.

Goethe's influence is particularly evident in Ivanov's theoretical writings. Thus his important essay "Manner, Personality, Style"[163] shows a striking similarity in its themes and organization to Goethe's essay "Einfache Nachahmung, Manier, Stil."[164] Its very title reminds one of Goethe's. Ivanov, like Goethe, considers "simple imitation" but a preliminary stage in the artistic process. As Goethe defines it, "Die einfache Nachahmung arbeitet . . . gleichsam im Vorhof des Stils." Ivanov is more severe in his critique. "It is an error," he writes, "to consider the artist's mission as being merely a passive reproduction of life, for then the mimetic element gains the upper hand, which, according to Plato, is the original sin of art, its negative pole." Like Goethe, Ivanov defines "Manier" as a predominantly "subjective" mode of expression and as such inferior to "style." According to him, style is achieved through "the complete objectification of the subjective content of 'Manier.'" He echoes Goethe's lofty evaluation of "style," if not in his exact words then certainly in his spirit, when he stresses that "art in the strictest sense of that term is achieved only at the moment marked by the triumph of style. . . ." But, he continues, "Such a lofty achievement is bought at the high cost of self-limitation." He closes his essay by citing a favorite Goethe dictum: "In der Beschränkung zeigt sich erst der Meister." In another essay, "Two Elements in Contemporary Symbolism,"[165] Ivanov identifies Goethe as the "originator (rodonachal'nik)" of "modern, realistic Symbolism," which "nourishes its roots in Goethe's creations." And he explains, "Goethe has interpreted the symbol in his Goethean objectively apprehending, observing, and at the same time mystical sense. Goethe approaches idealistic art with the only completely justified demand, equally acceptable to and sanctified by realistic art, the demand that the artist discover and affirm the universal and eternal type in the fleeting multiplicity of phenomena." Ivanov considers this to be the reason "why the contemporary 'realist-symbolist poet' hears a congenial, kindred message in Goethe's legacy passed on to the artist in the pages of *Wilhelm Meisters Wanderjahre.*" Here follow several quotations from the novel (partly in Ivanov's Russian prose paraphrase, partly in the original German) which illuminate and support his esoteric argument.

Many other examples of Ivanov's dependence on Goethe can be cited. His piece on the mystical poet Churlanov, for instance, draws for buttressing evidence on an impressive number of mystical, magical, religio-philosophical verses from *Faust* ("Prolog im Himmel," "Erdgeist," Ariel's song, etc.). Another example is the essay "On the Limits of Art,"[166] in which Ivanov poses the question "To whom should we turn for council and guidance in a discussion of the loftiest heights of art?" and answers, "To whom, indeed, but to that artist at home in realms that transcend the boundaries between art and nature, art and mysticism—to Goethe." There follows an excerpt from Goethe's *Novelle* (the taming of the lion by the boy),[167] which, Ivanov claims, "contains hints of that mind-boggling, transcendent art, the divine and magical activity of which is directed not toward the idol-creating powers of symbols but toward the liberation of the World-Soul," that is, toward the artistic realization of the Symbolists' highest ideal.

In addition to the countless "borrowings" from, quotations of, and references to Goethe throughout his writings,[168] Ivanov has left us a monograph on Goethe which is easily the most factual and perceptive study of the poet-philosopher by a Russian Symbolist. That monograph bears the programmatic title *Goethe at the Border of Two Centuries,*[169] "programmatic" because all Symbolists saw Goethe as standing, in his time, at the threshold of a new era just as they saw themselves, in their time, standing between a past they rejected and a future they saw "holding great promise as well as great peril."[170]

A reader of Ivanov's monograph acquainted with the Symbolists' thoughts on Goethe and his works will find in it a number of passages with a familiar ring. By way of Ivanov's many influential articles in leading journals, and perhaps even more effectively by way of the typically Russian night-long discussions and debates every Wednesday in Ivanov's St. Petersburg apartment called "the Tower" (bashnia), many of his ideas had become the common property of his guests, friends as well as opponents: poets, scientists, actors, philologists, philosophers, musicians, archeologists—all of them welcome in the sociable "Tower." In turn, he absorbed many of his guests' theories about and attitudes toward Goethe in these lively exchanges of ideas.

Ivanov's study, unlike most Symbolist statements on Goethe, is rich in reliable biographical material not only on Goethe himself but also on his predecessors and contemporaries who influenced him or with whom he had personal contact (Lessing, Rousseau, Winckelmann, Schiller, Napoleon, August Wolff, and many others), materials that Ivanov uses effectively to enliven and enrich his portrayal of Goethe and his interpretation of Goethe's works. The concise study deserves to be ranked with some of the best. It is remarkable how much factual material and original interpretation Ivanov succeeded in concentrating within the pages of this monograph. Ivanov's selections from Goethe's lyrics in support of his argument reach well beyond the Symbolists' canon of Goethe's works.[171] His Russian renderings of some of them (especially selected strophes of "Gesang der Geister über den Wassern," "Das Göttliche," and "Grenzen der Menschheit") show the inimitable touch of a gifted poet.

In his monograph, Ivanov sets for himself the formidable task of "surveying the lengthy process of Goethe's fully conscious formation of his intellectual, moral, and aesthetic personality." His view of this process differs fundamentally from that of Radical Democrats Chernyshevski and Pisarev, which was the generally accepted view in the nineteenth century and was to become the official Soviet view, with certain modifications. Chernyshevski had singled out Goethe's Sturm und Drang period as the time of the greatest flowering of Goethe's genius. Pisarev had denigrated Karl August's Duchy of Weimar as a prime example of the "deutsche Misere" that stultified Goethe's development. Both saw in Goethe's Italian journey the fateful aberration into a debilitating "Classicism." Ivanov counters them on every point. He downgrades Sturm und Drang to a period of questionable value in Goethe's development, calling on Goethe as a witness. Goethe himself, he tells us, had "condemned this epoch of exaggerated sentimentality, fruitless Titanic passions, and vapid daydreaming for its lack of creative purposefulness. . . . Goethe himself had promptly unmasked all his youthful impulsive strivings and dreams as symptoms of a chaotic barbarism [!]. He was irresistibly drawn to the sacred soil of Italy." At most, Ivanov would grant some value to Goethe's Sturm und Drang as a period of "preparation." Having passed through this stage of "confused vagabondism and chaotic rebellion against all norms, he [Goethe] could now develop those well-proportioned, harmonious forms of his classical works." Obviously, Ivanov is speaking here as the avowed "Classicist."

Having *downgraded* the period of Sturm und Drang, Ivanov *upgrades* the Duchy of Weimar into the most suitable environment for a poet like Goethe: "Weimar protected him from narrow patriotism and political chauvinism, concentrating his emotions and thoughts on the realm of panhuman values, inviting him to ponder exclusively religious matters [!], the secrets of nature and ideals of humanity, surrounding him with the most favorable outward influences for his development into a spiritually total man."

Ivanov celebrates Italy as the *locus classicus* of Goethe's maturation as man and artist: "Goethe's two years on classical soil developed to the utmost the pure facets of the precious crystal of Goethe's soul, and henceforth his creativity gained its power to shape and mold the soul of all Europe." With this unqualifiedly positive valuation of Goethe's Italian journey, Ivanov stands in opposition not only to the Radical Democrats but also to his fellow Symbolists Toporkov and Sergei Solov'ev. As we may recall, Toporkov saw Italy as the locus of Goethe's betrayal of the Dionysian side of his genius, and Solov'ev condemned Italy as the locus of Goethe's betrayal of the Christian church to the heathen gods.

The new creative powers, which, according to Ivanov, Goethe developed in Italy, produced the final version of his classical dramas *Iphigenie auf Tauris* and *Tasso*. One would expect Ivanov to praise these works as masterpieces without flaw, but we find instead deep-reaching criticism alongside sincere admiration. He does laud these works' "limpid verse developed under the influence of the sunlit Mediterranean world" for its crystalline clarity and plasticity and for its economy of expression. He likens *Iphigenie* to the "foremost examples of Attic literature. . . . There are in these verses no more and no less embellishments than we find on Ionian temples; the entire work seems aglow with the luminescence of sunlit marble."

After this praise, however, there follow Ivanov's misgivings. For him *Iphigenie* is not a tragedy. "Its tragicness remains sporadic, scattered, and is not carried to its logical climax. . . . Goethe does not aim at catharsis, which can be achieved only by means of tragic catastrophe. Instead this author strives to establish the mood of lucid, contemplative harmony by arranging a fortunate turn of events by means of the victory of noble and magnanimous sentiments over primitive, dark, barbarous impulses and prejudices." And thus, Ivanov concludes, "Goethe's work is not a tragedy, not even an Euripidean tragedy. It is instead a sermon on the humanism of the eighteenth century, based on an abstract optimism, dressed up in elegant Greek finery."

And why did Goethe fail to create a tragedy worthy of his great classical predecessors? Ivanov gives an answer that has a familiar ring: "Greek tragedy was motivated by the spirit of Dionysus. Goethe, however, was afraid of the Dionysian excess and frenzy and avoided it, as he did everything that broke the firm boundaries which the instinct of self-preservation had drawn around the human personality." And to clinch his argument, Ivanov once again calls Goethe for a witness. He cites Goethe's much-quoted confession that true tragedy would exceed his emotional strength and would destroy him. Goethe's inability to face up to stark tragedy and to express such tragedy in his works, Goethe's unwillingness to surrender to Dionysus in complete self-abandon, disappointed Ivanov as it did Bal'mont and Toporkov. Despite his appreciation of Apollonian form, reason, and measure, Ivanov intensely experienced the attraction of the Dionysian, irrational, chthonic, mysterious, magical forces in life, as did all the Symbolists to a lesser or greater extent—and not only the Russian Symbolists.

Goethe's *Tasso* does not satisfy Ivanov's definition of "Classical" tragedy, and for the same reason. In it Goethe again fails to build a tragic plot resulting in a true catharsis. Instead *Tasso* is, in Ivanov's view, an autobiographical *Bildungsdrama*, imbued with the optimistic spirit of humanism. It is a *Schauspiel* of self-liberation and self-education. Ivanov's interpretation demonstrates his ability to empathize with the poet, to perceive the covert impulses in Goethe's creations. His argument runs: "Reflecting in a work of art his personal situation and conditions, Goethe had learned to heal his psychic wounds." That was Goethe's primary aim in his *Tasso*. Portraying the endangered personality of Tasso, Goethe sought to free himself from the pathological traits he recognized as being inherent in genius, by "exteriorizing," by "objectifying," these traits. This Ivanov sees as an act of *self-liberation*. As for *self-education*, that function was served by Goethe's portrayal of the worldly-wise, practical Antonio as a "positive" hero, a worthy foil to Tasso: "Depicting Antonio, he [Goethe] forced himself to be fair toward the 'cold, unfeeling world of high society' [Ivanov paraphrases here a famous line of Pushkin]. He fulfilled his wish to combine in his personality the creative power inherent in the outwardly weak, hypersensitive Tasso with the powerful will and practical common sense that lend to his portrayal of Antonio such strong and beautiful lineaments."

Ivanov discerns the same basic creative drives in Goethe's novel *Wilhelm Meister*, in the *Lehrjahre* as in the *Wanderjahre*, namely, Goethe's penchant for covert autobiography and for pedagogy. He values this work as a "book of symbolic didacticism." The form and structure of the *Wanderjahre* he puts down as an unmitigated failure, too confused, too tangled, overburdened with too much farfetched detail. The novel's importance he sees in what he calls "Goethe's legacy," in the "Pedagogische Provinz," and above all in Goethe's thoughts on social problems. "Goethe," he writes, "had grasped the conditions of labor and production, had properly understood the just demands of the working class, and based on these observations and perceptions had projected the ideal of a classless society in which everyone is required to work and where a central authority dictates to each and every one his particular task and sets for him his conditions of life in keeping with his labor and with an eye to increased productivity." Startled, I seem to hear him paraphrase Karl Marx's *Manifesto* rather than "Goethe's legacy." But Ivanov is quick to assure us that for him "the Second Part of 'Meister' is something akin to Plato's 'Republic,'" an assurance which, of course, does not altogether rule out Marx's influence on his interpretation of Goethe's message.

In the *Lehrjahre*, the figure and fate of Mignon attracts Ivanov's special attention and elicits a sensitively empathetic response. In that "bewitching fairy tale," as he calls the Mignon scenes, he hears "an ineffable music, which reminds one of something kindred, something infinitely beautiful, something over which we have shed tears, something lost and long, long forgotten." Here speaks Ivanov the Romantic (who he certainly was despite his "Classicism," or rather in an astounding symbiosis with it), and here is re-created something of the mood and melody of the Mignon song which he so deeply felt. In the *Wanderjahre*, Makarie is singled out as Goethe's embodiment of "*Das Ewig-Weibliche*, enthroned on high, clothed in the sun's radiance, and circling round about her, like planets in their orbits, the tirelessly striving devotees of self-renunciation, of *Entsagung*."

Ivanov defines the "basic idea and profoundest theme" of the entire novel as the "depiction of a dark, labyrinthian path along which, in a prolonged errancy, the hero of the novel is moving, vaguely conscious of the ultimate goal, which, however, remains hidden from his view for a long time." In this novel "Goethe seeks to affirm his central idea (which is the same as for his *Faust*), that a person, destined for something noble and good, will attain by way of self-education and self-conquest a clear, comprehensive vision of his immediate, realistic, and with it productive assignment and mission." Yet this "comprehensive vision," this "first active, productive contact with reality," far from implying a widening and broadening of the field of activity, represents its extreme limitation. Previously, Wilhelm imagined himself to be lord over a spacious realm, but that lordship proved altogether illusory. Now he finds himself confined in a very limited circle of activity [as a surgeon], but within that circle his lordship is real and his activity genuinely alive. This "legacy" marks for Ivanov this novel as a forward-looking, truly prophetic masterpiece in which the author ranges far beyond his time and attempts answers to problems facing Ivanov and his generation.

Ivanov's interpretation of Goethe's *Wahlverwandtschaften* is paradigmatic for the Symbolists' attitude toward this work. He passes severe judgment on Goethe's "betrayal of his own better self" in his support of the institution of marriage as sanctioned by church and state. "Goethe," he writes, "sincerely or partly dissimulating (we really do not know how), joins the ranks of the defenders of social mores, opposing the laws of nature. He does this truly 'against reason and fate' and with utter inconsistency in logic. But, of course," Ivanov insists, "the real value of this great work does not rest on this patched-on, uncharacteristic moralizing." Its immense value is to be found in that "miracle of Goethe's sensitively penetrating portrayal of characters, his rendering of situations," and above all in his descriptions of love: "These are always unusual in their bewitching power and clairvoyance . . . but his 'Elective Affinities' are the ultimate revelation of love's secrets, of its cosmic roots."

Again we have in this interpretation of the *Wahlverwandtschaften* that combination of praise and criticism typical of the Symbolists' attitude toward Goethe. They are not willing or able to accept his balanced judgment and sound common sense. Instead they criticize him for his "ambivalence toward all things" or are even prepared to condemn him for "self-betrayal."

Ivanov is greatly impressed with Goethe's ballads as genuine mythopoetic masterpieces. "Their beauty has not been surpassed by any of the great balladeers . . . because only in them is revealed a vision of the secrets of nature." Thus, in "Der Fischer," Ivanov finds "uncovered the very soul of the element 'water,' as irresistibly alluring, bewitchingly captivating, sweetly fateful as it was known to the ancient seers and creators of myths." In "Erlkönig" he hears "the 'king's' last magical incantations before the gates of his realm fall shut forever," clearly a parallel to Briusov's portrayal of the "departing king" in his poem "On the Square." [172] In the ballads of Goethe's late period, Ivanov admires "the easy filiation of this Germanic murk with India's mysticism . . . for instance, in his 'Prayer of Paria' [Des Paria Gebet]," [173] in which he finds the profoundest revelation by the poet about nature and spirit, whereas Goethe's "Bride of Corinth" [174] combines for Ivanov "with equally unforced ease antiquity and Romanticism." Through this "mask of Greek Romanticism [!] Goethe conveys one of his deepest insights into the secrets of love." He has uncovered " 'das offene Geheimnis,' that love is more potent than death, that nature ordains the union of lovers destined for one another, and that accidental death can never prevent that fated union."

Ivanov dwells at some length on the "productive friendship of Goethe and Schiller." Comparing and contrasting these two geniuses, he effectively develops and sharpens many lineaments of his image of Goethe. A representative example of his method is his comparison of Goethe's and Schiller's concepts of the "Symbol," which gives us an idea of his approach to this subject of central importance to the Symbolists: "The word 'Symbol,' " Ivanov explains, "had at first a different meaning for Goethe than it had for Schiller. Goethe understood with it, first and foremost, the 'Urphänomen.' In each phenomenon he recognized unchanging traits, distinguishing characteristics for a multitude of analogical phenomena." From this it follows for Ivanov that "every phenomenon [in Goethe's definition] appears as a concrete representative of an eternal type, as its *Symbol*." The type, in turn, "is for Goethe the living essence or idea of things, the idea being indwelling in things. Goethe conceives of the idea as "the 'form of things,' as energy, as one of the aspects of the world's soul."

Having defined Goethe's initial concept of the Symbol, Ivanov contrasts it to Schiller's view: "For Schiller," he states (agreeing with the generally held opinion), "the idea is *not* indwelling in things, as Goethe had assumed, following in the footsteps of Aristotle. Rather, for Schiller the idea transcends things, as Plato had taught. Things for Schiller do not completely mirror the idea. Art is symbolic insofar as it reflects the transcendental idea."

Despite this radical difference in Goethe's and Schiller's concepts of the Symbol, Ivanov sees them gradually converging. He reminds us that Goethe had not been a systematic philosopher with a strict methodology: "[Goethe] did not leave us a comprehensive statement of his views in a logically consistent form." Thus it does not surprise Ivanov to find "that with the passing years the sharpness of [Goethe's and Schiller's] initial disagreement was smoothed over. When Goethe, completing the Second Part of his *Faust*—under the influence of Schelling, who taught that every art is symbolic and nature itself creates nothing but symbols—wrote the famous line 'Alles Vergängliche ist nur ein Gleichnis,' their dispute was ended. Schiller would have had no objections to this formulation."

Ivanov's image of Goethe is truly imposing, monumental. He sees Goethe's life, his intellectual and emotional growth, as "repeating the development of European mankind" and traces the poet-philosopher's profound influence on his time and beyond to the fact that Goethe "experienced within the framework of his personal life the entire history of the European spirit. . . . Surveying the totality of the colossal activity of this superhuman, all-encompassing spirit, we realize that while Goethe nourished and transformed his own epoch, he also posed questions his contemporaries were quite unable to understand fully. And more, he was already *answering* questions that in his time had not even been *raised*."

The insightful psychologist Ivanov makes us aware by means of substantive evidence that Goethe lived his life both as an introspective subjectivist *and* as the precise, objective observer of the world of nature and of men. He singles out the "one thing above all others which Goethe demanded of himself—*clarity* [iasnost']. Goethe wanted his physical and spiritual eye to reflect nature *clearly*. It seemed to him that by learning to know a mineral, to apperceive its essential nature, he was learning to know himself. That was Goethe's way of encompassing the world; he diminished his ego in order to receive into his soul the entire universe, clearly, without subjective distortion."

Like Belyi, Ivanov stresses Goethe's "religiosity," but unlike Belyi he does not distort Goethe's faith into Orthodox Christianity: "When Goethe calls himself a Christian (and he does this repeatedly), we must be aware that for him a Christian can at the same time be an *immanentist*, more exactly, that he *must* be one, Goethe being convinced that he understands Christianity correctly and spiritually."

Ivanov's discussion of Goethe's highly personal relation to God reveals a wide-ranging acquaintance with and a probing examination of Goethe's statements, in poetry and prose (especially in the "Pedagogische Provinz" [175] of *Wilhelm Meisters Wanderjahre*), on the esoteric subject that Goethe himself has comprehensively defined as "Gott und Welt": man's relationship to his God and God's relationship to his creation, the world. The deeper Ivanov delved into Goethe's beliefs, the more convinced he became that Goethe's creed was "deeply mystical, permeated with a profound feeling for the ineffable, tender delicacy of the divine mystery, evident for Goethe's eye in every object and event." Ivanov rejects the possibility of adequately defining Goethe's relationship with the divine by the term "pantheism," "so commonly used and so empty of meaning." He recognized only one difference between the message of the New Testament and Goethe's faith, albeit a very important one: "The New Testament transfers man's natural existence in and with God to the hereafter, in other words, it feels the power of evil in *this* life." Goethe, on the other hand, while acknowledging the existence of evil in the world, denies it ultimate power. Goethe firmly believes that "the presence of evil in the life of the universe turns out to be, in the end, productive of the good against evil's own will, because it awakens the life-affirming powers of untiring striving." With this definition of Goethe's concept of evil, Ivanov gives at the same time his definition of Mephistopheles, that incarnation of evil, whom Goethe had characterized as "ein Teil von jener Kraft, / Die stets das Böse will und stets das Gute schafft." [176] We may remember that Dostoevski had categorically rejected that definition of evil on the basis of his Greek Orthodox faith as well as his personal keen observation of evil's true nature. [177] Ivanov neither rejects nor affirms it; he only *records* it as Goethe's answer to the perennially debated question, "What is evil?"

Goethe's vision of God continued to preoccupy Ivanov. [178] He strives to define it. The following is a summary of his effort:

For Goethe, God is Something or Someone supremely alive, far more alive than all living things. . . . He is Someone most pure and lofty who calls on the spirit of man to transcend itself in an unceasing enhancement, *Steigerung*. . . . He is Someone who joyfully welcomes every human being at every stage of his development. . . . Yet He is Someone who continually recedes, who evades every attempt to fathom, to define, to name Him, though being willing to accept the very best and holiest of definitions, of appellations man is capable of at every new stage in his spiritual growth. . . . Thus God remains eternally above and in advance of man, who continues to strive untiringly to reach Him.

Ivanov singles out Goethe's religiosity as the basic enlivening, energizing force in all his creative activities as artist, as historian, [179] as natural scientist. Much like Belyi, Ivanov stresses Goethe's revulsion for the "mechanistic" methods in the natural sciences prevalent in Goethe's time as they continued to be in Ivanov's. "Goethe," he writes, "despised the ongoing favorite practice of scientists to examine nature as if it were a soulless mechanism. He liked to tell them [in Faust's words] that nature would never yield its secrets to their prying instruments, to levers and to screws." [180] Goethe's own approach to nature was empathetic, reverent. Ivanov perceives "Goethe's contemplation and study of nature" as "bordering on religious meditation." [181] He firmly believes that "Goethe's deeply religious soul" was the ultimate source from which flowed his incomparable power to divine the "secret laws of nature," active in man as in beast, in plant as in the mineral world, as in the greatest works of art, "all of these being, for Goethe, parts of God's all-uniting, all-embracing universe."

This monograph concludes with a discussion of *Faust*. Limitation of space, Ivanov points out, precluded consideration of the vast body of the *Faust-Forschung*. He could give only his "very personal interpretation of the basic concepts of the mighty creation, a personal synthesizing view of its general meaning." But it is precisely such a "personal interpretation" of Goethe's masterpiece that is of the greatest importance in the context of my study, worthy of a detailed summary.

Again—as in the case of Ivanov's analysis of *Iphigenie*, *Tasso*, and *Wilhelm Meisters Wanderjahre*—the autobiographical element in the work is stressed. "Unquestionably, Goethe's contemplation of his own questing search of the right way has inspired him to represent himself in the phantasmagoric milieu of the transitional period from the medieval to the modern age. All the inexhaustible energy of his spirit, all his sensuous cravings, find their loftiest expression in Faust's spiritual as well as egoistical impulses and desires. . . . In his *Faust*, Goethe has *potentiated* a mirror image if not of his entire personality then certainly of its most salient traits." This "potentiation," this *Steigerung*, makes Faust appear before us as a *symbol* of mankind. In his spiritual strivings, in his sensuous yearnings, Faust is for Ivanov a foremost representative "of a new individualism." Faust's intense, complex nature opens him up to the devilish enticements of the Mephistophelian sphere of phallic sexuality: naked lust, promiscuity, perversion. It leads him to the witch's kitchen, to the witch's sabbath on the Brocken.

Ivanov insists that there is but one way by which the "noble spirit can achieve contact with the immanent content [Ivanov's term for "matter," for the physical world] while preserving its transcendental form and thus remain his 'noble self.'" That way, in his characteristically arcane formulation, is by "the kiss of Mother Earth, who creates from out of itself the image of the Eternal Woman." [182]

Ivanov's interpretation of Faust's wager is equally "personal" and highly debatable. However, he leaves no room for debate. Categorically he states, "Faust's wager is not with Mephisto, it is with God," and continues: "Faust accepts the wager's conditions before *God*, that condition being eternal, untiring striving. A moment of self-satisfaction, of rest, of stagnation, of loss of will to reach ever higher stages in self-development suffice to end Faust's terrestrial life without, however, *surrendering him into the power of evil*."

Why? Because at the very instant the yearning for a higher life reawakens in Faust's soul, at that instant his signature under the words 'Then I am yours [Mephisto's]' is null and void, and he is again not the devil's but God's." Herein, in Faust's ability to rekindle in his soul his "higher spirit," Ivanov finds the key for Goethe's granting Faust, despite his transgressions, ultimate salvation. Faust experiences this recapturing of his better self in the scene "Witch's Kitchen" in contemplation in the magic mirror, of the image of the most beautiful of all women,[183] and again in the "Walpurgisnight" scene when, dancing with the witches, his attention is suddenly riveted on the apparition of Gretchen.[184] It also happens in Ivanov's reading of Faust's apotheosis: "And once again [as in the "Witch's Kitchen"], there rises before Faust the transcendent form . . . with which his whole being yearns to unite; that yearning is called love, the transcendent form—woman. Faust recognizes in the train of spirits following Mater Gloriosa his beloved Gretchen and, irresistibly attracted, follows her because the 'Eternal Feminine' draws us to it."

In his discussion of the Second Part, Ivanov counters the multitude of Russian critics who condemned it for its "dark" and "obfuscating" allegory. He finds no "allegorical emblems" in it. Instead he finds "expressed in synthesizing symbols the most diverse powers and fates: the decrepit Holy Roman Empire . . . ; the rebirth of antique beauty and its symbiosis with northern Romanticism (Helena learns to speak in rhymes instructed by Faust) giving birth to the most modern lyric poetry (Euphorion-Byron); successes in the natural sciences; the freedom of the Dutch people in the land of canals."

As much as Ivanov admires this unprecedented achievement by the Symbolist-poet Goethe in presenting that sweeping panorama of historical events reaching from the fall of Troy to the battle of Missolunghi and Byron's death, a panorama of some three thousand years, Ivanov would not dwell on this symbolico-historical plane; he is intent on delving into deeper, mystical strata of Goethe's masterpiece. "In the very center of the Second Part of *Faust*, as in the center of the novel *Wilhelm Meister*," Ivanov discovers, "the idea of the Eternal-Feminine." He celebrates it as the "most mysterious legacy of Goethe to future generations."

As we know, Ivanov is not the only Symbolist to find this idea and this idol as an important motif in Goethe's creations, yet he does give it a highly personal interpretation. As already pointed out, he extols it as the symbol of "Mother Earth." "The Earth herself," he explains, "as a third" * sacred image of the Eternal Feminine, attracts Faust and sanctifies his eternal striving."

---

*The other two "sacred images" are Helena, the ideal of *external* (physical) beauty, and Gretchen, the ideal of *internal* beauty, of *Seelenschönheit*, as represented in Act IV, Scene "Hochgebirg" (*Hamb. Ausg.*, 3:304).

In the light of my discussion of Ivanov's attitude toward Goethe's *Faust*, it is not surprising to find him affirming Faust's "eternal striving." Recalling its unconditional condemnation by Dostoevski, Bal'mont, Briusov, and Sergei Solov'ev, one can readily recognize Ivanov's high valuation of it as a determined effort at an unequivocal vindication, a "Rettung," of Goethe's ideal. Ivanov centers our attention on Faust's social activity, on his "technological achievements," which had been denigrated by Bal'mont.[185] He celebrates Faust as the leader of "those new people who carry their heads high in a newly won freedom on free soil and that now belongs to labor [!]." Faust's doubts and cares and his pangs of conscience are minimized in Ivanov's interpretation: "The earth has become a new world, work is aboiling; the weak and backward perish, the old family system [Baukis and Philemon are its symbols], the traditional values and truths are destroyed. . . . Nature yields to liberated human energy, and Faust is deeply satisfied with having realized his plans, with his triumph over the elements, a triumph that has opened the way to all-embracing freedom and bliss in communal labor." Faust's encounter with Dame Care is mentioned only in a brief aside, and Faust's culpable involvement with the brutalities of Mephisto and his three ruthless "mighty companions" receives no mention whatever.

Ivanov leaves no doubt as to his purpose. His interpretation is an unambiguous glorification of Goethe's optimism and activism, of Goethe's ideal of purposeful, socially conscious striving. It is meant to serve as a counterpoise to the negative approach by his contemporaries and by preceding generations to Goethe's most valuable "legacy." In his opinion, "too many of them have misunderstood Goethe, have criticized the author of *Werther* and of *Faust* as a prophet of extreme nihilism." Ivanov does not mention any of the Russian fellow Symbolists by name, as he might well have done. Instead, he singles out for criticism the French author Alfred de Musset: "Characteristic are the curses that Musset heaps in his morbid *Confessions d'un Enfant du Siècle* on Byron and on Goethe, these spiritual poisoners [according to Musset] of the soul of his generation." In Ivanov's opinion, such critics as Musset quite erroneously denigrate "the sum total of Faust's life as a sorry self-deception, as the pitiable death of a blind old man who in his 'eternal striving' had utterly forgotten that all striving, in the end, is but much ado about nothing." Ivanov considers it "far more appropriate to see the last days of Faust as a warning of the dangers inherent in crassly materialistic cultures" and predicts that "the twentieth century will read anew Goethe's creations and will find in them a very different message than did the people of the past era."

Ivanov's prediction proved to be prophetic. The Soviets and their fellow travelers the world over did give Goethe's masterpiece a "new reading" to find in it welcome corroboration of their Marxist-Leninist dialectic materialism. Would Ivanov have approved that reading? Available textual evidence gives an ambiguous answer. There are statements by Ivanov, some of which I have quoted,[186] that have a distinctly Marxian ring. On the other hand, he has repeatedly warned against the dangers inherent in crass materialism and has welcomed the reawakening of the religious spirit he sensed in his troublous times. This much is certain: In 1924 Ivanov left the Soviet Union on a mission to Italy and never returned to his homeland. He died in Rome, an expatriate, in 1949.[187]

Summary and Conclusion

In the crosscurrents of the Symbolists' opinions of Goethe, one can readily identify certain themes common to virtually all of them. They see Goethe standing in his time, as they in theirs, at the "great divide" (na rubezhe), leaving the past behind and ushering in the new, "modern" era. They recognize in him the "distant forebear" of their movement and agree that his aesthetics anticipate the basic principles and essential concepts of modern Symbolism. To Ellis, Goethe is the "prophet and inspirer of almost all present-day aesthetics and present-day Symbolism." As he sums up, "In the realm of poetry the principle of Symbolism as it had been established by Goethe, after a long series of misconceptions and aberrations, is now once again understood by us as Goethe understood it, and Goethe's poetics appear once again basically as our own poetics." The great majority of the Symbolists honor Goethe as their "great teacher and guide," and some of them—Bal'mont, for instance, and the Metner brothers and Ivanov—even hail him as the "wise physician" who has the power to cure through contact with his vital, harmonious nature the modern artist of his various ills developed in his unnatural, debilitating "hothouse" existence.

Typical of the Symbolists is their desire to delve below the surface appearances in Goethe's personality to his "true," innermost self, to grasp the "reality beyond realities," or, in Ivanov's Latin motto, to penetrate "de realibus ad realiora." They tend to regard the Olympian calm, the Apollonian measure and balance in Goethe's life and art, as a mere facade behind which hides the "real" Goethe. They like to emphasize, even to magnify out of all proportion, the mystical, irrational, Dionysian traits in Goethe, and some of them, not finding in him the sought-for "depths," a "sense for the tragic, the nocturnal side of life," turn abruptly from praise to censure—Bal'mont, for instance, and even so judicious a devotee of Goethe as Ivanov.

But there are also traits in Goethe's personality and events in his life on which the Symbolists are deeply divided. The Italian journey is such an event, and Goethe's "religiosity" is such a trait. Some of them, Sergei Solov'ev and Toporkov in their lead, consider the years spent by Goethe in Italy as a time of aberration and self-betrayal, while others, particularly the Metners and

Ivanov, celebrate these years as a time of the fullest flowering of Goethe's genius. As to Goethe's "religiosity," there are again sharply contrasting opinions. Merezhkovski, for instance, extols Goethe as "the prophet of a religion of the future which will unite Christianity with Nietzschean individualism," Andrei Belyi strives to make of the "self-assured heathen" (as Tolstoi saw Goethe) an orthodox Christian. Ellis sees Goethe as "the mightiest poet-mystic of our age," and Ivanov discovers in Goethe's "deeply religious soul" the ultimate source of inspiration for all of Goethe's many-sided activities as artist, philosopher, historian, and natural scientist. On the other hand, in sharpest disagreement with these voices, Sergei Solov'ev denies Goethe all affinity with the religious, Christian world view, a fatal flaw which according to Solov'ev grew ever more dominant with Goethe's advancing age and ultimately condemned him to the "realm of chaos and eternal night" as the traitor who, in his Grecophilia, had turned his back on the "church of the Crucified One" to worship the heathen gods.

Most of the Symbolists, while recognizing Goethe's *Faust* as a supreme artistic achievement, especially its symbolic Second Part, are either unwilling or unable to empathize with Goethe's optimism, his activism, and specifically his glorification of Faust's "eternal striving" (Bal'mont and Briusov foremost among these). The outstanding exceptions are Aleksandr Blok and Viacheslav Ivanov. Blok faults Goethe not for excessive optimism and activism but for his *lack* of activism and of commitment to the cause of humanism. He censures Goethe for his passivity, his indecisiveness, his "inveterate ambivalence toward all things." Viacheslav Ivanov, in contrast, praises Goethe for his progressive stance, his socially conscious activism, as expressed by the poet-philosopher not only in his *Faust* but in even greater detail and prophetic depth in his *Wilhelm Meister* novel, especially in the *Wanderjahre*.

Generally, the Symbolists concentrate their attention on Goethe's late works, in his poetry as in his prose. The closing lines of *Faust*: "Das Ewig-Weibliche / Zieht uns hinan" and "Alles Vergängliche / Ist nur ein Gleichnis" run as important leitmotivs through their belletristic and essayistic writings, and the lines from the late poem "Das Vermächtnis," "Das Wahre war schon längst gefunden / Hat edle Geisterschaft verbunden / Das alte Wahre fass es an!" are repeatedly cited to buttress with Goethe's authority the soundness of their conservative world view. Among Goethe's early works, only the Sturm und Drang ballads are singled out as truly mythopoetic creations and the "Erdgeist" scene from *Faust* as a powerfully evocative statement of their vitalistic, predominantly irrational, intensely emotional life's philosophy.

All too many of the Symbolists, in their frenzied search for ultimate truth, for "der Weisheit letzten Schluss," make themselves guilty of grievous distortions of the Goethe image but are also rewarded by some perceptive insights into Goethe's personality and work, as, for instance, Belyi into Goethe's methods and achievements as a natural scientist, specifically in his *Farben-lehre*. The best balanced, lifelike portrayals of the poet-philosopher are the product of devoted, detailed study of his life and work by Viacheslav Ivanov and Emili Metner. Ivanov's monograph on Goethe can serve as an admirable summation as well as a much-needed "correction" of the Symbolists' image of the poet.

As any interpretation of so complex a personality and opus as Goethe's, the Symbolists' portrayal of him is certain to rouse criticism. Thus, Victor Zhirmunski characterizes them all as "not attuned to the problems and images created by Goethe" and deplores their distortion of the Goethe image:

In the epoch of the decline of the bourgeois culture, Goethe appears as a Symbolist and a mystic, as a predecessor of Nietzsche, as a theosoph, as a devotee of Catholicism, of the Hellenic cult of Dionysus, and of the Eastern mysteries. The Russian Symbolists depict their Goethe as a mirror image of themselves, and for that reason their Goethe reminds us, in turn, of Baudelaire and Nietzsche, of Tiutchev and Novalis, of Vladimir Solov'ev and Rudolf Steiner. In this distortion all historically progressive and impor-tant elements in Goethe's creations have vanished without a trace.[188]

Clearly, this is an all-too-sweeping, ideologically biased criticism. In the Symbolists' statements, "the historically progressive and important elements in Goethe's creations" do not "vanish without a trace," certainly not in Ivanov's interpretations of *Faust* and *Wilhelm Meister*. And yet Zhirmunski does put his finger on a central weakness of the Symbolists: they do tend to distort their Goethe image, to a greater or lesser extent, into a likeness of themselves. Unquestionably, there is much room for disagreement with their view of Goethe, but the following facts will stand up to any challenge: They have contributed some important new facets to the Russian image of Goethe. They have reactivated the Romantic interpretation and lofty evaluation of him, and above all, they have focused on him once again—after a hiatus of half a century—the attention of the Russian reading public. They have rekindled his influence on Russian life and letters, which to the present day has hardly diminished, in proof of which I cite the presence of Goethe and his works in the writings, belletristic and essayistic, of such diverse authors as Anatoli Lunacharski, Aleksandr Solzhenitsyn, Mikhail Bulgakov, and Boris Pasternak, to name but these four from among many notable figures who con-tinued or began to write after the great October Revolution, that ultimate "divide" in Russian history. For further evidence of Goethe's presence on the Soviet literary stage, one may recall the impressive celebrations of the Goethe anniversaries of 1932, 1949, and 1982. Such enduring influence in the tur-bulent history of Soviet Russia is highly significant and deserves a definitive study.

Notes

Preface

1. V. Zhirmunski, *Gete v Russkoi Literature* (*Goethe in Russian Literature*) (Leningrad, 1937), 5.
2. M. Gorlin, "Goethe in Russland," *Zeitschrift für slawische Philologie* 9 (1932): 335–36. (Italics added.)

Chapter One. I. S. Turgenev: *A Study in Ambivalence*

1. V. Terras, "Turgenev and Western Realism," *Comparative Literature* 22/1 (1970): 35. Soviet critic L. V. Pumpianski also speaks of Turgenev's "extraordinary knowledge of Western life, which was without equal among Russian writers of his epoch," and singles out his "systematic contact with European culture as one of the most important characteristics of Turgenev's development," in contrast to Leo Nikolaevich Tolstoi, in whose development such systematic preoccupation with Western cultures and literatures was singularly absent. Cf. "Turgenev and the West," in N. L. Brodski, *I. S. Turgenev, Materialy i Issledovaniia; Sbornik* (Orlov, 1940), 96. Henceforth cited as Brodski, *Materialy*.
2. I. S. Turgenev, *Polnoe Sobranie Sochineni i Pisem v Dvatsati Vosmi Tomakh* (Moscow and Leningrad, 1960–67), vol. 14, "Pervoe Predstavlenie Opery G-zhi Viardo v Veimare," p. 292. Henceforth cited as *P.S.S.*, followed by volume and page. Translations are mine unless otherwise indicated.
3. *P.S.S.* 14:291.
4. T. G. Masaryk, *The Spirit of Russia*, ed. G. Gibian (New York, 1967), 279.
5. I. S. Turgenev, *Pis'ma v Trinadtsati Tomakh* (Moscow and Leningrad, Akademia Nauk, 1961–67), 1:173. Henceforth cited as Turgenev, *Pis'ma* followed by volume and page. Translations are mine unless otherwise indicated.
6. Translated by Turgenev, *P.S.S.* 1:65–66.
7. Turgenev, *Pis'ma* 1:176.
8. *P.S.S.* 14:106.
9. Turgenev, *Pis'ma* 1:249–50. Letter to Louis and Pauline Viardot, November 8, 1846, from St. Petersburg.
10. Ibid., 211–14. Turgenev accepts the essay "Die Natur," the main subject of the letter, as being by Goethe, in keeping with the *Stand der Forschung* at that time. For vivid accounts of Turgenev's contacts with the Berlin salons of Rahel Varnhagen, Bettina von Arnim, and the Frolows, consult, among other sources, N. M. Gut'iar, *Ivan Sergeevich Turgenev* (Moscow, 1907), esp. chap. 1; V. N. Gorbacheva, *Molodye Gody Turgeneva* (Moscow, 1926); and A. Yarmolinski, *Turgenev: The Man, His Art, and His Age* (New York and London, 1926).

11. *Goethes Werke. Hamburger Ausgabe*, 6th ed. (Hamburg, 1962), 3:13. Henceforth cited as *Hamb. Ausg.*, followed by volume and page.

12. *P.S.S.* 14:106–7.

13. Act II, Scene 1, *Hamb. Ausg.* 5:98.

14. Letter of December 13, 1867, in Turgenev, *Pis'ma* 7:14 (italics in the original).

15. "I am and always have been a 'gradualist,' . . . a man expecting reform *only from above*. I oppose revolution on principle" (Letter to the journal *Vestnik Evropy [The European Messenger]*, January 2, 1880, in *P.S.S.* 15:185. Italics added.

16. Turgenev, *Pis'ma* 7:14.

17. For another example, see the letter to Pauline Viardot in which Turgenev quotes the same lines and comments, "C'est tout bonnement un fait, une vérité qu'il énonçait *en observateur exact de la nature qu'il Goethe etait*" (ibid., 1:343; Italics added). With "nature" is meant "human nature"; no reference to Goethe the natural scientist is implied.

18. Zhirmunski, *Gete v Russkoi Literature*, 361.

19. K. Schütz, *Das Goethebild Turgeniews. Sprache und Dichtung*, no. 75 (Stuttgart, 1952), 122.

20. Letter of February 14, 1870, in Turgenev, *Pis'ma* 8:193.

21. See, for example, his letter to A. A. Fet, November 29, 1869, in ibid., 137.

22. For example, by Ludwig Pietsch and Friedrich Bodenstedt. Pietsch: "Mit der deutschen poetischen Literatur schien er gründlich vertraut und speziell von einer imponierended Goethefestigkeit" (*Nord und Süd*, 1878, p. 246); Bodenstedt: "Es mag hierbei bemerkt werden, dass Goethes *Faust* Turgeniews Lieblingsdichtung war, deren ersten Teil er fast auswendig wusste . . ." (*Russkaja Starina*, 1887, p. 444).

23. Schütz, *Goethebild*, 134–44; E. Rosenkranz, "Turgeniew und Goethe," *Germanoslavica* 2/1 (1932–33): 76–91.

24. Cf. the autobiographical sketch "Ivan Sergeevich Turgenev," in *P.S.S.* 15:204.

25. Yarmolinski, *Turgenev*, 16.

26. See, for instance, his letters to Pauline Viardot and Tatiana Bakunin.

27. For a detailed account of Schiller's influence on young Turgenev, see. T. P. Dehn, "Des jungen Turgeniews Verhältnis zu Schiller," in *I. S. Turgeniew und Deutschland. Materialien und Untersuchungen*, ed. G. Ziegengeist (Berlin, 1965), 193–203.

28. Erich Hock, an authority on Turgenev and German literature, observes, "Ob Turgeniew schon früher [before 1833] ein Werk Goethes mit Hingebung gelesen und mit Ernst studiert hat, lässt sich nicht ausmachen." Cf. Erich Hock, *Turgeniew und die deutsche Literatur* (Göttingen, 1955), 9.

29. David Magarshak, *Turgenev: A Life* (London, n.d.), 33.

30. *P.S.S.* 14:9.

31. See *Pis'ma K. D. Kavelina i I. S. Turgeneva k A. I. Gertsen*, ed. M. Dragomanov (Geneva, 1892), passim.

32. *P.S.S.* 14:100.

33. Ibid., 10, in the autobiographical essay "Vmesto Vstupleniia."

34. August Wilhelm Zumpt (1815–1877), classical scholar. Among his works are *Commentationes Epigraphica, Studia Romana*, and *Das Kriminalrecht der römischen Republik*, all published after Turgenev's years at Berlin University.

35. August Böckh (1785–1867), professor of Greek, archeology, and philology, was appointed to a professorship at Berlin University in 1811 and served five times as its rector.

36. *P.S.S.* 14:8.

37. Cf. ibid., 6:389–95: "Vospominaniia o N. V. Stankevich," p. 390: "Ia khodil tuda molchat', razinia rot, i slushat'."

38. In Varnhagen von Ense's (Rahel's husband) *Tagebücher*, ed. L. Assing, vols. 1–14 (Leipzig, 1861–70). See esp. 1:235, 4:32, 4:45, 11:227, and 13:111: "Er [Turgenev] erzählte uns seine Geschichte. . . . Die Literatur ist schwach in Russland, doch entstehen neue Zeitschriften. Grosse Zunahme des Ansehens und der Einwirkung von Goethe in Russland (Besuch, Oktober, 1856)."

39. Cf. André von Gronicka, *The Russian Image of Goethe*, vol. 1: *Goethe in Russian Literature of the First Half of the Nineteenth Century* (Philadelphia: University of Pennsylvania Press, 1968), 169–79.

40. *P.S.S.* 1:338: "Pesnia Klerkhen iz tragedii Gëte 'Egmont'"; pp. 65–66: "Rimskaia Elegiia (Gëte. XII)"; pp. 30–37: "Posledniaia stsena pervoi chasti 'Fausta' Gëte." It seems not to have been noticed that the "verse-sketch" (nabrosok) "Chto ty serdtse, moë serdtse" (ibid., 328) is based on Goethe's poem "Neue Liebe, neues Leben." In a later period Turgenev translated Goethe's ballad "Vor dem Gericht" (1869) and the poem "Finisches Lied" (1874); the poem served as a text for Pauline Viardot's "Romances." Cf. I. S. Chistov, "Stikhotvornye teksty dlia romansov Poliny Viardo," in *Turgenevski Sbornik: Materialy k Polnomu Sobraniiu Sochineni i Pisem I. S. Turgeneva* (Leningrad, 1964 ff.), 4:203.

41. Schütz, *Goethebild*, 18.

42. Yarmolinski, *Turgenev*, 77.

43. Ibid., 75.

44. *P.S.S.* 14:208, in the essay "Vstrecha moia s Belinskim."

45. Vladimir Grigorievich Benedictov (1807–1873), the "laureate" member of the "Pushkin Pleiade." Cf. Gronicka, *The Russian Image of Goethe*, 1:95.

46. *P.S.S.* 14:22–64: "Vospominaniia o Belinskom."

47. Ibid., 23 (italics in the original).

48. *P.S.S.* 1:214–56: "*Faust*, trag. soch. Gëte. Perevod pervoi i izlazhenie vtoroi chasti" (St. Peterburg, 1844).

49. Cf. G. B. Prokhorov, "Tvorcheskaia Istoria Romana *Rudin*," in Brodski, *Materialy*, 127.

50. Yarmolinski, *Turgenev*, 80.

51. Terras, "Turgenev and Western Realism," 31: "Turgenev's aesthetic has its romantic traits. His roots lay . . . in romanticism." See also Prokhorov, in Brodski, *Materialy*, 123: "Turgenev byl i ostalsia v svoei estetike na idealisticheskikh pozitsiiakh Shellinga i Gegelia."

52. In a letter to Botkin and Nekrasov of July 25, 1855, Turgenev writes in sharp criticism of Chernyshevski's *Master Thesis*: "The Aesthetic Relationship of Art and Reality": "This is my accusation against it: In his opinion art is . . . only a substitute for reality and life and in effect is good only for immature people. Say what you will, this idea lies at the very foundation of his argument. And in my view this is nonsense. No, brother, his book is both untrue and harmful" (*Pis'ma* 2:300–301). But in November 1856 Turgenev strikes a more restrained tone in a letter to Druzhinin: "He [Chernyshevski] does not understand poetry . . . but—how shall I put it?—he does understand the needs of contemporary life. . . . I regard Chernyshevski as useful. Time will show whether I am right or wrong" (ibid., 3:29–30).

53. Cf. S. M. Petrov, *I. S. Turgenev* (Moscow, 1968), 148–49.

54. In a letter to Leo Nikolaevich Tolstoi, Turgenev uses a vivid image to drive home his dislike of all systems: "Systems are like the tails of truth, but truth, like a

lizard, leaves its tail in your hand while it scurries off knowing full well that in quick time it will grow another." Letter of January 3, 1857, in *Pis'ma* 3:75.

55. *P.S.S.* 12:310: "Predislovie k Romanam." Cf. Isaiah Berlin: "The conscious use of art for ends extraneous to itself, ideological, didactic, or utilitarian, and especially as a deliberate weapon in the class war, demanded by the Russian radicals of the 1860s, was detestable to him [Turgenev]." "Father and Children: Turgenev and the Liberal Predicament," in *The New York Book Review* 20, nos. 16–18; quotation is from no. 16, pp. 39–40.

56. *P.S.S.* 1:214–56. All subsequent quotations are from this essay unless otherwise indicated. Translations are my own.

57. Cf., for example, Letter to P. Polonski of September 1870, in which Turgenev speaks of Germany's "greed for conquest" and of the Franco-Prussian War as the "embryo of more terrible wars to come" (*Pis'ma* 8:280). See also Boris Zaitsev, *Zhizn' Turgeneva* (Paris, 1949), 187: "Turgenev loved Germany, but the Germany of *Asia* and Heidelberg, of Baden-Baden, and of Goethe's Weimar. That Germany ended with the victorious war [Franco-Prussian]. . . . If Napoleon III was bad, then Bismarck with his crude and stupid military clique was disgusting [to Turgenev]."

58. *P.S.S.* 1:207. Comparison of this evaluation with Belinski's in his essay "Stikhotvoreniia Lermontova" (*Polnoe Sobobranie Sochineni*, ed. Vengerov, St. Petersburg, 1900, 6:38) shows Turgenev to be derivative.

59. In his letter to Pauline Viardot, Turgenev had characterized Goethe's Iphigenia figure as "d'une simplicité antique, chaste et calme—*peut-être trop calme* . . ." (*Pis'ma* 1:249; italics added).

60. Italics added. E. Hock states categorically: "Das Hochklassische Werk Goethes lässt sich . . . mit Turgeniews realistischer Konzeption nicht in Einklang bringen" (*Turgeniew und die deutsche Literatur*, 198).

61. However, Turgenev is fully aware that Romanticism as a literary "school" postdates Sturm und Drang.

62. Cf. Gronicka, *The Russian Image of Goethe*, 1:97.

63. Turgenev uses throughout the term "egoistic," which in most instances should be read as "egocentric."

64. "Der eigentliche Widerspruch in Turgeniews Aufsatz wurzelt darin, dass seine Vorstellung von der dichterischen Freiheit, von dem Wesen des Dichtertums überhaupt, noch nicht geklärt und ausgereift ist" (Hock, *Turgeniew und die deutsche Literatur*, 22).

65. Henry James has called Turgenev a "Romantic Realist."

66. This is the central theme of Isaiah Berlin's Romanes Lecture at Oxford in 1970 with the title "Turgenev and the Liberal Predicament." The full text was carried in *The New York Review of Books*, 20:16–18.

67. Cf. Masaryk, *The Spirit of Russia*, 284: "Turgenev tried to surmount Faust's 'apotheosis of personality,' thus attempting to overcome the legacy of both Goethe and Byron."

68. Turgenev is referring here to the scene "Vor dem Tor" and specifically to "Bauern unter der Linde" (*Hamb. Ausg.* 3:36–38).

69. I find myself being supported on this point by Soviet critic K. G. Chshmshkian in his informative study *I. S. Turgenev—Literaturnyi Kritik* (Erivan, 1957), 19.

70. *Hamb. Ausg.* 3:61–67.

71. Ibid., 23–24.

72. This pair of adjectives may strike one as a *contradictio in adjecto*, yet with Turgenev it is not. He sees Mephisto here both as a personification and as a supra-

human generalization, a symbol of negation, of evil, a concept that is expressed very precisely by the Russian term "otvlechënnyi," i.e., "abstract."

73. Schütz even goes so far as to maintain that in Turgenev's *Faust* study "Faust und Mephisto sich allmählich vom deutschen Hintergrund ablösen und russische Gestalt und Form annehmen. Der deutsche Faust und der deutsche Mephisto verwandeln sich im Geiste Turgeniews in russisches Fleisch und Blut. Sie beide verkörpern nun nicht mehr nur deutsche Menschen mit ihren Eigentümlichkeiten, sondern verwandeln sich zum Prototypen des 'überflüssigen Menschen'" (Schütz, *Goethebild*, 96). This much is certainly true: In his study of Goethe and his drama, Turgenev is also scrutinizing the problematical nature of his compatriots, the Russian intelligentsia and the great number of "superfluous people" in its midst.

74. *P.S.S.* 8:169–73. All subsequent quotations are from this text in my translation.

75. Schütz, *Goethebild*, 102–3. Cf. also *Hamb. Ausg.* 8:337 (*Zur Farbenlehre*—"Physiologische Farben," 38): "So setzt das Einatmen schon das Ausatmen voraus und umgekehrt, so jede Systole ihre Diastole. Es ist die ewige Formel des Lebens."

76. Turgenev bases his judgment mainly on Friedrich Theodor Vischer's "Die Literatur über Goethes Faust," in *Hallische Jahrbücher für Kunst und Wissenschaft* (Leipzig, 1838–40). Vischer's essay appeared in nos. 6–67 of the journal, from January 10 to March 19, 1839.

77. See p. 16.

78. In a letter to L. N. Tolstoi he writes, "I am a writer in a transitional time—and as such am of value only to those people who find themselves in a transitional situation" (*Pis'ma* 3:43).

79. *Hamb. Ausg.* 3:348.

80. Cf., for example, Chshmkian, *Turgenev*, 49, among many others.

81. For a comparison of the German Faust figure with its Russian counterpart, see Konrad Bittner, *Die Faustsage im russischen Schrifttum. Prager Deutsche Studien* (Reichenberg im Breisgau, 1925).

82. Philosophers, historians, literary historians, and critics have made much of this "otherness," above all, of course, the Slavophiles. Among modern critics we may point to Masaryk, *The Spirit of Russia*. In our special field, Schütz's study *Das Goethebild Turgeniews* illustrates this tendency.

83. In his informative essay "Turgenev and the West," L. V. Pumpianski goes into considerable detail showing "how all the leading ideas of the epoch were absorbed and transformed [tvorcheski pererabotyvalis'—lit.: were creatively reworked] by the Russian intelligentsia of the 1840s: the philosophies of Hegel and Feuerbach, the poetry of the Romanticists and Heine, the novels of George Sand—even including the debates in the Paris Chamber of Deputies and of the French Socialists in the times of Louis Philipp." He concludes: "This breadth of intellectual vision of the Russian intelligentsia of the 1840s was indeed unique compared with the intellectual horizon of the Western intellectuals." Brodski, *Materialy*, 90–207; quotation from p. 102.

84. See Gronicka, *The Russian Image of Goethe*, 1:190ff., and passim.

85. Ibid., 169–79.

86. Turgenev gives Vronchenko his due as a conscientious and industrious translator but faults the translation for not being "a living spring that pulses freely and easily from the innermost depths of the earth; it is a well from which water is being laboriously pumped with much screeching and wheezing. One is constantly moved to exclaim: Bravo, another difficulty overcome! . . . While, of course, one should not

even be conscious of difficulties." Goethe's *Faust* "simply exceeded Vronchenko's powers," and not surprisingly, for "the creations of such a sharply profiled, passionate, and deeply poetic personality as Goethe's can be adequately rendered only by a fellow poet." But alas, Vronchenko "is not a poet, not even a versifier."

87. Vronchenko's text with Turgenev's marginalia has been preserved in the library of the Institute of the Academy of Sciences. These marginalia have been published by M. Kleman in *Literaturnoe Nasledsto* 4–6 (Moscow and Leningrad, 1932): 943–57: "Anmerkungen I. S. Turgeniews zu der Übersetzung des *Faust* von Vronchenko." Zhirmunski has also reproduced some of Turgenev's annotations (*Gete v Russkoi Literature*, 540–41); he even ventures the opinion that Turgenev's "furious reaction" to Vronchenko's translation, and especially to his commentary, may well have been the main impulse for the *Faust* essay.

88. *Hamb. Ausg.* 1:358. Turgenev, quoting from memory, is not quite accurate; Goethe's text: "Nichts ist innen! Nichts is aussen / Denn was innen ist—ist draussen!"

89. *P.S.S.* 5:423–27: "Neskol'ko slov o stikhotvoreniiakh F. N. Tiutcheva" (quotation from p. 424).

90. *P.S.S.* 5:424.

91. Schütz, *Goethebild*, p. 63 and passim.

92. Bem also believes that Russian critics have ascribed too much importance to this essay and proceeds with a roll call of those critics whose praise of Turgenev's critical effort he finds excessive: "Ich glaube nicht, dass N. Brodski recht hat, wenn er behauptet, er [*Faust* essay] enthalte eine 'glänzende Charakteristik der deutschen Literatur des 18. Jahrhunderts' und wenn E. Rosenkranz meint, darin 'meisterhafte Charakterschilderungen der Hauptpersonen der Goetheschen Tragödie' zu sehen. . . , ich glaube auch nicht, dass M. Kleman im Recht ist, wenn er in dem Aufsatz Turgeniews 'eine bedeutsame Etappe in der Geschichte der Auslegung des Goetheschen Drama auf russischem Boden' zu erkennen geneigt ist." Cf. A. Bem, "Faust bei Turgeniew," *Germanoslavica* 2 (1932–33): 360.

93. *Germanoslavica*, p. 360.

94. To his "Hamlet–Don Quixote" essay, for example, as I have shown. Cf. pp. 17–19.

95. "Parasha. Rasskaz v. Stikhakh" (1844), in *P.S.S.* 1:75–101.

96. As quoted by Hock, *Turgeniew und die deutsche Literatur*, 13, from Bem, "Faust bei Turgeniew," 364.

97. Bem, "Faust bei Turgeniew," 363.

98. "Parasha," p. 98, Strophes LX and LXI.

99. "Parasha," p. 98: "Moi Viktor ne byl Don Zhuanom."

100. Turgenev refers us explicitly to Pushkin's heroine. Cf. "Parasha," p. 76, Strophe II.

101. Bem, "Faust bei Turgeniew," 363.

102. "Parasha," Strophe XIII and passim.

103. Ibid., p. 87, Strophe XXXII, quoted in Arthur Luther's translation. Cf. *Germanoslavica*, Jhrg. II (1932–33). I realize that the *Faust* essay (1845) appeared a year after the publication of "Parasha" (1844) but contend that during the writing of that poem the figure of Goethe's Mephisto was present in Turgenev's mind.

104. No extravagant attire for Turgenev's devil. He does not introduce himself, Mephisto fashion, as "edler Junker, in rotem, goldverbrämten Kleide, / Das Mäntelchen von starrer Seide, / Die Hahnenfeder auf dem Hut" *Hamb. Ausg.* 3:52.

105. "Parasha," pp. 98–99, Strophe LXII, in Luther's translation.

106. A. Pushkin, *Evgeni Onegin*. Other influences have been pointed out: Push-kin's *Count Nulin* and *The Little House in Kolomn* (*Domik v Kolomne*) as well as Lermontov's *Fairy Tale for Little Children* (*Skazka dlia Detei*), *Sashka*, and *Kaznacheisha*.

107. A comparison of Turgenev's and Pushkin's style is offered by L. A. Bulash-kovski in his comprehensive study *Russki Literaturnyi Iazyk Pervoi Poloviny XIX Veka* (Kiev, 1957), 99–101.

108. *P.S.S.* 4:7–20.

109. Cf. S. M. Petrov in his *I. S. Turgenev* (Moscow, 1968), 35: "The aristo-cratic readers saw in the juxtaposition of Khor' and Kalinych to Goethe and Schiller an unheard-of insolence."

110. *P.S.S.* 1:534.

111. The group includes *Hamlet of the Shchigry District* (1849), *Iakov Pasynkov* (1855), and *Rudin* (1855). However, there are a number of minor works that do not yield any new material relevant to my study, for example, *Andrei Kolosov* (1844), *The Diary of a Superfluous Man* (*Dnevnik Lishnego Cheloveka*, 1847), *Two Friends* (*Dva Priiatelia*, 1853), and *Correspondence* (*Perepiska*, 1854).

112. "Parasha," p. 85, Strophe XXVIII.

113. *Gamlet Shchigrovskogo Uezda*, *P.S.S.* 4:270–96. All quotations are from this text and in my translation unless otherwise indicated.

114. As in "Parasha," the veil that is to hide the autobiographical nature of the narrative is all too transparent. The editor of the latest edition of Turgenev's collected works comments: "Behind the tormenting reflections of 'Hamlet' one recognizes Turgenev's thoughts on his own fate" (*P.S.S.* 4:591).

115. Henceforth referred to as Shchigry Hamlet.

116. Turgenev wrote this scathing criticism of the "Kruzhki" while still under the immediate impact of Belinski, who was sharply critical of the "circles." In a letter to Mikahil Bakunin he wrote: "I am happy from the bottom of my heart that the circle no longer exists in which there was much that was beautiful but little that was of lasting substance, in which a handful of people brought happiness to each other but also mutu-ally tormented one another" (Letter of February 16, 1840, in *Pis'ma Belinskogo* [Moscow, 1914], 11:486). And to Nikolai A. Bakunin he wrote: "Worst of all, the members of these circles always, being estranged from all that is not within their narrow confines" (Letter of December 9, 1841, in ibid., 12:77).

117. Friedrich Hegel, *Encyklopädie der philosophischen Wissenschaften* (1817), a basic text intensively studied in Moscow's philosophical circles. Cf., for example, *P.S.S.* 4:503.

118. See pp. 83–95.

119. A. A. Grigor'ev, "I. S. Turgenev i Ego Deiatel'nost,'" in *Literaturnaia Kritika* (Moscow, 1858), 248–49 (italics in the original).

120. *P.S.S.* 4:192–234. All quotations are from this text in my translation unless otherwise indicated.

121. "Resignation, Eine Phantasie," in *Schillers sämtliche Werke* (Berlin and Leipzig, n.d.), 1:136–39.

122. Chernyshevski had proclaimed the complete incompatibility of his and Dobroliubov's views with those of Turgenev and the other liberals and had coined the provocative slogan "We or they!"

123. *P.S.S.* 4:541, as quoted from I. I. Panaev's "Zametki novogo poeta" in the *Otechestvennye Zapiski*, 1855.

124. Turgenev is thinking of Chernyshevski, Dobroliubov, and other Radical Democrats.

125. *P.S.S.* 4:237–368. All subsequent quotations are from this text in my translation unless otherwise indicated.

126. In his "Preface to [My] Novels" (1880) Turgenev wrote: "Beginning with *Rudin* I have striven to depict conscientiously and without prejudice in the respective types [among them, of course, Rudin] what Shakespeare calls the body and pressure of time" (*P.S.S.* 12:303). For the Shakespeare quotations, see *Hamlet*, III.ii. For the complex textual history of Turgenev's novel, see G. Prokhorov, "Tvorcheskaia Istoria Romana *Rudin*," in Brodski, *Materialy*, 108–35.

127. P. V. Annenkov wrote in his *Literary Recollections*, "Turgenev was preoccupied, throughout a decade, with the creation of one and the same type—the highminded person—beginning with the year 1846 [actually 1845], when *The Three Portraits* were written, right up to *Rudin*, which appeared in 1856 [actually 1855], in which the image of that type found its full embodiment." *Literaturnye Vospominaniia* (Moscow, n.d.), 479.

128. *P.S.S.* 7:7–50. All subsequent quotations are from this text.

129. Bem, "Faust bei Turgeniew," 365–68.

130. Schütz, *Goethebild*, 106–7.

131. Vera mistakes her lover for Mephisto in Goethe's words: "Was will er an dem heiligen Ort? . . ." *Hamb. Ausg.* 3:144.

132. Cf. p. 15.

133. For Turgenev's emotions on returning to Spasskoe, see the first letter of the novella.

134. Schütz, *Goethebild*, 111. The recollections stirred in the protagonist in reading Goethe's *Faust* are Turgenev's own memories of his Berlin days: "I [Paul] recalled everything: Berlin and student days and Fräulein Klara Stich and Seidelmann in the role of Mephisto and the music of Radzivil. . . . My youth stood before me a phantom; it ran like *fire*, like *poison* through my veins. My heart leaped and would not be still; something plucked at its chords, and yearnings surged anew. . . ." Once again we have here a typical expression of Turgenev's ambivalent attitude toward that seminal Romantic period, the Berlin experience of his youth. (Italics added.)

135. From among the numerous studies of the novella genre and its structure, see E. K. Bennett, *A History of the German Novelle from Goethe to Th. Mann* (Cambridge, Eng., 1934); W. Silz, *Realism and Reality: Studies in the German Novelle of Poetic Realism* (Chapel Hill, N.C., 1954); and most recently, Henry H. H. Remak, *Novellistische Struktur: Der Marschall von Bassompierre und die schöne Krämerin* (*Bassompierre, Goethe, Hofmannsthal*) (Bern and Frankfurt am Main, 1983).

136. Schütz, *Goethebild*, 106.

137. *Hamb. Ausg.* 3:53.

138. *P.S.S.* 7:392. See also Brodski, *Materialy*, 94 and passim.

139. *Hamb. Ausg.* 3:348.

140. Ibid., 18.

141. Ibid., 1:102.

142. The close resemblance of Turgenev's portrayal of Ladanov (Vera's grandfather) to Goethe's depiction of Faust in his *Studierzimmer* seems to have escaped notice. Ladanov is shown withdrawn to his study, busy with chemistry, anatomy, and cabalistics, striving to extend the span of human life, imagining himself in contact with spirits and capable of conjuring up the dead. "His neighbors saw in him a sorcerer." One is vividly reminded in this description of the "sorcerer" Faust, immersed

in alchemical and cabalistic pursuits, conjuring spirits—transported, to be sure, into modern times.

143. *P.S.S.* 7:71–120. All the following quotations are from this text in my translation unless otherwise indicated.

144. Ibid., 426.

145. Ibid., 424: "The tale of 'Asia' was conceived by Turgenev at a time of sharp ideological and psychological crisis . . ."; and ibid., 440–41: "The fate of his own daughter troubled the writer [Turgenev] and forced him again and again to ponder, with deep pain, the problem of the situation of 'illegitimate' children. The texts of the story (both the final as well as the draft) contain many details that are traceable to the life story of Pauline."

146. Ibid., 435.

147. N. M. Gut'iar, *Ivan Sergeevich Turgenev* (Moscow, 1907), 366–67.

148. The central problem developed by Turgenev is his deep-seated doubt in his ability to surmount his dilettantism, to break through into serious art. Turgenev's concern is pointedly articulated in N. N.'s conversations with the pseudo-artist Gagin. I was unable to detect any hint of Goethe's influence (thematically) on this facet of the novella.

149. The term "chameleon" could be applied to Lermontov's figure with equal justice.

150. That similarity, so apparent in the descriptions of Asia, may well be blurred or even canceled out for many a reader by Turgenev's rather labored effort in that long and ponderous chapter 8 to "explain" Asia's character and behavior by her illegitimate birth and "strange, unusual education." Here the need to "objectify" personal experiences and anxieties almost thwarted the artistic intent in this predominantly lyrico-Romantic novella.

151. For example, by Chernyshevski in his "Russki Chelovek na Rendes-vous," as quoted in *P.S.S.* 7:435.

152. For my discussion of that relationship, see Gronicka, *The Russian Image of Goethe*, 1:84–86; quotation is from p. 85.

153. *P.S.S.* 7:125–294.

154. Cf. Petrov, *I. S. Turgenev*, 137: "In *A Nobleman's Nest*, Turgenev took leave of this past and turned his gaze toward the new generation, in which was ripening the future of Russia. . . . Having completed work on *Nobleman's Nest*, Turgenev began to plan the novel *On the Eve*." Petrov goes on to quote Turgenev: "To the tale 'On the Eve' I have given that title in view of the time of its appearance. . . . It was at that time that a new life began in Russia."

155. The theme and mood of the Lemm episodes have been traced to the influence on Turgenev of "the tradition of German Romantic literature of the 1820s to 1830s, which drew extensively on the musical sphere for the psychological characterization of the heroes." Wilhelm Wackenroder's influence is singled out, specifically that of his "Das musikalische Leben Joseph Berglingers," in Wackenroder, *Herzensergiessungen eines kunstliebenden Klosterbruders* (Jena, 1904). Cf. editor's "Notes" in *P.S.S.* 7:485.

156. Cf. Turgenev in his essay "On the Occasion of *Fathers and Children*": "I am a rooted, incorrigible Westerner. I never did deny this, nor do I deny it now. Nevertheless, I have set forth with special pleasure in the figure of Panshin (in 'A Nobleman's Nest') all the comical and cheap facets of Westernism. I had the Slavophile Lavretski 'crush him on every point'" (*P.S.S.* 14:100).

157. Cf. Turgenev's letter to I. S. Aksakov (November 1859): "A central theme

216 Notes

of my tale [*On the Eve*] is the need of *consciously* heroic natures . . . so that the cause can move forward" (*Pis'ma* 3:368; italics in the original).

158. Heroes and heroines of the novels *On the Eve* (*Nakanune*, 1860), *Fathers and Children* (*Ottsy i Deti*, 1862), and *Unplowed Soil* (November 1876), respectively.

159. Erich Hock (*Turgeniew und die deutsche Literatur*, 34) essentially agrees: "Die Ablehnung des Goetheschen 'Egoismus' ist ja nur eine durch die Zeitsituation bedingte Befangenheit, die dem Gefühl einer ernst genommenen sozialen Pflicht entspringt, während die tiefer liegende unbewusste Quelle des Dichtertums schon das Gemeinsame mit dem Genius Goethes ahnt."

160. For a conscientious listing of Goethe quotes and references in Turgenev's works, see Schütz, *Goethebild*, 149–52.

161. *P.S.S.* 10:44–71; quotation from p. 63. Even though farfetched, this reference to Goethe is another instance of the insistent presence of the German poet's works in Turgenev's mind.

162. *Hamb. Ausg.* 2:242 ("Noten und Abhandlungen zum besseren Verständnis des West-Östlichen Divans. Entschuldigung").

163. *P.S.S.* 12:28 (italics added).

164. Ibid., 15:66–76. All quotations are from this text in my translation unless otherwise indicated.

165. See p. 3 above. For quotation, see *Hamb. Ausg.* 3:13.

166. See p. 3 above.

167. Cf., for example, "On the Occasion of *Fathers and Children*," in *P.S.S.* 14:106.

168. *Hamb. Ausg.* 1:359.

169. In Goethe's meaning of that term: a poem in immediate response to an intense personal experience ("Mailied," "Auf dem See," "Auf Kieseln im Bache"), not as a formal exercise in celebration of a birthday, wedding, or death, often requested or even ordered by a patron, the type of "Gelegenheitsgedicht" flourishing in the Baroque period.

170. This is probably one reason why Turgenev took part only halfheartedly in the Schiller cult prevalent in intellectual and artistic circles of contemporary Russia. See E. Kostka, *Schiller in Russian Literature* (Philadephia, 1965), 25–27 and passim.

171. *Hamb. Ausg.* 9:590.

172. *Eckermanns Gespräche mit Goethe*, ed. H. H. Houben (Leipzig, 1939), 154.

173. Ibid., 38.

174. Turgenev uses the term "typical" positively, but the terms "symbolical" and "allegorical," generally, pejoratively.

175. *P.S.S.* 14:107, among many other relevant passages.

176. Turgenev singles out *Faust*, Part One for special praise because it was written by Goethe "without a plan" (*P.S.S.* 1:228; see also ibid., 234).

177. Ibid., 235.

178. I. Turgenev, *Sobranie Sochineni* (Moscow, 1962), 7:36. Or compare the dismal vision of mankind and its habitat in the novella *Phantoms*: "The entire globe with its population, with that ephemeral, impotent humanity, oppressed by poverty, sorrow, and sickness, chained to this clump of dust . . . these people-flies, a thousand times more insignificant than flies, their dwellings pasted together out of dirt, these tiny traces of their puny, monotonous labors, of their ludicrous struggle against immutable, inexorable fate . . ." (*P.S.S.* 7:25).

179. "Der Bräutigam," in *Hamb. Ausg.* 1:386.

180. "In ein Stammbuch," in ibid., 259.

181. *P.S.S.* 7:26.

182. Ibid., 13:76–135. Or consider the enigmatic figure of Ellis in *Phantoms*: "Really, what is that creature, Ellis?" the author asks. "Is she an apparition, a wandering soul [skitaiushchaia dusha], an evil spirit, a sylphid, a vampire—what is she?" (*P.S.S.* 7:28).

183. *Hamb. Ausg.* 3:103.

184. *P.S.S.* 7:51: "Poezdka v Poles'e."

185. *Hamb. Ausg.* 3, esp. pp. 282–84. In contrast to Turgenev, Shevyrëv had recognized the importance and beauty of the "Classico-Romantic Phantasmagoria" shortly upon its appearance in 1827. See my *Russian Image of Goethe*, 1:125–34.

186. Hock, *Turgeniew und die deutsche Literatur*, 88.

Chapter Two. *Crosscurrents of Opinion*

1. Afanasi Fet, *Moi Vospominaniia, 1848–1889* (Moscow, 1890), 401–2.

2. See Gronicka, *The Russian Image of Goethe*, 1:208.

3. Vasili Botkin, "Germanskaia Literatura v 1843 godu," in *Polnoe Sobranie Sochineni* (St. Petersburg, 1891), 2:275–91. Henceforth cited as Botkin, *Soch.*

4. Ibid., 2:278.

5. Ibid.

6. Ibid.

7. "Russkaia Literatura: A. A. Fet" (1856), in Botkin, *Soch.* 2:372.

8. Ibid., 355.

9. Ibid., 372.

10. "Shakespeare," in Botkin, *Soch.* 2:79.

11. Ibid., 68.

12. "Russkaia Literatura: A. A. Fet." In Botkin, *Soch.* 2:370.

13. Ibid., 371.

14. Ibid., 394. For Goethe's quotation, see *Jubiläums-Ausgabe* (Stuttgart and Berlin, n.d.), 34:12.

15. A. Druzhinin, *Sobrannye Sochineniia A.V. Druzhinina* (St. Petersburg, 1865), 7:233–34. Henceforth cited as Druzhinin, *Soch.*

16. Ibid., 14.

17. Ibid., 6:719.

18. "Grecheskie Stikhotvoreniia," in ibid., 11.

19. Ibid.

20. Ibid., 718.

21. *Edinburgh Review* 42/84 (August 1825): 409–49, art. 7: "Wilhelm Meister's Apprenticeship, a Novel. From the German of Goethe. In three volumes. Edinburgh, 1824."

22. *Bibliotheka dlia Chteniia*, no. 2, 1854.

23. *Edinburgh Review* 42/84 (August 1825): 416.

24. Ibid., 417.

25. Ibid.

26. Ibid., 425.

27. Ibid., 441.

28. Ibid.

29. Ibid., 414.

30. Ibid., 415.

31. Ibid.

32. Ibid., 433–34.

33. Ibid., 449.

34. Druzhinin, *Soch.* 6:718.

35. Ibid., 5:359. Druzhinin, however, still credits Jeffrey with having "drawn attention to many aspects of Goethe's personality and work heretofore completely unknown in England" and praises him for having "dealt the deathblow to those short-sighted German admirers of Goethe who grow enthusiastic over every letter [of the alphabet: bukvoi] by him . . . and who, in their slavish adoration of the master, continue to interpret the immortal thinker from their narrow German point of view" (ibid.).

36. Ibid., 357.

37. Ibid., 355 (italics in the original).

38. Ibid., 7:219.

39. Only Heine and Börne were associated with the "Young Germans."

40. Druzhinin probably refers here to Feuerbach, Ludwig Börne, and theologian David Friedrich Strauss.

41. The river in the underworld, the waters of which brought oblivion.

42. Druzhinin, *Soch.* 7:219.

43. Ibid., 5:355.

44. Ibid., 7:219.

45. Ibid., 221.

46. Ibid., 222.

47. The other leading figure is Nikolai Aleksandrovich Dobroliubov. I have examined his collected works, *Sobranie Sochineni* (Moscow and Leningrad, 1964ff.), and have not been able to find any noteworthy statement by him on Goethe.

48. Cf. Dmitri Chizhevski, *Hegel bei den Slawen. Wissenschaftliche Buchgesellschaft* (Darmstadt, 1961), 344.

49. Cf. Chizhevski, *Aus Zwei Welten. Beiträge zur Geschichte der Slawisch-Westlichen Beziehungen* (The Hague, 1956), 14.

50. Anatoli Lunacharski, *On Literature and Art* (Moscow, 1965), 44.

51. B. I. Bursov, *Chernyshevski as Literary Critic* (Moscow and Leningrad: Akademiia Nauk, 1918), 15–16.

52. Zhirmunski, *Gete v Russkoi Literature*, 372. For the quotation from Chernyshevski, see *Polnoe Sobranie Sochineni v Piatnadtsati Tomakh* (Moscow, 1944ff.), 4:48. Henceforth cited as *Pol. Sob.*, with volume and page following.

53. Chernyshevski, *Pol. Sob.* 1:358, Note of January 20, 1850.

54. Ibid.

55. Ibid.

56. Ibid., 140, Note of October 5, 1848, and p. 150, Note of October 18, 1848.

57. Ibid., 244, Note of February 25, 1849.

58. Ibid., 285, Note of June 10, 1849.

59. Ibid., 166, Note of November 9, 1848.

60. Ibid., 295, Note of July 8, 1849.

61. Ibid., 11:696–99.

62. For comments on Huber, see ibid., 1:217, 232. For comments on M. Vronchenko, see ibid., 227, 228.

63. Ibid., 187, Note of December 3, 1848. Chernyshevski corroborates my thesis of Goethe's influence on Lermontov's *Hero of Our Times*. See *The Russian Image of Goethe*, 1:91: "Bela, Princess Mary, Vera, all of them [are] sisters in suffering to Gretchen!"

64. Chernyshevski, *Pol. Sob.* 1:456 (italics added). For Goethe quotation, see *Hamb. Ausg.* 1:30.

65. Ibid., 11:269.

66. Ibid., 269–70.

67. Ibid., 269. For Goethe quotation, see *Hamb. Ausg.* 3:108.

68. Ibid., 12:123–25; see also pp. 165, 187, 221, 269, 314, 357, 400. For Goethe quotation, see *Hamb. Ausg.* 1:271.

69. Ibid., 3:137.

70. Ibid., 21–22.

71. Ibid., 4:507.

72. Ibid., 12:125; see also 2:51: "Goethe's drama may seem strange to those who are unable to transfer themselves into the epoch of striving and doubt which finds expression in the figure of Faust."

73. Ibid., 15:199. Letter to A. N. and M. N. Chernyshevski (his sons), of March 8, 1878 (italics in the original).

74. Ibid., 4:160.

75. Ibid., 178.

76. Ibid., 2:257–58.

77. Ibid., 7:441.

78. Ibid., 6:274–75. For Goethe quotation, see *Hamb. Ausg.* 1:269.

79. Ibid., 2:798.

80. Ibid., 3:783–93; also in the journal *Zven'ia* (Moscow and Leningrad, 1933), 97–117: "Chernyshevski, 'Primechaniia k Perevodu *Fausta*." The following quotations are from these "Notes" (Primechaniia) unless otherwise indicated. Chernyshevski does not seem to have known firsthand the Second Part of *Faust*. His references to that part are critical in the extreme. The following judgment is typical: "Unfortunately, the Second Part, written or revised in the days of Goethe's spiritual decrepitude [vo vremia nravstvennoi driakhlosti], was unsuccessful, and only the First Part of the plan—the presentation of the private world—was accomplished in the manner of a true genius" (Chernyshevski, *Pol. Sob.* 3:792).

81. Ibid., 2:473, 506.

82. Ibid., 3:266.

83. This quotation and the following quotations are from "Predislovie: Dlia Podrug ili Druzei Avtora," in ibid., 12:677–79 (italics added).

84. See the essay "Lessing, Ego Vremiia, Ego Zhizn' i Deiatel'nost'" ("Lessing, His Times, His Life, and His Activity"), in ibid., 4:5–221. Chernyshevski had planned a full-scale biography of his idol as well as a detailed interpretation and evaluation of all his works. The project remained incomplete. The interpretative part was never written.

85. Ibid., 10.

86. Ibid., 8.

87. Ibid., 9.

88. Ibid., 153.

89. Ibid., 10.

90. Ibid., 160.

91. Ibid., 150.

92. Ibid., 172.

93. Ibid., 153.

94. Ibid.

95. Ibid., 4:99.

96. Ibid., 176.
97. Ibid., 177.
98. Ibid.
99. Ibid., 179.
100. Ibid., 161.
101. Ibid., 15:323. Letter to his son, A. N. Chernyshevski, of March 7, 1881. See also the letter to his daughter, O. S. Chernyshevskaia, of March 1878 in ibid., 239.
102. See Gronicka, *The Russian Image of Goethe*, 1:179–220, for my discussion of Belinski's attitude toward Goethe. The quotation is from p. 219: "Goethe is a poet of the past and is dead in the present; he is a king dethroned."
103. Dmitri Ivanovich Pisarev, *Izbrannye Proizvedeniia* (Leningrad, 1968), 284. Henceforth cited as Pisarev, *Izb. Pro.* The following quotations are from the essays "The Realists" ("Realisty"; ibid., 224–366) and "Heinrich Heine" ("Genrich Geine"; ibid., 470–521).
104. Ibid., 231.
105. Ibid., 319.
106. Ibid., 333.
107. Ibid., 374.
108. Ibid., 316 (italics in the original).
109. Ibid., 343.
110. Ibid., 238.
111. Ibid., 228.
112. Dmitri Ivanovich Pisarev, *Polnoe Sobranie Sochineni v Shesti Tomakh* (St. Petersburg, 1909–13), vol. 3, "Nasha Universitetskaia Nauka," p. 46. Henceforth cited as Pisarev, *Pol. Sob.*
113. Pisarev, *Izb. Pro.*, 331.
114. Pisarev, *Pol. Sob.*, vol. 2, "Russki Don-Kikhot," p. 223.
115. Pisarev, *Izb. Pro.*, 279.
116. Ibid., 283.
117. Ibid., 279.
118. Ibid., 283.
119. Ibid., 501 (italics in the original).
120. Ibid., 498. Pisarev refers here sarcastically to Goethe's lyric masterpiece the *West-Östliche Divan*. See, *Hamb. Ausg.* 2:7–270.
121. Pisarev, *Izb. Pro.*, 265.
122. Ibid.
123. Ibid.
124. Ibid. (italics in the original).
125. Ibid., 501–2 (italics in the original).
126. Ibid., 320.
127. Ibid., 321.
128. Ibid.
129. Ibid., 322.
130. Ibid.
131. Ibid.
132. Nicholas V. Riasanovsky, *Russia and the West in the Teaching of the Slavophiles: A Study of Romantic Ideology* (Cambridge, Mass., 1952).
133. A. I. Gertsen, *Polnoe Sobranie Sochineni i Pisem*, ed. M. K. Lemke, vol. 11: *Byloe i Dumy*, p. 11 (italics in the original).

134. See, for example, O. Miller, *Slavianstvo i Evropa* (St. Petersburg, 1877).
135. Riasanovski, *Russia and the West*, 33.
136. Ibid., 166.
137. I examined the following edition: Aleksei Stepanovich Khomiakov, *Polnoe Sobranie Sochineni*, 8 vols. (Moscow, 1900–1904).
138. Sergei Timofeevich Aksakov, *Sobranie Sochineni v Piati Tomakh* (Moscow, 1966), vol. 2: *Vospominaniia*, pp. 115, 128–29.
139. Ibid., 2:155–56.
140. There are scattered comments in the essays "O sovremennom literaturnom spore," *Rus'*, 1883, no. 7; and in "Obozrenie sovremennoi russkoi literatury," *Russkaia Beseda*, 1857, book 1, pp. 1–39.
141. Dmitri Chizhevski, *Hegel bei den Slawen* (Darmstadt, 1961), 246.
142. Now collected in *Sochineniia Konstantina Aksakova*, ed. E. A. Liadski (St. Petersburg, 1915), 1:129 "Novaia Liubov', novaia zhizn'" ["Neue Liebe, neues Leben"]; 1:130 "Na Ozere" ["Auf dem See"]; 1:130–32 "Utrennie Zhaloby" ["Morgenklagen"]; 1:132–34 "Magadeva i Baiadera" ["Der Gott und die Bajadere"]; 1:135 "Tishina na more" ["Meeres Stille"]; 1:135 "Shchastlivyi Put'" ["Glückliche Fahrt"]; 1:135–36 "Rybak" ["Der Fischer"]; 1:136–37 "Pevets" ["Der Sänger"]; 1:136–42 Four selections from *Faust*; 1:142 "Peremena" ["Wechsel"]; 1:142–43 "Spasenie" ["Rettung"]; 1:144 "Elegiia" [the fourteenth Roman Elegy]; 1:144–46 "Poseshchenie" ["Der Besuch"]; 1:146–48 "Korintskaia Nevesta" ["Die Braut von Korinth," the first twelve strophes only].
143. For originals, see *Hamb. Ausg.*, 1:19 and 239, respectively.
144. See Gronicka, *The Russian Image of Goethe*, 1:185–86.
145. V. G. Belinski, *Pis'ma Belinskogo* (Moscow, 1914), 1:341, Letter to Stankevich of September 29, 1839.
146. Ibid., 2:69. For S. E. Raich, see Gronicka, *The Russian Image of Goethe*, 1:76, 116, 155, 156.
147. See *Sochineniia Konstantina Aksakova*, 1:129.
148. See Gronicka, *The Russian Image of Goethe*, 1:54–55. For Goethe quotation, see *Hamb. Ausg.*, 1:96.
149. See especially the sources mentioned in n. 140.
150. See Gronicka, *The Russian Image of Goethe*, 1:145–50. Kireievski's interest in and closeness to Rozhalin finds ample expression in his correspondence from abroad. See Gershenson edition of I. Kireievski's *Collected Works* (*Sobranie Sochineni*) (Leningrad, n.d.), 1:38–39, 45, 48, 52–53, 56–57; 2:218.
151. See the A. I. Koshelëv edition of Kireievski's collected works: *Polnoe Sobranie Sochineni Ivana Vasil'evicha Kireievskago* (Moscow, 1861), vol. 1: "V otvet A. S. Khomiakovu," p. 190.
152. Ibid., 2:209, "Faust, tragediia. Sochinenie Gete. Perevod pervoi i izlozhenie vtoroi chasti, M. Vronchenko. 1844 g." (St. Petersburg, n.d.). Kireievski's review appeared first in the journal *Moskvitianin* in 1845.
153. Kireievski, *Polnoe Sobranie Sochineni*, 2:209.
154. Ibid., 210.
155. Ibid., 210–11.
156. Ibid., 210.
157. See Gronicka, *The Russian Image of Goethe*, 1:125–34.
158. See pp. 19–20.
159. Kireievski, *Polnoe Sobranie Sochineni*, 2:213.
160. Ibid., 212–13.

161. Ibid., 189–90.

162. Ibid., 1 : 190. Wilhelm Goerdt, in his study of Kireievski's philosophy, identifies Wolfgang Menzel's influence on this view of Goethe as an unreliable, ever-changing character. He quotes Menzel's *Die Deutsche Literatur* (1836), part 3, p. 363: "So sehen wir Göthes [!] Talent, wie das Chamäleon, in allen Farben wechseln." See Wilhelm Goerdt, *Vergöttlichung und Gesellschaft* (Wiesbaden, 1968), 77.

163. Goerdt, *Vergöttlichung und Gesellschaft*, 77: "Nicht Poesie als Poesie, nicht das *pulchrum* als *verum* wünscht der 'Industrialismus,' sondern die Poesie als Politik, die der Gesellschaft die je nötigen schönen Illusionen, die Illusionen als das Schöne liefert. Das ist ein so wesentliches Epiphänomen der industriellen Gesellschaft, dass seinem Zwang sogar der grosse Goethe, der geniale Schöpfer des poetischen und philosophischen, allmenschlichen und 'modernen' *Faust*, sich nicht entziehen kann." In this passage Goerdt summarizes Kireievski's thought on this theme with great precision.

164. Kireievski, *Polnoe Sobranie Sochineni*, vol. 2: "Obozrenie sovremennogo sostoianiia literatury," p. 25.

165. Ibid.

166. Ibid., vol 2: "Deviatnadtsatyi Vek," p. 66 (italics in the original).

167. Ibid., 25 (italics in the original). It is not clear whether with this statement Kireievski joins the critics of *Faust* or whether he credits *Faust* with being the last example of great art, still capable of adumbrating in artistic form its decline and death.

168. Ibid., 1 : 67.

169. Ibid. (italics in the original).

170. Ibid.

171. Ibid., vol. 2: "Obozrenie sovremennogo sostoiania literatury," p. 57.

172. Ibid., 34 (italics in the original).

173. Apollon Aleksandrovich Grigor'ev, *Sobranie Sochineni*, ed. V. T. Savodnik (Moscow, 1915). Henceforth cited as Grigor'ev, *Sob. Soch. Vypusk (Issue)* II: "Kriticheski Vzgliad na Osnovy, Znachenie i Priemy Sovremennyi Kritiki Iskusstva" (1858), 92.

174. Grigor'ev, *Sob. Soch.*, *Vypusk* X: "I. S. Turgeniev i ego deiatel'nost'" (1859), 65 (italics in the original).

175. Afanasi A. Fet., *Rannie Gody Moei Zhizni* (Moscow, 1893), 153.

176. As quoted by Zhirmunski, *Gete v Russkoi Literature*, 394, from *Materialy dlia biografii*, ed. V. Kniazhnina (1917), a source that was unavailable to me.

177. A. Grigor'ev, "Stikhotvoreniia A. A. Feta," *Otechestvennye Zapiski*, February 1850, pp. 49–72. The following quotations are from this source unless otherwise indicated.

178. For Goethe's poem, see *Hamb. Ausg.* 1 : 369/370.

179. See Grigor'ev, *Sob. Soch.*, *Vypusk* X, 89.

180. Ibid., *Vypusk* II, 98. For Goethe quotation, see *Hamb. Ausg.*, 3 : 110.

181. A. Grigor'ev, *Literaturnaia Kritika*, (Moscow, 1858), 317.

182. Ibid., 126.

183. Grigor'ev, "Stikhotvoreniia Feta," 51. For Goethe's poem, see *Hamb. Ausg.* 1 : 30.

184. See *Jubiläums-Ausgabe*, 2 : 52.

185. Grigor'ev, "Stikhotvoreniia Feta," 60. For Goethe's poem, see *Hamb. Ausg.*, 1 : 268.

186. Grigor'ev, *Sob. Soch.*, *Vypusk* II, 98. For Goethe quotation, see *Hamb. Ausg.* 3 : 110.

187. See Goethe, *Jubiläums-Ausgabe*, (Stuttgart and Berlin, 1902ff.) 1:57–58.
188. These quotations are from Grigor'ev, "Stikhotvoreniia Feta," passim.
189. Grigor'ev, *Literaturnaia Kritika*, 143.
190. These quotations are from Grigor'ev, "Stikhotvoreniia Feta," passim.
191. Grigor'ev, *Literaturnaia Kritika*, 138 (italics in the original).
192. Ibid., 151.
193. Ibid., 188.
194. Ibid., 187–88.
195. Grigor'ev, *Sob. Soch.*, *Vypusk* II, 8–9.
196. Grigor'ev, *Literaturnaia Kritika*, 313. For the Goethe quotation, see *Wilhelm Meisters Wanderjahre*, book 3, chap. 1, *Hamb. Ausg.*, 8:318.
197. Grigor'ev, *Literaturnaia Kritika*, 310. For the Goethe quotation, see *Hamb. Ausg.*, 8:317.
198. Grigor'ev, *Sob. Soch.*, *Vypusk* II, "O Pravde i Iskrennosti v Iskusstve," pp. 20–21. For the Goethe quotation, see *Faust* Part II, Act 3, *Hamb. Ausg.*, 3:298. The quotation is not exact; it should read "Ikarus, Ikarus, Jammer genug."
199. Grigor'ev, *Sob. Soch.*, *Vypusk* II, 20–21. Grigor'ev repeated this thought verbatim in "Lermontov i Ego Napravlenie," *Sob. Soch.*, *Vypusk* VII, 4–5.
200. Grigor'ev, *Sob. Soch.*, *Vypusk* II, "O Pravde i Iskrennosti v Iskusstve," p. 3.
201. Ibid., 66.
202. Ibid., *Vypusk* VI, "Vzgliad na Russkuiu Literaturu," p. 24.
203. Ibid., *Vypusk* IX, "Russkaia Iziashnaia Literatura v 1852 Godu," p. 114.
204. Ibid., *Vypusk* II, "O Pravde i Iskrennosti v Iskusstve," p. 3.
205. Ibid., 3–4.
206. Ibid.
207. Compare, for example, Uvarov's portrayal of Goethe as a Proteus, or Baratynski's famous eulogy of Goethe. See Gronicka, *The Russian Image of Goethe*, 1:29 and 95–96, respectively.
208. Grigor'ev, *Sob. Soch.*, *Vypusk* II, 3–4.
209. Ibid., 4.
210. Ibid., 4–5.
211. Ibid. (italics in the original).
212. Grigor'ev refers here to the lines "Oftmals hab' ich auch schon in ihren Armen gedichtet / Und des Hexameters Mass leise mit fingernder Hand / Ihr auf den Rücken gezählt. Sie atmet in lieblichem Schlummer, / Und es durchglühet ihr Hauch mir bis ins Tiefste die Brust" (*Hamb. Ausg.*, 1:160).
213. Grigor'ev, *Sob. Soch.*, *Vypusk* IX, "Russkaia Iziashnaia Literatura v 1852 Godu," p. 114 (italics in the original).
214. Ibid., *Vypusk* II, "O Pravde i Iskrennosti v Iskusstve," p. 4.
215. A. Grigor'ev, "Stat'ia Lorda Dzheffri" (1854), in *Moskvitianin*, 2:174 (italics added).
216. Ibid., 178.
217. Grigor'ev, *Sob. Soch.*, *Vypusk* II, "O Pravde i Iskrennosti v Iskusstve," p. 32 (italics in the original).
218. Ibid.
219. See above, pp. 53–55.
220. Grigor'ev, "Stat'ia Lord Dzheffri," 2:178. The following quotations are from this source; all italics are in the original.
221. With this claim, Grigor'ev anticipates Friedrich Engels's all-but-identical

thesis, which was to become one of the maxims of Marxist-Leninist literary criticism.

222. Other members usually included in this group or standing close to it are Lev Aleksandrovich Mei (1822–1862), Aleksei N. Pleshcheev (1825–1893), and Iakov Petrovich Polonski (1819–1898).

223. Zhirmunski, *Gete v Russkoi Literature*, 440. *Hamburg Ausg.* 1:156.

224. A. Fet, "O Stikhotvoreniiakh F. Tiutcheva," *Russkoe Slovo*, no. 2 (1859): 64.

225. V. P. Botkin, *Polnoe Sobranie Sochineni* (St. Petersburg, 1891), 2:370.

226. Mandelstam's wife, Nadezhda, echoing her husband's valuation of the translation, speaks of "the miraculous meeting of poetic minds such as one finds in the case of Zhukovski, whose translations brought a new element into Russian poetry or of other translated verse . . . such as A. K. Tolstoi's rendering of Goethe's 'Bride of Corinth,' which we liked so much." Cf. N. Mandelstam, *Hope Against Hope: A Memoire* (New York, 1976), 73. In sobering contrast, I would quote Ivan Turgenev's reaction: "And with it all, I simply cannot stomach his [A. Tolstoi's] verses! They have the mark of rhetoric all over them . . . are lifelessly bombastic, correct—and completely false. What kind of poet is this anyway? What has he made of the poor 'Braut von Korinth' of Goethe!" (*Pis'ma*, 7:250).

227. Fet, *Rannie Gody Moei Zhizni* (Moscow, 1893), 16. Hence cited as *Rannie Gody*.

228. Ibid., 209.

229. Grigor'ev, "Stikhotvoreniia Feta," 54–55.

230. Fet, *Rannie Gody*, 192. The term "objective truth," coined by Grigor'ev as a central concept of his "organismic aesthetics" and used widely by the Pure Poets, denotes the true artist's ability to depict all aspects of life without ideological bias, free of subjective mannerisms, in "organic" contact with the object (aspect) depicted, a term quite close to Goethe's "Stil" in his essay "Einfache Nachahmung der Natur, Manier, Stil."

231. Ibid.

232. Grigor'ev is among those who attest to this influence. See, for example, his discussion of Fet's poetry in "Stikhotvoreniia Feta," 49–72.

233. For these translations, see *Polnoe Sobranie Stikhotvoreni A. A. Feta* (St. Petersburg, 1901), 3:95: "Prekrasnaia Noch'" ("Die schöne Nacht"); pp. 102–3: "Na Ozere" ("Auf dem See"); p. 353: "Maiskaia Pesnia" ("Mailied"); pp. 112–13: "Novaia Liubov'—Novaia Zhizn'" ("Neue Liebe, neues Leben"); p. 114: "Nochnaia Pesnia Putnika" ("Wandrers Nachtgesang"). Henceforth cited as Fet, *Pol. Sol.*

234. Ibid., 3:322: "Lesnoi Tsar'" ("Erlkönig"); p. 360: "Pevets" ("Der Sänger"); pp. 110–11: "Rybak" ("Der Fischer"). He also translated "Pazh i Mel'nichikha" ("Der Edelknabe und die Müllerin"), pp. 104–6, and "Iunosha i Mel'nichnyi Ruchei" ("Der Junggesell und der Mühlbach"), pp. 107–9.

235. A. Fet, "O Stikhotvoreniiakh F. Tiutcheva," *Russkoe Slovo*, no. 2 (1859): 70.

236. A. Fet, "Po Povodu Statui G-na Ivanova," *Khudozhestvennyi Sbornik*, 1866, 89.

237. Ibid., 88–89.

238. A. Fet, "Dva Pis'ma o Klassicheskom Obrasovanii," *Literaturnaia Biblioteka*, April 1867, 56. Henceforth cited as "Dva Pis'ma."

239. A. Fet, *Faust: Faust, Tragediia Gëte. Perevod A. Feta* (St. Petersburg, 1889), 2 vols. in 1. Fet began the translation in the fall of 1879, encouraged by his gifted nephew Peter Borisov. See A. Fet, *Moi Vospominaniia, 1848–1889* (Moscow, 1890), 2:367: "Upon Boris' departure for the Lyceum, I dared to begin the translation

of *Faust* and was able to continue it with completely unexpected effortlessness." He finished it in 1883.

240. *Hamb. Ausg.*, 3:146–49.

241. Zhirmunski, *Gete v Russkoi Literature*, 551. For a detailed analysis, see Wilma Pohl, *Russische Faust-Übersetzungen. Veröffentlichungen des slawisch-baltischen Seminars der westfälischen Wilhelms-Universität* (Münster, 1962), 94–105.

242. Grigor'ev, "Stikhotvoreniia Feta," 53, 69.

243. Fet, *Rannie Gody*, 209.

244. Fet, *Pol. Sob.*, 4:219–66, 8:261–64.

245. Cf., for example, lines in ibid., p. 223.

246. Cf., for example, lines in ibid., p. 263: "Kazhdoe chuvstvo byvaet poniatnee mne noch'iu." ("Every feeling I sense more readily at night.")

247. A. Fet, "Iz-za Granitsy," *Sovremennik* 61/2 (1857): 243.

248. Fet, *Rannie Gody*, 213.

249. Fet, *Moi Vospominaniia*, part 1, 1848–63; part 2, 1863–89 (Moscow, 1890). For quotation, see 2:172. As a motto for the first part of these recollections, Fet chose the lines from Goethe's "Vorspiel auf dem Theater," *Faust*: "Greift nur hinein ins volle Menschenleben! / Ein jeder lebt's, nicht vielen ist's bekannt / Und wo ihr's packt, da ist's interessant," which Fet rendered very successfully: "Staraisia pocherpat' iz zhizni to liudskoi.' / Vse ei zhivut, ne vsem ona izvestna; / A gde ni oglianis', povsiudu interesna."

250. Fet, *Pol. Sob.*, 3:119–99.

251. Fet, "O Stikhotvoreniiakh Tiutcheva," 64.

252. Fet, *Moi Vospominaniia*, 2:391–92. I have not been able to locate the passage in Turgenev's letters.

253. Fet, "Dva Pis'ma," 54.

254. Ibid., 57. For the Goethe quotation, cf. also Goethe, *Wilhelm Meisters Wanderjahre. Hamb. Ausg.*, 8:65: "*Vom Nützlichen durchs Wahre zum Schönen*" (italics in the original).

255. Fet, "O Stikhotvoreniiakh Tiutcheva," 64.

256. Fet, *Moi Vospominaniia*, part 2:236. Italics in the original.

257. Fet, *Rannie Gody*, 214.

258. Zhirmunski, *Gete v Russkoi Literature*, 440, 448, and 454, respectively.

259. D. S. Mirski, *A History of Russian Literature* (New York, 1949), 219.

260. A. P. Maikov, *Polnoe Sobranie Sochineni*, ed. P. V. Bykov (St. Petersburg, 1914). For translations of Goethe lyrics, see ibid., 1:206: trans. of "Kennst du das Land . . ."; pp. 206–7: trans. of "An Lida"; pp. 207–8: trans. of "Lilli"; p. 277: An improvisation on Goethe's "Augen, sagt mir, sagt, was sagt ihr . . ."; 2:43–48: trans. of "Der neue Pausias und sein Blumenmädchen," under the title "Poet i Tsvetochnitsa: The Poet and His Flower Girl"; pp. 48–51: A free paraphrase ("pereskaz") of "Alexis und Dora." The last two items support Zhirmunski's contention that the "classicist Maikov [had an] outspoken predilection for the classicist Goethe."

261. Cf. Joseph Matl, "Goethe bei den Slawen," *Jahrbücher für Kultur und Geschichte der Slawen*, n.f., 8/1 (1932).

262. A. K. Tolstoi, *Polnoe Sobranie Sochineni Grafa A. K. Tolstogo* (St. Petersburg, 1907), 1:449–57. Henceforth cited as Tolstoi, *Pol. Sob. Soch.* The translation of the "Braut" was first published in the *Vestnik Evropy* in March 1868.

263. All these quotations are from a letter to Tolstoi's bride, S. A. Miller, of November 30, 1867. Cf. A. K. Tolstoi *Sochineniia* (St. Petersburg, 1908), 4:128–29 (italics in the original).

264. Cf. Tolstoi, *Pol. Sob. Soch.* 4:229.

265. A. K. Tolstoi, *Sobranie Sochineni* (Moscow, 1963), vol. 2 ("Dramatiche-skie Proizvedeniia"): "Prologue," 9–20; the play, 20–120; "Epilogue," 656–58. The following quotations are from these pages unless otherwise indicated.

266. Tolstoi, *Sochineniia*, 4:143.

267. Ibid., 2:611.

268. Ibid., 4:149, letter from Karlsbad, August 5, 1869.

269. Ibid., letter from Karlsbad, August 13, 1869.

270. Ibid., 4:226, letter of November 3, 1869.

271. Ibid., 150, letter of August 18, 1870.

272. Ibid., 169, letter from Sorrento to his bride, May 11, 1873.

273. Ibid., 152, letter of May 9, 1871.

274. Ibid., 116, letter from Weimar, September 4, 1869.

275. Ibid., 151–52.

276. Zhirmunski, *Gete v Russkoi Literature*, 454. Zhirmunski is also thinking here of Tolstoi's "Epilogue" to his *Don Juan*, which—as we remember—depicts the reprobate and libertine shriven of his sins of seduction and murder, dying a pious death, signaling the victory of the "good spirits" over Satan and his minions.

Chapter Three. *Fëdor Mikhailovich Dostoevski*

1. Karl Nötzel, *Das Leben Dostoewskijs* (Osnabrück, 1967), 208.

2. Joseph Matl, "Goethe bei den Slawen," *Jahrbücher für Kultur und Geschichte der Slawen*, n.f., 8/1 (1932): 46.

3. Zenta Maurina, *Dostoewskij. Menschengestalter und Gottsucher* (Memmingen, 1952), 15.

4. Ilja Kostovski, *Dostoevski and Goethe, Two Devils–Two Geniuses: A Study of the Demonic in Their Works*, trans. D. Hitchcock (New York, 1974), 33 and 128, respectively. With the term "pyramid," Kostovski refers to Goethe's concept of personality in its development. See also Hans von Rimscha, *Dostoewskij, ein Antipode Goethes* (Coburg, 1949). Rimscha launches his argument from Hermann Hesse's dictum "Europe ist zu einem Schlachtfeld zwischen Goethe und Dostoejewski geworden [shortly after the first World War] und dieser Kampf wird über den Untergang des Abendlandes entscheiden."

5. A few of the many relevant works are Hermann Hesse, *Blick ins Chaos* (1920); Stefan Zweig, *Drei Meister: Dostoewskij, Balzak, Dickens* (1919); Alfred Döblin, *Goethe und Dostoewskij* (1921); and Jakob Wassermann, "Einige allgemeine Bemerkungen über Dostoewskij," *Vossische Zeitung*, August 1921.

6. Fritz Strich, *Goethe and World Literature* (New York, 1949), 83.

7. Cf. F. Dostoevski, *Pis'ma*, ed. S. A. Dolinin, vol. 1, 1832–67; vol. 2, 1867–71; vol. 3, 1871–81 (Moscow and Leningrad, 1928–59). Henceforth cited as Dostoevski, *Pis'ma*, followed by volume and page. Dolinin minimizes the importance of Dosteovski's references to Goethe, characterizing them as "a debt conventionally paid to a world-renowned writer" (ibid., 1:466).

8. Gene Fitzgerald, in *Slavic and East European Journal* 20 (November 4, 1976): 472–73.

9. Zhirmunski, *Gete v Russkoi Literature*, 657 n. 1.

10. Dostoevski, *Pis'ma* (ed. S. A. Dolinin).

11. Cf. *Dostoewskij. Gesammelte Briefe, 1833–1881*, ed. Friedrich Hitzer (Munich, n.d.), 653. For a study of Dostoevski's attitude toward Dickens, see N. M.

Lary, *Dostoevsky and Dickens* (London, 1973). It should be pointed out that young Dostoevski's enthusiasms ranged widely, embracing such diverse authors as Homer and Balzac, Hugo and Shakespeare, Corneille and Racine, and E. T. A. Hoffmann. All these and many more inspired the youthful writer at different times without muting or distorting his very personal voice.

12. Dostoevski, *Pis'ma* 1:56–58, letter to his brother Mikhael of January 1, 1840.

13. Ibid., 4:196, letter of August 18, 1880. For Dostoevski's friendship with Berezhedski and Shidlovski, see Joseph Frank, *Dostoevsky: The Seeds of Revolt (1821–1849)* (Princeton, N.J., 1976), 79–100. Henceforth cited as Frank, *Dostoevski*.

14. Dostoevski, *Pis'ma* 1:56–58. Dostoevski's admiration of Schiller remained undiminished. Risen to fame and influence, he exhorted his Russian compatriots in "Some Remarks on Schiller," published in his periodical *Vremia* (*Time*; March 1862), to hold Schiller in the highest esteem "because to him it was given not only to be a great poet but to be *our* poet; his poetry appeals more to the heart than that of Goethe or of Byron" (italics in the original). For a thorough study of Dostoevski's relationship to Schiller, see Edmund Kostka, *Schiller in Russian Literature* (Philadelphia: University of Pennsylvania Press, 1965), 214–50. See also D. Chizhevski, "Schiller v Rossii," *Novyi Zhurnal* 45 (1956): 109–35; and idem, "Schiller und die Brüder Karamazow," *Zeitschrift für slawische Philologie* 6, parts 1–2:1–42.

15. Dostoevski, *Pis'ma* 1:47. With the term "short lyrics" (mel'kie stikhotvoreniia) Dostoevski refers to Goethe's Sturm und Drang poems.

16. Ibid., 89, letter of April 1, 1846.

17. Cf. *Literaturnoe Nasledstvo: F. M. Dostoevski. Novye Materialy i Issledovaniia* (Moscow: 1973), 86:328.

18. F. Dostoevski, *Dnevnik Pisatelia za God 1876* (Paris, n.d.), 11:146.

19. The only words of Werther that Dostoevski can possibly be referring to are the following: "Ich trete an das Fenster, meine Beste, und sehe, und sehe noch durch die stürmenden, vorüberfliehenden Wolken einzelne Sterne des Himmels! Nein, ihr werdet nicht fallen! der Ewige trägt euch an seinem Herzen, und mich. *Ich sehe die Deichselsterne des Wagens, des liebsten unter allen Gestirnen*. Wenn ich nachts von dir [Lotte] ging, wie ich aus deinem Tore trat, stand er gegen mir über. Mit welcher Trunkenheit habe ich ihn oft angesehen, oft mit aufgehobenen Händen ihn zum Zeichen, zum heiligen Merkstein meiner gegenwärtigen Seligkeit gemacht!" *Hamb. Ausg.* 6:122 (italics added).

20. Letter of April 17, 1877, to S. E. Luria, in Dostoevski, *Pis'ma* 3:264.

21. Cf., for example, letters of August 18, 1880, and December 19, 1880, in ibid., 4:196 and 222, respectively.

22. An interesting parallel in the plot of the two works is both authors' use of the seasons in their relation to the unfolding action. Spring, summer, autumn, and winter accompany and accentuate the changing mood of the tales as they progress, or rather descend, to their hibernal denouement.

23. Victor Terras, *The Young Dostoevski: A Critical Study* (The Hague, 1969), 17.

24. Frank, *Dostoevsky*, 153.

25. See F. Dostoevski, *Polnoe Sobranie Sochineni v Tridtsati Tomakh* (Leningrad, 1972ff.), 1:318. Henceforth cited as Dostoevski, *Pol. Sob. Soch.*, followed by volume and page.

26. Cf. *Literaturnoe Nasledstvo*, 86:12.

27. Dostoevski, *Pol. Sob. Soch.* 3:169–442. Numbers in parentheses in the text refer to pages in this volume.

28. Cf., e.g., G. F. Kogan, "Chernovoi nabrosok k romanu 'Unizhennye i Oskorblennye,'" *Literaturnoe Nasledstvo*, vol. 86. See also A. S. Dolinin's article comparing these two figures in his *F. M. Dostoevski. Materialy i Issledovaniia* (Leningrad, 1935).

29. Dostoevski "solves" her parentage in the "epilogue" much in the fashion of the popular, sentimental suspense novels of the time (Dostoevski, *Pol. Sob. Soch.* 3:436–42).

30. Dostoevski lends clearly Mephistophelian traits to his portrait of the prince (Nelli's purported father), especially in his description of his lewdness, lasciviousness, and general moral depravity (ibid., 359–69).

31. *Hamb. Ausg.* 3:32–42. "Des Pudels Kern," 46.

32. Victor Terras has established an influence of this Goethean scene on Dostoevski's much earlier novella *The Double* (1846). Cf. Terras, *The Young Dostoevski*, 151.

33. It might be noted that the heroine of *The Idiot*, Nastasia Filipovna, went under the name of Mignon in an early manuscript of that novel. Cf. *Iz Arkhiva F. M. Dostoevskago. Idiot. Neizdannye Materialy*, ed. P. N. Sakulina and N. F. Bel'chikova (Leningrad, 1931), 212.

34. Dostoevski did write a parody of Part Two, but he did so in a fictional context as an effective device to add a characteristic trait to his portrayal of his tragi-comical protagonist Stepan Trofimovich Verkhovenski, that "liberal" progenitor of the devils. He has Stepan Trofimovich write this "phantasmagoric" poem "in Berlin in his earliest youth." Dostoevski characterizes this poem as a "strange creation, but a type of work frequently written in the 1830s," that is, by the Russian Romanticists. Cf. Dostoevski, *Pol. Sob. Soch.* 10:9–10. Dostoevski's irony is clearly directed not at Goethe's work but at its feeble imitation by such "Romantic" authors as young Stepan Trofimovich.

35. For example, T. G. Masaryk, *Studie o F. M. Dostoevskom* (Praha, 1932); A. Lunacharski, "Russki Faust," *Voprosy Fil. i Psikh.*, 3. Book, 1902; N. Misheev, "Russki Faust," *Russki Filosofski Vestnik*, nos. 53–57.

36. In his portrayal of Ivan, Dostoevski makes no reference to Faust. It is as if he intentionally avoided the use of Faust's name, much like Thomas Mann avoided the mention of Nietzsche's name in his *Faust* novel, although he readily admitted that Nietzsche was a prime model for his Faustian figure, Leverkühn. Cf. *Die Entstehung des Doktor Faustus. Roman eines Romans* (Berlin, 1949), 34: "Da ist die Verflechtung der Tragödie Leverkühns mit derjenigen Nietzsches, dessen Name wohlweislich in dem ganzen Buch nicht erscheint, eben weil der euphorische Musiker an seine Stelle gesetzt ist, so dass es ihn nun nicht mehr geben darf."

37. *Hamb. Ausg.* 3:44 (italics added).

38. In accordance with Greek Orthodox tradition, Dostoevski equated the "Word" of the Gospel with Jesus Christ as the source of the loftiest morality and most profound wisdom. Cf. Dostoevski, *Pol. Sob. Soch.* 15:82, 338, 442.

39. Dostoevski, *Pis'ma* 3:177, letter of June 10, 1875.

40. Katharina Schütz, *Das Goethebild Turgenews. Sprache und Dichtung*, no. 75 (Stuttgart, 1952), 56.

41. *Hamb. Ausg.* 3:344.

42. With the term "Euclidian," Dostoevski does not point merely to the great geometrician but rather to the entire pagan culture of Greece, which for him stands in fateful conflict with the culture of Orthodox Russia. He recognizes the Euclidian mentality of the Greeks as the ultimate source of Western hubric intellectualism and mate-

rialism, of its atheism, of its arrogant reliance on the godlike powers of man. Strich persuasively argues that this "European deification of man, begun by the Greeks and continued in European humanism, intensified in Faust, Napoleon, and Byron, . . . culminating in the idea of [Nietzsche's] superman" (Strich, *Goethe and World Literature*, 287).

43. Dostoevski, *Pol. Sob. Soch.* 14:214–15.

44. Ibid., 214.

45. Ibid., 15:83–84 and passim.

46. Ibid., 14:215.

47. Ivan identifies Smerdiakov with the devil. He feels that this devil is part of himself, "sitting in his soul" (ibid., 242; 15:54).

48. *Hamb. Ausg.* 3:57.

49. Dostoevski wrote to N. A. Liubimov, editor of the journal *Staraia Russ'* (*Old Russia*), explaining this paradoxical attitude of Ivan toward the devil: "Denying the reality of the apparition, he [Ivan] affirms it as soon as the vision has vanished. Tormented by his agnosticism [!], he (subconsciously) yearns—at the same time— that the apparition not be merely the figment of his imagination but rather something palpable, substantial . . ." (Dostoevski, *Pis'ma* 4:190).

50. *Hamb. Ausg.* 3:47.

51. *Dostoevski . . . Literaturnoe Nasledstvo* 83:618.

52. The original title was "Zapuganaia," literally, "one frightened to death," which characterizes more aptly the fate of the heroine. Cf. Dostoevski, *Dnevnik Pisatelia za God 1876* (Paris, n.d.), 15:414–57. Quotations are from these pages in my translation, unless otherwise indicated.

53. Dostoevski neatly combines here two of Mephisto's self-characterizations, i.e., "*Ich bin ein Teil des Teils, der anfangs alles war,* / *Der Teil der Finsternis, die sich das Licht gebar . . .*" (*Hamb. Ausg.* 3:47) and "*Ein Teil von jener Kraft,* / *Die stets das Böse will und stets das Gute schafft*" (ibid., italics added).

54. *Dnevnik Pisatelia za God 1873* (Paris, n.d.), 14:219–33; quotation from p. 230.

55. *Dnevnik Pisatelia za God 1876*, 15:5–8.

56. D. S. Mirsky, *A History of Russian Literature* (New York, 1949), 220.

57. Dostoevski, *Pol. Sob. Soch.* 15:336, 442–43; *Hamb. Ausg.* 3:16–19, 43–44.

58. *Hamb. Ausg.* 3:52.

59. Cf. Dostoevski's letter of August 10, 1880, to N. A. Liubimov, quoted in "Notes to *The Brothers Karamazov*," in Dostoevski, *Pol. Sob. Soch.* 15:465; see also ibid., 15:81.

60. Dostoevski, *Pol. Sob. Soch.*, vol. 10. Pages of quotations are given in parentheses in the text. I have avoided the much-used title *The Possessed* as misleading. It is of particular importance to our interpretation to keep in mind that Dostoevski conceived the conspirators, with Pëtr Verkhovenski at their head, as *devils* (Besy) who *possessed* Russia. See, among other evidence, Dostoevski's letter of October 21, 1870, to Maikov, in *Pis'ma* 2:291: "The devils left the Russian man and entered the herd of swine. . . ." Dostoevski follows here the account in the *Gospel according to Luke*, a passage he also uses as motto for his novel.

61. For a detailed account of the gradual development of the Stavrogin figure through the many plans and sketches, see Dostoevski, *Pol. Sob. Soch.* 12:178ff.

62. Frank, *Dostoevsky*, 258. Dolinin, in his *Dostoevski: Reminiscences of His Contemporaries*, cites Doctor Ianovski's report of his conversation with Dostoevski in

which the writer confides that he had borrowed money from Speshnev and now feels bound to him as in a devil's pact. "I have taken money from Speshnev," Ianovski quotes him, "and now I am *with him* and *am his*. . . . Do you understand, henceforth I have my own Mephisto!" See A. Dolinin, ed., *F. M. Dostoevski v Vospominaniiakh Sovremennikov* (Moscow, 1964).

63. In *The Devils*, Dostoevski draws liberally on the records of the Nechaev and to a lesser degree on the Petrachevski conspiracies. For detailed analysis, see Dostoevski, *Pol. Sob. Soch.* 12:192–218.

64. Terras, *The Young Dostoevski*, 110.

65. See N. Leer, "Stavrogin and Prince Hal: The Hero in Two Worlds," *Slavic and East European Journal* 6/2 (1962): 99–116.

66. The fact that Goethe's *Faust* is not named as a source in Dostoevski's notes, plans, or the final version of *The Devils* in no way discredits the drama's influence on the novel, for many of the most important influences remain equally unmentioned, for example, Ogarëv, Speshnev, and Steerforth, the demonic hero of Dicken's *Life of David Copperfield*, to mention but a few at random (cf. G. Katkov, "Steerforth and Stavrogin: On the Sources of *The Possessed*," *Slavonic and East European Review* 5 [1949]: 25–37). Dostoevski even seems to enjoy teasing his readers about his sources. Thus he has Alësha ask himself as he is leaving Ivan after a harrowing conversation: "Pater Seraphicus—that name he [Ivan] must have taken from somewhere, but where did he get it from?" (241). This question has been answered by more than one critic as being from Goethe's *Faust*, Part 2, "Bergschluchten." For a suggestion of another possible, source, see Dostoevski, *Pol. Sob. Soch.* 15:563–64.

67. V. Ivanov, *Borozdy i Mezhi* (Moscow, 1916), 66 (italics added).

68. Dostoevski, *Pol. Sob. Soch.* 11:136.

69. Paraphrase of lines 1112–17 of Goethe's *Faust*, *Hamb. Ausg.* 3:41.

70. Ibid., 112.

71. For Stavrogin's rape of Matrësha, see the "Tikhon chapter," in Dostoevski, *Pol. Sob. Soch.* 11:5–30.

72. In an early "note" (probably 1870), Dostoevski sketches the "main thought of the prince" as "Christianity will save the world. . . . Furthermore, Christianity exists in Russia only as [Greek] Orthodoxy, therefore Russia will save the world . . . if it will believe! If not, then it will decompose much like Europe" (ibid., 12:187).

73. The following details and quotations are from the Tikhon chapter, in ibid., 11:5–30. Dostoevski regarded this chapter as essential to his novel but could not publish it because of stringent censorship. For a detailed account of Dostoevski's effort to publish, see ibid., 12:237–53.

74. There is a striking similarity of Stavrogin's quandary to Ivan's futile efforts of solving the riddle of the devil's existence as a real being or as a figment of his overwrought imagination.

75. Dostoevski "borrowed" these traits of Stavrogin from Speshnev, that unforgotten companion of his youth, and put them to his artistic purpose in the novel. For models of Stavrogin, see Dostoevski, *Pol. Sob. Soch.* 12:227–28.

76. Ibid., 10:84. Pages of all subsequent quotations are indicated parenthetically in the text.

77. Gronicka, *The Russian Image of Goethe*, 1:74–92.

78. Ibid., 89–91.

79. Dostoevski, *Pol. Sob. Soch.* 12:229.

80. M. Y. Lermontov, *Sobrannye Sochineniia v Chetyrëkh Tomakh* (Moscow: Akademiia Nauk., 1956), 4:364.

81. The Switzerland theme is once again a "borrowing" from Speshnev's life, and once again the biographical material is transformed to serve Dostoevski's artistic intentions in setting the stage for Stavrogin's tragic end.

82. *Hamb. Ausg.* 3:356–64.

83. Ibid., 364.

84. Viacheslav Ivanov had recognized the nature of Stavrogin's pact with his devil even without knowledge of the Tikhon chapter, which had not been published at the time. Stavrogin, he writes, "has betrayed the sacred trust bestowed on him in a decisive moment of his horrible past which is hidden from us [now revealed in the Tikhon chapter]. He befriends the Satanists, holds discourse with Satan, and clearly surrenders himself to him. He gives to him his self [ia], which he had promised to Christ, and finds himself emptied [opustoshënnym], thus anticipating a 'second death' while still alive, the complete obliteration of personality in his living body" (Ivanov, *Borozdy i Mezhi*, 69).

85. Cf. Kurt May, *Faust Zweiter Teil, in der Sprachform gedeutet* (Munich, 1962), 82–83 and passim.

86. E. C. Brody, "The Liberal Intellectual in *The Possessed*," *Germano-Slavica* 2/4 (Fall 1977): 253–72, traces in detail Stefan Trofimovich' Verkhovenski's character and role in the novel, with special attention to his relationship with his son and his generation, as direct progenitor of the radicalism of the 1860s and 1870s. See also Dostoevski's letter to A. A. Romanov (Crown Prince Alexander III) in *Pis'ma* 3:50: "Our Belinskis and Granovskis would not believe it if told that they are the fathers of Nechaevs. It is this kinship and continuity of thought, developing from fathers to sons, that I wanted to express in my work [*The Devils*]."

87. *Hamb. Ausg.* 3:112.

88. Ibid., 342 and 341, respectively.

89. Ibid., 342.

90. Ibid., 356.

91. Dostoevski, *Pol. Sob. Soch.*, "Rukopisnye redaktsii," 15:202.

92. *Hamb. Ausg.* 3:304.

93. Dostoevski, *Pol. Sob. Soch.*, vol. 6. Pages of quotations are given parenthetically in the text.

94. *Hamb. Ausg.* 3:52.

95. Ibid., 84.

96. Ibid., 144.

97. Walter H. Sokel, *The Writer in Extremis: Expressionism in Twentieth-Century German Literature* (Stanford, Calif., 1959), 151.

98. Ivanov does not mention Maria's encounter with Stavrogin in the salon of his mother (Dostoevski, *Pol. Sob. Soch.*, 10:146–47), where the sudden appearance of her lover rouses in her emotions of horror mixed with rapturous joy, "of both terror and ecstasy," clearly reminiscent of Gretchen's reaction to Faust's sudden appearance in the dungeon. But here, together with the striking similarity, there is an equally striking contrast: Gretchen's Faust is unable to free her, while Stavrogin, having an all-but-hypnotic power over Maria at this moment, leads her gently out of *her* dungeon, those hostile surroundings of Mrs. Stavrogin's drawing room.

99. Ivanov, *Borozdy i Mezhi*, 67.

100. *Hamb. Ausg.* 3:143.

101. Cf. Alfred L. Bem, " 'Faust' v Tvorchestve Dostoevskogo," in *Bulletin de L'Association Russe Pour les Recherches Scientifiques à Prague* (Prague, 1937), vol. 5 (10), section des sciences philosophiques, historiques et sociales, no. 29, 109–35.

102. Strugovshchikov's translation was published in the 1830s in almanacs as well as in the *National Notes* edited by Belinski. It appeared separately in 1856.

103. Bem, " 'Faust' v Tvorchestve Dostoevskogo," 130.

104. Dostoevski, *Pol. Sob. Soch.*, vol. 16. Following quotations are from this volume, unless otherwise indicated.

105. *Hamb. Ausg.* 3:120.

106. Fritz Strich argues that "the 'prolonged, persistent' area of Mephisto [*sic*] is filled with tears and despair because he has nothing but damnation to pronounce on Gretchen," and he considers this to be "a highly characteristic divergence from Goethe's Mephisto" (Strich, *Goethe and World Literature*, 288–89). Disagreeing, I would suggest that—in keeping with Dostoevski's manner of composition as exemplified, for instance, in Ivan Karamazov's dialogue with the devil in which the devil verbalizes Ivan's thoughts and feelings—Satan is here verbalizing and intoning Gretchen's anguish, longings, and despair.

107. Ibid., 287.

108. Ivan Aleksandrovich Goncharov, *Oblomov*, trans. Ann Dunningen (New York, 1963), 523. I give a free paraphrase of Dunningen's translation on the basis of the Russian original: I. A. Goncharov, *Oblomov*, in the 4th vol. of *Sobranie Sochinenii* (Moscow, 1959). For a study of *Oblomov* as an anti-Faust, see Yvette Louria and Morton I. Seiden, "Ivan Goncharov's *Oblomov*, the Anti-Faust as Christian Hero," *Canadian Slavic Studies* 3/1 (Spring 1969): esp. 46–51.

109. *Hamb. Ausg.* 3:359. See also J. P. Eckermann, *Gespräche mit Goethe* (Stuttgart, n.d.) 2:212–13. Here Goethe comments as follows on these verses: "In diesen Versen ist der Schlüssel zu Fausts Rettung enthalten: in Faust selber eine immer höhere und reinere Thätigkeit bis ans Ende, und *von oben die ihm zu Hilfe kommende ewige Liebe. Es steht dieses mit unserer religiösen Vorstellung durchaus in Harmonie, nach welcher wir nicht bloss durch eigene Kraft selig werden, sondern durch die hinzukommende göttliche Gnade*" (italics added).

110. The editor of Dostoevski's collected works gives the following summary of Raskolnikov's literary filiation: "In critical literature the image of Raskolnikov has been likened . . . to the figures of Faust [!], of Franz Moor, of the Byronesque rebellious heroes [Manfred, Corsar], to Balzac's Rastignac, to Stendhal's Julien Sorel, to Pushkin's Hermann, to Hoffmann's Medardus, and to other exponents of Romantic 'Titanism'. . . , the typical character of which has received a new, more profound sociopsychological interpretation in Dostoevski's novels under the influence of the Russian milieu" (cf. Dostoevski, *Pol. Sob. Soch.* 7:343).

111. Frank, *Dostoevsky*, 198.

112. Masaryk speaks of Dostoevski's "falsifying" Goethe's Faust figure. Cf. *The Spirit of Russia*, 221.

113. *Hamb. Ausg.* 3:48.

114. In his "Faust Fragment" of the *17th Literaturbrief*. Cf. *Lessings Werke* (Berlin and Leipzig, n.d.), 4:58–60.

115. See the informative article by V. V. Dudkin and K. M. Azadovski, "Dostoevski v Germanii (1846–1921)," in *Literaturnoe Nasledstvo*, vol. 86: *Dostoevski. Novye Materialy i Issledovaniia* (Moscow: 1973).

116. Lev Shestov, on the other hand, argues that it was Dostoevski, that "cruel genius," who gave Nietzsche the courage to spell out his message: "With certainty it can be stated [!] that the German philosopher [Nietzsche] would never have reached in his 'Geneologie der Moral' such courage and sincere honesty [otkrovennost'] in his

interpretation if he had not felt Dostoevski's support" (107–8). And again: "Dostoevski and Nietzsche left humaneness for brutality and on their standard inscribed the strange words Wille zur Macht" (*sic*! 241; see also 139, 218, 237, 288, and passim). Certainly, there is the voice of the "underground man" in Dostoevski's many-voiced *Lebenswerk*, of the underground man whom Shestov quotes with such relish, especially his words of unmasked egoism: "Let the world perish if only I can drink my tea." But there are also Dostoevskian voices proclaiming, in sharpest contrast to Nietzsche's, profound compassion and love for the "insulted and the injured," the voices of the meek (smirënnye) and the pure-at-heart and the wise, the voices of Prince Myshkin, of Sonia, of Alësha, of the Pater Seraphicus Zosima, of Tikhon, voices that Shestov not only mutes in his interpretation but totally silences as being of no account, or rather as contradicting his untenable thesis. This work is a headstrong attempt to crush the philosophies of idealism as well as of positivism and to establish as the only "true" philosophy the "philosophy of tragedy." To help reach this fateful goal, poor Dostoevski is strapped on a Procrustean bed. Cf. L. Shestov, *Dostoevski i Nitshe: Filosofia Tragedii* (St. Petersburg, 1909), and also the English version, *Dostoevski, Tolstoy, and Nietzsche* (Athens, Ohio, 1969).

117. *Dnevnik Pisatelia za God 1880* (Paris, n.d.), 16:499–527, esp. 501–2 and 524–27.

118. One can imagine Dostoevski's reaction to Goethe's "Ode to Prometheus" of his Sturm und Drang period with its more than Faustian superbia: "Hier sitz' ich, / forme Menschen / Nach meinem Bilde, / Ein Geschlecht, das mir gleich sei, zu leiden, / zu weinen, / Zu geniessen und zu freuen sich / Und dein nicht zu achten, / Wie ich" (*Hamb. Ausg.* 1:44–46).

Chapter Four. *Leo Nikolaevich Tolstoi*

1. Marina Chistiakova, "Tolstoi i Gëte," in *Zven'ia. Sbornik Materialov i Dokumentov po Istorii Russkoi Literatury* (Moscow and Leningrad, 1933), 2:129.

2. Lev Kopelev, *Zwei Epochen deutsch-russischer Literaturbeziehungen* (Frankfurt am Main, 1973), "Tolstoj und Goethe. Dialog zweier Epochen," 24 and 45, respectively.

3. Ibid., 22.

4. Diary entry of July 9, 1854, in L. Tolstoi, *Polnoe Sobranie Sochineni*, Jubilee edition, 90 vols. (Moscow, 1929–58), 47:10. Henceforth cited as Tolstoi *P.S.S.*, followed by volume and page.

5. Entries in the "Journal of Daily Studies": "March 3rd [1847] 8–10:00 read Faust—fulfilled the assignment [ispolnil]"; "March 5th [1847] 6–8:00 Faust—fulfilled the assignment"; "March 6th [1847] 6–8:00 Faust—overslept [prospal]"; "March 9th [1847] Sunday 1 to 2:00 Faust—did not carry out assignment"; "March 10th [1847] Monday 6–8:00 Faust [no indication of completion]." Cf. ibid., 46:249, 250.

6. As recorded by D. P. Makovitski in his "Zapiski" (Notes), the original of which was not available to me. They are excerpted in ibid., 55:561–62; for quotation, see p. 562.

7. Letter to M. M. Lederle, October 25, 1891, in ibid., 66:68.

8. Ibid., 46:55.

9. In the introduction to his "Recollections" (Vospominania) he expresses his dislike of *Childhood*, *Boyhood*, and *Youth* as altogether derivative books. "During their composition," he writes, "I had been far from independent [samostoiatel'nyi] in

my style, finding myself under the influecne of two authors, Sterne (his *Sentimental Voyage* [!]) and Töpfer (*Bibliothèque de mon oncle*), both of whom had made a tremendous impression on me at the time." Ibid., 34:348.

10. Entry of September 29, 1856, in ibid., 47:93.

11. Entry of July 6, 1854, in ibid., 7.

12. Entry of July 9, 1854, in ibid., 10.

13. Entry of July 10, 1854, ibid.

14. Entry of July 14, 1854, in ibid., 13 (italics added).

15. Entry of May 31, 1855, in ibid., 43.

16. Letter of November 23, 1856, in ibid., 60:124.

17. Diary entry of June 19, 1857, in ibid., 47:135 (italics added).

18. Entry of July 16, 1857, in ibid., 144.

19. Entry in *Zapisnye Knizhki* (*Notebooks*), October 1857, in ibid., 219 (italics added).

20. Diary entry of April 13, 1861, in ibid., 48:32 (italics added).

21. Nikolai Nikolaevich Tolstoi, born 1823, died October 2, 1860.

22. From April 13 to 17, 1861.

23. Diary entry of April 14, 1861, in Tolstoi, *P.S.S.* 48:33. It would be interesting to know whether the guide had made Tolstoi aware of this coincidence. For Zhukovski's visits to Weimar and the Goethe house, cf. Gronicka, *The Russian Image of Goethe*, 1:34–45. Following is Zhukovski's description of Goethe's house with his reference to the "pyramid": "The diminutive size of [Goethe's] bedroom. . . . The stuffiness in the long-unventilated chambers. The bedpan. The pretty calendar in its case. . . . Bust of the [Russian?] Empress. A pyramid made of cardboard: *Sensuality* in green color, *intellect* in yellow, *imagination* in red. Poems and diary. Inkspots. Goethe's drawings" (ibid., 43).

24. Letter of March 8, 1861, in Tolstoi, *P.S.S.* 60:370–71.

25. Entry of March 9, 1865, in ibid., 48:59.

26. Letter of November 3, 1874, in ibid., 62:121.

27. *Mysli Mudrykh Liudei*, in ibid., 40:67–396.

28. Schopenhauer quotations are almost as frequent as those from Tolstoi's favorite sources: the Talmud, the New Testament, the writings of Lao-tse, Confucius, Marcus Aurelius.

29. Following are the quotations with volume and page of Tolstoi, *P.S.S.*: "True virtue never looks backward on its shadow—fame" (40:214); "Perfection is an attribute of God. Striving for perfection is an attribute of man" (41:138); "Nature does not know a halt to its movement and punishes every kind of inactivity" (41:593); "One must grow old to become kinder. I never meet with an error which I myself have not already committed" (42:377); "Man gets to know himself not through thought but in action. Only in his efforts to fulfill his duty does he recognize his true worth" (42:174); "Be attentive to the present. Only in the present do we fathom eternity" (42:259. This quotation is introduced by the notation "According to Goethe"); "When we deal with our fellow men as they deserve to be treated, we make them worse than they are. But when we deal with them as if they were better than they actually are, we force them to become better persons" (41:231).

30. I. M. Ivakin, "Zapiski," in *Literaturnoe Nasledstvo* 69:100, note of March 16, 1889.

31. Among Tolstoi's selections for his "Krug Chteniia" (Circle of Reading) Goethe is not represented.

32. Tolstoi's characterization of Goethe in a letter to his aunt Aleksandra Andreevna of August 29, 1891, in Tolstoi, *P.S.S.* 66:34.

33. Chistiakova, "Tolstoi i Gëte," 118.

34. Diary entry of June 2, 1863, in Tolstoi, *P.S.S.* 48:54.

35. Ibid., 13:13–880.

36. Ibid., 230–31.

37. Ibid., 18:184 (italics added).

38. Diary entry of July 3, 1905: "I have experienced three attitudes in married life: (1) The marriage is indissoluble, whether you be happy or not, suffer as you would suffer your own body, and there are no emotional transports [poryvov], no despairing, no romancing; (2) harmony of souls, passion, poetic love, Werther, sufferings of love; (3) if husband or wife does not like the partner, separate and take a new mate" (ibid., 55:151).

39. See, for example, R. Schweiche, "Der naturalistische Roman bei den Russen und bei den Franzosen," in *Neue Zeit* 5 (1887); Christiana Stulz, "Betrachtungen über *Anna Karenina*," in *Leo Tolstoi. Aufsätze und Essay* (Halle, 1960). Relevant excerpts also in *Literaturnoe Nasledstvo; Tolstoi i Zarubezhnyi Mir* 75, book 1:489–90.

40. Masaryk, *The Spirit of Russia*, 3:167.

41. Ibid., 204–5.

42. Ibid.

43. Chistiakova, "Tolstoi i Gëte," 121. We have a listing of books Tolstoi used in his work on the novel. It consists of diaries, memoires, travelogues, journals, lexica, and works on history, philosophy, and theology. Neither *Faust* nor *Hermann und Dorothea* appears on this list. In fact, not a single belletristic work is mentioned, with the sole exception of Madame de Staël's novel *Delphine*. Cf. Tolstoi, *P.S.S.* 16:141–46.

44. Chistiakova, "Tolstoi i Gëte," 121. Cf. also P. Biriukov, *Lev Tolstoi. Biografia* (Moscow, n.d.), 2:111: "He [Tolstoi] read Shakespeare, Goethe, and Molière and then turned to Sophocles and Euripides."

45. Letter of February 17, 1870, in Tolstoi, *P.S.S.* 61:226–27.

46. "Zapiski na Otdel'nykh Listakh," February 2, 1870, in ibid., 48:344.

47. Tolstoi is probably referring here to Adam Smith's classical study of England's economy, *An Inquiry into the Nature and Causes of the Wealth of Nations* (1776).

48. "Notebook Number 3," entry of February 21, 1870, in Tolstoi, *P.S.S.* 48:111–12.

49. Letter of April 13, 1897, in ibid., 70:68. Already in 1870 Tolstoi had compared "the Europeans' admiration for Greek literature with the admiration of a clever sectarian [raskol'nik] for the words of a meaningless song, for the Apokalypse." Cf. "Notebook Number 3," entry of February 21, 1870, in ibid., 48:112.

50. Thomas Mann, "Goethe und Tolstoi. Fragmente zum Problem der Humanität," *Gesammelte Werke in Dreizehn Bänden* (Frankfurt am Main, 1960), 9:58–173. Quotation from pp. 130–31. For my discussion of Thomas Mann's view of Tolstoi and Goethe, see *Thomas Mann, Profile and Perspectives* (New York, 1970), esp. 35–36 and 42–43.

51. Kopelev, *Zwei Epochen*, 24.

52. Pëtr Iakovlevich Chaadaev (1793–1856), leader of the Westernizers with strong ties to Roman Catholicism.

53. Letter to I. P. Biriukov (Tolstoi's biographer) of December 24, 1905, in Tolstoi, *P.S.S.* 76:68.

54. Diary entry of October 20, 1906, in ibid., 55:263 (italics in the original).

55. Ibid., 79:207. *Goethe Kalender auf das Jahr 1909* (Weihnachten 1908 von Otto Julius Bierbaum im Dietrich Verlag herausgegeben). The items referred to by

Tolstoi appear on the following pages of the calendar: (1) on 74–75; (2) on 88; (3) on 92; (4) on 98–99; (5) on 103.

56. E. Simmons, *Leo Tolstoy* (Boston, 1946), 536. Zhirmunski places the "conversion" somewhat later, in the early 1880s. Cf. Zhirmunski, *Gete v Russkoi Literature*, 421.

57. Admirers of Tolstoi have written eloquent *apologia* for his sweeping critique of art. The following excerpts from Anatol France's encomium on Tolstoi's death may serve as an example: "No! Tolstoi does not condemn art. Whatever he said, whatever he did, he never condemned it—he elevated, he extolled it! . . . He vainly strove to free himself of it. Art is within him, art indwells in his very flesh, in every drop of his blood." And addressing the shade of the departed, Anatol France exclaimed, "You are greater than a Messiah, you are a Homer, you are a Russian Goethe!" As quoted in "Tolstoi i Zarubezhnyi Mir," in *Literaturnoe Nasledstvo* 75:128.

58. To quote Tolstoi: "About fifteen years ago [ca. 1882], I began writing about art, thinking, when I embarked on this work, that I would finish it without interruption; but then I realized that my thoughts on the subject at that time were as yet so unclear that I was quite unable to express them to my satisfaction. Since then I have uninterruptedly pondered the subject and have started to write on it six or seven times, but every time, having written down a considerable amount, I found myself unable to finish the work and abandoned it. Now I have finally finished it, and—no matter how poorly—I hope that my fundamental idea about the false path on which the art of our time has been moving, and about the causes of this aberration, and about the true mission of art, is correct and that my labors . . . will not have been in vain and that sooner or later art will abandon the false path on which it finds itself" (Tolstoi, *P.S.S.* 30:185). All subsequent quotations, unless otherwise indicated are from the essay *What is Art?* comprising vol. 30 of Tolstoi, *P.S.S.*

59. "On Gogol' [o Gogole]," in ibid., 38:51.

60. Tolstoi warns us not to confuse "religious consciousness" with "the religious cults, the Catholic, the Protestant, and so forth."

61. "As an animal instinctively chooses what it needs, even so man, if only his natural qualities be uncorrupted, will unerringly choose from among a thousand objects the true subject of art which he needs . . . but it is not so for people whose taste had been spoiled by education and life."

62. In an essay with the telling title "Komu u Kogo Uchit'sia Pisat', Krestianskim Rebiatam u Nas, Ili Nam u Krestianskikh Rebiat?" (Who Is to Learn from Whom How to Write, the Peasant Boys from Us or We from the Peasant Boys?), in Tolstoi, *P.S.S.* 8:307–25.

63. Ibid.

64. *Kalos*: "beautiful"; *agathos*: "good"; *k -kai*: "and."

65. In the essay "O Tom Chto Nazyvaiut Iskusstvom" (About What One Calls Art), Tolstoi, *P.S.S.* 30:268.

66. In the first version of *What Is Art?* in ibid., 320.

67. In the essay "Rech' o Narodnykh Izdaniakh" (Speech on Popular Editions), in ibid., 25:527.

68. To quote Tolstoi, "I count my artistic productions as belonging to the sphere of bad art, with the only exception of the story 'God Sees the Truth' and 'The Prisoner of the Caucasus.'"

69. Diary entry of May 28, 1889, in ibid., 50:86.

70. See, among some other sources, Edmund K. Kostka, *Schiller in Russian Literature* (Philadelphia, 1965).

71. Diary entry of October 11, 1906, in Tolstoi, *P.S.S.* 55:305. Kopelev is right to point out that Tolstoi's love for Schiller blinded him to many facets of Schiller's life philosophy and aesthetics which were in clear contradiction to his own, Schiller's Grecophilia, for one. Cf. Kopelev, *Zwei Epochen*, 23. I would add Schiller's pathos and fondness for "poetic" devices: metaphor, allegory, hyperbole.

72. *Lev Tolstoi v Vospominaniakh Sovremennikov* (*Tolstoi in the Recollections of His Contemporaries*) (Moscow, 1960), 2:63. The quotation is reproduced as reported by Vladimir Gregorovich Chertkov. Tolstoi can be thinking here only of Faust's love for Helena, an interesting instance of a perhaps subconscious interaction in his mind of his puritanism with his Grecophobia.

73. First draft of *What Is Art?* Another version of this passage runs as follows: "Goethe has written forty-two volumes. From among these one can select barely three truly artistic creations; everything else is either very poor art or not art at all but imitations of art. . . . And yet the critics, mindful that Goethe is a famous writer, try to find in these poor novels and dramas imaginary qualities, discuss them, and invent suitable theories. And promptly there appear the imitators of his worthless creations."

74. A. B. Gol'denveizer, *Vblizi Tolstogo* (*Near Tolstoi/In the Company of Tolstoi*) (Moscow, 1922), 1:30.

75. Tolstoi, *P.S.S.* 35:216–75.

76. Georg Gibian, in *Tolstoi and Shakespeare* (The Hague, 1957), uses that very term. In Gibian's sound judgment, Tolstoi's condemnation of Shakespeare was "entirely too sweeping and went far beyond the bounds of reasonable rebuttal" (ibid., 21).

77. Tolstoi, *P.S.S.* 35:265.

78. Ibid. In a passage not included in the final version, Tolstoi shows surer historical grasp: "This campaign [Shakespeare's glorification] was begun by Lessing and continued by Herder, Goethe, then by Schlegel and finally by Gervinus" (ibid., 569).

79. Ibid., 266.

80. Ibid., 270.

81. Ibid., 570.

82. *Hamb. Ausg.* 5:99. *Torquato Tasso*. Like many of his predecessors, Tolstoi liked to use Goethe quotations to start or to buttress his arguments and, like they, often quoted inaccurately. Thus, he quotes this famous passage as follows: "Man sieht die Absicht und man wird verstimmt" (Tolstoi, *P.S.S.* 35:238). Other favorite quotations of Tolstoi were "Ein guter Mensch in seinem dunklen Drange / Ist sich des rechten Weges wohl bewusst" (*Hamb. Ausg.* 3:18, "Prolog im Himmel") and "Du glaubst zu schieben und du wirst geschoben" (ibid., 129, "Walpurgisnacht"). He placed this latter quote at the head of his pedagogical journal, *Iasnaia Poliana*. It would have served better as a motto for *War and Peace* as the most succinct expression of Tolstoi's deterministic view of history, of what he called "the law of predetermination," which he so insistently expounds in his novel. In the brief essay "A Few Words to *War and Peace*" he stresses that "the activity of [Napoleon, Kutuzov, et al.] was of interest to me only as an illustration of that law of predetermination which, in my opinion, guides history" (Tolstoi, *P.S.S.* 24:193).

83. An obvious allusion to Nietzsche's *Jenseits von Gut und Böse*.

84. Tolstoi, *P.S.S.* 35:570.

85. Compare also Zhirmunski, *Gete v Russkoi Literature*, 421–22: "In this evaluation [of Goethe] he [Tolstoi] partly coincides with the revolutionary-democratic critics, especially with the most extreme representatives of the egalitarian and utilitarian tendencies of the petit-bourgeois democrats." Zhirmunski considers Tolstoi's re-

jection of Goethe and his works to be more radical and all-embracing than that of "his predecessors from the revolutionary camp" (ibid.).

86. Tolstoi did not include the last two quoted passages in the final version of *What Is Art?* They are preserved in the "Manuscript No. 11." Cf. Tolstoi, *P.S.S.*, vol. 30.

87. Letter to N. N. Strakhov of December 28, 1880, in ibid., 63:38. And again: "In the course of fifty years I had taken up Shakespeare's works several times and had experienced without fail that same feeling of revulsion, boredom, and quandary [otvrashchenie, skuku i nedoumenie]" (ibid., 35:217).

88. Ibid., 53:97.

89. Ibid., 124–25.

90. See pp. 154–55, above: Goethe as the proselytizer of Shakespeare.

91. Diary entry of September 24, 1906, in Tolstoi, *P.S.S.* 55:248.

92. Diary entry of February 21, 1897, in ibid., 53:138–39.

93. For the following quotations from Makovitski's "Notes," see ibid., 55: 561–62.

94. Makovitski's note of October 19, 1906, in ibid., 562.

95. Letter to Aleksandra Andreevna Tolstoi of August 29, 1891, in ibid., 66:34.

96. Diary entry of May 31, 1909, in ibid., 57:77.

97. According to Makovitski's "Note" of November 11, 1909, in ibid., 55:562.

98. Kopelev, *Zwei Epochen*, 26.

99. Chistiakova, "Tolstoi i Gëte," 127–28.

100. Diary entry of September 24, 1906, in Tolstoi, *P.S.S.* 55:246.

101. *Literaturnoe Nasledstvo* 75, book 2:371.

102. Fedor Stepun, *Dostoevsky und Tolstoy* (Munich, 1961), 156.

103. I. Ivoshkevich, "Slovo o Tolstom" (A Word About Tolstoi), in *Literaturnoe Nasledstvo* 75, book 2:195.

104. Romain Rolland, *Vie de Tolstoi* (Paris, 1911), 178. T. Motylova quotes Rolland on his high esteem for Tolstoi: "He occupies a place in my heart next to Shakespeare, Goethe, and Beethoven, whom he *forced* himself to underestimate" (italics in the original). I have not been able to locate Rolland's original passage. For T. Motylova's quote, cf. *Literaturnoe Nasledstvo* 69:143 in "Tolstoi i Sovremennye Zarubezhnye Pisateli."

105. Diary entry of October 11, 1906, in Tolstoi, *P.S.S.* 55:305.

106. Critics have commented on Tolstoi's intolerant stance, Romain Rolland among them. To quote him: "Tolstoi se sert de toutes armes, et frappe au hazard, sans regarder au visage ceux qu'il frappe. Bien souvent, il arrive—comme dans toutes les batailles—qu'il blesse tels de ceux qu'il eût été de son devoir de défendre: Ibsen ou Beethoven. C'est la faute de son emportement, qui ne lui laisse pas le temps de réfléchir assez avant d'agir, de sa passion qui l'aveugle souvent sur la faiblesse de ses raisons, et—disons-le—c'est aussi la faute de sa culture artistique incomplète" (Rolland, *Vie de Tolstoi*, 116).

Chapter Five. *The Russian Symbolists*

1. Aleksandr Blok, *Polnoe Sobranie Sochineni v Vos'mi Tomakh* (Moscow and Leningrad, 1960–63), vol. 8, "Literaturnye Itogi, 1907," 211.

2. Valeri Briusov, *Sobranie Sochineni v Semi Tomakh* (Moscow, 1975), 6:352–53. Henceforth cited as Briusov, *Sob. Soch.*

3. In sharp contrast, the Futurists and the Nichevoki radically broke with the

past. Maiakovski ranked the newspaper higher than the works of classical authors; A. Kruchenyke (to quote but one of the many voices) asks, "Why borrow from the mute Germans? [beziazykikh nemtsev]." N.B.: The word for German, *Nemets*, is frequently traced to "nemoi"—"dumb," "mute," "speechless." "Do not indulge in imitation," he exhorts his fellow poets. "Throw Pushkin, Dostoevski, Tolstoi, and others [Goethe, of course, included] from the steamship of contemporaneity [s parokhoda sovremennosti]." *Osvobozhdenie Slova* (*Liberation of the Word*) *Manifesty i Programmy Russkikh Futuristov* (Munich, 1913), vol. 27: "Novye Puti Slova [New Paths of the Word]," 50–51.

4. Oleg Maslenikov, *The Frenzied Poets: The Russian Symbolists* (New York, 1968), 5. See also V. Zhirmunski, *Nemetski Romanticism i Sovremennaia Mistika* (*German Romanticism and Contemporary Mysticism*) (St. Petersburg, 1914).

5. Aleksandr Blok, *Iskusstvo i Revolutsiia* (Moscow, 1979), 168–69, 323. James West, in his informed study *Russian Symbolism: A Study of Vyacheslav Ivanov and the Russian Symbolist Esthetics* (London, 1970), corroborates my findings; cf. esp. 2–3.

6. Andrei Belyi, *Arabeski. Kniga Statei* (Moscow, 1911), 458.

7. Briusov, *Sob. Soch.* 6:419.

8. Ellis (pen name of V. Kobylinski), "O Shusnosti Simvolizma" (On the Essence of Symbolism), in *Russkie Simvolisty* (Moscow, 1910), 14–16.

9. "From the real to the more real. Through the real to the more real." See note 10.

10. *Borozdy i Mezhi. Opyty Esteticheskie i Kriticheskie* (*Furrows and Field Boundaries. Studies Aesthetic and Critical*), "Mysli o Simvolizme" (Thoughts on Symbolism), 158.

11. Zhirmunski, *Gete v Russkoi Literature*, 587.

12. *Hamb. Ausg.* 2:271–81.

13. Viacheslav Ivanov, *Gete na Rubezhe Dvukh Stoleti* (*Goethe at the Divide of Two Centuries*) (Moscow, 1912), 142. That this "fragment" roused much discussion and speculation among Goethe's contemporaries is evidenced by Goethe's essay in Cotta's "Morgenblatt" (1816), written in reply to the many inquiries on the nature of this "rätselhafte Produkt." It spellbound the Russian Symbolists. We have translations of the enigmatic fragment by A. A. Sidorov, Boris Pasternak, and S. Shervinski (cf. *Gete. Sochinenii* [Moscow and Leningrad, 1932]). For a typical commentary, I quote from the introduction by G. A. Rachinski to Sidorov's translation: "The entire fascination of this insoluble riddle is to be found in its mysterious obscurity, which leaves ample room for the fantasies of a mystically attuned reader" (Rachinski, *Gete. Sochineniia*, p. xv).

14. *Hamb. Ausg.* 3:364.

15. Ibid., 24. Cf. R. Kluge, *Westeuropa und Russland im Weltbild Aleksandr Bloks. Slawistische Beiträge* (Munich, 1967), vol. 27, for an informed discussion of the Symbolists' "Lebensphilosophie," esp. 13ff.: "Entzieht sich auch seiner Natur nach dieses Denken einer genaueren Festlegung, so lassen sich doch gewisse gemeinsame Strukturen und Axiome . . . herausstellen . . . es wird ein irrationaler, sich stets wandelnder Ur- oder Lebensstrom angenommen, aus dem alles Dasein hervorgeht und in den es wieder zurückkehrt, seine Wirksamkeit ist ewiges Schaffen und Zerstören. Rationales, wissenschaftliches Denken wird zugunsten einer organischen Weltdeutung verworfen, schöpferische Intuition ist wertvoller als logische Untersuchung, Bekennen steht vor Erkennen."

16. Toporkov, *Trudy i Dni*, 2/1–2:8–18. All quotations are from these pages.

17. Ibid., 2/7:11–20. All quotations are from these pages.

18. This is a rare mention of Hölderlin in the work of the Russian Symbolists. More likely than not, such knowledge as they had of him they acquired by way of the French. I know of no Russian translation of Hölderlin extant at the time of the Symbolist movement (up to ca. 1920).

19. Cf. N. Metner, *Sechs Gedichte von Goethe für eine Singstimme und Klavier*, Op. 18 (Berlin, Moscow, and New York, 1910). Contents: Texts in German and Russian: 1. Die Spröde, 2. Die Bekehrte, 3. Einsamkeit, 4. Mignon, 5. Das Veilchen, 6. Jägers Abendlied, and others. Belyi in his review mentions "Im Vorübergehn," "Mailied," and "Elfenliedchen." Cf. Belyi, *Arabeski. Kniga Statei* (Moscow, 1911), 372ff. (N.B.: The family name, Metner, is also variously given as Mettner or Medtner.)

20. Belyi, *Arabeski*, 374–75.

21. N. Metner, *Muza i Moda. Zashchita Osnov Musikal' nogo Iskusstva* (Paris, 1978).

22. *Goethes Sämtliche Werke. Jubiläums-Ausgabe* (Stuttgart and Berlin, 1902), 1:253–54.

23. I draw here on Belyi's recollections. See especially his *Nachalo Veka* (*Beginning of an Epoch*) (Moscow, 1933); quotations are from this volume.

24. E. K. Metner, *Razmyshleniia o Gete. Razbor Vzgliadov R. Steinera v Sviazi s Voprosami Krititsizma, Simvolizma i Okkul'tizma. (Thoughts on Goethe: An Examination of R[udolf] Steiner's Views in Connection with the Problems of Criticism [Kant's], Symbolism, and Occultism)* (Moscow, 1916), book 1, p. 48.

25. Ibid., 83.

26. E. Metner, "Vvedenie" (Introduction), *Trudy i Dni* (Moscow, 1913), 2/1– 2:1–7. Quotations are from these pages unless otherwise indicated (italics in the original).

27. Konstantin Bal'mont, in *Zhizn'* (*Life*) 9 (1899): 12–16. Quotations are from this source (italics added).

28. Ibid., 7:171–77. The following quotations are from these pages (italics in the original).

29. See Chapter 3.

30. Valeri Briusov, *Sobranie Sochineni v Semi Tomakh* (Moscow, 1973ff.), 3:372.

31. Ibid., 339.

32. Ibid., 6:445.

33. Ibid., 205.

34. Ibid., 130.

35. Ibid., 178.

36. Ibid., 169–70.

37. Ibid., 1:545.

38. Ibid., 2:76–77. The following quotations are from these pages (italics added).

39. "I my s toboi letim ne k raiu / No v bezdnu, gde toska i mgla." Ibid., 2:77.

40. Cf. my discussion on pp. 136–38, above.

41. "Vstala ty v luchakh iz t'my! / No za mnoi klubilis' teni,— / *I vo mrake oba my!*" Ibid., 2:77, (italics added).

42. Briusov, *Sob. Soch.* 1:441–42. All quotations are from these pages.

43. "V rodnoi i v dikoi vole / Vsei prirody potonut'."

44. Briusov, *Sob. Soch.* 1:535.

45. Ibid., 63–64. Briusov specifies: "(Gete, Faust, chast' [part] 2)." The poem

was written in 1920, the year of Briusov's intense labors on Goethe's *Faust* and under the overpowering impact of the Russian Revolution.

46. Ibid., 2:106.

47. The list of other examples is long. See especially "Ariadne" (ibid., 3:199); "Legenda Let" ("The Legend of Past Times"; 3:135–36); "Iav'" ("Reality"; 3:173); "Skol'ziashchiia Terzina" ("The Gliding Tercine"; 3:372–73); "Bessonnaia Noch'" ("Sleepless Night"; 3:402–3).

48. "Germania. Otryvki" (Germany: Fragments), ibid., 1:338.

49. See my discussion on pp. 186–88, below.

50. We remember the impact of Goethe's "Mailied" on young Chernyshevski, by no means an uncritical admirer of Goethe, to mention but one example. See my discussion on pp. 59–61, above.

51. A favorite of Vissarion Belinski. See my discussion in Gronicka, *The Russian Image of Goethe*, 1:186ff.

52. *Stikhi o Liubvi* in Briusov, *Sob. Soch.* 1:57–64 (a selection).

53. I am thinking especially of the early poems of Stefan George, who had translated Baudelaire's *Flowers of Evil*.

54. K. Mochul'ski, *Valeri Briusov* (Paris, 1962), 37.

55. In the early phase, the terms *symbolism* and *decadence* were interchangeable.

56. Diary jotting of August 8, 1895, in Briusov, *Sob. Soch.* 1:574.

57. *Ognennyi Angel*, in ibid., 4.

58. Ibid., 4:402.

59. *Hamb. Ausg.* 3:196–201.

60. *Fiery Angel*, in Briusov, *Sob. Soch.* 4:225–28, esp. 227: "She [Helena] approached Dr. Faustus who rushed forward in the greatest excitement and thrust open his arms toward the apparition. This movement and gesture astonished me greatly, for it made me conclude that Faust himself was utterly surprised by the apparition." Briusov does not follow this up with the "paralyzation" of Faust by Helena—intentionally, to keep to his "style"?

61. *Hamb. Ausg.* 3:139–45.

62. Briusov, ibid., 4:286–90. It should also be mentioned that a considerable amount of autobiographical material has found its way into Briusov's depiction of his hero's highly problematical relationship with his amour, Renate, from Briusov's equally problematical love affair with schizophrenic Nina Petrovskoi. Cf. Mochul'ski, *Briusov*, 138.

63. Cf. *Gete, Sochineniia* (Moscow, 1932), 1:541–42.

64. Briusov, *Sob. Soch.* 3:491. In a special "note" Briusov informs us that he strove to improve on Lermontov's rendering by way of a more "faithful reproduction of the poem's rhythms" (ibid., 535).

65. Ibid., 6:103–9: "Fialka v Tigele" (The Violet in the Cooking Pot).

66. Ibid., 400: "I know French and Latin rather well, tolerably Italian, rather poorly German."

67. See pp. 99–100.

68. V. Briusov, *Gete, Faust. Perevod Valeria Briusova* (Moscow and Leningrad, 1928).

69. Wilma Pohl, *Russische Faust-Übersetzungen* (Mannheim am Glan, 1962), 112.

70. N. Vil'mont, *Gete i Ego Faust* (*Goethe and His Faust*) (Moscow and Leningrad, 1955), 33–34.

71. Zhirmunski, *Gete v Russkoi Literature*, 604.

72. Mochul'ski, *Briusov*, 43.

73. Ibid., 20, 143. "Sochetaniia slov" and "iarkopevuchikh stikhov" are phrases from Bruisov's poem "Profession de Foi." Here is one of its central strophes: "Byt' mozhet, vsë v zhizni lish sredstvo / Dlia *iarko-pevuchikh stikhov*, / I ty s bespechal'nogo detstva / Ishchi *sochetaniia slov*" (Perhaps, all in life is but a means / For *brilliantly melodious verses* / And from your sorrowless youth / You are to search *for combinations of words*). (Italics added.)

74. See pp. 170–71.

75. Briusov, *Sob. Soch.* 6:205.

76. Belyi, *Na Rubezhe Dvukh Stoleti* (*On the Border of Two Centuries*) (Chicago, 1966), 205.

77. Ibid., 174; also p. 81: Raisa reads to him "the songs [!] of Uhland and Heine and Goethe so understandable to my heart."

78. Ibid.

79. Ibid., 168.

80. Ibid., 331.

81. Ibid., 409. Cf. also Maslenikov, *The Frenzied Poets*, 43 and passim.

82. For my discussion of the Metner brothers, cf. pp. 166–67, above.

83. Cf. Belyi's autobiographical *Nachalo Veka* (Moscow, 1933). The following quotations, unless otherwise indicated, are from this volume.

84. Cf. Mochul'ski, *Andrei Belyi* (Paris, 1955), 29: "Pevets Vechnoi Zhenstvennosti sygral ogromnuiu rol' v ego [Belyi's] zhizni" ("The singer [!] of the Eternal-Feminine played a tremendous role in his [Belyi's] life").

85. See especially Solov'ev's poems "Das Ewig-Weibliche" and "Tri vstrechi" (Three Meetings), in *Stikhotvoreniia i Shutochnye Piesy* (Munich, 1968), vol. 18 of *Slawische Propyläen*, 163–64 and 170–80, respectively.

86. Translations by Solov'ev of relevant verses of Dante's *Vita Nuova* and of Petrarca's "Praise of and Supplications to the Most Holy Virgin" (*Stikhotvoreniia*, 195–96 and 197–201) are evidence of these two poets' influence on him.

87. *Hamb. Ausg.* 3:364.

88. Goethe's portrayal of Makarie borders on the mystical. He addresses her as the "Blessed," "the Saintly," "Die Heilige." When Wilhelm Meister dreams of her ascension to heaven, he feels himself "drawn heavenward." All those who come in contact with her are purified, enobled. Her "very presence calms injured feelings, settles disputes, brings order into chaos." See *Hamb. Ausg.*, vol. 8; esp. book 1, chap. 10; book 3, chap. 15, and "Aus Makariens Archiv."

89. Cf. also Briusov, *Sob. Soch.* 6:229, of the essay "Vladimir Solov'ev: The Meaning of His Poetry."

90. For an account of the "mystic brotherhood" of Belyi, Blok, and Sergei Solov'ev in ecstatic adoration of Liubov Dmitrievna, see Mochul'ski, *Belyi*, 67–68, 89ff., and passim.

91. "Krizis Zhizni" (St. Petersburg, 1918).

92. Cf. also Belyi's poem "Mladentsu" ("To the Child"), written in 1918, as quoted by Mochul'ski, *Belyi*, 243.

93. For a concise definition of Steiner's anthroposophy, cf. Maslenikov, *The Frenzied Poets*, 86–87.

94. The meeting occurred completely by chance on a train in Norway during Belyi's European trip with his wife Asia (daughter of Ivan Turgenev, Anna Alekseevna) in 1912.

95. As quoted by Mochul'ski, *Belyi*, 184 (italics in the original).

96. Ibid., 185.

97. Cf. *Aleksandr Blok i Andrei Belyi. Perepiska* (*A. Blok and A. Belyi: Correspondence*) (Moscow, 1940), 293. Also "Steiner has deeply entered my soul." Letter to Blok of May 14, 1912, ibid. Henceforth cited as *Perepiska*.

98. Maslenikov, *The Frenzied Poets*, 87.

99. Ibid., " 'Johannesbau' later rechristened the 'Goetheanum' and destroyed by fire in 1922."

100. Belyi: "I have passed through a terrible sickness; Friedrich Nietzsche, the sublime Schumann, Hölderlin—they went insane. And I?—I remained sane, casting off my old skin, and have experienced a resurrection to health." Cf. Mochul'ski, *Belyi*, 195.

101. *Perepiska*, 332. Belyi recalls in a letter to Blok of June 23, 1916, after a three-year break in their correspondence, "the wooden barracks in which we took our five-o-clock coffee, surrounded by half-crazy 'occult' old maids, in a cloud of nasty gossip, in an atmosphere of indescribably repulsive hostility and hatred. There was everything: death, decay, being buried alive, the grave, derision, slap-in-the-face, spit-in-the face. . . ."

102. In those terrible years, Belyi had become estranged from his closest friends, Metner and Blok, from his wife, who left him to remain in Dornach, and worst of all from himself as a poet. The poet's creative vision had turned into the deadening routine of abstract meditation and self-analysis in strict obeisance to the teacher's "rules." In a letter to Blok, Belyi describes Steiner's "rules": "Work starts with the purification of the *ethereal body.* . . . Central to everything is the motto '*Transubstantiate yourself!*' renew yourself from the very beginning—everything without embellishments [bez prikras]—and all over again!" *Perepiska*, 303 (italics in the original).

103. Belyi, *Simvolizm* (Moscow, 1910), "Problematika Kultury," 9. For Goethe quotation, cf. *Hamb. Ausg.* 3:364.

104. Ivanov quotes Belyi in his essay "Liniia, Krug, Spiral—Simvolizma," *Trudy i Dni*, 1/4–5:18.

105. Belyi, *Arabeski*, "Na Perevale" ("On the Divide") (Moscow: Musaget, 1911).

106. Mochul'ski, *Belyi*, 74: "The Symbolist movement in Russia is of course no mere literature and no mere art. All leading members of the movement—Minski, Merezhkovski, Belyi, Viacheslav Ivanov, Blok, Gippius—they all emphasize its religious nature. Let me put it more precisely. Symbolism is a religious tragedy of the Russian spirit at the great divide of our catastrophic era."

107. Belyi, *Arabeski*, "N. Mettner," 374.

108. Ibid., "Na Perevale," 264.

109. Ibid., "Simvolizm kak miroponimanie" ("Symbolism as an Understanding of the World"), 225.

110. Ibid., 226.

111. Ibid., "Friedrich Nietzsche," 62.

112. Ibid., 73.

113. Andrei Belyi, *Rudolf Steiner i Gete v Mirovozrenie Sovremennosti. Otvet Emiliiu Metneru na ego pervyi tom "Razmyshlenii o Gete"* (Moscow, 1917). The following quotations are from this work unless otherwise indicated (italics in the original).

114. Steiner's influence is pervasive in this work and Belyi does not attempt to hide it. To Blok he writes, "Dr. Steiner has become the best part of the soul of Andrei Belyi. I no longer differentiate as to what is my own and what is Steiner's [Steinerovskoe]" (*Perepiska*, 318).

115. See n. 24 for this chapter.

116. *Zur Farbenlehre. Goethes Werke. Weimarer Ausgabe*, 2d Part, vols. 1–5, ed. S. Kalischer (Weimar, 1890–97).

117. Belyi's intensive study of Goethe's *Farbenlehre* is not the only evidence of his interest in the nature of colors and their symbolical use in poetry (esp. Blok's) and in painting (esp. Vrubel's). In his collection of essays, *At the Divide of Two Centuries* (*Na Rubezhe Dvukh Stoleti*, Rarity Reprints No. 4) (Chicago, 1966), Belyi tells how, very early in their careers, he, Blok, and Sergei Solov'ev (nephew of the great Vladimir) had become fascinated with the use of colors in the *Apocalypse of Saint John*, and conjectures: "Had we studied Goethe's optics in those early days, we would surely have become Goetheists [my stali by Getistami]" (Belyi, *Nachalo Veka* 377).

118. See pp. 85–86.

119. I do not include Russian specialists in the field of Germanistics, a discipline that developed rapidly in Russia, partly under the influence of the pioneering work in linguistics by the Formalists and the Structuralists. Cf. V. Erlich, *Russian Formalism*, 3d ed. (The Hague, 1969).

120. Mochul'ski, *Aleksandr Blok* (Paris, 1948), 198–99. Maksim Gorki has this to say of these two elements in Blok's nature: "I think the 'German element' was inborn, was given him directly, while the Russian he absorbed intellectually under the influence of [Vladimir] Solov'ev and Moscow" (*Literaturnoe Nasledstvo* 70 [1963]: 625). Expressions of abiding love for Germany are frequent in Blok's letters. Cf. Blok, *Pis'ma Rodnym* (*Letters to Relatives*) (Moscow and Leningrad, 1923–27), 2:145, 179 and passim. The Romantic in Blok tends to idealize the land of his dreams. From Bad Nauheim he writes to his mother: "The kinship [rodstvennost'] I feel for Germany and its beauty astounds me, its customs, which I understand, and that lofty lyricism that informs everything here. . . . The native land of the Gothic spirit [a term of highest approbation with Blok] is Germany, not Italy, not France. Germany is the land closest in spirit to Russia. . . . If only the Germans would take Russia under their guardianship [opeka], then we could breathe easier, then the miserable life [in Russia] would come to an end. Only here is that genuine religiosity of life, that Gothic form of life, a life that knows how to sanctify [osviatit'] even its bureaucratic service to the state. So beautiful is Germany that nothing here offends." Quoted by M. A. Beketova in *Aleksandr Blok i Ego Mat'* (*A. Blok and His Mother*) (Moscow and Leningrad, 1930), 122.

121. Mochul'ski, *Blok*, 16.

122. Among her numerous translations listed by Blok in his autobiography there is no mention of a work by a German author. Cf. A. Blok, *Sobranie Sochineni v Vos'mi Tomakh* (Moscow and Leningrad, 1960–63), 7:9. Henceforth cited as Blok, *Sob. Soch.*

123. Blok's other favorites, aside from Russian authors, among them especially Pushkin, Gogol', Polonski, and Fet, were Ibsen, Strindberg, and Verhaeren. Friedrich Nietzsche's *Birth of Tragedy* had a decisive influence on him, as did Schopenhauer's pessimistic philosophy.

124. Blok, *Sob. Soch.*, "Autobiography," 7:13.

125. Cf. *Literaturnoe Nasledstvo*, 1937, 54. Blok refers here primarily to Solov'ev's verses dealing with his Sophia cult. The record of this central experience of his life Solov'ev has couched in a serio-jocular tone not unlike Goethe's in what he called the "sehr ernste Scherze" of the Second Part of *Faust* (the "Grablegung" scene, for instance). In a note, Solov'ev characterizes the poems as "jocular verses [shutlivye stikhi] composed to express the most important event . . . in my life." Cf. *Stikhotvo-*

reniia. Shutochnye Piesy, 179. It may be mentioned that a central theme of the poem "Das Ewig-Weibliche" is the same as that of Goethe's "Grablegung," namely, the duping of the devil.

126. Belyi corroborates: "Goethe, Dante, and Petrarca, inspired by their beloved, have been able to create the symbol of the Eternal Feminine. . . . Vladimir Solov'ev, uniting the contemplations of the Gnostics with the hymns of the poets, spoke the 'new word' announcing the approach to us of the holy image [lik] of the Eternal Woman. Here *at this point began Blok's poetry*" (Belyi, *Arabeski*, 459, italics added).

127. *Stikhi o Prekrasnoi Dame*, in Blok, *Sob. Soch.* 1:74–228.

128. Letter to Briusov, February 1, 1903, in ibid., 8:55. Cf. also Briusov, *Sob. Soch.* 6:432.

129. Blok, *Sob. Soch.* 6:95.

130. Blok speaks of the "immensely challenging undertaking" of a *Faust* translation. He never carried it out. (Ibid., 6:469.)

131. Liubov Dmitrievna Mendeleeva, his love and wife-to-be, was the "real" inspiration. Cf., for example, the "Unpublished Letter" to her: ". . . My long-lasting and deep faith in Thou, as in the terrestrial embodiment . . . of the Eternal Feminine" (ibid., 62). See also Kluge, *Westeuropa und Russland im Weltbild Aleksandr Bloks*, 63: "Diese Vergottung der Liebe und der Geliebten fanden für Blok in der Philosophie und Dichtung Vladimir Solov'evs wie auch Goethes . . . eine willkommene Bestätigung und Erhärtung. Blok formt aus diesen vorgefundenen Gedanken einen eigenartigen religiös-mystischen Kult um das 'Ewig-Weibliche' in Gestalt seiner schönen Dame."

132. *Perepiska*, 36.

133. Blok, *Sob. Soch.* 1:181. Henceforth volume and page of quotations from this source will be given parenthetically in my text unless otherwise indicated.

134. See esp. Blok's essay "On the Present-Day Condition of Russian Symbolism" (O Sovremennom Sostoianii Russkogo Simvolizma), in Blok, *Sob. Soch.* 6:425–36, esp. 433.

135. The "snows" is a reference to the lyric cycle, *The Snow-Mask* (*Snezhnaia Maska*), in ibid., 2:211–35.

136. Blok unmistakably links this figure to Solov'ev's Sophia. The Snow Maiden, even though she has "accepted as her kingdom the iron-gray city [St. Petersburg]" still "yearns for her native Egypt, for the aromatic lilies of the Nile" (ibid., 67–68). One remembers that Solov'ev's vision of Sophia appeared for the third and final time in her "native Egypt."

137. In the play *Balaganchik* (*Puppet Theater*), in ibid., 4:7–20.

138. The heroine of a lyric cycle (ibid., 1:185ff.) and of a play by that name (ibid., 1:329–40). In the play the Neznakomka is, at the same time, a "falling maiden-star" (paduchaia devazvezda). Forced from her celestial orbit, she falls to earth. There she turns "terrestrial," scorns the ethereal adulation of the "blue one," "wants terrestrial words," and gives herself to a very terrestrial gentleman ("Gospodin"). The final stage direction makes it clear that she ascends to heaven, there to shine once again as a "brilliant star." The playlet is less than successful, but it does convey by means of a traditional symbol the dual nature of Blok's "Eternal Woman" as a celestial being and as a Mondaine. Its tragic message, ruthlessly burlesqued, is that the "poet" remembers only the Neznakomka and cannot recall her as the worshiped idol, the heavenly star of his youth. The autobiographical implications are only too evident.

139. Briusov, *Sob. Soch.* 6:435–36.

140. Blok, *Sob. Soch.* 5:430.

141. Cf. the lyric cycle *Faima* (ibid., 2:254–95), and the play, *Song of Fate* (*Pesnia Sud'by*) (ibid., 4:103–67). Quotations are from these pages.

142. See especially the "Seventh Picture" of the *Song of Fate* (4:159–67).

143. The pronoun-adjective "Sei" is used only in formal context for special emphasis. The usual term is "etot."

144. This portrayal is not only of a modern Faust but also of the tragic fate of Blok's father. See Blok's autobiography in *Sob. Soch.* 7:7–16 and Mochul'ski *Blok,* 296–97.

145. "Krushenie Gumanizma," in Blok, *Sob. Soch.* 6:93–115; quotations are from pp. 94–96. This article was written in March or April 1919 under the impact of the October Revolution.

146. Cf. ibid., 7:260 and passim. See also *Zapisnye Knizhki* (*Notebooks*), book 26, 123–24: "Music creates the world, the spiritual body of the world, the flowing thought of the world." Cf. also Kluge, *Westeuropa und Russland,* 166ff. and passim.

147. *Notebooks,* book 23, July 8, 1909 (italics added).

148. A farfetched argument can be made that Blok's "Eternal Woman" did "return" as the prostitute Katia of the famous poem *The Twelve.* This figure, stripped of every vestige of myth, mystery, and magic, has not a hint about it of transcendence, no Romantic symbolism. With stark realism and bitter irony, the poet creates that final incarnation with which his vision of the celestial "Lady," by way of a long sequence of transformations, was destined to come to its end, left lying on a snowdrift like "discarded *carrion*" ("lezhi ty, *padal'*, na snegu!") stanza 6, italics added; Blok, *Sob. Soch.* 3:347–59.

149. Cf. Briusov, *Sob. Soch.,* "Aleksandr Blok," 6:434: "The fateful prediction took place [i.e., the First World War], but the prophecies were not fulfilled. There came the period of great disillusionment and disenchantment, resulting at times in sarcastic ridicule of the old sanctities [sviatyni]."

150. Blok, *Sob. Soch.* 3:347–59.

151. See n. 146 above.

152. Cf. Mochul'ski, *Blok,* 429: "For Blok in 1920, the revolution had long since ended; its 'music' had been replaced with the 'enveloping silence of the grave.'"

153. Cf. S. Solov'ev, "Ellinism i Tserkov'" ("Hellenism and the Church"), in *Bogoslovskie i Kriticheskie Lektsii* (*Theological and Critical Lectures*) (Moscow, 1913ff.): p. 6.

154. S. Solov'ev, "Simvolizm i Dekadenstvo," *Vesy* (*The Scales*), no. 5 (May 1909): p. 13.

155. S. Solov'ev "Hellenism and the Church," 6–7.

156. S. Solov'ev, "Gete i Khristianstvo" ("Goethe and Christianity") in *Bogoslovski Vestnik* (*The Theological Messenger*) (Moscow, 1917): p. 242.

157. S. Solov'ev, "Hellenism and the Church," 7 (italics in the original).

158. S. Solov'ev, "Goethe and Christianity," 250. The following quotations are from this source.

159. Maslenikov, *The Frenzied Poets,* 197.

160. Briusov, *Sob. Soch.,* "Viacheslav Ivanov. Andrei Belyi," 6:291–311; quotations from p. 295.

161. *Cor Ardens* (Ann Arbor, Mich., 1968), Kniga Pervaia (First Book): "Plameneiushchee Serdtse" ("The Flaming Heart").

162. *Kormchie Zvëzdy* (Ann Arbor, Mich., 1968). With one exception, mottoes are from "Anmutige Gegend," *Hamb. Ausg.* 3:146–49. The exception is the line "Ach, die Erde kühlt die Liebe nicht!" from "Die Braut von Korinth," ibid., 1:272.

163. "Manera, Litso, Stil'," in *Borozdy i Mezhi (Furrows and Boundaries)*. *Opyty esteticheskie i kriticheskie (Essays, aesthetical and critical)* (Moscow, 1916), 169ff. Quotations are from these pages.

164. *Hamb. Ausg.* 12:30–34.

165. *Po Zvëzdam*, "Dve Stikhii v Sovremënnom Simvolizme" (St. Petersburg, 1909), 247–90. All quotations are from Goethe, *Wilhelm Meisters Wanderjahre*, "Gesang," *Hamb. Ausg.* 8:255–56.

166. V. Ivanov, "O Granitsakh Iskusstva," *Trudy i Dni*, vol. 2, no. 7. Quotations are from these pages.

167. *Hamb. Ausg.* 6:491–513; the excerpt is from pp. 511–13.

168. I have referred to Ivanov's important essay on Dostoevski, in which he is the first to point out the influence of Goethe's Faust and Mephisto on Stavrogin and Pëtr Verkhovenski and of Goethe's Gretchen on Maria Timofeevna Lebiadkin in Dostoevski's *The Devils* (see above, pp. 124 and 134–35). I would also call attention to Ivanov's exchange of letters with M. O. Gershenzon. Here Ivanov draws liberally on *Faust* and the poems "Selige Sehnsucht" and "Vermächtnis," even closing his last letter by extolling Goethe's *Flammentod*: "There is but one way not to be 'ein trüber Gast / Auf der dunklen Erde,'" and that is "the fiery death in the spirit [ognennaia smert' v dukhe].' Dixi' (*Perepiska iz Dvukh Uglov [Correspondence from Two Corners]* [St. Petersburg, 1921], esp. 13–14, 28, 30, 33, 58). These letters were written in the summer of 1920 in the hospital "for the workers in science and literature," where the two friends had been lodged each in a "corner" of the same room.

169. V. Ivanov, *Gete Na Rubezhe Dvukh Stoleti* (Moscow, 1912). All quotations are from this source.

170. To quote Belyi in his essay "Na Perevale. At the Divide," in *Arabeski*, 241: "Our art is alive with the consciousness of some sort of insurmountable divide between us and the recent past; our art is the symbol of a crisis in mankind's worldview [mirosozertsaniia]. This crisis is deep, and we live with a vague and disturbing presentiment [my smutno predchustvuem] that we are standing on the border [na granitse] of two great periods in mankind's development." This essay was written in 1909, between the Revolution of 1905 and the First World War.

171. Especially in Ivanov's choice of poems and dramatic fragments with classical themes: "Prometheus Ode" and dramatic fragment, "Parzenlied," and "Alexis und Dora"—to give but a few examples.

172. See my discussion on p. 171.

173. *Hamb. Ausg.* 1:361.

174. "Die Braut von Korinth," in ibid., 1:268–73.

175. In the "pedagogische Provinz," Ivanov is particularly impressed with Goethe's discussion of the nature of religion in its historical development. He gives the following succinct synopsis of it as he understands it: "Reverence before God from *fear* Goethe does not consider worthy of being called a religion. The lowest level of religious consciousness Goethe considers to be reverence before God out of a feeling of *awe* before the divine; that is the level of the Old Testament, which considers the object of religion [i.e., God] as being loftier than man. The second level of religious consciousness [according to Goethe in Ivanov's interpretation] is the New Testament. Here the object of reverence stands next to man, on the same level with him. God has

become man in Christ. The third spiritual level of religious consciousness is the awe toward that which is lower than man; the possibility of such a relationship of man toward that which is below him is revealed only in Christianity, a Christianity received spiritually [Khristianstvo priniatoe v dukhe]."

176. *Hamb. Ausg.* 3:47.

177. See my discussion on pp. 121 and passim.

178. Ivanov's translation of Goethe's poem "Prooemion" (*Hamb. Ausg.* 1:357), of that inspired effort by Goethe to define the nature of God, is one of Ivanov's best. See V. Ivanov, *Gete Na Rubezhe Dvukh Stoleti*, 142–43.

179. Ivanov believes that Goethe was a greater historian than he has generally been given credit for. The reason why Goethe had not been given full credit was that Goethe was never attracted to historical pragmatism and thus had been out of step with the dominant trend of his time. Goethe's attention was focused not on the mechanics of history but on what Ivanov would call its "chemistry." Goethe the evolutionist could not perceive history other than as an evolutionary process of the spirit (*Geistesgeschichte!*). According to Ivanov, Goethe studied historical epochs in the interaction of their living forces, their style, and their symbolism, which revealed to him (Goethe) the forms of their highest culture: their ideas, their faiths, their ideals of art.

180. *Hamb. Ausg.* 3:28: "Geheimnisvoll am lichten Tag / Lässt sich Natur des Schleiers nicht berauben, / Und was sie deinem Geist nicht offenbaren mag, / Das zwingst du ihr nicht ab mit *Hebeln und mit Schrauben*" (italics added).

181. In his excellent Russian translation Ivanov quotes relevant passages from Goethe's essay "Über den Granit" in support of his contention that Goethe's contemplation of nature borders on religious meditation. One such passage is "Hier auf dem ältesten, ewigen Altare, der unmittelbar auf die Tiefe der Schöpfung gebaut ist, bring ich dem Wesen aller Wesen ein Opfer" (ibid., 13:256 and passim).

182. The Classicist Ivanov was profoundly influenced by the Demeter-Persephone cult of the ancient Greeks.

183. *Hamb. Ausg.* 3:78.

184. Ibid., 131.

185. For my discussion, see p. 169.

186. See pp. 195 and passim.

187. A definitive study from an unprejudiced point of view of the Symbolists' attitude toward the October Revolution (1917) and the Soviet Union has yet to be written.

188. Zhirmunski, *Gete v Russkoi Literature*, 596.

Bibliography

This bibliography includes only works that are cited in the text. For easy reference, items are listed under the chapters in which they occur and are grouped as primary and secondary sources. Within each group, the items are arranged alphabetically by authors.

Chapter One. I. S. Turgenev: A Study in Ambivalence

Primary Sources

Turgenev, I. *Polnoe Sobranie Sochineni i Pisem v Dvatsati Vosmi Tomakh*. Moscow and Leningrad, 1960–67.

———. *Pis'ma v Trinadtsati Tomakh*. Moscow and Leningrad, 1961–67.

———. *Sobranie Sochineni*. Moscow, 1962.

Turgenevski Sbornik; Materialy k Polnomu Sobraniiu Sochineni i Pisem I. S. Turgeneva. Leningrad, 1964ff.

Turgenev, I. *Parasha*. Translated into German by A. Luther. *Germanoslavica* 2 (1932–33).

Secondary Sources

Annenkov, P. *Literaturnye Vospominaniia, 1813–1887*. Leningrad, 1960.

———. "Molodost' I. S. Turgeneva." *I. S. Turgenev v Vospominaniakh Ego Sovremennikov i Ego Pis'makh*. Edited by Brodski. Moscow, n.d.

Bem, A. "Faust bei Turgeniew." *Germanoslavica* 2 (1932–33).

Berlin, I. "Father and Children: Turgenev and the Liberal Predicament." *The New York Book Review* 20, nos. 16–18.

Bittner, K. *Die Faustsage im russischen Schrifttum. Prager Deutsche Studien*. Reichenberg im Breisgau, 1925.

Brodski, N. *I. S. Turgenev, Materialy i Issledovaniia; Sbornik*. Orlov, 1940.

———. *Tvorcheski Put' Turgeneva. Sbornik Statei*. Petrograd, 1923.

Brumfield, W. "Bazarov and Rjazanov: The Romantic Archetype in Russian Nihilism." *Slavonic and East European Journal* 21/4 (Winter 1977).

Bulashkovski, L. *Russki Literaturnyi Iazyk Pervoi Poloviny XIX Veka*. Kiev, 1957.

Chshmkian, K. *I. S. Turgenev—Literaturnyi Kritik*. Erévan, 1957.

Dehn, T. "Des jungen Turgeniews Verhältnis zu Schiller." *I. S. Turgeniew und Deutschland. Materialien und Untersuchungen*. Edited by G. Ziegengeist. Berlin, 1965.

Eckermanns Gespräche mit Goethe. Leipzig, 1939.

Ense, Varnhagen von. *Tagebücher*. Edited by L. Assing. Leipzig, 1861–70.

Gabel', O. "Tvorcheskaia Istoria Romana *Rudin*." *Literaturnoe Nasledstvo*, vol. 55.

Gebhard, R. *Iwan Turgenjew in seinen Beziehungen zu Shakespeare. Jahrbuch der deutschen Shakespeare Gesellschaft*, vol. 45.

249

Gettmann, R. *Turgenev in England and America*. Urbana, Ill., 1937.
Glagan, O. *Die russische Literatur und Iwan Turgenjew*. Berlin, 1872.
Goethes Werke. Hamburger Ausgabe. 6th ed. Hamburg, 1926.
Gorbacheva, V. *Molodye Gody Turgeneva*. Moscow, 1926.
Grigor'ev, A. "I. S. Turgenev i Ego Deiatel'nost'." *Literaturnaia Kritika*. Moscow, 1958.
Gut'iar, N. *Ivan Sergeevich Turgenev*. Moscow, 1907.
Gutman, D. *Turgenev i Gëte*. Elabizh, 1959.
Hock, E. *Turgeniew und die deutsche Literatur*. Göttingen, 1955.
Kagon-Klaus, E. *Hamlet and Don Quixote: Turgenev's Ambivalent Vision*. The Hague, 1975.
Kavelin, K. and Turgenev, I. *Pis'ma k A. I. Gertsen*. Edited by M. Dragomanov. Geneva, 1892.
Kleman, M. "Anmerkungen I. S. Turgeniews zu der Übersetzung des *Faust* von Vronchenko." *Literaturnoe Nasledstvo* 4–6. Moscow, 1932.
Kostka, E. *Schiller in Russian Literature*. Philadelphia, 1965.
Laage, K. E. *Theodor Storm und Iwan Turgenjew. Persönliche und literarische Beziehungen, Einflüsse, Briefe, Bilder*. Heide, 1967.
Magarshak, D. *Turgenev: A Life*. London, n.d.
Masaryk, T. *The Spirit of Russia*. Edited by G. Gibian. New York, 1967.
Muratov, A. *I. S. Turgenev Posle 'Otsov i Detei' (60-e Gody)*. Leningrad, 1972.
Petrov, S. *I. S. Turgenev*. Moscow, 1968.
Prokhorov, G. "Tvorcheskaia Istoria Romana *Rudin*," in Brodski, *Materialy*. Orlov, 1940.
Pumpianski, L. "Turgenev i Zapad," in Brodski, *Materialy*.
Rosenkranz, E. "Turgeniew und Goethe." *Germanoslavica* 2/1 (1932–33).
Rozanov, F. *Tvorchestvo Turgeneva*. Moscow, 1920.
Schütz, K. *Das Goethebild Turgeniews. Sprache und Dichtung*. No. 75. Stuttgart, 1952.
Terras, V. "Turgenev and Western Realism." *Comparative Literature* 22/1 (1970).
Vischer, F. "Die Literatur über Goethes Faust." *Hallische Jahrbücher für Kunst und Wissenschaft* (Leipzig, 1838–40), nos. 6–67.
Vronchenko, M. *"Faust," Trag. Soch. Gëte. Perevod Pervoi i Izlazhenie Vtoroi Chasti*. St. Petersburg, 1844.
Waddington, P. *Turgenev and England*. London, 1980.
Wiegand, K. *I. S. Turgenjews Einstellung zum Deutschtum. Veröffentlichungen des Slawischen Instituts an der Friedrich-Wilhelm-Universität*. Lichtenstein, 1968.
Yarmolinski, A. *Turgenev: The Man, His Art, and His Age*. New York and London, 1926.
Zaitsev, B. *Zhizn' Turgeneva*. Paris, 1949.
Zhirmunski, V. *Gete v Russkoi Literature*. Leningrad, 1937.
Ziegengeist, G. *I. S. Turgeniew und Deutschland: Materialien und Untersuchungen*. Berlin, 1965.

Chapter Two. Crosscurrents of Opinion

Primary Sources

Aksakov, K. *Sochineniia Konstantina Aksakova*. Edited by E. A. Liadski. St. Petersburg, 1915.

————. "O Sovremennom Literaturnom Spore." *Rus'* 7 (1883).

Aksakov, S. *Sobranie Sochineni v Piati Tomakh*. Moscow, 1966.

Belinski, V. *Pis'ma Belinskogo*. Moscow, 1914.

Botkin, V. *Polnoe Sobranie Sochineni*. St. Petersburg, 1891.

Chernyshevski, N. *Polnoe Sobranie Sochineni v Piadnadtsati Tomakh*. Moscow, 1944ff.

Dobroliubov, N. *Sobranie Sochineni*. Moscow and Leningrad, 1964ff.

Druzhinin, A. *Sobranie Sochineniia A. V. Druzhinina*. St. Petersburg, 1865.

————. *Biblioteka Dlia Chteniia*. St. Petersburg, 1854.

Fet, A. *Polnoe Sobranie Stikhotvoreni A. A. Feta*. St. Petersburg, 1901.

————. *Moi Vospominaniia, 1848–1889*. Moscow, 1890.

————. *Rannie Gody Moei Zhizni*. Moscow, 1893.

————. "O Stikhotvoreniiakh F. Tiutcheva." *Russkoe Slovo* 2 (1859).

————. "Po Povodu Statui G-na Ivanova." *Khudozhestvennyi Sbornik*, 1866.

————. "Dva Pis'ma o Klassicheskom Obrasovanii." *Literaturnaia Biblioteka*, April 1867.

————. "Iz-za Granitsy." *Sovremennik* 61/2 (1857).

————. *Goethes Faust. Faust, Tragediia Gëte. Perevod A. Feta*. St. Petersburg, 1889.

Grigor'ev, A. *Sobranie Sochineni*. Moscow, 1856ff.

————. *Stikhotvoreniia i Poemy*. Moscow, 1978.

————. *Estetika i Kritika*. Moscow, 1979.

————. *Literaturnaia Kritika*. Moscow, 1858.

————. *Vospominaniia*. Leningrad, 1980.

————. *I. S. Turgenev i Ego Deiatel'nost' Po Povodu Romana 'Dvorianskoe Gnezdo'*. Moscow, 1915.

————. "Stikhotvoreniia A. A. Feta." *Otechestvennye Zapiski*. Section "Kritika." February 1850.

————. "Stat'ia Lorda Dzheffri." *Moskvitianin* 2 (1854).

Khomiakov, A. *Polnoe Sobranie Sochineni*. Moscow, 1900–1904.

————. *Izbrannye Sochineniia*. Edited by N. S. Arsen'eva. New York, 1955.

Kireievski, I. *Polnoe Sobranie Sochineni Ivana Vasil'evicha Kireievskago*. Edited by A. I. Koshelëv. Moscow, 1861.

————. *Russland und Europa*. Translated into German by Nikolai von Bubnoff. Stuttgart, 1948.

Maikov, A. *Polnoe Sobranie Sochineni*. Edited by P. V. Bykov. St. Petersburg, 1914.

Mei, L. *Polnoe Sobranie Sochineni s Kritiko-biograficheskim Ocherkom*. St. Petersburg, 1911.

————. *Stikhotvoreniia i Dramy*. Edited by S. A. Reiser. Leningrad, 1947.

Pisarev, D. *Polnoe Sobranie Sochineni v Shesti Tomakh*. St. Petersburg, 1909–13.

————. *Izbrannye Proizvedeniia*. Leningrad, 1968.

————. *Heinrich Heine. 10 Essays von D. I. Pisarev*. Vienna, 1965.

Tolstoi, A. K. *Polnoe Sobranie Sochineni Grafa A. K. Tolstogo*. St. Petersburg, 1907.

————. *Sochineniia*. Ed. S. A. Vengerov. St. Petersburg, 1908.

————. *Sobranie Sochineni*. Moscow, 1963.

Secondary Sources

Berdiaev, N. *Aleksei Stepanovich Khomiakov*. Moscow, 1912.

Bolshakoff, S. *The Doctrine of the Unity of the Church in the Works of Khomyakov and Moehler*. London, 1946.

Bursov, B. *Chernyshevski as Literary Critic.* Moscow and Leningrad, 1918.

Chizhevski, D. *Aus Zwei Welter. Beiträge zur Geschichte der Slawisch-Westlichen Literarischen Beziehungen.* The Hague, 1961.

Chizhevski, D. *Hegel bei den Slawen. Wissenschaftliche Buchgesellschaft.* Darmstadt, 1961.

Christoff, P. *An Introduction to Nineteenth-Century Russian Slavophilism: A Study in Ideas.* The Hague, 1961.

Dalton, M. *A. K. Tolstoy.* New York, 1972.

Demidova, N. *Pisarev.* Moscow, 1969.

Gleason, A. *European and Muscovite: Ivan Kireievsky and the Origins of Slavophilism.* Cambridge, Mass., 1972.

Goerdt, W. *Vergöttlichung und Gesellschaft. Studien zur Philosophie von Ivan V. Kireievskij.* Wiesbaden, 1968.

Grossman, L. *Tri Sovremennika: Tiutshev, Dostoevski, Apollon Grigor'ev.* Moscow, 1922.

Gustafson, R. *The Imagination of Spring: The Poetry of Afanasij Fet.* New Haven, 1966.

Jeffrey, F. (Lord). "Wilhelm Meister's Apprenticeship, a Novel. From the German of Goethe. In three volumes. Edinburgh, 1824." *The Edinburgh Review* 42/84, art. 7 (August 1825).

Lehmann, J. *Der Einfluss der Philosophie des deutschen Idealismus in der russischen Literaturkritik des 19. Jahrhunderts: Die 'organische' Kritik Apollon A. Grigoriews. Beiträge zur neueren Literaturgeschichte* 3/23. Heidelberg, 1975.

Lirondelle, A. *Le Poète Alexis Tolstoi. L'homme et l'Oeuvre.* Paris, 1912.

Lotman, L. *Afanasy Fet.* Boston, 1976.

Lunacharski, A. *On Literature and Art.* Moscow, 1965.

Mandelstam, N. *Hope Against Hope: A Memoire.* New York, 1976.

Mashinski, S. *Sergei Timofeevich Aksakov.* Moscow, 1959.

Matl, J. "Goethe bei den Slawen," *Jahrbücher für Kultur und Geschichte der Slawen.* New Series 8/1 (1932).

Miller, O. *Slavianstvo i Evropa.* St. Petersburg, 1877.

Mirski, D. *A History of Russian Literature.* New York, 1949.

Müller, E. *Russischer Intellekt in europäischer Krise: Ivan V. Kireiewskij, 1806–1856.* Cologne, 1966.

Ozerov, L. *A. A. Fet. O Masterstve Poeta.* Moscow, 1970.

Plotkin, L. *Pisarev i Literaturno-obshestvennoe Dvizhenie Shestidesiatykh Godov.* Leningrad, 1969.

Pohl, W. *Russische Faust-Übersetzungen. Veröffentlichungen des slawisch-baltischen Seminars der westfälischen Wilhelms-Universität.* Münster, Meisenheim am Glau, 1962.

Reichel, H. *Studien zum slawophilen Weltbild Konstantin Aksakows.* Bonn, 1966.

Riasanovski, N. *Russia and the West in the Teaching of the Slavophiles: A Study of Romantic Ideology.* Cambridge, Mass., 1952.

Simkin, Ia. *Zhizn' Dmitriia, I. Pisareva. Lichnost' i Publitistika.* Rostov, 1969.

Smirnov, V. *The Aksakoffs: Their Life and Literary Activity.* St. Petersburg, 1895.

Smolitsch, I. *Ivan Vasil'evich Kireievskij. Leben und Weltanschauung, 1806–1856. Ein Beitrag zur Geschichte des russischen Slawophilentums.* Breslau, 1934.

Solov'ev, E. *D. I. Pisarev, Ego Zhizn' i Literaturnaia Deiatel'nost'. Biograficheski Ocherk.* St. Petersburg, 1894.

Tsubenko, V. *Mirovozrenie D. I. Pisareva*. Moscow, 1969.
Zernov, N. *Three Russian Prophets: Khomiakov, Dostoevski, Soloviev*. London, 1944.

Chapter Three. Fëdor Mikhailovich Dostoevski (1821–1881)

Primary Sources
Dostoevski, F. *Polnoe Sobranie Sochineni v Tridtsati Tomakh*. Leningrad, 1972ff.
———. *Pis'ma*. Edited by S. A. Dolinin. Moscow and Leningrad, 1928–59.
———. *Dostoewskij. Gesammelte Briefe, 1833–1881*. Edited by F. Hitzer. Munich, n.d.
———. *The Possessed*. Translated by C. Garnett. London, 1970.
———. *Dnevnik Pisatelia za God 1873, 1876, 1880*. Paris, n.d.
———. *F. M. Dostoevski. Novye Materialy i Issledovaniia. Literaturnoe Nasledstvo*. No. 86. Moscow, 1973.
———. *Iz Arkhiva F. M. Dostoevskago. Idiot. Neizdannye Materialy*. Moscow and Leningrad, 1931.
Goncharov, I. *Oblomov. Sobranie Sochineni*. Moscow, 1959.
———. *Oblomov*. Translated by A. Dunningen. New York, 1963.

Secondary Sources
Bem, A. "'Faust' v Tvorchestve Dostoevskogo." *Bulletin de l'Association Russe pour les Recherches Scientifiques a Prague*, vol. 5 (10). Section des sciences philosophiques, historiques et sociales. Prague, 1937.
Brody, E. "The Liberal Intellectual in *The Possessed*." *Germano-Slavica* 2/4 (Fall 1977).
Chizhevski, D. "Schiller und die Brüder Karamasow." *Zeitschrift für slawische Philologie* 6, parts 1–2. (1958).
———. "Schiller v Rossii." *Novyi Zhurnal* 45 (1956).
Dolinin, A. *F. M. Dostoevski. Materialy i Issledovaniia*. Leningrad, 1935.
———, ed. *F. M. Dostoevski v Vospominaniiakh Sovremennikov*. Moscow, 1964.
Dudkin, V., and Azadovski, K. "Dostoevski v Germanii (1846–1921)." *Dostoevski. Novye Materialy i Issledovaniia. Literaturnoe Nasledstvo*, vol. 86. Moscow, 1973.
Fitzgerald, G. Review of N. M. Lary's *Dostoevsky and Dickens*. *Slavic and East European Journal* 20/4 (1976).
Frank, J. *Dostoevsky: The Seeds of Revolt (1821–1849)*. Princeton, N.J., 1976.
Fridlender, G. *Dostoevski i Mirovaia Literatura*. Moscow, 1979.
Holthusen, J. "Die Figur der Mignon bei Dostoewskij." *Zeitschrift für Slawische Philologie* 23 (1954).
Ivanov, V. *Borozdy i Mezhi*. Moscow, 1916.
Katkov, G. "Steerforth and Stavrogin: On the Sources of *The Possessed*." *Slavonic and East European Review* 5 (1949).
Kostovski, I. *Dostoevski and Goethe, Two Devils—Two Geniuses: A Study of the Demonic in Their Works*. Translated by D. Hitchcock. New York, 1974.
Lary, N. *Dostoevsky and Dickens*. London, 1973.
Leer, N. "Stavrogin and Prince Hal: The Hero in Two Worlds." *Slavic and East European Journal* 6/2 (1962).
Louria, Y., and Seiden, M. "Ivan Goncharov's Oblomov: The Anti-Faust as Christian Hero." *Canadian Slavic Studies* 3/1 (Spring 1969).

Lukacs, G. *Der Russische Realismus in der Weltliteratur*. Berlin, 1949.
Lunacharski, A. "Russki Faust." *Voprosy Fil. i Psikh*, 3. Book. 1902.
Lyngstad, A. *Dostoevskij and Schiller*. The Hague, 1975.
Magarshak, D. *Dostoevsky*. New York, 1963.
Mann, T. *Die Entstehung des Doktor Faustus. Roman eines Romans*. Berlin, 1949.
Masaryk, T. *Studie o F. M. Dostoevskom*. Prague, 1932.
Matl, J. "Goethe bei den Slawen." *Jahrbücher für Kultur und Geschichte der Slawen*, New Series, 8/1 (1932).
Maurina, Z. *Dostoewskij. Menschengestalter und Gottsucher*. Memmingen, 1952.
May, K. *Faust Zweiter Teil, in der Sprachform gedeutet*. Munich, 1962.
Mirsky, D. *A History of Russian Literature*. New York, 1949.
Misheev, N. "Russki Faust." *Russki Filosofski Vestnik*. Nos. 53–57.
Muchnic, H. "Dostoevsky's English Reputation." *Smith College Studies in Modern Languages* 20/3–4 (1939).
Natova, N. *Dostoevski v Bad Ems*. Berlin, 1971.
Nötzel, K. *Das Leben Dostoewskijs*. Osnabrück, 1967.
Rimscha, H. von. *Dostoewskij, ein Antipode Goethes*. Coburg, 1949.
Schubart, W. *Dostoewskij und Nietzsche. Symbolik ihres Lebens*. Lucerne, 1939.
Shestov, L. *Dostoevski, Tolstoy, and Nietzsche*. Athens, Ohio, 1969.
Simmons, E. *Fedor Dostoevsky*. New York, 1969.
Sokel, W. *The Writer in Extremis: Expressionism in Twentieth-Century German Literature*. Stanford, Calif., 1959.
Strich, F. *Goethe and World Literature*. New York, 1949.
Terras, V. *The Young Dostoevski: A Critical Study*. The Hague, 1969.
Troyat, H. *Dostoievsky*. Paris, 1960.
Turrian, M. *Dostoewskij und Franz Werfel; vom östlischen zum westlichen Denken*. Bern, 1950.

Chapter Four. Leo Nikolaevich Tolstoi (1828–1910)

Primary Sources
Tolstoi, L. *Polnoe Sobranie Sochineni*. Jubilee Edition. 90 vols. Moscow, 1929–58.

Secondary Sources
Bayley, J. *Tolstoy and the Novel*. London, 1966.
Bibliographia Proizvedeni L. N. Tolstogo. Moscow, 1955.
Bierbaum, J., ed. *Goethe Kalender auf das Jahr 1909*. Munich, 1909.
Biriukov, P. *The Life of Tolstoy*. London and New York, 1911.
Chertkov, V. *The Last Days of Tolstoy*. London, 1922.
Chistiakova, M. "Tolstoi i Gëte." *Zven'ia. Sbornik Materialov i Dokumentov po Istorii Russkoi Literatury*. Moscow and Leningrad, 1933.
Davis, H. *Tolstoy and Nietzsche*. New York, 1929.
Eikhenbaum, B. *Lev Tolstoi*. Leningrad, 1928–31.
Gibian, G. *Tolstoi and Shakespeare*. The Hague, 1957.
Gol'denveizer, A. *Vblizi Tolstogo*. Moscow, 1922.
Gorlin, M. "Goethe in Russland." *Zeitschrift für Slawische Philologie* 10 (1933).
Gudzi, N. *Kak rabotal Tolstoi*. Moscow, 1936.
———. *L. N. Tolstoi, 1828–1910*. *Russkie Pisateli*. Moscow, 1949.
Hamburger, K. *Leo Tolstoi. Gestalt und Problem*. Bern, 1950.

Ivakin, I. "Zapiski." *Literaturnoe Nasledstvo* 69 (1956).

Ivoshkevich, I. "Slovo o Tolstom." *Literaturnoe Nasledstvo* 75 (1962).

Kersten, G. *Gerhart Hauptmann und Lev Nikolaevich Tolstoj. Studien zur Wirkungs-geschichte von L. N. Tolstoj in Deutschland, 1885–1910.* Wiesbaden, 1966.

Knight, G. *Shakespeare and Tolstoy.* London, 1934.

Kopelev, L. "Tolstoj und Goethe. Dialog zweier Epochen." *Zwei Epochen deutsch-russischer Literaturbeziehungen.* Frankfurth am Main, 1973.

Lashkin, V. *Tolstoi i Chekhov.* Moscow, 1975.

Lev Tolstoi v Vospominaniakh Sovremennikov. Moscow, 1960.

Lunacharski, A. *Tolstoi i Marks.* Letchworth, Eng., 1979.

Makovitski, D. "U Tolstogo (1904–1910). Iasnopolianskie Zapiski," in Tolstoi's *Polnoe Sobranie Sochineni*, vol. 55.

Mann, T. "Goethe und Tolstoi. Fragmente zum Problem der Humanität." *Gesammelte Werke in Dreizehn Bänden.* Vol. 9. Frankfurt am Main, 1960.

Maud, A. *Leo Tolstoy.* New York, 1975.

Merezhkovski, D. *Tolstoi as Man and Artist, with an Essay on Dostoevski.* New York, 1902.

Motylova, T. "Tolstoi i Sovremennye Zarubezhnye Pisateli." *Literaturnoe Nasledstvo* 69 (1956).

Rolland, R. *Vie de Tolstoi.* Paris, 1911.

Rozanova, S. *Tolstoi i Gertsen.* Moscow, 1972.

Shcheglov, V. *Graf Lev Nikolaevich Tolstoi i Fridrikh Nittsshe.* Iaroslavl', 1898.

Shifman, A. *Lev Tolstoi i Vostok.* Moscow, 1971.

Shklovski, V. *Lev Tolstoy.* Moscow, 1978.

Simmons, E. *Leo Tolstoy.* Boston, 1946.

Tolstaia, A. *Tolstoy: A Life of My Father.* New York, 1973.

Tolstaia, S. *Dnevniki.* Moscow, 1978.

Troyat, H. *Tolstoy.* Garden City, N.Y., 1967.

Chapter Five. The Russian Symbolists

Primary Sources

Bal'mont, K. *Polnoe Sobranie Sochineni.* Moscow, 1907–14.

———. "Neskol'ko Slov o Tipe Fausta." *Zhizn'* 7 (1898): 171–77.

———. "Izbrannik Zemli." *Zhizn'* 9 (1899): 12–16.

Belyi, A. *Arabeski. Kniga Statei.* Moscow, 1911.

———. *Nachalo Veka.* Moscow, 1933.

———. *Na Rubezhe Dvukh Stoleti.* Rarity Reprints No. 4. Chicago, 1966.

———. *Rudolf Steiner i Gete v Mirovozrenie Sovremennosti. Otvet Emiliiu Metneru na Ego Pervyi Tom "Rasmyshlenii o Gete."* Moscow, 1917.

———. *Simvolizm. Kniga Statei.* Moscow, 1910.

Blok, A. *Polnoe Sobranie Sochineni v Vos'mi Tomakh.* Moscow and Leningrad, 1960–63.

———. *Iskusstvo i Revoliutsiia.* Moscow, 1979.

———. *Pis'ma Rodnym.* Moscow and Leningrad, 1923–27.

Blok, A., and Belyi, A. *Perepiska.* Moscow, 1940.

Briusov, V. *Sobranie Sochineni v Semi Tomakh.* Moscow, 1973ff.

———. *Gete, Faust. Perevod Valeria Briusova.* Moscow and Leningrad, 1932.

———. "Novye Techeniia v Russkoi Poezii. Akmeizm." *Russkaia Mysl'* 2/4 (1913).

Ellis (V. Kobelinski). "O shusnosti Simvolizma." *Russkie Simvolisty.* Moscow, 1910.
Gete. Sochineniia. Moscow and Leningrad, 1932.
Goethe, *Jubiläums-Ausgabe.* Stuttgart and Berlin, 1902ff.
————. *Weimarer-Ausgabe.* Weimar, 1890–97.
Ivanov, V. *Cor Ardens.* Ann Arbor, Mich., 1968. Microfilm.
————. *Gete Na Rubezhe Dvukh Stoleti. Istoria Zapadno-Evropeiskoi Literatury XIX Veka.* Moscow, 1912.
————. *Kormchie Zvëzdy.* Ann Arbor, Mich., 1968. Microfilm.
————. "O Granitsakh Iskusstva." *Trudy i Dni*, 2/7. Moscow, 1914.
————. "Opyty Esteticheskie i Kriticheskie." *Borozdy i Mezhy.* Moscow, 1916.
————. "Dve Stikhii v Sovremennom Simvolizme." *Po Zvëzdam. Stati i Aforizmy.* St. Petersburg, 1909.
————. "Zavety Simvolizma." *Apollon*, no. 8. St. Petersburg, 1910.
————. "Vvedenie." *Trudy i Dni*, 1/1. Moscow, 1912.
Ivanov, V., and Gershenson, M. *Perepiska iz Dvukh Uglov.* St. Petersburg, 1921.
Maiakovski, V. *Polnoe Sobranie Sochineni v 13 Tomakh.* Moscow, 1955–61.
Metner, E. *Razmyshleniia o Gete. Razbor Vzgliadov R. Steinera v Sviazi s Voprosami Krititsizma, Simvolizma i Okkul'tizma.* Moscow, 1916.
————. "Vvedenie." *Trudy i Dni*, vol. 2, nos. 1–2. Moscow, 1913.
Metner, N. *Muza i Moda. Zashchita Osnov Muzykal'nogo Iskusstva.* Paris, 1978.
————. *Sechs Gedichte von Goethe für eine Singstimme und Klavier.* Berlin, Moscow, and New York, 1910.
Osvobozhdenie Slova. Manifesty i Programmy Russkikh Futuristov. Munich, 1913.
Solov'ev, S. "Ellinism i Tserkov'." *Bogoslovskie i Kriticheskie Lektsii.* Moscow, 1913ff.
————. "Gete i Khristianstvo." *Bogoslovski Vestnik.* Moscow, 1917.
————. "Simvolizm i Dekadenstvo." *Vesy*, no. 5 (May 1909).
Solov'ev, V. *Stikhotvoreniia. Shutochnye P'esy. Slawische Propyläen. Texte in Neu- und Nachdrucken*, vol. 18. Munich, 1968.
Toporkov, A. "Gete i Fikhte." *Trudy i Dni*, 2/7. Moscow, 1914.
————. "Lesnoi Tsar'." *Trudy i Dni*, 2/1–2. Moscow, 1913.

Secondary Sources
Symbolist Journals Examined:
Apollon (St. Petersburg) 1909–17.
Mir Iskusstva (St. Petersburg) 1899–1904.
Novyi Put' (St. Petersburg) 1903–4.
Pereval (Moscow) 1906–7.
Severnyi Vestnik (St. Petersburg) 1882–98.
Skify (Moscow) 1917–18.
Trudy i Dni Musageta (Moscow) 1912–16.
Vesy (Moscow) 1904–9.
Voprosy Zhizni (St. Petersburg) 1905.
Zolotoe Runo (Moscow) 1906–9.

Beketova, M. *Aleksandr Blok.* Moscow, 1922–30.
————. *Aleksandr Blok i Ego Mat'.* Moscow and Leningrad, 1930.
Chizhevski, D. *Anfänge des russischen Futurismus.* Wiesbaden, 1963.
Erlich, V. *Russian Formalism.* 3d ed. The Hague, 1969.

Gorodetski, S. "Vospominaniia o Bloke." *Pechat' i Revolutsiia*. Moscow, 1922.
Istoriia Russkoi Literatury Kontsa XIX i Nachala XX Veka. Bibliograficheski Ukazatel'. Moscow and Leningrad, 1963.
Kluge, R. *Westeuropa und Russland im Weltbild Aleksandr Bloks. Slawistische Beiträge*. Edited by A. Schmaus. Vol. 27. Munich, 1967.
Knigge, A. *Die Lyrik Vl. Solov'evs und ihre Nachwirkung bei A. Belyi und A. Blok*. Amsterdam, 1973.
Kruchenykh, A. "Novye Puti Slova." *Osvobozhdenie Slova* 27:50ff.
Literaturnoe Nasledstvo. Vols. 27–28: *Simvolizm*. Leningrad, 1937.
Maslenikov, O. *The Frenzied Poets: The Russian Symbolists*. New York, 1968.
Mochul'ski, K. *Aleksandr Blok*. Paris, 1948.
———. *Andrei Belyi*. Paris, 1955.
———. *Valeri Briusov*. Paris, 1962.
Mohrenshildt, D. "The Russian Symbolist Movement." *PMLA* 53 (1938).
Pertsova, V., and Serebrianski, I., eds. *Maiakovski. Materialy i Issledovaniia*. Moscow, 1940.
Piast, V. *Vospominaniia o Aleksandre Bloke*. Leningrad, 1923.
Poggioli, R. *The Poets of the Advance Guard: The Poets of Russia 1890–1930*. Cambridge, Mass., 1960.
Pohl, W. *Russische Faust-Übersetzungen*. Mannheim am Glan, 1962.
Rice, M. *Valeri Briusov and the Rise of Russian Symbolism*. Ann Arbor, Mich., 1975.
Schmidt, A. *Valeri Briusovs Beitrag zur Literaturtheorie*. Munich, 1963.
Shaginian, M. "Volia k Vlasti." *Trudy i Dni*, 2/7. Moscow, 1914.
Shestov, L. *Vladimir Solov'ev. Sovremennye Zapiski. Book 33*. Paris, 1928.
Sidorov, A. "Gete i Perevodshiki." *Trudy i Dni*, 2/7. Moscow, 1914.
Stepun, F. *Viacheslav Ivanov. Sovremennye Zapiski. Book 62*. Paris, 1936.
Struve, G. "Blok and Gumiliov." *Slavic and Easteuropean Review* 25 (1946–47).
Vil'mont, N. *Gete i Ego Faust*. Moscow and Leningrad, 1955.
Wellek, R. *A History of Modern Criticism*, 1750–1950. New Haven, 1955ff.
West, J. *Russian Symbolism: A Study of Vyacheslav Ivanov and the Russian Symbolist Esthetics*. London, 1970.
Zhirmunski, V. *Nementski Romanticism i Sovremennaia Mistika*. St. Petersburg, 1914.
———. *Drama Aleksandra Bloka "Rosa i Krest." Literaturnye Istochniki*. Leningrad, 1964.

Index

A. INDEX OF NAMES

(Bold face numbers indicate a running account of the person's view of Goethe.)